Sociology, History and Education
a reader

Sociology, History and Education

a reader

edited with an introduction
by P. W. MUSGRAVE

Methuen & Co Ltd
II NEW FETTER LANE · LONDON · EC4

First published 1970 by Methuen & Co Ltd
11 New Fetter Lane, London EC4
© 1970 by P. W. Musgrave
Printed in Great Britain by
Richard Clay (The Chaucer Press) Ltd,
Bungay, Suffolk

Distributed in the U.S.A.
by Barnes & Noble Inc.

Contents

Acknowledgements

The editor and publishers wish to thank the following for permission to reproduce the articles listed below: Aldine Publishing Company for 'The Evolving Economics of Pre-Industrial Apprenticeship' by M. J. Bowman, and 'Determinants of the Incidence of Literacy in Rural Nineteenth-Century Russia', by A. Kahan (both articles are reprinted from C. Arnold Anderson and Mary Jean Bowman (eds), *Education and Economic Development*, Chicago, 1965); The American Sociological Association for 'The Gentleman Ideal and the Maintenance of a Political Élite', by R. H. Wilkinson (*Sociology of Education*, Vol. XXXVII, 1963); Dr G. Baron and the Institute of Education, Leeds University for 'Some Aspects of the Headmaster Tradition' by Dr Baron (*Leeds Researches and Studies*, Vol. XIII, June 1956); Faber & Faber Ltd for 'Public School Town in the Nineteenth Century', by T. W. Bamford (*British Journal of Educational Studies*, Vol. VI, November 1957), 'The Influence of Religion on Educational Policy, 1902–1944', by C. Cannon (*B.J.E.S.*, Vol. XII, May 1964), 'Constant Factors in the Demand for Technical Education, 1860–1960', by P. W. Musgrave (*B.J.E.S.*, Vol. XIV, May 1966), and 'The Anti-Intellectual Tradition in the West', by J. Wellens (*B.J.E.S.*, Vol. VIII, November 1959); Cambridge University Press for 'Literary Culture: Some General Considerations', by J. Goody and I. Watt (*Comparative Studies in Society and History*, Vol. V, 1962–3, and *Literacy in Traditional Societies* edited by Professor Goody (C.U.P., 1968) and 'Japan and England: A Comparative Study', by L. Stone ('Education and Modernization in Japan and England', by Stone and Jansen, *Comparative Studies in Society and History*, Vol. XI, 1966–7); Jonathan Cape Ltd and Alfred A. Knopf, Inc, for 'Two Concepts of Childhood', by P. Ariès, translated by R. Baldick (*Centuries of Childhood*, C.U.P., 1962); The Association of Teachers in Colleges and Departments of Education for 'Some Variations on the Teacher's Role', by C. Cannon (*Education for Teaching*, No. 64, May 1964); Evans Brothers Limited for 'The Changing Status of the Teacher in England and Wales', by A. Tropp (*The Yearbook of Education*, edited by Professor Philip Vernon, 1953); The National Foundation for Educational Research for 'Metallurgy and the Department of Science and Art, 1870–1900', by P. W. Musgrave (this chapter is based on the article, 'Curriculum Development in Further Education: Two Case Studies' from *Technical Education Abstracts*, Vol. IX, No. 3,

January–March 1969); Routledge & Kegan Paul Ltd and the Indiana University Press for 'Population Changes and the Status of the Young', by F. Musgrove (*Youth and the Social Order*, R.K.P., 1964); Routledge & Kegan Paul Ltd and the London School of Economics for 'Latin and the Élite Tradition in Education', by F. Campbell (*British Journal of Sociology*, Vol. XIX, Sept. 1968); The Sociological Review for 'Middle-Class Families and Schools, 1780–1880: Interaction and Exchange of Function between Institutions', by F. Musgrove (*Sociological Review*, Vol. VII, November 1959); University of North Carolina Press for 'Latin Language as a Renaissance Puberty Rite', by W. J. Ong (*Studies in Philology*, Vol. LVI, April 1959); University of Chicago Press for 'The Impact of Printing on European Education', by E. L. Eisenstein (an extract from the article 'Some Conjectures about the Impact of Printing on Western Society and Thought: A Preliminary Report' from the *Journal of Modern History*, Vol. XL, March 1968); Universities Quarterly for 'The Seminar', by I. Watt (*Universities Quarterly*, Vol. XVIII, September 1964); the editors of the *Vocational Aspect of Secondary and Further Education* for 'The Definition of Technical Education, 1860–1910', by P. W. Musgrove (Vol. XVI, 1964).

The publishers would also like to thank Professor Musgrave for permission to reproduce: 'A Model for the Analysis of the Development of the English Educational System from 1860'.

Editor's Introduction

SOCIOLOGISTS AND HISTORIANS often illustrate their mutual misunderstanding by making critical statements about each other's work. In this situation E. H. Carr has suggested that 'the more sociological history becomes, and the more historical sociology becomes, the better for both'.[1] It follows that before presenting the aims of, and a brief commentary on, the contents of this Reader, which relates to the apparently dangerous, but potentially fruitful, dialogue between history and sociology, there should be some consideration of the interrelationship of these two disciplines.

History and sociology

THE DIFFERENT FOCI OF THE TWO DISCIPLINES

Historians and sociologists have their central interests in common, since both examine the actions of human beings in various social situations, the aims and values that seem to be behind behaviour, and the changes that occur through time in aims, values and behaviour. Yet practitioners in these two disciplines have different goals. Hence they ask different questions of the same data and use different methods in their attempts to solve their problems. If for the purposes of analysis we were to invent an imaginary, typical historian, we should probably think of a scholar who tended to concentrate on the detailed study of single cases or of one nation within one relatively short period of time, whereas any similar imaginary sociologist would be interested in broad comparisons of several cases or societies over a long time scale.

The important point to stress here is that despite their differing foci these two disciplines both use similar modes of explanation. All explanations that are open to objective checks, whether in history, sociology or any other discipline, include three common elements.[2] There is, firstly, some investigation of the determining conditions of the event or process that is to be explained. What, for example, were the conditions that led to a certain war or to the establishment of

---

[1] E. H. Carr, *What is History?*, (Pelican edn, London, 1964), p. 66.
[2] C. G. Hempel, 'The Function of General Laws', *Journal of Philosophy*, Vol. XXXIX, No. 1 (January 1942), pp. 40–8.

a specific educational system of an élitest kind? Secondly, there is one or more hypotheses of a universal nature as, for instance, the following: continuous economic rivalry ultimately leads to armed conflict, or rigidly stratified societies establish schools to which few of the lower social orders are allowed entry. Finally, there are reasoned statements that connect the determining conditions to the universal hypothesis in the circumstances under investigation. In the examples given here, the problems to be solved might be the linking of determining conditions and general hypotheses in the cases of the outbreak of the First World War, or the establishment of the state system of secondary education in England. Any historical or sociological explanation that carries weight will contain all three elements in greater or lesser measure but because of their differing interests, historians and sociologists will stress different parts of the explanatory process. The sociologist will make the universal hypotheses more explicit, while the historian will emphasize more fully the details of the case and often allow the universal hypotheses upon which his explanation depends to remain implicit in his argument.

Causality is clearly an important concept to both. Yet cause has legitimately different meanings to different people. As academic disciplines become separate they develop traditional interests and ideas of what is an acceptable explanation in their particular fields of interests. Historians on the whole have focused on the richness of detail in any train of events and have tended to look for causes in the behaviour of individuals.[1] Thus, to continue the examples used above, a historian might well say that the Kaiser played a part in starting the war in 1914, or that Sir Robert Morant greatly influenced the establishment of state grammar schools in the first decade of this century. Implicit here are certain psychological hypotheses about how individuals usually behave in such circumstances. Sociologists, on the other hand, tend to concentrate on the social conditions at the time, seeing the individuals more as the agents of forces over which they had a limited range of control. In the economic circumstances of the time the Kaiser had one possible, even probable, course of behaviour open to him: namely to start a war. Or, again, with his upbringing and in the stratified class system of early twentieth-century England, Morant would have had little option but to extend the existing socially exclusive schools by creating a state system of secondary education. Here emphasis is put on determining conditions and on making the assumed universal hypothesis at least clear, if not always stated in a rigorous form.

The historian, then, tends to take universal hypotheses for granted, while the sociologist is seeking to develop them or even, in the few areas where much work has been done, to test them. The historian is, however, interested in change and may try to establish a trend in events. He will sometimes be concerned to establish why a trend began or persisted. Why, for instance, was Germany a growing

[1] For this paragraph, see P. Gardiner, *The Nature of Historical Explanation* (Oxford, 1952); M. White, 'Historical Explanation', *Mind*, Vol. LII, No. 207 (July 1943), pp. 212–29.

problem in Europe after, say, 1860? The important point to notice here is that trends have not the same logical status as universal hypotheses, and it is with the latter that theoretical disciplines like sociology are largely concerned. However, the German problem could be of interest to a sociologist in two ways. He might form a hypothesis based on this trend which he could then try to falsify in other historical settings in an endeavour to establish some more general, or even universal, hypothesis of the following order – that under certain conditions of economic stress, autocratic governments use aggressive foreign policies that may cause, or help to bring about a war.

Many sociologists today, however, are somewhat less ambitious and are content to try to establish what are called theories of the middle range. In the historical context such theories would be confined to one historical period and even, perhaps, to one society rather than to all periods or all societies. Thus, an explanation of the nature of the growth of secondary education might be different for a capitalist and for a socialist society, or for a developed and an underdeveloped nation.

If we return to our imaginary practitioners, then, on the one hand, there is the sociologist moving from the particular to the general and back again to the particular, fining away the detail in order to discover the general principles that are believed to be at work, and constantly attempting to falsify this explanation by testing it on other historical periods and other societies. On the other hand, there is the historian digging even deeper into the evidence that relates to his chosen problem in order to give a fuller picture of what happened in all its complex profusion. Neither approach is better nor worse than the other, providing both are technically sound and follow the method of logical explanation outlined above. The two disciplines are different merely in that they each seek different goals.

But, as Carr indicated in the quotation cited earlier, history and sociology can help each other since both often view the same data from their own perspectives and, if the two views can be brought together, there is at least the chance of a fuller view of the particular problems under consideration. Two advantages should follow. A deeper understanding is a possibility since the question has now been investigated by two disciplines whose findings have been integrated. But secondly, each discipline should be able to view its own findings in the light of the results of the other. The historian will criticize the sociological interpretation on the grounds that this theory does not cover all the cases or that the concepts used are ill-defined, thus forcing the sociologist to greater theoretical rigour and conceptual clarity. The sociologist will, in his turn, compel the historian to stand back and view his chosen period from a wider perspective and will, in addition, offer such new concepts as social mobility or some new technique which may well be statistical in nature. As a result the historian will feel bound to rework his original material and thereby, perhaps, come to a fuller understanding.

THE USES OF HISTORY IN SOCIOLOGY

Sociology is seen by many to be a study of contemporary societies that is mainly undertaken by means of questionnaires. However, the whole rationale of this Reader is that sociologists can, and often must, use historical material in their attempts to understand the workings of social systems. Therefore, it is necessary to indicate what uses sociologists make of history in their work. As a starting-point we should remember that the early sociologists rarely gathered contemporary empirical material. For example, when Max Weber wished to investigate the part religious belief played in the birth of capitalism he based his book, *The Protestant Ethic and the Spirit of Capitalism*, on a wide-ranging examination of historical material, much of it culled from primary sources. Weber ultimately developed a hypothesis to explain his problem and, at least to his own satisfaction, he proved his hypothesis, though since his time his conclusion has been constantly and fruitfully questioned by both historians and sociologists.

Very often sociologists develop hypotheses as a result of their theorizing which can only, or perhaps can most easily, be tested on historical material. For example, sociologists who are interested in theories of social change have no laboratory available to test their conclusions. Unlike their colleagues investigating small group behaviour under rigidly controlled conditions, they are driven perforce to examine past instances of historical change in the hope that they may elucidate general processes and develop hypotheses that have a wider relevance than to the historical case studies out of which they arise. The process of history as established by historical research is here providing a laboratory for the development of sociological theory. An example in this Reader is the paper in which Kahan reports investigations concerning the spread of literacy in nineteenth-century rural Russia, and shows briefly how the very simple hypothesis that 'literacy increased to the degree that the rural population was exposed to contact with urban areas' was developed and tested.

Frequently such rigorous testing of hypotheses is not done. A proposition is stated as a result of theoretical considerations and then the instances drawn from the immense range of available and relevant historical material are cited either as mere illustrations or in order to give the appearance of substantiating what has been stated. In this Reader, Campbell's paper on 'Latin and the Élite Tradition in Education' is an example. There are dangers for the unwary in this use of history, since the material that is used may not be a representative sample of all that is available. The evidence chosen may be that in favour of the proposition under examination, while unfavourable material may either consciously, or more often unconsciously, be omitted. If the historical examples quoted are used merely in an illustrative fashion, there is nothing but gain, since the case rests on its inherent logic and not on the examples cited. But, if such instances are used as proof, then the argument will need careful consideration to note whether or not opposing evidence exists which ought to have been taken into account.

The process of comparison is vital to such a theoretical study as sociology, and history very often can provide comparative material for the sociologist. Perhaps the crucial test of the worth of any hypothesis is whether or not replication is possible in a comparable situation. In sociology, one way of replicating work is the testing of its application to another culture which may be contemporaneous with the culture in which the hypothesis was first developed. It may, however, mean using another time period, either earlier in the history of the same culture or in the history of a totally different society. An excellent example of a series of such complex comparisons is that undertaken by Stone in the paper included in this Reader in which he is concerned with examining the part played by education as a precondition for an industrial revolution. To investigate this problem he compares historical data relating to various periods in the history of both Japan and England.

At a more technical level sociologists borrow concepts and techniques from historians. Such a historical idea as feudalism has become central to much sociological thinking about the early roots of capitalism and hence to considerations of the movement towards an industrialized society. Again, sociologists can learn much from historians about the techniques of handling primary source material. In several papers included in this Reader extensive use is made of such evidence; for example, Charmian Cannon relies greatly on reports of parliamentary debates in her study of the influence of religion on education in early twentieth-century England. Great care is needed in interpreting this type of material. Indeed, on the whole sociologists have tended to use such secondary material as historical monographs rather than carry out their own original historical research, partly because of the very time-consuming nature of the latter type of enquiry, but also because very few have developed the necessary skills for handling such data. Thus, of the papers included here, Goody and Watt in their study of the consequences of literacy rely heavily on secondary material, while Musgrave relies extensively on original sources in his examination of the various factors in the demand for technical education over the last century in Britain, though historians might question the methods whereby he uses this material.

This process of borrowing is mutual, as historians are now borrowing concepts and techniques from sociologists. Examples may be found in this Reader. Kahan, a historian, for example, uses the concept of the market and also elementary statistical techniques in a sociological manner in order to study the spread of literacy in nineteenth-century Russia. We can see that not only do sociologists use, for their own purposes, the fruits of specialist study by historians, but also that there is some historical work (for example, the paper just mentioned) that is to them truly sociological in nature.

SOME PROBLEMS OF THE SOCIOLOGICAL USE OF HISTORY

The use of historical material in sociology does, however, raise a number of methodological problems. The first of these relates to the often repeated claim that history deals with unique happenings. In a narrow sense this is true.[1] No parliament contains the same members twice, if only because at the second time of looking they are all that much older and have, since last observed, undergone a variety of new experiences. In addition, every parliament varies in length and usually also in its composition by party. Yet despite such differences we all recognize a new parliament as a member of its genus. The historian tends to focus on the unique parliament, whereas the sociologist is operating at another level of analysis, being interested in whether the unique parliament can illuminate some general hypothesis relating to all parliaments or all parliaments of a certain type, for example, all those dominated by right-wing parties. It is relevant at this point to quote Duverger who has written of two categories of history; he speaks of 'institutional' and 'evential' histories. The former focuses on changing institutions, while the latter concentrates on detailed series of happenings: 'The former is a genuine historical sociology, while the latter provides raw material for the social sciences.'[2] To take this stance makes the problem of uniqueness manageable, because once again the difficulty is clearly seen to be due to the different aims that historians and sociologists have when they use the same or similar material. The former focuses on the more unique aspects of the events under examination, while the latter stresses those aspects of the same happenings wherein similarities may be found.

Yet another problem follows because the sociologist must now decide at what level of analysis he is operating. The historian is concerned with a period of time and the explanation of what happened within it and why this occurred. In most cases no one central theory will organize his approach to these questions. What he includes or excludes from his account will depend largely upon what his interests are and what question he is tackling. Thus, the account by an art historian of the seventeenth century in England will be different from that by a constitutional or economic historian, though there will be some overlap. For example, the rise of the middle class will probably figure in each of the three accounts. The sociologist, on the other hand, aims to falsify laws consciously, so the laws must perforce be explicit.[3] The substance of the analysis will therefore relate to the nature of the law concerned. In addition the time scale and form of enquiry will also determine how deep the sociologist goes, though naturally he has a scientific duty to take notice of all relevant evidence. Any one piece of

---

[1] See P. Winch, *The Idea of a Social Science* (London, 1958), pp. 24–33.

[2] M. Duverger, *Introduction to the Social Sciences* (London, 1964), p. 62.

[3] C. B. Joynt and N. Rescher, 'The Problem of Uniqueness in History', *History and Theory*, Vol. I, No. 2 (1961), pp. 150–62, is relevant to this and the last paragraph.

contradictory data has to be quoted and explained or the theory recast to take it into account.

Since, then, at some level events and institutions are not unique, we can use that basic method of sociology, namely comparison. In setting similar cases from different cultures beside one another, the sociologist hopes to isolate factors that lead to the similarities or differences between societies. An example of this method is the paper already mentioned by Stone in which he illuminates the part played by education in the process of industrialization by examining the experience of two societies, namely Japan and England. Such comparisons raise very definite methodological problems. Basically the hope is that a result will be achieved akin to that resulting from an experiment in a laboratory. After such experiments, statements of the following order are possible: if two chemicals A and B of given strengths are mixed in specified proportions in water of given purity and heated to a certain temperature, then chemical C of a certain strength will form. Under the controlled conditions of the laboratory this will always occur. But when we use history as our laboratory, how can we control all the conditions prevailing in so exact a fashion? Even assuming, as I believe, that Stone selected a good sample of data, how can he hold constant a myriad of potentially important factors in such complex and changing societies as Japan or England during their periods of industrialization? He probably cannot, but all sociologists who work in this field have to be as careful as possible, with the object of achieving, in some measure, the degree of control that is possible in the scientist's laboratory.[1]

Another problem in comparative work is similar to one met by anthropologists who face the possibility of taking an ethnocentric view of the culture that they are studying. When a sociologist examines an historical culture and uses a conceptual tool, such as the idea of bureaucracy that has been developed in twentieth-century Western society, he, like the anthropologist using the concept of the nuclear family, cannot be sure that he is not creating a reality that never existed in the culture that he is analysing. Perhaps this problem is best exemplified in the paper by Father Ong that is included in this Reader. He applies the concept of a puberty rite, developed among 'primitive' cultures, to historical data relating to Europe in the period after the Rennaissance. By doing so he certainly throws new light on what was happening in the school classrooms of that period. Yet, when we use similar methods of analysis, we must beware of creating a conjectural history that bears no relation whatsoever to what, by most other criteria, seems to have occurred.

The very fact that history is about time and the order of events raises a further

---

[1] For problems of comparison, see S. M. Lipset, 'History and Sociology: Some Methodological Considerations', in S. M. Lipset and R. Hofstadter (eds), *Sociology and History: Methods* (New York, 1968); and J. T. Flint, 'A Handbook for Historical Sociologists', *Comparative Studies in Society and History*, Vol. X, No. 4 (July 1968). This latter paper is an examination of the methods used in G. E. Swanson, *Religion and Regime: A Sociological Account of the Reformation* (Ann Arbor, 1967).

methodological problem. This concerns the way in which history is divided into periods so that we speak, for example, of the Tudor period or the Industrial Revolution. In essence, to categorize a given stretch of time in such a way is to make the hypothesis that there is an important and identifiable break in the flow of history. In other words, there is a big enough discontinuity to make what occurred before seem very different in certain ways from what followed. In the two cases just cited, there were changes in the mechanisms of government after the Tudors came to power, and in the rate of expansion in industry after about 1760, that marked these periods off from the years immediately before. Many sociologists who are interested in social change, in why the before became the after, are attracted to using history to test out their theories. They are, therefore, concerned with the before and after, which means that they are driven to identify the points at which discontinuities in the process of history occur.

Various criteria have been used for determining periods in history. Marx saw a general pattern of history shaped by the changing relationships of man to the instruments of production; in this way he identified periods of slavery, feudalism, capitalism, and predicted one of socialism. Some economic historians divide their fields of interest according to the stage of development of economic theory; thus, they have used such periods as those of mercantilism or *laissez-faire*. Another economic historian, Rostow, has divided the process of economic growth into stages and applied these to a number of national case-studies; he speaks of the traditional society, the preconditious stage, take-off and the drive to maturity.[1] It is only by considering a number of examples such as these that a sociologist can grasp the answer to his problem of determining what criteria to use in deciding on periods. The nature of the hypothesis or theory being tested, or of the question being asked, will play the vital role in determining which discontinuities are important, since any era may be analysed along several dimensions, in each of which different discontinuities will be found. Certainly, major breaks such as the Reformation may affect most or all dimensions, but often sociologists are working along specialized lines which have their own rationale. For example, in the paper included here by Musgrave on English educational history since 1860, the periods used are those relevant to his problem, namely the discovery of a pattern in the changes in educational structure over the years considered, and the discontinuities that he discovers may be of no service in any other field than that of the sociology of education.

Finally, there is an epistemological problem. Every established discipline tends to have a central mode of justifying statements as true or false, although they may also borrow subsidiary methods from other disciplines. Physical scientists warrant their truths by experiment, although they use mathematical techniques in assessing and ordering their results. Mathematicians use deduction as their warrant. Sociologists have increasingly built a positivistic tradition that relies on an experimental approach and calls on the help of statistical techniques

[1] W. W. Rostow, *The Stages of Economic Growth* (Cambridge, 1960).

(recently of great complexity) in manipulating their data. Historians, however, have adopted on the whole a qualitative rather than quantitative approach, weighing pieces of evidence in an attempt to reconstruct the historical reality. The position taken earlier was that there is an area of research where historians and sociologists are doing much the same thing; where historians are using a theoretical approach, more usually associated with sociological work, to order their evidence and where sociologists must re-create a historical reality before they can begin to test their perhaps somewhat general hypotheses. In this area of overlap between the two disciplines, there is more chance that the modes of justification will have something in common. The sociologist will, perforce, put less stress on quantification than his fellow-sociologist working on contemporary data, while the historian will put more weight on making explicit the structuring theories or hypotheses than will his brother historian working on other historical problems.

An attempt must be made to summarize these introductory remarks. The problem for the sociologist using historical material is to replicate something approaching experimental conditions in order to reveal 'the logic of the situation'.[1] His method is to develop by trial and error; that is, through repeated falsification of hypotheses, a model which is 'sociological in concept and historical in execution'.[2] Because of the necessity of saving valuable time, he will most often be a user of secondary historical material, but research into original sources may become essential to answer some of his questions. From this process of using historical material and doing historical research is born the true 'historical sociology' or 'sociological history'. The question of which of the two emphases is given may be influenced by a combination of such factors as the tradition in which the worker has been trained, the nature of the problem concerned and of the evidence available, and, last but by no means least, the researcher's own predilections.

Aims and contents of this Reader

The main aim of this Reader, as far as the pure sociologist is concerned, is to introduce a particular sociological genre which has gone rather out of fashion in recent years. There have been a number of substantive areas where sociologists have made history one of the main sources of their data, or a major field of research. The outstanding examples are, perhaps, the sociologies of knowledge and of science, where such central problems as the way in which styles of thought alter with changes in the social structure clearly force recourse to history. There has also been, however, a certain amount of work in this style that relates to the specific field of the sociology of education. In this latter context, the aim is to provide a wide range of relevant material that assists in the greater understanding

[1] K. Popper, *The Poverty of Historicism* (London, 1957), p. 149.
[2] W. J. Cahnham and A. Boskoff (eds), *Sociology and History* (New York, 1965), p. 560.

of the place of education, whether as a structure or as a process, in various types of social system. This may be presumed to be the general hope of all those working in the substantive area of the sociology of education.

THE CHOICE OF MATERIAL

These aims provide the criteria for the choice of the papers included here. An attempt has been made to provide as wide a coverage of the methods and uses of historical material and techniques as is possible in a substantive area where there may be more relevant material than in many other areas, but where, nevertheless, there is by no means an excess. Thus, there are, on the one hand, several papers characterized by what may be termed the narrative style, but which have great sociological relevance. Such is Bamford's account of the relationship of school and urban community in nineteenth-century Rugby. On the other hand, there is the more theoretical paper by Musgrave, in which he examines education in England in the nineteenth century with the object of contributing towards at least the conceptual framework for the analysis of social change, if not of constructing a model of such change. Again, there are a number of empirical papers, both qualitative and quantitative in character. Musgrove's paper on the family comes under the first heading in that he weighs evidence from many sources to substantiate his hypothesis that the educative function of the family was in some important respects transferred to the school during the early nineteenth century, while his paper on the status of the young in Britain since about 1780 illustrates the more quantitative approach.

This Reader also aims to show how sociological concepts may be used on historical material in this particular substantive area. A large number of concepts are used in the material presented here. In addition to those already referred to so far, such as the interrelationship of social institutions (Musgrove) and puberty rites (Ong), four other important concepts that are commonly used in contemporary sociology are illustrated here.

Firstly, there is the idea of the definition of the situation used by Musgrave in the paper mentioned above on social change. In fact, this concept is, as will be seen, central to the way in which the material chosen for the Reader is presented. Secondly, there is the concept of ideology; a paper by Wellens on anti-intellectualism shows the way in which this concept may be used. Next, Baron's examination of the changing role of the headmaster in the nineteenth century, and Cannon's perhaps rather amusing account of the development of the role of the woman teacher of physical education during the twentieth century, indicate the way in which the concept of role may be employed as the organizing concept in the sociological analysis of historical data. Finally, Tropp's use of the concept of status, in his account of the changing status of the teacher over the last century, shows the important part that the sociological use of history can play in considering such a contemporary problem as that of the professionalism of an occupation, and also the immense implications for the making of practical policies that such an analysis can have.

THE OUTLINE OF THE READER

The principle used here to organize the material presented is that an examination of the definition of the child and of education in all its aspects can provide an advantageous starting-point for an analysis of the overall position of education as an institution in any society, and of the interrelationships between education and various other social institutions. Furthermore, such social definitions are worked out as educational organizations at the various levels of the educational system' for instance, as schools or universities, and also in the processes that occur within such organizations – for example, in teaching methods.

In Part One, therefore, a number of definitions of education are presented which relate mainly to Britain or even to England. Such definitions result in a higher or lower status being given to education, and in Part Two the overall position of education is examined in a number of societies. More particularly, some attention is given to the development of literacy as a worthwhile skill and the consequences of this for education. Part Three presents work that relates education to other social institutions, such as the economy, the family and the polity. Lastly, in Part Four there are a number of papers showing the way in which definitions of the child and of education are transformed into expected behaviour in such positions as headmaster or teacher. By this final stage we have moved from considering rather abstract social definitions of education to examining how these definitions are translated into behaviour in the classroom where teacher and child interact.

PART ONE

Definitions of the Child and of Education

IF THE DEFINITIONS of the child and of education ruling at any moment in time can be isolated, we have a starting-point for an analysis of the main influences upon the educational system and of the processes at work within it. Questions such as the following may be asked: who are those who make the definitions, or oppose or agree with them, and who has the power to translate these definitions into educational structures and organizations? And how do these definitions affect the processes at work within the organizations that are established? Some answers to such questions will be given in the second and third parts of this Reader. Definitions of the child and of education also rule the goals given to those who run schools, and the behaviour expected of the pupils that they teach. Studies examining this process are included in the last part. Furthermore, if we follow the ways in which such definitions have changed through time, we may reach some understanding of the ways in which processes of social change relate to education.

This approach is illustrated here by five extracts. In the first Musgrave is concerned to understand the way in which education in England has changed since 1860 and tries to construct, if not a model, at least a conceptual framework, that throws light upon this process, while at the same time contributing in some small measure to the more general sociological problem of how to conceptualize social change. Musgrave uses definitions of education from official sources. Ariès, however, in his study of the definitions of the child which were prevailing in early modern Europe, searched original sources such as paintings, plays and various other types of literary work. In the brief passage quoted here he summarizes his findings on two views of the child that still influence the way we behave towards children and the behaviour that we expect of them. All such roles are accorded a status and Musgrove shows in his paper, included in Part One, how the status of the child in Britain, since about 1780, has first fallen and then risen. He mainly deploys demographic evidence, but also uses literary and anthropological data to substantiate his hypothesis.

Definitions of education are made within the ethos of their time. Over the period since the process of industrialization in Britain began there has been a marked antipathy to things intellectual, especially among those who have had political and economic power. Wellens traces the origin of this state in a brief comparative study. He contrasts the somewhat different versions of this anti-intellectual tradition in Britain and the United States with the apparently more intellectual tradition of the U.S.S.R. As Wellens indicates, anti-intellectualism has had a marked effect on the way in which education and the economy are linked. Clearly one moderating factor here is the definition given to technical education. In the final paper in this section Musgrave provides a case study of the way in which one particular definition of education changed through the comparatively brief period of half a century, admittedly one of rapid economic and social change. He also traces in detail the influence of the ideology that Wellens describes on one mediating definition – that of technical education, and also, by implication, its influence upon the growth of one particular sector of the educational system.

I   A Model for the Analysis of the Development of the English Educational System from 1860[1]

P. W. MUSGRAVE

The development of the educational system of a country is one specific but central example of social change. Historians and sociologists have rarely examined the changing structure of English education in sociological terms,[2] and among those who have done so only one has specifically related his analysis to a model of social change. Duncan Mitchell used the changing social class structure in England over the last century and a half as his central analytical theme.[3] While social class was vitally important in England during this period, to use it as the central analytical concept obviates the possibility of relating this specific example of social change to any more general theoretical model and thereby stands in the way of relating the understanding gained in this specific field to general theories of social change. More particularly, this method fails to identify other important foci in the process of educational development and of social change.

The problem to be considered here, namely the development of the English educational system since 1860, raises certain difficulties of delimiting boundaries since the term 'educational system' as used in common parlance includes several sub-sectors, for instance, both the private and the maintained schools or organ-

---

[1] Paper given to the Research Group on the Sociology of Education at the Sixth World Congress of Sociology, Evian, September 1966. I wish to thank Professor Raymond Illsley, James C. Kincaid and Gordon W. Horobin, all of the University of Aberdeen, for their comments on an earlier version of this paper.

[2] See, however, A. E. Dobbs, *Education and Social Movements, 1700–1850* (London, 1919); O. Banks, *Parity and Prestige in English Secondary Education* (London, 1955); S. F. Cotgrove, *Technical Education and Social Change* (London, 1958).

[3] G. Duncan Mitchell, 'Education, Ideology, and Social Change in England', in G. K. Zollschan and W. Hirsch (eds), *Explorations in Social Change* (London, 1964). For a somewhat similar approach, though not related specifically to the theory of social change, see D. V. Glass, 'Education and Social Change in Modern England', in M. Ginsberg (ed.), *Law and Opinion in England in the Twentieth Century* (London, 1959).

First printed as pp. 65-82 of Vol. IV of Transactions of the Sixth World Congress of Sociology, *(1970).*

izations giving both secondary and higher education. Furthermore, other social institutions, such as the family, or the economy, as in the case of apprenticeship, undertake simultaneously some of the same functions as the educational system. For the purposes of this analysis the educational system will be taken to include all those social systems, at whatever level, specifically created to educate.

I

THE DEFINITION OF THE SITUATION

Central to the model to be used here is the idea of the definition of the situation. Such a definition indicates in a general form the forces at work in an institutional sphere and is derived from the value system of those who bring power to bear on the formulation of the definition. Actors in the sphere to which the definition is relevant take their goals from it.[1]

In this case the definitions to be considered are those of education taken from Acts of Parliament, official reports or speeches in parliament. From these definitions action has followed. A critic might consider these definitions to be interpretations of the ideology of the ruling class. However, certainly since the Parliamentary Reform Act of 1832, there has been enough real power conflict in British politics for definitions of this type to represent compromises between conflicting interests within a dialogue that assumed a higher-level consensus of values about the nature of a democratic system. These definitions were the end-product of a bargaining process, a 'truce situation'.[2] In this context political parties can be said to inhabit a plural society, and their different value systems from time to time may allow a measure of consensus, which may or may not be marked by an agreed definition of the situation.[3] Where agreement is not reached, the truce situation will be broken when the next change of political power occurs. What can be already seen, and this will become even clearer, is that this process of definition contains within itself the possibility of further change.

From this definition of the situation goals are given to the relevant institutional sphere, in this case to the educational system or to that part of the system for which the definition is operant. As a result of these goals positions are created and norms evolve that govern the roles of the actors filling the new positions. The assumption here is that the goals given influence the system and not vice versa. The possibility that the educational system will influence the nature of its own goals must be considered at a later stage.

Thus, as a result of a defining of the situation a process is started by which an educational system is either established or reorganized in such a way that it attains the goals given to it. Manpower and materials are claimed in order to fill

[1] See T. Parsons, *Essays in Sociological Theory* (Glencoe, 1954), pp. 143–5.
[2] J. Rex, *Key Problems of Sociological Theory* (London, 1961), pp. 127–9.
[3] J. Rex, 'The Plural Society and Social Theory', *B.J.S.* (April 1959).

the positions created for teachers and to provide for the capital and current physical resources that are needed so that the system may adapt to goals defined for it. These resources will need co-ordination, and some administrative element will be necessary to integrate the efforts made to attain the goals laid down explicitly or implicitly by the definition. Finally, the system must ensure that the pattern established is maintained in two ways. Firstly, it must socialize its members, whether newly recruited or already present, into the norms now operating and must attempt to keep the behaviour of its members within the range of role behaviour permitted by these norms. Secondly, the system must take measures to see that its products, namely educated beings, meet the requirements laid upon it by the definition. These two needs clearly demand the institutionalization of conditions of employment in certain roles, for example that of teacher at primary or at secondary level, behind which lie specific levels of education.

The norms and roles in the system will rarely be specified in exact detail and, therefore, a socially permitted range of indeterminacy will exist within which small differences are possible. This range enables the system to manage a certain amount of tension without a redefinition of the situation, but it also permits cumulative movement towards either limit of the permitted range. This, or indeed any other form of experiment within the range, allows the development of autonomous change. Such a process is very important for the analysis of the English educational system in view of the fact that it grew in a prevailing atmosphere of *laissez-faire*. As a result much scope for freedom has been usual at every level of the educational system.

So far a brief description has been given of a stationary model of the Parsonian type using those functional dimensions of the situation, namely goal-attainment, adaptation, integration and pattern-maintenance, that Smelser has used for historical analysis elsewhere.[1] Here, however, the Parsonian terms have been used to analyse an administrative process. Care has been taken to allow for the possibility that future change may be generated within the model itself in two ways. Firstly, there is the chance of autonomous development of change within the system itself, and secondly, the definition of the situation has been seen as a result of a power struggle leading to a truce situation which could be changed by an alteration in the power brought to bear, or by a change in the values governing the use of that power.

II

THE PROBLEM OF CHANGE

The various social changes that influence such institutions as the educational system can be put into certain categories. Thus, changes may be placed on a continuum with the poles major and minor; the demarcation line between the

[1] N. J. Smelser, *Social Change in the Industrial Revolution* (London, 1959).

two categories is arbitrary, the criterion being some measure of the effect of the change. An example of major change is the educational reorganization eventually needed to cope with the demands of the economy as a result of the Industrial Revolution. The minor changes that occur within a system can be absorbed within the range of indeterminacy allowed by the present definition of the situation, but can also be of a cumulative nature, eventually creating such strain that some redefinition of the situation becomes essential for a continuance of the system, albeit in a new form. An example here is the cumulative growth of the educational system within the framework erected as a result of the 1870 Elementary Education Act. By the end of the century the educational system had evolved beyond the limits of the original definition. In addition, the different parts of the system (for example, the secondary and the technical sectors) were developing at very different rates. As a result a radical redefinition of the situation was essential. In fact, as is often the case, there were exogenous factors such as changes in the power structure and the value system governing its use that hastened the necessary redefinition.

A second continuum against which changes can be categorized is that of sudden/gradual. Here the criterion is the rate of realization of impact. The effect of modern war is sudden. In 1939 the outbreak of war was rapidly followed by the mass evacuation of children from large urban areas, and this led to the closing of many schools. Gradual change is illustrated by the effect of industrialization on a social system. The structure of the various parts of a system must readjust to meet such a major gradual change. In the case of England during this period the family came to hand over part of its educative function to several parts of the educational system including, for instance, the schools.[1]

Lastly, changes may be either general to the whole social system (or to a large part of it, including the institution under consideration), or may be particular to that institution. The outbreak of a war or the process of industrialization are general changes, while a technical improvement in teaching methods such as the introduction of structural mathematics or the Initial Teaching Alphabet are particular changes only affecting the educational system. Under contemporary conditions this latter type of change is usually sudden in impact, as the existence of educational journals and the holding of technical exhibitions speed up the diffusion of such cultural innovations.

Whether the change is generated within the system or comes from without, strains will appear at an operational level within the system. Thus, at a social-system level the educational system may fail to meet the demands put on it by other institutions; for example, the supply of physicists may not meet the demands of the economic or military systems, or, again, the nature of education for girls may not meet the needs of a society in which marriage is taking place

[1] F. Musgrove, 'The Decline of the Educative Family', *Universities Quarterly* (September 1960), and 'Middle-Class Families and Schools, 1780–1880', *Sociological Review* (1959). (Included in this Reader, Part Three, No. 1.)

at an earlier age. At the institutional level one part of the educational system may not meet the needs of another. For example, the secondary system may produce more youths able and wanting to undertake higher education than the tertiary level can absorb. This latter case is an example of the potentialities going to waste which are inherent in a given level of differentiation of the system.

Autonomous change may develop within the interstices of the system. Where there is indeterminacy in norms and tolerances of slight deviance, ambiguity exists, exploitable by those with a slightly different definition of the situation from the agreed one. In this case, as Lockwood has said, 'Authority is never given, but is always contingent upon its exercise.'[1] If sufficient tolerance exists, there is the possibility that either to meet their own slightly different values or to meet external needs by short-cutting official action, an individual or a group of individuals may redefine the situation and act upon their new definition. A classic example of this was the development of the Department of Science and Art in the second half of the last century. This department was established in 1853 to further the teaching of science and art, as applied to industry, to members of the lower classes who had left school, but by 1899 when its more or less complete autonomy was ended, its activities were, in the main, aimed at teaching science to middle-class boys of secondary school age.[2] Eisenstadt has christened groups of this nature that have values at odds with those governing the existing definition of the situation as 'anti-systems'.[3]

III

REDEFINITION OF THE SITUATION

When the strains, either at the social-system level or at institutional level, become sufficiently intense, activity akin to Smelser's collective behaviour occurs.[4] The system is at present functioning inadequately. New or somewhat different beliefs are brought to bear on the situation and ultimately a redefinition of the situation is made. The important question here is the determination of 'the threshold values beyond which equilibrium will break down'.[5] As Moore has pointed out, the idea of 'the threshold' stresses that the trigger cause of a great change may be 'a small change in one element'.[6] The result of this redefinition will be a new truce situation, a resultant of the new balance of power of a political

[1] D. Lockwood, 'Social Integration and System Integration', pp. 246–7, footnote 2, in G. K. Zollschan and W. Hirsch, op. cit.

[2] See P. W. Musgrave, *Technical Change, Education and the Labour Force* (Oxford, 1967), Chaps. 6 and 7, *passim.*

[3] S. N. Eisenstadt, 'Institutionalization and Change', *A.S.R.* (April 1964), p. 247.

[4] See N. J. Smelser, *Theory of Collective Behaviour* (London, 1962), especially Chaps. 1 and 4.

[5] T. Parsons, 'A Functional Theory of Change', in A. and E. Etzioni (eds), *Social Change* (New York, 1964), p. 97.

[6] W. E. Moore, 'Discontinuities in the Theory of Change', *A.S.R.* (April 1964), p. 334.

nature either at social-system or at institutional level. The nature of this new definition will be governed by the relative strength of the various vested interests, whether for or against change, that bear upon the particular situation. At this point the influence of pressure groups such as professional associations can be important. The resulting definition will embody the value systems of these various interests as filtered through the conflict leading to the new truce situation. Thus the 1944 Education Act was more egalitarian than the 1902 Education Act had been, reflecting the move from a more ascriptive to a more achievement-oriented society, the symbol of which was the rise of the Labour Party between these dates.

The result of a redefinition of the situation can be examined by using again the Parsonian functional dimensions. There will be a redeployment of manpower and resources to meet the new goals, a new mode of integration and new norms to maintain the rearranged system. On the whole the redefinition will probably result in a more differentiated system. Social change has usually proceeded in the direction of complexity; the increasingly fine division of labour is the paradigm case. This does not seem a logical imperative of change. For example, the educational system of a depopulating area in the north of Scotland may grow less differentiated. However, the same sources of this social change are simultaneously bringing increasing differentiation to the educational systems of Aberdeen, Glasgow, London or even of parts of Canada, that is, in the areas receiving the migrating population.

This increasing differentiation makes the task of integrating the system more complex and increases the chance of autonomous change in two ways. If the range of indeterminacy in norms is increased to allow individuals more scope to deal with the more complex system, there is even more chance of agreed autonomous change through constant re-interpretation within the allowed limits of the norms. A case in point was the frequent revision of the Elementary Code between the 1860s and 1890s and, again, the publication of various Regulations in the first decade of this century to interpret the 1902 Education Act. Important and agreed changes were generated within the administrative system itself. If, however, an attempt is made to control the greater complexity of the system by tighter bureaucratic control, there is a greater chance of disagreement with the now explicit norms; truce situations will be less durable and, hence, there will be a more frequent need for redefinition of the situation.

The model has so far described the process of change, but not why the system did not go into a state of uncontrolled and accelerating change. An institution interlocks with other institutions and it is in this fact that we must seek the explanation of why change proceeds at a relatively controlled rate. Some of these institutions are at any moment more salient for the institution under consideration than are others and therefore bring more power to bear on the establishment or the breaking and re-establishing of truce situations. Thus, in the case of the educational system, religion was salient until around the middle of the nineteenth century, though it has maintained much influence during this century despite the so-called 'decline in religion'.[1] After the 1860s the class structure became more salient.[2] Over the whole period the salience of the economy has grown gradually greater until, since 1945, it has probably had as much salience for education as has social class.[3] Symbolic of this struggle for salience between these two institutions is the nicely balanced argument that this country cannot afford to reorganize secondary education on a comprehensive basis in the name of equality because of the possible disruption of the flow of highly educated manpower to the economy. In general the economy has a great salience with regard to the educational system, since the national income must be a certain size before a significant proportion can be devoted to the creation of a developed educational system, and this is true whether the schools are state-provided or not. Yet, paradoxically, in an industrialized society once the national income is of a certain size, or, perhaps, when it starts to grow at more than a certain rate, the presence of an educational system becomes vital to maintain the system either as stable or in growth. It may be that one institution has greater salience for one part of the educational system than for others, either at one moment or through time; the economy has had great salience for technical education throughout the whole of the last century.[4]

Before applying the model, one point remains. So far the assumption has been made that the educational system does not influence its own goals or, to put it in another way, that education is a resultant but not a determinant of culture. This assumption must be relaxed to account for such cases as the growth of technologies, such as metallurgy, brought about by research in pure science within the universities which was completely autonomous, owing nothing to demands from the economy. The model can account for these and similar changes because their ultimate effect is through the transmission of this new knowledge beyond the educational system. Hence the value system outside the educational system is changed, and there is a demand for a redefinition of the situation to meet the new value system and, possibly, a new power structure.

IV

The next step is to trace out the way in which the definition of the educational situation has changed over the last century. There is only space here to treat in a brief way the parts of the educational system that have now become the primary

[1] See Charmian Cannon, 'The Influence of Religion on Educational Policy, 1902–1944', *Br. J. of Educ. Studies* (May 1964), especially pp. 154–60. (Included in this Reader, Part Three, No. 6.)

[2] See Brian Simon, *Education and the Labour Movement, 1870–1920* (London, 1965), *passim*.

[3] See S. F. Cotgrove, op. cit.

[4] P. W. Musgrave, 'Constant factors in the Demand for Technical Education since 1860', *B.J.E.S.* (May 1966). (Included in this Reader, Part Three, No. 4.)

and secondary sectors, though any complete treatment would deal with the various forms of infant, higher and technical education.[1]

Prior to the passing of the 1870 Elementary Education Act the educational system was simple in form. What elementary schools existed were mainly financed by voluntary societies of a religious nature; secondary education was provided by private proprietary schools or by grammar and other schools on ancient foundations that were often inefficient. There was no central organization controlling this rudimentary system and criticism was growing by the middle of the century, partly because of various structural strains but also because the facts about the schools were now more fully known and this in itself influenced values. As part of the 1851 decennial Census, Horace Mann had compiled a report, 'Education in England and Wales', which revealed the low proportion of children then attending any school. During the period 1859–68 three Royal Commissions considered the educational system of the country. In the reports of these commissions may be found the definitions of the educational situation, by the ruling class of the time, for the education of its own children and those of the other social classes. The working class had little direct influence on these definitions. The middle class, however, could bring some influence to bear because a generation after the 1832 Reform Act it had representatives in parliament who had begun to make it understood that the British economy needed an efficient educational system to meet contemporary conditions, and more particularly the growth of foreign competition.

In 1861 the Newcastle Commission defined elementary education in terms of the ability to read 'a common narrative', writing 'a letter that shall be both legible and intelligible' and knowing 'enough of ciphering to make out, or test the correctness of a common shop bill', together with a little geography and the ability 'to follow the allusions and the arguments of a plain Saxon sermon'[2] – in other words a Christian version of 'the three Rs' for boys and girls up to the age of 10 or 12.

In the report of the Clarendon Commission (1864) the upper class defined its own education in terms of a mainly classical diet, but wished to add some mathematics and science.[3] It should be noted that this education was defined mainly in terms of boys. However, it is in the report of the Taunton Commission (1868) that one finds the first plan for the organization of what today would be called secondary education, a term that Matthew Arnold in his role of H.M.I. was introducing into English educational discourse as a result of his comparative studies of European educational systems. For the first time stress was put on the secondary education of girls, by this Commission. Their report suggested three

---

[1] For a short treatment of this latter field, see P. W. Musgrave, 'The Definition of Technical Education, 1860–1910', *Vocational Aspect* (summer 1964). (Included in this Reader, Part One, No. 5.)

[2] *Report of R.C. on the State of Popular Education in England*, Vol. I (1861), p. 243.

[3] See *Report of R.C. on the Revenues and Management of Certain Colleges and Schools* (1864).

grades of school: the first was for the children of the upper and professional classes and would continue to the age of about 18. It was seen as giving 'something more than classics and mathematics'. The second-grade schools stopped at 16 and were mainly to serve the mercantile and higher commercial classes. Their curriculum was, therefore, seen as containing 'a certain amount of thorough knowledge of those subjects which can be turned to practical use in business'; Latin was barely tolerated by this class of people. The third-grade schools were for the upper working class ('The smaller tenant farmers, the small tradesmen, the superior artisans') and their needs were described as 'very good reading, very good writing, very good arithmetic'.[1]

The definitions of the educational situation contained in these commissions represented the truce situation of the time and influenced the patterns of implementation of the Acts that followed the three reports. In fact, the Newcastle Commission's immediate influence was upon the Revised Code (of Regulations for Elementary Education) of 1862, but this Code in its changing forms was, after 1870, administered under the Elementary Education Act which founded the state educational system in England. Legislation relating to the second field followed both the other commissions and led to the some reorganization and expansion of education at this level.

The truce situation in the elementary sector had been hard to reach because of the difficulty of satisfying the various religious bodies concerned with educational provision. By the 1880s the religious denominations were beginning to question the definition subsumed under the 1870 Act. As a result the Cross Commission was set up to examine the working of the Elementary Education Act. Two further strains led to a questioning of the whole settlement of the 1870s. There was, firstly, a strain between the educational system and another institutional area, namely the economy. This was due to the relatively slow growth of secondary education when measured against the needs of the economy. This led to the development of post-elementary education, secondary in character, within the elementary sector. Secondly, there was a strain within the educational system itself due to the very diffuse growth of technical education both before, and particularly after, the 1889 Technical Instruction Act, which was the first Act to define fully the situation for technical education. Most of this latter development was under the control of the Department of Science and Art which appeared to follow a policy completely divorced from that of any other educational body. There was obviously a need for an overall redefinition of the situation to eliminate these strains. In 1894 the Bryce Commission on Secondary Education was set up. Its report in 1895 was soon followed by two major Acts.

The Bryce Commission had recommended a central department to co-ordinate the educational system. There was a need to integrate the educational activities of the Elementary Education Department, the Department of Science and Art and the educational section of the Charity Commission, which had been respon-

[1] *Schools Inquiry Commission*, Vol. I (1868), pp. 15–21.

sible since the Taunton Commission for much of the reorganization of the private sector of secondary education. This was achieved by the Education Act of 1899 which established the Board of Education. The 1902 Education Act established a new truce situation between those with the main vested interest in the provision of schools (more particularly between the various religious denominations), and also between the central government and various forms of local authority. In addition this act paved the way for the establishment and growth of a state-provided secondary system. The Bryce Commission had expressed its desire that the 'freedom, variety (and) elasticity' of the English system should be preserved.[1] There were therefore the minimum number of specific definitions of the situation in the Act.

The range of tolerance was wide and the various codes and handbooks that flowed from the new Board set the direction of growth of the system without much difficulty. The Elementary Code of 1904 saw the purpose of this branch of education to be 'to form and strengthen the character, and to develop the intelligence of the children entrusted to it', a much wider definition than that of the Newcastle Commission. The Regulations for Secondary Schools, also issued in 1904, spoke of a 'general' and 'complete' education, 'up to and beyond the age of 16'. Furthermore, the 1902 Act led to an increased differentiation of the state educational system as it authorized local authorities to establish training colleges for teachers. By 1913 twenty such colleges had been founded.

One of the most remarkable provisions of the 1902 Act was the creation of a Consultative Committee. This body of eminent people (who were, in the main, educationalists) was to consider contemporary educational issues referred to it by the government, and make recommendations. In fact the presence of this body created within the system the possibility of continuous redefinition of the educational situation, or at least of the part currently being studied by the Committee. Prior to the outbreak of the First World War, the system envisaged by the 1899 and 1902 Acts was being developed, and it was only after the war that reappraisal began. A massive redefinition occurred under the impact of several forces. Firstly, the whole value system of British society had become more egalitarian and, therefore, the goals of the educational system were defined in very different terms from those of the pre-war era. Secondly, the severe economic depressions of the inter-war period brought into clearer light the dysfunctional way in which the educational system, in certain important respects, was serving the economy. Lastly, a more scientific educational technology had evolved; this was typified by the application of psychology, and particularly psychological testing, to the field of education.

The reappraisal of the social system that was triggered off by the Second World War led to a further attempt to redefine the educational situation in the 1944 Education Act, which forms the legal basis of the present system. The bases of this act lie in the definitions of education generated by three of the reports made

[1] R.C. on Secondary Education, Vol. I (1895), p. 326.

by the Consultative Committee during the inter-war years. Thus, in 1931 the Committee, with Sir W. H. Hadow as Chairman, reported on primary education, and saw its main task as being the provision, to children between 7 and 11, of 'what is essential to their healthy growth – physical, intellectual and moral'. The curriculum was to be 'thought of in terms of activity and experience rather than knowledge to be acquired and facts to be stored'.[1]

This redefinition was clearly a direct, though perhaps even more liberal, descendant of the 1904 Elementary Code. The rethinking that was going on in the secondary sector was much more radical. It was possible to receive schooling from the ages of 5–18 completely within the Elementary Code. In 1926 the Hadow Report on 'The Education of the Adolescent' stated that 'between the age of eleven and (if possible) that of fifteen, all . . . who do not go forward to "secondary education" in the present narrow sense of the word, should go forward none the less to what is, in our view, a form of secondary education, in the truer and broader sense of the word'. The term 'elementary' was to be abolished and there were to be two stages to schooling – primary and secondary. The new, wider secondary education was to be given mainly in either the already existing grammar schools or in the envisaged modern schools, in which 'the courses of instruction, though not merely vocational or utilitarian, should be used to connect the school work with the interests arising from the social and industrial environment of the pupils'.[2]

The redefinition of secondary education as for all children, and of the curriculum as much wider in scope than the mere three Rs of the nineteenth-century elementary school was reinforced by the Spens Report on 'Secondary Education', published late in 1938. In addition, the Consultative Committee, while rejecting the establishment of a multilateral type of school, perhaps comparable to the U.S. high school, recommended the creation of a third type of secondary school, the Technical High School.[3] Many of these recommendations were contained in the wartime coalition government's white paper 'Educational Reconstruction', published in 1943, though probably the clearest presentation of the definition of the educational situation by educationalists at the time is to be found in the Report of the Secondary Schools Examinations Council, with Cyril Norwood as chairman, on 'The Secondary Curriculum and Examinations'. This report was published ten days after the white paper on reconstruction, which it must have influenced. The Norwood report justified the Spens recommendations of three school types and tried to underpin the argument on psychological grounds by discovering three types of mind to fit the three types of schools.[4]

[1] *Report of the Cons. Committee of the B. of E. on The Primary School* (1931), pp. 92–3.
[2] *Report of the Cons. Committee on The Education of the Adolescent* (1926), pp. xxi–xxiii and 175.
[3] *Report of the Cons. Committee on Secondary Education* (1938), pp. xix–xxi.
[4] *Report of the Sec. Sch. Exam. Council on Curriculum and Examinations in Secondary Schools* (1943), pp. 2–3.

The 1944 Education Act was born of these redefinitions, though not all were made explicit. The important switch from codes to stages was clear: 'The statutory system . . . shall be organized in three progressive stages to be known as primary education, secondary education and further education.'[1] The word 'elementary' was cut out of the educational vocabulary. Yet there was no definite legislation on how the secondary level was to be organized, nor did further education include the universities. The assumed definition of the situation was that there should be a tripartite system as the Spens and Norwood Reports had recommended, though this assumption was very quickly challenged.[2] The apparent truce situation of 1944 did not seem to meet the more egalitarian value system of the Labour Party which now wielded more power at both national and local levels.

Since 1944 the educational situation has not been redefined legally, but a constant and varied number of redefinitions[3] have been made, amidst a growing state of strain between the educational system and other social institutions. During this time changes in social institutions have occurred that reflect changes in the relevant value systems. The influential values can be traced in the way the various committees have examined these strains. A brief analysis of the influence of various institutions at the present time follows.

The saliency given to the economy at present can be seen in the Crowther Report's invention of and plea for 'numeracy', and in the case of less able children, in the Newsom Report's stress on the practical, mathematical and scientific sides of the curriculum.[4] The economy, particularly in an age of full employment and with the new stress on research, needs highly educated manpower at all levels. So influential is this demand that the Robbins Committee put as the first objective of 'any properly balanced system' of higher education 'instruction suitable to play a part in the general division of labour'.[5] At all levels the social functions of education are now given at least as much weight as its individual functions. Furthermore, the logic of the development of the occupational structure, as the proportion of labour employed in the tertiary sector rises, now has a strong autonomous influence on the direction and rate of development of the demands for specific types of manpower from the educational system. This growing realization within the economy of the need for trained manpower played a part in the passing of the Industrial Training Act (1964), and the gradual growth of training within industry as a result of this Act will raise the problem

[1] Education Act, 1944, Part II, 7.
[2] Compare the Min. of Educ's *A Guide to the Educational System of England and Wales* ('three main alternative types of secondary education') (1945), with *The New Secondary Education* ('no set guides for organization') (1947).
[3] *Reports of the Min. of Educ's Cent. Adv. Council*, '15 to 18' (Crowther, 1959); *Half our Future* (Newsom, 1963), and *Report of the Committee on Higher Education, Higher Education* (Robbins, 1963).
[4] '15 to 18', pp. 268–81; *Half Our Future*, pp. 128–51. See also *From School to Further Education* (Brunton Report), Scottish Educ. Dept. (1963).
[5] *Higher Education*, p. 6.

of defining the boundary between the economy and the educational system at this point.

Manpower problems are often expressed in demographic terms. However, perhaps the main institutional changes that can be analysed in such terms are those concerning the family. The impact on education of changes in the size, age structure and life cycle of the English family were noted by the Crowther Committee as an influence bearing on any redefinition of the education of girls, and by the Newsom Committee as an important factor in differential social class learning. The latter committee also examined the function of education in relation to changes in contemporary moral values and, hence, in the future quality of family life.[1] At this point there is a link with another social institution – organized religion, which because of the history of the English educational system has a vested interest in any future redefinition. Despite a recent temporary re-definition by administrative regulation of the financial position of the various denominations, little overt attempt has been made to examine what the next truce situation will be *vis-à-vis* the churches.

Finally, social class has been given much attention in post-war thought on education, particularly since the Central Advisory Council's report on 'Early Leaving' (1954) showed the close connection between social class and those leaving selective secondary schools at the minimum legal age before the first external examination. Yet the decreasing importance given to social class in any ideological sense is clear, since social class was mainly used in the 'Early Leaving', Crowther and Robbins (though this is not so true of the Newsom) Reports in the analysis of the loss of talent, a problem given importance in an economic context. Furthermore, much of the present consideration of the reorganization of secondary education, an issue dodged by Crowther and Newsom, has been pursued along similar lines, though the ideological argument of egalitarianism has also been important.

The brief analysis of the saliency of the various social institutions impinging on English education today indicates that the redefinition of the educational situation that seems imminent will be much more influenced by economic interest and much less by organized religion that has been the case at any of the three major truce situations reached over the last hundred years. Indeed, so salient is the economy that the universities may find themselves defined merely as one group of organizations within the general tertiary sector, rather than as special organizations outside the general definition of the educational situation.

V

The main characteristic of the model described here is the idea of the definition of the situation. The advantage of such a starting-point is that the model is of

[1] '15 to 18', pp. 28–35; *Half Our Future*, p. 35, Chaps. 7 and 22, *passim*.

general application at both macro- and micro- level. Implicit in the argument is a denial of the statement that 'each of the special sociologies has its own statics and dynamics and its own empirical problem of discovering uniformities in the processes which sustain or alter the structure with which it is concerned'.[1] The position taken here is that a general model can help uncover those uniformities which are of more importance in one specific institutional area than in another.

If the definition of a situation in one particular area, e.g. education, is examined, the particular set of values that governs the goals of that system can be discovered. Yet such a definition, when embodied in legal or quasi-legal form, constitutes a truce situation and hence is liable to change. In addition, change can come because of the range of tolerance permitted by most of such definitions or, where the range is narrow, from the antagonism caused by excessive rigidity. The agents of change in this model are the actors in the situation who may set up 'anti-systems' or reinterpret regulations within the allowed range – the men have been brought back in.[2]

Here the model has been only partially demonstrated. Further work might convert description into theory. We need to know which power groups were important either consistently or at certain stages in the establishment of truce situations, and which strains were crucial in the process of development. A closer analysis might clarify the concept of 'the threshold' and indicate how much strain, either of the unitary or of a cumulative nature, is needed to trigger off a redefinition of the situation. The accumulation of discreet changes often seems to occur within such an institutional area as the educational system, particularly in a country like England where the range of tolerance has been wide, and detailed work on such processes might be worthwhile. Any theory, however limited in its predictive value, would have to give some explanation of rates and paths of change. A necessary step in its evolution would be its testing on comparative historical data. This is important if only because, as Ginsberg has said, 'societies differ greatly in plasticity'.[3] Part of the reason for this may well be that the attitude to change differs by society, and it could be that societies differ in their attitude to the changing of any one institutional area, for example, to changes in the educational system.

With more space it would be possible to show how after each major redefinition resources had been claimed for the educational system, how integration had been achieved and how the pattern of the system had been maintained. But several results have been achieved. The analysis has led to the posing of some questions, crucial both to the theory of social change and to an analysis of the history of English education. Some of the important definitions have been

[1] J. Rex, in a review of W. E. Moore, *Social Change*, *Sociological Review* (November 1965), p. 349.
[2] See G. C. Homans, 'Bringing Men Back In', *A.J.S.* (December 1964).
[3] M. Ginsberg, 'On Social Change, *B.J.S.* (September 1958), p. 214.

isolated and the pattern of redefinition made clear. It would seem that two of the categories of change described above have been of major importance in the development of the English educational system, namely – major, gradual, general change and minor, sudden, particular change, especially in the latter case where the change is of a cumulative nature.

2 Two Concepts of Childhood

P. ARIÈS

In medieval society the idea of childhood did not exist; this is not to suggest that children were neglected, forsaken or despised. The idea of childhood is not to be confused with affection for children: it corresponds to an awareness of the particular nature of childhood, that particular nature which distinguishes the child from the adult, even the young adult. In medieval society this awareness was lacking. That is why, as soon as the child could live without the constant solicitude of his mother, his nanny or his cradle-rocker, he belonged to adult society. That adult society now strikes us as rather puerile: no doubt this is largely a matter of its mental age, but it is also due to its physical age, because it was partly made up of children and youths. Language did not give the word 'child' the restricted meaning we give it today: people said 'child' much as we say 'lad' in everyday speech. The absence of definition extended to every sort of social activity: games, crafts, arms. There is not a single collective picture of the times in which children are not to be found, nestling singly or in pairs in the *trousse* hung round women's necks,[1] or urinating in a corner, or playing their part in a traditional festival, or as apprentices in a workshop, or as pages serving a knight, etc.

The infant who was too fragile as yet to take part in the life of adults simply 'did not count': this is the expression used by Molière, who bears witness to the survival in the seventeenth century of a very old attitude of mind. Argan in *Le Malade imaginaire* has two daughters, one of marriageable age and little Louison who is just beginning to talk and walk. It is generally known that he is threatening to put his elder daughter in a convent to stop her philandering. His brother asks him: 'How is it, Brother, that rich as you are and having only one daughter, *for I don't count the little one*, you can talk of putting her in a convent?'[2] The little one did not count because she could disappear.

---

[1] Père Michault, *Doctrinal du temps présent*, edited by T. Walton (1931), p. 119: 'Puis vecy une femme grausse, Pourtant deux enfants en sa trousse.' Painting by Van Laer (1592–1642), reproduced in Berndt, No. 468.

[2] *Le Malade imaginaire*, Act III, Scene III. Cf. Montaigne, *Essais*, II, 8.

First printed as the Conclusion to Part One, Centuries of Childhood, *by P. Ariès, translated from the French by R. Baldick (Jonathan Cape, London, 1962), pp. 128–33.*

The quotation from Molière shows the continuance of the archaic attitude to childhood. But this survival, for all that it was stubborn, was precarious. From the fourteenth century on, there had been a tendency to express in art, iconography and religion (in the cult of the dead) the personality which children were seen to possess, and the poetic, familiar significance attributed to their special nature. We have followed the evolution of the *putto* and the child portrait. And we have seen that in the sixteenth and seventeenth centuries the child or infant – at least in the upper classes of society – was given a special costume which marked him out from the adults. This specialization of the dress of children and especially of little boys, in a society in which clothes and outward appearances had considerable importance, bears witness to the change which had taken place in the general attitude towards children: they counted much more than Argan's brother imagined. In fact, *Le Malade imaginaire*, which seems as hard on little children as do certain remarks by La Fontaine, contains a whole conversation between Argan and little Louison: 'Look at me, will you!' 'What is it, papa?' 'Here!' 'What?' 'Haven't you anything to tell me?' 'If you wish, I can tell you, to amuse you, the story of the Ass's skin, or else the fable of the Fox and the Crow which I was taught not so long ago.' A new concept of childhood had appeared, in which the child, on account of his sweetness, simplicity and drollery, became a source of amusement and relaxation for the adult.

To begin with, the attitude was held by women, women whose task it was to look after children – mothers and nannies. In the sixteenth-century edition of *Le Grand Propriétaire de toutes choses* we are told about the nanny: 'She rejoices when the child is happy, and feels sorry for the child when he is ill; she picks him up when he falls, she binds him when he tosses about, and she washes and cleans him when he is dirty.'[1] She brings the child up and teaches him to talk:

She pronounces the words as if she had a stammer, to teach him to talk better and more rapidly . . . she carries him in her hands, then on her shoulder, then on her lap, to play with him when he cries; she chews the child's meat for him when he has no teeth so that he can swallow profitably and without danger; she plays with the child to make him sleep and she binds his limbs to keep them straight so that he has no stiffness in his body, and she bathes and anoints him to nourish his flesh . . .

Thomas More dwells on the subject of the schoolboy being sent to school by his mother:

When the little boy will not rise in time for her, but lies still abed and slugg, and when he is up, weepeth because he hath lien so long, fearing to be beaten at school for his late coming thither, she telleth him then that it is but early days, and he shall come time enough, and biddeth him: 'Go, good son, I warrant thee, I have sent to thy master myself, take thy bread and butter with thee, thou shalt not be beaten at all.'

[1] *Le Grand Propriétaire de toutes choses* (1556).

Thus she sends him off sufficiently reassured not to burst into tears at the idea of leaving her at home, but she does not get to the bottom of the trouble and the late arrival will be well and truly beaten when he gets to school.[1]

Children's little antics must always have seemed touching to mothers, nannies and cradle-rockers, but their reactions formed part of the huge domain of unexpressed feelings. Henceforth people would no longer hesitate to recognize the pleasure they got from watching children's antics and 'coddling' them. We find Mme de Sévigné admitting, not without a certain affectation, how much time she spends playing with her granddaughter: 'I am reading the story of Christopher Columbus's discovery of the Indies, which is entertaining me greatly; but your daughter entertains me even more. I do so love her . . . she strokes your portrait and caresses it in such an amusing way that I have to kiss her straight away.'[2] 'I have been playing with your daughter for an hour now; she is delightful.' And, as if she were afraid of some infection, she adds, with a levity which surprises us, for the death of a child is something serious for us and nothing to joke about: 'I do not want her to die.' For, as we have seen from Molière, this first appreciation of childhood went with a certain indifference, or rather with the indifference that was traditional.

The 'coddling' attitude towards children is even better known to us by the critical reactions it provoked at the end of the sixteenth century and particularly in the seventeenth century. Peevish persons found insufferable the attention paid to children. Montaigne bristles: 'I cannot abide that passion for caressing new-born children, which have neither mental activities nor recognizable bodily shape by which to make themselves lovable, and I have never willingly suffered them to be fed in my presence.' He cannot accept the idea of loving children 'for our amusement, like monkeys', or taking pleasure in their 'frolickings, games and infantile nonsense'.[3]

Another example of this state of mind, a century later, is to be seen in Coulanges, Mme de Sévigné's cousin.[4] He was obviously exasperated by the way his friends and relatives fussed over their children, for he composed a song dedicated to 'fathers of families', urging them not to spoil their offspring or allow them to eat with adults.

It is important to note that this feeling of exasperation was as novel as 'coddling', and even more foreign than 'coddling' to the indifferent attitude of people in the Middle Ages. It was precisely to the presence of children that Montaigne and Coulanges, like Mme de Sévigné, were hypersensitive; it should be pointed out that Montaigne and Coulanges were more modern than Mme de Sévigné in so far as they considered it necessary to keep children apart from adults. They held that it was no longer desirable that children should mingle with adults,

---

[1] Quoted by Jarman, *Landmarks in the History of Education* (London, 1951).
[2] Mme de Sévigné, *Lettres*, 1 April 1672. Cf. letter of 19 August 1671.
[3] Montaigne, *Essais*, II, 8.
[4] Coulanges, *Chansons choisies* (1694).

especially at table; no doubt because if they did they were 'spoiled' and became ill-mannered.

The seventeenth-century moralists and pedagogues shared the dislike felt by Montaigne and Coulanges for 'coddling'. Thus the austere Fleury, in his treatise on studies, speaks very much like Montaigne:

When little children are caught in a trap, when they say something foolish, drawing a correct inference from an irrelevant principle which has been given to them, people burst out laughing, rejoice at having tricked them, or kiss and caress them as if they had worked out the correct answer. It is as if the poor children had been made only to amuse the adults, like little dogs or little monkeys.'[1]

The author of *Galatée*, the manual of etiquette commonly used in the best colleges, those of the Jesuits, speaks like Coulanges: 'Those persons are greatly at fault who never talk of anything but their wives, their little children and their nannies. "My little son made me laugh so much! Just listen to this . . ." '[2]

M. d'Argonne, in his treatise on education, *L'Education de Monsieur de Moncade* (1690), likewise complains that people take an interest in very small children only for the sake of their 'caresses' and 'antics'; too many parents 'value their children only in so far as they derive pleasure and entertainment from them'.

It is important to remember that at the end of the seventeenth century this 'coddling' was not practised only by people of quality, who, in fact, were beginning to disdain it. Its presence in the lower classes was noted and denounced. J.-B. de La Salle in his *Conduite des écoles chrétiennes* (1720) states that the children of the poor are particularly ill-mannered because 'they do just as they please, their parents paying no attention to them, even treating them in an idolatrous manner: what the children want, they want too'.

In the moralists and pedagogues of the seventeenth century, we see that fondness for childhood and its special nature no longer found expression in amusement and 'coddling', but in psychological interest and moral solicitude. The child was no longer regarded as amusing or agreeable: 'Every man must be conscious of that insipidity of childhood which disgusts the sane mind; that coarseness of youth which finds pleasure in scarcely anything but material objects and which is only a very crude sketch of the man of thought.' Thus Balthazar Gratien in *El Discreto*, a treatise on education published in 1646 which was still being translated into French in 1723.[3] 'Only time can cure a person of childhood and youth, which are truly ages of imperfection in every respect.' To be understood, these opinions need to be put back in their temporal context and

---

[1] Fleury, op. cit.

[2] G. Della Casa, *Galatée*, French translation (1609), pp. 162–8.

[3] B. Gratien, *El Discreto*, Huesca (1646), French translation of 1723 by Père de Courbeville, S. J.

compared with the other texts of the period. They have been interpreted by some historians as showing ignorance of childhood, but in fact they mark the beginning of a serious and realistic concept of childhood. For they do not suggest that people should accept the levity of childhood: that was the old mistake. In order to correct the behaviour of children, people must first of all understand it, and the texts of the late sixteenth century and the seventeenth century are full of comments on child psychology.[1] The authors show a great solicitude for children, who are seen as witnesses to baptismal innocence, comparable to the angels, and close to Christ who loved them. But this interest calls for the development in them of a faculty of reasoning which is still fragile, a determined attempt to turn them into thinking men and good Christians. The tone is sometimes grim, the emphasis being laid on strictness as opposed to the laxity and facility of contemporary manners; but this is not always the case. There is even humour in Jacqueline Pascal, and undisguised tenderness. In the texts published towards the end of the century, an attempt is made to reconcile sweetness and reason. Thus the Abbé Goussault, a counsellor at the High Court, writes in *Le Portrait d'une honnête femme*:

> Familiarizing oneself with one's children, getting them to talk about all manner of things, treating them as sensible people and winning them over with sweetness, is an infallible secret for doing what one wants with them. They are young plants which need tending and watering frequently: a few words of advice offered at the right moment, a few marks of friendship and affection given now and then, touch them and bind them. A few caresses, a few little presents, a few words of cordiality and trust make an impression on their minds, and they are few in number that resist these sweet and easy methods of making them persons of honour and probity.[2]

The first concept of childhood – characterized by 'coddling' – had made its appearance in the family circle, in the company of little children. The second, on the contrary, sprang from a source outside the family: churchmen or gentlemen of the robe, few in number before the sixteenth century, and a far greater number of moralists in the seventeenth century, eager to ensure disciplined, rational manners. They too had become alive to the formerly neglected phenomenon of childhood, but they were unwilling to regard children as charming toys, for they saw them as fragile creatures of God who needed to be both safeguarded and reformed. This concept in its turn passed into family life.

In the eighteenth century, we find those two elements in the family, together with a new element: concern about hygiene and physical health. Care of the body was not ignored by seventeenth-century moralists and pedagogues. People

---

[1] As can be seen in the 1586 *ratio* of the Jesuits and in Jacqueline Pascal's regulations for the little girls brought up at Port-Royal.
[2] Goussault, *Le Portrait d'une honnête femme* (1693).

nursed the sick devotedly (at the same time taking every precaution to unmask malingerers), but any interest shown in healthy bodies had a moral purpose behind it: a delicate body encouraged luxury, sloth, concupiscence – all the vices in fact!

General de Martange's correspondence with his wife gives us some idea of a family's private life and preoccupations about a century after Mme de Sévigné.[1] Martange was born in 1722 and married in 1754. He shows great interest in everything concerning his children's life, from 'coddling' to education; he watches closely over their health and even their hygiene. Everything to do with children and family life has become a matter worthy of attention. Not only the child's future but his presence and his very existence are of concern: the child has taken a central place in the family.

[1] *Correspondence inédite du général de Martange, 1756–1782*, edited by Bréard (1898).

3 Population Changes and the Status of the Young[1]

F. MUSGROVE

During the past two hundred years young people in English society have moved through three broad status phases: the first, from the 1780s to the 1860s, was a period of high status, the second, from the 1860s to the 1910s, a period of low; the third, from the 1920s up to the present time, a high status phase. 'Young people' between the ages of 10 and 20, no longer young children, but not yet 'adults' chronologically, socially or legally, have enjoyed a status which has varied with population changes and economic opportunity. The best indices of their status are probably the amount of marriage among them and the extent of their independent income.

The status of the young has often been equated with the extent to which they are protected from adult society. Such an assessment shows increasing status throughout the nineteenth century with every successive Factory and Education Act, culminating in the last thirty years of the century, when the regulation or prohibition of juvenile employment was extended to a wider range of industry (including agriculture), when compulsory education was introduced, and children were finally protected from their parents by Mundella's 'Children's Charter' of 1889 and the work of the N.S.P.C.C.

This is a proposition which calls for critical reappraisal. Protective measures are a two-edged device: while they may signify concern for the welfare of the young, they also define them as a separate, non-adult population, inhabiting a less than adult world. The need for protection and distinctive treatment underlines their less than adult status. The young were extensively withheld from the economy and given compulsory schooling after 1870 when the economy no longer required their services on the scale that had prevailed over the previous century. The economy's diminished scope for juvenile labour was already evident in the sixties: not only was the demand decreasing, but it was shifting from the im-

[1] This chapter is based on the author's 'Population Changes and the Status of the Young in England since the Eighteenth Century', *Sociological Review*, Vol. II (1963).

First printed as Chapter Four of Youth and the Social Order (*Routledge & Kegan Paul, London, 1964*), *pp. 58–85.*

portant, central industries like agriculture to employment more marginal to the economy, like domestic service. The statutes of 1870 and 1880 which introduced compulsory education were largely superfluous acts of rescue; they signalized for the young a displacement which had already occurred from a pivotal position in the nation's economic life.[1]

Demographic influences

The rising status of the young in the Western world, measured by the protective provisions and welfare facilities increasingly at their disposal, has been attributed at least in part to their diminishing proportion of the total population. They are held to have acquired a scarcity-value.

'The present high status of childhood was not possible until a more economical rate of reproduction and the small-family system came generally to prevail.'[2] Their continuing scarcity is held to augur well for their position in the future: 'Many interesting consequences are likely to flow from the scarcity of children. They will probably be very much appreciated. Consideration will be given to them in building play space, guarding them from traffic, in providing nurseries for them in department stores.'[3] Similar arithmetic of population has been seen to underlie the rise of the child-centred family – particularly the *bourgeois* family – of Victorian France and England: 'La famille, réduite à la famille conjugale, s'est repliée sur les enfants qui constituent son noyau: c'est le triomphe du malthusianisme démographique.'[4] With the limitation of family size of which Malthus would have approved the child moved to a central, even a dominant, position in family life: 'Toute l'énergie du groupe est depensée pour la promotion des enfants, chacun en particulier, sans aucune ambition collective: les enfants, plutôt que la famille.'[5]

Even if we take protective legislation and the provision of educational and welfare services as the main criteria of the status of the young, this demographic explanation does not accord with the facts of nineteenth-century history. Protection and welfare came when the family was larger, and the proportion of young people in the population greater, than ever before or since. Charles Booth referred to the 'remarkable increase' in the number of children under 15 years of age to every 100 men aged 25 to 65, between 1851 and 1881: there were 179 in 1851, 181 in 1861, 185 in 1871 and 190 in 1881.[6] Dependent (unoccupied) children under the age of 15 years were increasing more rapidly than population:

[1] Cf. A. B. Hollingshead, op. cit., pp. 149–50: 'The establishment of high schools in the late nineteenth and early twentieth centuries may have been a response to the loss of economic functions of adolescents in American culture.'

[2] J. H. S. Bossard, *The Sociology of Child Development* (1954), p. 613.

[3] W. F. Ogburn and M. F. Nimkoff, *Handbook of Sociology* (1953), p. 337.

[4] Philippe Ariès, *L'Enfant at La Vie Familiale sous L'Ancien Régime* (1960), p. 317.

[5] Ibid., p. 457.

[6] Charles Booth, 'Occupations of the People of the United Kingdom 1801–1881', *Journal of the Statistical Society* (June 1886).

by 12·7 per cent compared with 11·9 per cent between 1851 and 1861, by 15·8 per cent compared with 13·1 per cent between 1861 and 1871, and by no less than 18·7 per cent compared with 14·5 per cent between 1871 and 1881. (In the latter decade, of course, the welfare provisions themselves were causing a greater number to be unoccupied.) The proportion of children (both dependent and occupied) under 15 years in the total population increased steadily: 35·4 per cent in 1851, 35·7 per cent in 1861, 36·1 per cent in 1871 and 36·6 per cent in 1881. By 1881 the young were never so abundant and never so protected. (Never before had they been so richly displayed – in Little Lord Fauntleroy outfits, sailor suits and Eton collars.) The declining birth-rate came after extensive measures for child welfare, and not before – when the cost of welfare, particularly to the middle-class family, proved to be extremely onerous.[1]

The growing concern for the welfare of children is more satisfactorily related to the falling mortality rates at the end of the eighteenth century than to the falling birth-rate at the end of the nineteenth.[2] Even the child-centred middle-class family to which Ariès refers can be seen at the earlier period: the seventeen children of the Edgeworth household were not too numerous to constitute the family's central concern, around whom domestic life was organized. (William Cobbett's farm is another good example of the child-centred, educative household, which was by no means uncommon at this time.)

Certainly the moralists and educationists of late-eighteenth-century England were unanimous that the (middle-class) child had never before been treated with such consideration and solicitude. 'The domestic discipline of our ancestors has been relaxed by the philosophy and softness of the age,' maintained Gibbon; 'and if my father remembered that he had trembled before a stern parent, it was only to adopt with his son an opposite mode of behaviour.'[3] Clara Reeve[4] and Mrs Sherwood[5] gave similar testimony; the Rev William Jones saw the importance given to the young as productive of 'a new generation of libertines, some of whom are such monsters of ignorance, insolence and boundless profligacy as never existed before in a Christian country'.[6] Both Hannah More and William Barrow attributed the changed standing of children to the pernicious influence of the French Revolution. The former regretted that

not only sons but daughters have adopted something of that spirit of independence, and disdain of control, which characterizes the time . . . The rights

---

[1] See J. A. Banks, *Prosperity and Parenthood* (1954), Chap. XI, 'The Cost of Children'.
[2] Cf. D. E. C. Eversley, *Social Theories of Fertility and the Malthusian Debate* (1959), p. 80. Bernard Shaw suggests that the power of children in the home declined as a consequence of the reduction of family size: 'Two adult parents, in spite of a home to keep and an income to earn, can still interfere to a disastrous extent with the rights and liberties of one child' (Preface to *Misalliance*, 1910).
[3] E. Gibbon, *Works* (Vol. I), *Autobiography*, p. 112.
[4] *Plans of Education* (1792), p. 39.
[5] S. Kelley (ed.), *Life of Mrs Sherwood* (1854), pp. 40 and 46.
[6] W. Jones, *Letters from a Tutor to his Pupil* (1775) (1821 edn), p. 8.

of man have been discussed till we are sometimes wearied with the discussion. To these have been opposed, as the next stage in the progress of illumination, and with more presumption than prudence, the rights of women. It follows, according to the actual progression of human things, that the next influx of that irradiation which our enlighteners are pouring in upon us, will illuminate the world with grave descants on the rights of youth, the rights of children, the rights of babies.[1]

William Barrow was of the opinion that the new age's solicitude for the young begot all too often 'the character known amongst us by the appellation of a Jacobin or a Democratist'.[2]

A sensitive awareness of the nature and the needs of childhood, reflected in the literature of the age,[3] long preceded the spread of modern methods of birth control among the middle classes and the reduction of family size. Declining child mortality rates in the later eighteenth century made children worth taking seriously: when they were more likely to survive to manhood, there was more point in taking pains with their early training and education. The serious training for a career provided by apprenticeship had traditionally started only at the age of 14; Rousseau in the 1760s had recommended that systematic education was pointless before puberty. (The reasons he advanced were partly psychological, but he was fully aware of the likelihood that an early investment in education would be wasted.)[4] The considerable resources put into Infant and Preparatory schools after the 1820s make sense only in the light of declining mortality rates among their inmates.

The 'cruelty' with which children were treated in the eighteenth century owes much to the demographic circumstances of the age. Methods of hardening the young were devised in an attempt to combat the high rates of infant mortality. Severity was doubtless hallowed by puritan and stoic traditions; but the quasi-medical practice of hardening had been advocated by the physician, John Locke, and found ready acceptance in an age which discovered the principle of inoculation:[5] to be fortified against a disease one should first suffer its less virulent form or analogue.

[1] Hannah More, *Strictures on the Modern System of Female Education* (1801 edn), Vol. I, pp. 172–3.

[2] See W. Barrow, *Essay on Education* (1802).

[3] See W. Walsh, *The Use of Imagination: Educational Thought and the Literary Mind* (1959). Cf. J. Dunbar, *The Early Victorian Woman* (1953), p. 29.

[4] J. J. Rousseau, *Emile* (1762), Bk IV: 'The way childhood is spent is not great matter . . . But it is not so in those early years when a youth really begins to live.'

[5] Although modern vaccination was not originated by Dr Jenner until 1799, inoculation against smallpox was introduced from Turkey in 1722 by Lady Mary Wortley Montagu with results which appear to have impressed the general public. Goldsmith in *She Stoops to Conquer* (1773) made Mrs Hardcastle declare: 'I vow, since inoculation began, there is no such thing to be seen as a plain woman' (Act 2). In fact it does not appear to have had much effect on rates of mortality: see G. Talbot Griffith, *Population Problems in the Age of Malthus* (1926), pp. 249–50.

Locke recommended fresh air, exercise, plain diet and 'not too warm or strait clothing' for the young; he also urged that 'the head and feet (must be) kept cold, and the feet used to cold water and exposed to wet'.[1] Rousseau went further, rebuking Locke for his moderation: he would have the young lie on damp grass, go without sleep, and sleep on the hardest of beds – 'the best way to find no bed uncomfortable'. These views were propagated in the educational manuals of the day. George Chapman, for instance, maintained that children should be trained to 'bear fatigue and all the inclemencies of the weather', sleep on hard beds, be almost continuously in motion, go with wet feet, and be left in the dark so that it would have no terrors for them.[2]

There is no doubt that in the most enlightened and progressive households such advice was widely heeded. Edgeworth followed this advice in rearing his own children, Thomas Day carried out elaborate experiments to harden the orphans Lucretia and Sabrina to the point where one or the other would be worthy to become Mrs Day. (Neither responded satisfactorily. The lady whom he eventually married proved her fitness by tramping Hampstead Heath in the snow to cure her enfeebled constitution.)

Mrs Gaskell has told how her aunt subjected an adopted child to a process of hardening by tossing her in a blanket and appearing before her dressed up as a ghost.[3] Southey's sister was hardened out of existence. She was dipped every morning in a tub of the coldest well water.

> This was done [says Southey] from an old notion of strengthening her: the shock was dreadful, the poor child's horror of it every morning when taken out of bed was even more so; I cannot remember having seen it without horror; nor do I believe that among all the preposterous practices which false theories have produced there was ever a more cruel and perilous one than this.[4]

In fact, the rise in the later eighteenth century of the practice of hardening for essentially medical reasons opens up a new age of hope and importance for the young: they were no longer treated with the comparative indifference and neglect which arose from a sense of helplessness in the face of inexorably high rates of infant mortality. They were not now abandoned to their fate, until their capacity to survive had been demonstrated.

It is probable that in the eighteenth century fewer than half the children born survived to manhood.[5] There is no evidence of marked differences between the social classes: children's stories, which had a wide circulation, written for upper- and middle-class children prepared parents and children for the latter's probable

---

[1] *Thoughts concerning Education*, Sec. 30.
[2] George Chapman, *Treatise on Education* (1790), pp. 115 and 122.
[3] E. C. Gaskell, *Life of Charlotte Brontë* (1857), pp. 55–6.
[4] C. C. Southey (ed.), *Life and Correspondence of Robert Southey* (1949 edn), Vol. I, pp. 28–9.
[5] *Report of the Royal Commission on Population* (1949), p. 6.

early death.[1] In these circumstances children were of little account before they reached puberty. Rousseau asked what was the point of a rigorous education 'which sacrifices the present to an uncertain future . . . and begins by making the child miserable, in order to prepare him for some far-off happiness which he may never enjoy?'[2] The basis of this advice to upper- and middle-class parents was the alleged fact that 'of all the children who are born, scarcely one half reach adolescence, and it is very likely that your pupil will not live to be a man'. (Even a century later Trollope's Dr Thorne would not have early education made exacting for similar reasons: 'Why struggle after future advantage at the expense of present pain, seeing that the results were so very doubtful?'[3])

In the later eighteenth century and throughout the nineteenth, child mortality rates declined. While the significance of the eighteenth-century decline for population growth may be disputed,[4] no leading demographer would deny that it occurred. The middle and upper classes could avail themselves more easily than the working classes of improved housing, sanitation and medical care;[5] the survival rate among their children up to 15 years of age was 83 per cent in 1871; in the population at large, while it was much improved on the rough estimate of 50 per cent a century earlier, it was still only 63 per cent.[6] It seems likely that the social class differential had widened in the course of the nineteenth century. In 1830 79 per cent of the children of clergymen in the diocese of Canterbury survived their first 15 years, in 1871 85 per cent did so.[7]

There is no necessary correspondence between falling mortality rates among young people and the growth of suitable employment opportunities for them. There can be little doubt that by the 1870s middle-class children, by surviving in greater numbers, constituted a growing burden on their parents while they were growing up and an increasing problem to place in acceptable work when their education was completed. It is probable that a social class differential in fertility existed much earlier in the century – Glass has computed negative correlation coefficients between fertility and status in twenty-eight London boroughs which were not notably smaller in 1851 than in 1911 or 1931;[8] never-

---

[1] See James Janeway, *A Token for Children* (1671), Thomas White, *A Little Book for Little Children* (1702 edn), Henry Jessey, *A Looking-Glass for Children* (1672), and James Whitaker, *Comfort for Parents* (1693).

[2] *Emile*, Bk II.

[3] A. Trollope, *Dr Thorne* (1858), Chap. 3.

[4] See H. J. Habakkuk, 'English Population in the Eighteenth Century', *The Economic History Review* (1953), Vol. 4, 2nd series.

[5] Cf. J. Hole, *Homes of the Working Classes* (1866), p. 17, for details of social class differences in mortality in 1864.

[6] C. Ansell, *Statistics of Families* (1874). Ansell's enquiry was among 54,635 upper and professional class children. The figure for the general population is from the Carlisle Tables.

[7] Ibid.

[8] D. V. Glass, 'Fertility and Economic Status in London', *Eugenics Review* (1938), 30. But cf. D. Heron, *On the Relations of Fertility in Man to Social Status* (1906): 'the intensity of the fertility-status relationship doubled between the middle of the nineteenth century and the beginning of the twentieth'. T. H. C. Stevenson thought that if analysis could be

theless, it is from the seventies that the average size of the middle-class family began its steep decline. The birth-control movement was a symptom of the superabundance of the young in relation to family resources and to the needs of the economy. 'It may be possible to bring ten children into the world, if you only have to rear five, and, while one is "on the way", the last is in the grave, not in the nursery. But if the doctor preserves seven or eight of the ten, and other things remain equal, the burden may become intolerable.'[1] But other things did not even remain equal: it was unfortunate for the young that they were most abundant when the economy, whether at the level of professional or of manual employment, offered diminishing opportunities for youth and relative inexperience.

The needs of the economy

In the later eighteenth century and the first half of the nineteenth, parents valued children more highly as their chance of survival improved; employers valued them more highly as technological changes gave them a position of pivotal importance in new industries. As the traditional system of apprenticeship broke down because of its irrelevance in the eighteenth century, and the legal requirement to serve an apprenticeship to a trade was repealed in 1814, the young were liberated to find their true level of importance in the changing economy. Debased forms of 'apprenticeship' – particularly parish apprenticeship – within industry still often prevented the young worker from achieving his true economic wage and the social independence that went with it. But this form of exploitation, often by parents and relatives rather than by plant owners, became less common in the early decades of the nineteenth century. The new industries were heavily dependent on the skills and agility of the young.

Moreover, before the population aged in the later nineteenth and the twentieth centuries, there were greater opportunities for young people to secure top appointments: promotion was not blocked by a glut of older men. Jousselin has contrasted the opportunities which the young enjoyed in the later eighteenth and early nineteenth centuries with their frustrations today: 'Du fait du vieillissement de la population, la situation de jeunesse s'est profondément modifiée. Il leur est beaucoup plus difficile d'accéder aux postes de responsabilité et d'initiative. On ne connaît plus de généraux de 20 à 30 ans, ni de préfets ayant l'âge des gouverneurs de l'ancien régime.'[2]

In remote areas, away from large urban reservoirs of labour, young people were a particularly large proportion of the labour force in early-nineteenth-century

---

pushed far enough back, 'a period of substantial equality between all classes might have been met with'. 'The Fertility of Various Social Classes', *Journal of the Royal Statistical Society* (1920).

[1] T. H. Marshall, 'The Population Problem during the Industrial Revolution', *Economic History: Economic Journal Supplement* (1929).

[2] Jean Jousselin, *Jeunesse Fait Social Méconnu* (Toulouse, 1959), p. 8.

factories, partly because the pauper apprentice was the most freely mobile economic unit. But even where labour was abundant and there was less need to employ parish apprentices, young people were often a high proportion of the employees. Forty-eight per cent of the 1,020 workpeople of M'Connel and Kennedy in Manchester in 1816 were under 18 years of age.[1]

The demand at this time was particularly for working-class youth; but middle-class youth – at least the males – were also needed as commerce expanded even more rapidly than industry and called for a great army of white-collar workers.[2] Only gradually, in the closing decades of the century, were 'accountants', for example, distinguished from 'book-keepers' (and Upper Division civil servants from Lower Division)[3] and required to undertake prolonged education and training before receiving the economic rate for the work they did.[4]

In the new industries parents were often appendages to their children, heavily dependent on their earnings. When the farm labourer moved his family to the town, it was commonly for what his children could earn: his own employment might be as a porter, or in subsidiary work such as road-making, at a wage of 10s.–13s. a week; his child (and wife) could earn more on the power looms or in throstle-spinning.[5] As Mr Carey commented in Disraeli's *Sybil* (1845): 'Fathers and mothers goes for nothing. 'Tis the children gets the wages, and there it is.' The fathers of the poor families imported from Bedfordshire and Buckinghamshire were fit only for labourers. There must have been many a Devilsdust 'who had entered life so early that at 17 he combined the experience of manhood with the divine energy of youth'.

Apprenticeship and experience in traditional industries were a handicap in James Keir's chemical works at Tipton, founded in the 1780s;[6] Andrew Ure noted in 1836 that 'Mr Anthony Strutt, who conducts the chemical department of the great cotton factories at Belper and Milford . . . will employ no man who has learned his craft by regular apprenticeship'.[7] Samuel Oldknow's spinning mill at Mellor depended on youthful labour; subsidiary industries (lime-kilns, coal-mining, farming) had to be provided for redundant fathers;[8] at Styal the Gregs had to develop an industrial colony to provide employment for the adult dependants of their juvenile and female workers. What shocked middle-class commentators on factory life in mid-Victorian England as much as the alleged

[1] T. S. Ashton, *The Industrial Revolution* (1948), p. 116.

[2] Commercial clerks increased by 61 per cent 1861–71 and by 88 per cent 1871–81 while all occupied males increased by 13 per cent and 32 per cent.

[3] *First Report of the Civil Service Inquiry Commission* (The Playfair) (1875) recommended an Upper Division recruited from the universities distinct from a Lower Division of routine clerks.

[4] Until the Census of 1891 accountants were not distinguished from book-keepers. In 1880 the Institute of Chartered Accountants, in 1885 the Society of Accountants and Auditors were founded.

[5] See N. J. Smelser, *Social Change in the Industrial Revolution* (1959), p. 185.

[6] W. H. B. Court, *The Rise of the Midland Industries* (1938), pp. 230–2.

[7] Andrew Ure, *Philosophy of Manufactures* (1861 edn), p. 21.

[8] G. Unwin, *Samuel Oldknow and the Arkwrights* (1924), Chap. XI.

immorality was the independence of the young. In London girls of 14 working in the silk or trimming departments earned 8s. or 10s. a week: 'if they had cause to be dissatisfied with the conduct of their parents, they would leave them'.[1] Similar independence was to be found in the Birmingham metal trades: 'The going from home and earning money at such a tender age (of 7 or thereabouts) has – as might be expected – the effect of making the child early independent of its parents . . .'[2] The Factory Commissioners reported in 1842 that by the age of 14 young people 'frequently pay for their own lodgings, board and clothing. They usually make their own contracts, and are in the proper sense of the word free agents.' (Even the Poor Law provisions of the Speenhamland System had a similar effect in the early decades of the century. As Mr Assistant Commissioner Stuart stated in the *Report* from the Commissioners on the Poor Laws (1834): 'Boys of 14, when they become entitled to receive parish relief on their own account, no longer make a common fund of their income with their parents, but buy their own loaf and bacon and devour it alone. Disgraceful quarrels arise within the family circle from mutual accusations of theft.'[3])

While factory legislation was at least a potential threat to the earnings and power of the young, the Acts of 1833 extended their independence by destroying the vestigial authority of parents in the textile – particularly the spinning – mills. Virtually autonomous family units, under the headship of the father, had infiltrated intact into some of the textile factories: Andrew Ure[4] reported in the 1830s that 'Nearly the whole of the children of 14 years of age, and under, who are employed in cotton mills, belong to the mule-spinning department, and are, in forty-nine cases out of fifty, the immediate dependants, often the offspring or near relations of the spinner, being hired and dismissed at his option.' The spinner paid his piecers and scavengers from his own wages. (In the mines outside Northumberland and Durham the young worker in 1840 was often even more completely under his father's authority; in South Wales 'the collier boy is, to all intents and purposes, the property of his father (as to wages) until he attains the age of 17 years, or marries.' Butties received 'apprentices' at the age of 9 for twelve years – a system likened by witnesses to the African slave trade.[5]) The early regulation of the employment of the young, and particularly their shortened and staggered hours of work, had the effect, along with technological change, of removing them from the control of the head of the family who developed a more specialized role which 'no longer implied co-operation with, training of, and authority over dependent family members'.[6]

[1] Charles Bray, 'The Industrial Employment of Women', *Transactions of the National Association for the Promotion of Social Science* (1857).

[2] J. S. Wright, 'Employment of Women in Factories in Birmingham', *Transactions of the N.A.P.S.Sc.* (1857).

[3] Vol. IX, p. 54.

[4] Andrew Ure, op. cit., p. 290.

[5] *First Report of the Commissioners (Mines)* (1842), pp. 40 ff.

[6] N. J. Smelser, op. cit., p. 265. For the administrative complexities which the educational clauses entailed, see A. A. Fry 'Report of the Inspectors of Factories on the Effects

The importance of the young to the economy is reflected in the high birth-rate which was particularly buoyant in the later eighteenth and early nineteenth centuries. This is not simply to say that children were begotten for the benefit of what they could earn while still children; in an expanding economy they were valued as a longer term proposition. Talbot Griffith rejected as 'scarcely tenable' the theory that the high birth-rate of the period[1] was caused by the economic value of children,[2] but conceded that

> The feeling that the new industries would provide employment for the children at an early age and enable them possibly to help the family exchequer would tend, undoubtedly, to make parents contemplate a large family with equanimity and may have acted as a sort of encouragement to population without the more definite incentive implied in the theory that it was the value of children's work which led to the increase of the population.[3]

Marshall was more inclined to see significance for the birth-rate in children's earnings:

> By 1831 the birth-rate, measured in proportion to women aged 20–40, got back for the first time to the level of 1781 (this is a guess); by 1841 it had slumped far below it (this is a fact). Now it is only fair to older theories to point out how this fall by stages, slow at first and then rapid, reflects the history of child labour and the Poor Law.[4]

Glass, on the other hand, found little or no connection between the employment of children aged 10–15 and fertility between 1851 and 1911 in the forty-three registered countries.[5] The value of children for their earnings *whilst still children* is doubtless an inadequate explanation of the changing birth-rate; but the value of children more broadly conceived, as likely, in a buoyant economy, to constitute an insurance against misfortune in later life and old age, is an explanation not inconsistent with Arthur Young's argument that population is proportional to employment.[6]

---

of the Educational Provisions of the Factories' Act', *Journal of the Statistical Society* (1839).

[1] 34·4 births per 1,000 living in 1780, 35·4 1785–95; 34·2 1796–1806, cf. 31·1 in 1700, 27·5 in 1710 and 30·5 in 1720. See G. Talbot Griffith, op. cit., Table 5, p. 28.

[2] Ibid., p. 103.

[3] Ibid., p. 105. Talbot Griffith saw economic expansion as having a direct effect on the age of marriage and hence indirectly on the birth-rate (p. 106).

[4] T. H. Marshall, loc. cit., p. 454.

[5] D. V. Glass, 'Changes in Fertility in England and Wales 1851 to 1931' in L. Hogben (ed.), *Political Arithmetic* (1938): 'Correlations between fertility and child labour yielded coefficients of +0·489 ±0·116 for 1851, +0·291 ±0·140 for 1871, and +0·043 ±0·152 for 1911. Of these coefficients only that for 1851 is significant.'

[6] Arthur Young, *Political Arithmetic* (1774): 'People scarce—labour dear. Would you give a premium for population, could you express it in better terms? The commodity wanted is scarce, and the price raised; what is that but saying that the value of *man* is raised? Away! my boys – get children, they are worth more than ever they were.'

Habakkuk has attributed the growth in population during the Industrial Revolution primarily to 'specifically economic changes', and in particular to 'an increase in the demand for labour', but has pointed out that the way in which this demand operated (whether directly on the birth-rate or indirectly through the lower age of marriage) remains open to question.[1] The experience of Ireland, as Talbot Griffith realized, provides the key to this problem. It was an embarrassment to Griffith's argument that in relatively insanitary Ireland population increased between 1780 and 1840 at almost twice the rate experienced in England; inadequate statistics made it impossible for him to prove or disprove his contention that a declining rate of child mortality was the primary reason. On the other hand, the comparative lack of industrial development in Ireland seemed to nullify the argument that the primary reason was increased demand for labour.[2] This latter difficulty is overcome if we regard Ireland-with-England – or at least Ireland-with-Lancashire – as a single field of employment, as the Irish themselves clearly did. The relatively unskilled jobs available in the textile industry were particularly suited to Irish immigrants; and before 1819 movement into Lancashire was easy – easier than moving in from elsewhere in England – since the Irish were regarded as having no place of 'settlement' and so could not be removed by the Poor Law authorities if they became a charge upon the rates. But these were not young children seeking employment. Undue concentration on the earnings of *young* children has bedevilled the question of the value of offspring. At this time in Ireland – and in England too – 'a large family was regarded less as a strain upon resources than as the promise of comfort and material well being in middle and old age'.[3]

Children were of value even and perhaps particularly as they grew up into adult life and work, as an insurance against misfortune, against sickness and old age. They were not an entirely reliable insurance, particularly with increased geographical mobility and the dispersal of the family; their unreliability, at least in London, was commented on by Mayhew in the middle of the nineteenth century[4] and by Booth at the end. Booth was under the impression that this unreliability had become more marked in recent years:

The great loss of the last twenty years is the weakening of the family ties between parents and children. Children don't look after their old people according to their means. The fault lies in the fact that the tie is broken early. As soon as a boy earns 10s. a week he can obtain board and lodging in some family other than his own, and he goes away because he has in this great liberty.[5]

[1] H. J. Habakkuk, loc. cit.
[2] G. Talbot Griffith, op. cit., p. 66.
[3] K. H. Connell, 'Land and Population in Ireland 1780–1840', *The Economic History Review* (1949), 2nd series, Vol. II.
[4] See Peter Quennell, *Mayhew's London* (1949), pp. 54 and 76.
[5] Charles Booth, *Life and Labour of the People in London* (Final Volume, 1903), p. 43.

The importance of children was undermined in the later nineteenth century by the growth of alternative forms of insurance. Indeed, 'insurance' in a broad sense – whether paid-up premiums, private means or a working wife – has demographic significance as a substitute for children. Children seen as insurance help to explain the apparent paradox, discussed by Stevenson, that in the nineteenth century high mortality appeared to promote large families rather than vice versa. Many were born when comparatively few survived: additional births were necessary to effect replacements. This was particularly the case when there was no other form of insurance against misfortune: among miners, whose wives were excluded from employment after the 1840s, child mortality rates were high, but so was fertility. High child mortality rates were also experienced in the families of the textile workers, but fertility was low also; it is arguable that replacements were not so necessary when wives were commonly at work. The low fertility of couples of independent means had perplexed nineteenth-century demographers. Stevenson considered that their low fertility was the most remarkable case of all: 'In their case, presumably, those anxieties and difficulties which militate against fertility are at a minimum, but fertility is also at a minimum.'[1] Once the rates of infant mortality had fallen, it was safe to assume that even a small family would survive to carry on the family name and estate.

Children were of diminishing value to couples who were covered by insurance. The birth-rate at the end of the nineteenth century slumped not only among the professional and middle classes but among artisans and skilled mechanics, many of them among the infertile textile families, who in large numbers joined Friendly Societies such as the Oddfellows, Manchester Unity (1810), the Foresters (1834), the Rechabites, Salford Unity (1835), the Hearts of Oak (1842) and the National Deposit Friendly Society (1868). By 1872 the Friendly Societies probably had some four million members, compared with one million trade unionists – and the latter had sickness, employment and sometimes superannuation schemes too.[2] The decline in claims for lying-in benefit by members of the Hearts of Oak gives some indication of their declining fertility: between 1881 and 1904 the proportion of claims to membership declined by 52 per cent.[3] It is likely that they had less need of this benefit precisely because they were members of a provident society.

By the last quarter of the nineteenth century the status of the young was being undermined as a consequence of their earlier importance. Their value had resulted in their super-abundance. As Yule and Habakkuk have observed, the

[1] T. H. C. Stevenson, 'The Fertility of Various Social Classes in England and Wales from the Middle of the Nineteenth Century to 1911', *Journal of the Royal Statistical Society* (1920), Vol. 83.

[2] See P. H. J. Gosden, *The Friendly Societies of England 1815–1875* (1961). See also Charles Booth, *Life and Labour of the People in London* (1889), Vol. I, pp. 106–11. The Hearts of Oak charged a comparatively high subscription of 10s. a quarter; they provided £20 on a member's death, £10 on the death of a member's wife, sickness allowances beginning at 18s. a week, lying-in benefit of 30s. and superannuation of 4s. a week.

[3] See Sidney Webb, *The Decline of the Birth Rate* (1907), pp. 6–7.

children who are produced in response to favourable economic circumstances may still be there when the circumstances have deteriorated: 'the present demand is met only by a delivery of the commodity some twenty years later; by that time the "commodity" may not be required'.[1] Yule speaks of 'a very large and quite abnormal increase' in the labour force aged 20–55 years in the last twenty years of the century; as young workers the 'bulge' had entered the labour market in the late sixties and the seventies.[2] This increase was 'not produced by any present demands for labour, but in part by the "demand" of 1863–73 . . .': the birth-rate in the sixties and seventies was as high as in the quarter-of-a-century after 1780.[3] Moreover, in the second half of the nineteenth century the survival rates among older children and adolescents improved much more rapidly than among children aged 0–4 years. While the annual mortality per thousand declined by 11·3 per cent among boys aged 0–4 years (from 71 to 63) between 1841–5 and 1891–1900, the decline among boys aged 5–9 declined by 53·2 per cent (from 9·2 to 4·3), and among boys aged 10–14 by 53·0 per cent (from 5·1 to 2·4).[4] Thus while adolescents were a better 'proposition', since they were more likely to live and so justify what was spent on their upbringing and education, the wastage among them was small at the very time that the economy had a diminishing need for their services.

This is the prelude to the introduction of compulsory education between 1870 and 1880. Not only was there a 'bulge' in young people, but advances in technology were in any case displacing the young worker. In some industries, too, extended factory legislation greatly diminished his value in the eyes of employers: the administrative complications raised by part-time schooling deterred mine-owners from employing boys under 12 after the Mines Act of 1860;[5] the Factory Acts Extension Act of 1867 and the Workshops Regulation Act of the same year had similar consequences in a wide range of industries including the metal trades, glass and tobacco manufacture, letterpress printing and bookbinding.[6] The textile industry, on the other hand, which had greatly reduced its child labour force after the Act of 1833, maintained a high proportion of juvenile workers after the Act of 1844 which simplified the administration of part-time work.[7] Agriculture also took the Gang Act of 1867 and the Agricultural Children Act of 1873 in its stride – chiefly by ignoring them.

[1] G. Udny Yule, 'On the Changes in Marriage- and Birth-Rates in England and Wales during the Past Half Century', *Journal of the Royal Statistical Society* (1906), Vol. 69.

[2] While the population increased by 11·7 per cent 1881–91 the working population aged 20–55 increased by 14 per cent; the increases 1891–1901 were 12·2 per cent and 19 per cent respectively.

[3] 34·1 1851–60; 35·4 1871–80; cf. 29·9 1891–1900. See G. Talbot Griffith, op. cit., Table 5, p. 28.

[4] S. Peller, 'Mortality, Past and Future', *Population Studies* (1948), Vol. I.

[5] 23 and 24 Vict. c. 151. See A. H. Robson, *The Education of Children in Industry in England 1833–1876* (1931), p. 159.

[6] A. H. Robson, op. cit., pp. 204–5.

[7] The Act of 1844 reduced the minimum age of employment from 9 to 8 and limited the daily hours of children to 6½ which could be worked either before or after the dinner hour.

Technical changes in many industries were in any case breaking the earlier dependence on juvenile labour: steam power in the lace[1] and pottery[2] industries was being substituted for children's energy and dexterity; the dramatic decline in the proportion of young people engaged in agriculture in the second half of the century has been similarly attributed in part to technical development: 'A new class connected with the application of science to agriculture has sprung into being . . .'[3] Young people were no longer central to the economy; they were moving ever more on to the periphery, into marginal and relatively trivial occupations: street-trading, fetching and carrying, and particularly indoor domestic service.

The decline in the proportion of young people (under the age of 15) had set in before the 'slight dose of compulsory education' introduced by the Education Act of 1870[4] and the more effective Education Acts of Sandon and Mundella in 1876 and 1880. In 1851 young people under 15 were 6·9 per cent of the occupied population; in 1861 workers of this age were 6·7 per cent of all occupied, in 1871 6·2 per cent, in 1881 they were 4·5 per cent.[5] The following table gives the percentage of workers under 15 years of age in selected industries between 1861 and 1881:

Percentage of Under-15s in Selected Industries

	1861	1871	1881
Agriculture	7·6	7·2	5·5
Mining (males only)	11·9	9·5	5·7
Metal trades	7·9	5·5	3·1
Quarrying and brickmaking (males only)	7·3	5·9	3·8
Bricklayers and labourers (males only)	3·2	2·8	2·2
Textiles and dyeing	15·4	15·7	12·2
Indoor domestic service	8·8	8·9	7·7

Perhaps the most remarkable decline in the proportion of employed young people was in the country's major industry, agriculture. This industry, of course, was experiencing considerable difficulties at this time and its manpower contracting; but while the total number employed in agriculture declined by 24 per cent between 1851 and 1881, the number of young people under 15 declined by no less than 40 per cent. Under-15s in agriculture were 21 per cent of all young workers in 1851, 13·7 per cent in 1881. An opposite trend is marked in the case of indoor domestic service: under-15s in this employment were 11·6 per cent of all

[1] A. H. Robson, op. cit., p. 133.

[2] M. W. Thomas, *Young People in Industry* (1945), p. 85.

[3] Charles Booth, 'Occupations of the People of the United Kingdom 1801–81', *Journal of the Statistical Society* (June 1886).

[4] 'By 1876 50 per cent of the whole population was under compulsion, but in the boroughs the percentage was as high as 84.' See H. C. Barnard, *A Short History of English Education* (1947), p. 197.

[5] All calculations in this section are based on Charles Booth, loc. cit.

young workers in 1851, 19·7 per cent in 1881. In spite of compulsory education, while the employed population increased by 38 per cent between 1851 and 1881, young people employed in indoor domestic service increased over the same period by 55 per cent.

But in spite of the growing numbers of young people still employed in certain industries, while the total number of employed people in England and Wales increased by 12·4 per cent between 1861 and 1871, the number of under-15s employed increased by only 2·5 per cent. This is not because a greater proportion was attending school. What alarmed investigators in the sixties, and provided powerful arguments in the campaign for compulsory education, was not only the apparent decline in the proportion of children attending school but a decline also in the proportion at work. The consequence was an increasing proportion of young people in the very margin of society, outcast and neglected. 'And what are these neglected children doing if they are not at school?' asked James McCosh, after reviewing the evidence relating to Manchester, in a paper to the National Association for the Promotion of Social Science in 1867. 'They are idling in the streets and wynds; tumbling about in the gutters; selling matches; running errands; working in tobacco shops, cared for by no man . . .'[1]

Inquiries conducted by the Manchester Statistical Society and by the Education Aid Society in the 1860s had produced disquieting statistics. With a decreasing importance to the nation's economy, the young had an exiguous existence in the interstices of adult society. In 1834 there had been in Manchester and Salford 967 day pupils at school for every 10,000 inhabitants; in 1861 there were only 908. The Manchester Statistical Society found in a survey conducted in 1865 that among the children aged 3–12 in their sample, over a half were neither at school nor at work. The Education Aid Society found in 1862 in widely separate districts of Manchester that in 2,896 families investigated, out of every fifteen children aged 3–12, one was at work, six were at school, but eight were neither at school nor at work.[2] (There were in these families a further 2,882 children over the age of 12: while 81·3 per cent of these were at work, and 1·5 per cent at school, 17·2 per cent were neither at school nor at work.) Compulsory education was a necessity by the 1870s not because children were at work, but because increasingly they were not.

The age of marriage

Between the 1780s and the 1860s young people, particularly the working-class young, were able to approximate to adult status because of their importance to the economy. Superfluous apprenticeship was an artifice which kept a diminish-

[1] James McCosh, 'On Compulsory Education', *Transactions of the National Association for the Promotion of Social Science* (1867).

[2] See E. Brotherton, 'The State of Popular Education', *Transactions of the National Association for the Promotion of Social Science* (1865). Also J. Hole, *Homes of the Working Classes* (1866).

ing proportion in unmerited subordination, particularly in the regions of most rapid social change;[1] in 1863, before the National Association for the Promotion of Social Science, its remaining vestiges were roundly attacked as 'a species of slavery', 'incompatible with the free institutions of this country', which, 'unsuited to the present advanced state of society', 'should be discontinued as a worn-out vestige of the past . . .' These were not strictures on 'parish apprenticeship', but on normal apprenticeship for which high premiums might be charged, which might require seven years' training for 'what might be acquired by a sharp lad in three or four'.[2] The early nineteenth century offered youth a dominant and not a subordinate economic role. The young, in their 'teens, could attain an independence which gave them virtually adult status, a situation reflected in, and further confirmed by, the tendency to early marriage.

The independence and early marriage of young industrial workers were severely disapproved of by (middle-class) social commentators and legislators. The resentment of the high status of the young (and of employed women) echoed through the parliamentary debates on the regulation of factory employment. Social workers were surprised that people who worked long hours under conditions which the middle classes would have found distasteful did not feel sorry for themselves. Fanny Herz found young women factory workers 'exceeding tenacious of their independence and jealous to a surprising degree of even the appearance of condescension or patronage in the conduct of those who would approach them with the kindest intentions . . .'[3] Lord Ashley, in the course of the debates on the Ten Hours Bill, wished to regulate the conditions whereby women were 'gradually acquiring all those privileges which are held to be the proper portion of the male sex' and which promoted a 'perversion as it were of nature which has the inevitable effect of introducing into families disorder, insubordination and conflict'.[4]

Early marriage, the reflection and confirmation of the high status of young industrial workers, was generally deplored. Factory work was condemned for the young not because wages were low, but because they were high. 'From the same cause, namely high wages, very many early and improvident marriages take place.'[5] 'The Census returns of 1861', runs a typical lament of the period, 'show

[1] See Report of the Schools Inquiry Commission (1868), Vol. 9: 'In the West Riding, there is so great a demand for juvenile labour, that the custom of paying premiums to masters with apprentices is almost obsolete. Indeed, indentures of apprenticeship are far less common than they were. Boys are seldom bound to masters; they begin to receive wages almost immediately after they enter a shop . . .' (pp. 222–3).

[2] George Hurst, 'On the System of Apprenticeship', Transactions of the National Association for the Promotion of Social Science (1863). See W. Lucas, A Quaker Journal (1934 edn), Vol. I, p. 44, for an account of a pointlessly long, expensive and futile tutelage in the early nineteenth century even for the profession of chemist.

[3] Fanny Herz, 'Mechanics Institutes for Working Women', Transactions of the National Association for the Promotion of Social Science (1859).

[4] Parliamentary Papers, 3rd series, Vol. 73, col. 1096.

[5] R. Smith Baker, 'The Social Results of the Employment of Girls and Women in Factories and Workshops', Transactions of the National Association for the Promotion of

that among the population of Bolton, 45 husbands and 172 wives were coupled at the immature age of "15 or under"; in Burnley there were 51 husbands and 147 wives; in Stockport 59 husbands and 179 wives in the same category.'[1]

This tendency to early marriage dated from the later eighteenth century and has been attributed to the breakdown of traditional apprenticeship with its requirement of celibacy, to changes in the organization of farming, particularly to the decline of the custom of labourers 'living in', to the higher earnings of the young, and, more doubtfully, to the system of poor-law allowances.[2] Because of the few hindrances to early marriage and the high birth rate of the period the later eighteenth century and the early nineteenth have been described as 'an almost, if not quite, unique epoch in the history of the human race'.[3]

These circumstances prevailed in Ireland equally with England; and the social history of Ireland illustrates even more vividly than the history of England the close connection between the status of the young and the amount of marriage among them. The contrast between the Ireland of the later eighteenth century which Arthur Young described in his *Tour of Ireland* (1780) and the Ireland which American anthropologists described in the 1930s[4] is between a country with independent youth and early marriage and a country with subordinate youth and remarkably belated marriage.

Arthur Young was impressed by the independence of young people and the early age at which they married. The reclamation of waste land and the subdivision of land were important economic circumstances behind these developments. 'There is no doubt at all that in the late-eighteenth and early-nineteenth centuries the Irish married while unusually young.'[5] But whereas in 1841 only 43 per cent of males aged 25–35 were unmarried, in 1926 the percentage was 72. In the meantime the economic circumstances that had made early marriage possible had dramatically changed; in particular the shift from tillage to livestock production after the Famine, and the virtual cessation of the subdivision of land after 1852. By the 1920s, while 45 per cent of English males aged 25–30 were unmarried, 39 per cent of American, and 49 per cent of Danish, 80 per cent of Irish males of this age were still single.[6]

Wherever social and economic institutions restrict the freedom of young people past puberty to marry, their social standing is depressed. The institutions may be as varied as protracted compulsory schooling, apprenticeship, exclusion from employment, the dowry, the bride-price, the monopoly of wives by elderly polygynists or exchange-marriage. A bride-price or a dowry which is paid by

---

Social Science (1868). Cf. Fanny Herz, loc. cit., 'Owing to the liberal wages they earn, many of our young factory women become their own mistresses at a very early age . . .'

[1] R. A. Arnold, 'The Cotton Famine', *Transactions N.A.P.S.Sc.* (1864).
[2] G. Talbot Griffith, op. cit., pp. 112–22.
[3] See A. M. Carr-Saunders, *Population* (1925), pp. 38–41.
[4] Conrad M. Arensberg and Solon T. Kimball, *Family and Community in Ireland* (1940).
[5] K. H. Connell, loc. cit.
[6] C. M. Arensberg and S. T. Kimball, op. cit., pp. 103–4.

parents enables the latter to regulate and impede the progress of youth towards adult status; exchange-marriage, whereby a man could marry only when his father supplied him with one of his daughters to give in exchange for a bride, was practised by the Tiv of Nigeria until 1927 and effectively diminished the status of the young.[1]

Arensberg and Kimball have described how in County Clare in the 1930s farmers arranged their children's marriages with a keen eye to economic advantage. Marriage conferred status, and until marriage, whatever his chronological age, a man remained a 'boy'. 'Even at 45 or 50, if the old couple have not yet made over the farm, the countryman remains a "boy" in respect to farm work and in the rural vocabulary.' 'It goes without saying that the father exercises his control over the whole activity of the "boy". It is by no means confined to their work together.'[2] Groups of 'young' (i.e. unmarried) men, unlike the 'cuaird' of older men, discuss no serious adult concerns; their main activity together is gambling. They have been effectively reduced to a condition of social subordination and irresponsibility.

The position since 1870

The depressed status of youth between 1870 and 1914, already foreshadowed in the sixties in their increasing exclusion from the central concerns of the economy and signalized in the imposition of compulsory schooling in 1870, is further reflected in the rising average age of marriage. The proportion of married males and females between the ages of 15 and 24 rose from 13·1 per cent in 1851 to 16·6 per cent in 1861, reaching a peak of 17·4 per cent in 1871; thereafter the proportion declined to 16·0 per cent in 1881, 10·5 per cent in 1891, 11·0 per cent in 1901, and the nadir of 9·7 per cent in 1911.[3] Recovery thereafter was faltering in the twenties and thirties, marked from the period immediately preceding the Second World War: 12·7 per cent in 1921, 10·4 in 1931, 20·1 in 1947.

The diminished proportion of young people married after 1870 was particularly marked in the middle classes – a reduction of status particularly keen for middle-class girls who had as yet no compensation in widespread access to superior occupational statuses. As Hetty Widgett observed to Ann Veronica: 'They used to marry us off at seventeen. They don't marry us off now until high up in the twenties. And the age gets higher. We have to hang about in the interval. There's a great gulf opened, and nobody's got any plans what to do with us. So the world is choked with waste and waiting daughters.'[4] The average age of those professional men and gentlemen generally who married between 1840 and 1870 was 29·9 years, four and a half years above the average for all classes of workmen.[5]

[1] M. Mead (ed.), *Cultural Patterns and Technical Change* (1953), pp. 114–43.

[2] C. M. Arensberg and S. T. Kimball, op. cit., p. 56.

[3] Calculated from *Papers of the Royal Commission on Population* (1950), Vol. 2, *Reports and Selected Papers of the Statistics Committee*, pp. 195–7.

[4] H. G. Wells, *Ann Veronica* (1909), Chap. 2.   [5] C. Ansell, op. cit., p. 45.

The recovery of youthful marriage in the forty years after 1911 was greater than the decline in the forty years before. The proportion of males ever-married aged 20–24 declined by 38·6 per cent between 1871 and 1911: from 23·3 to 14·3 per cent; between 1911 and 1951 it rose by 66·4 per cent, from 14·3 to 23·8 per cent.[1] The recovery among young women has been more striking: the rate of marriage among young women aged 20–24 fell by 30 per cent between 1871 and 1911, from 34·8 to 24·3 per cent of the age group; it rose by 100 per cent (from 24·3 to 48·2 per cent) between 1911 and 1951. (The increase in the rate among girls aged 15–19 – 266 per cent – is still more remarkable.)

Titmuss, drawing heavily on the work of Hajnal, has claimed that 'These increases in the amount or quantity of marriage – in the apparent popularity of the institution of marriage – are . . . quite remarkable. They are also quite unprecedented in the history of vital statistics over the last hundred years.'[2] This is misleading: to claim that 'the amount of marriage' began to increase after 1911 and that the institution of marriage was never so popular as in the last fifteen years would require that the proportion ever-married in the population-at-risk – all those over the age of 15 – had risen. In fact, there has been remarkably little variation over the past century: 59·3 per cent in 1851, 64·3 per cent in 1871, 59·7 per cent in 1911 and 63·8 per cent in 1931. The proportion of spinsters in the age group 45–54 was 12·2 per cent in 1851, 12·1 per cent in 1871, 15·8 per cent in 1911, 16·4 per cent in 1931, and in 1951, at 15·1 per cent, almost as high as in 1911 and higher than at any time in late-Victorian and Edwardian England. What has recurred in the mid-twentieth century is the popularity of *youthful* marriage. It is a sensitive index of the changing status of the young.

The young have attained a new significance in the nation's economy since the thirties. It is true that they remain ever longer at school – although the really significant fact of educational history since 1944 is not the (belated) raising of the school leaving age to 15, but the refusal to raise it to 16. It is possible that in the 1960s, as in the 1870s, the young will pay the price of their importance and comparative abundance in the previous twenty years.[3] As the bulge moves on to the labour market, the school leaving age will in all likelihood be raised, as foreshadowed in the 'Crowther' Report, *15 to 18* (1959), and the grammar-school Sixth Forms, the universities and other institutions of higher education still further expand.

Since the twenties, and more particularly since the mid-thirties, the young have had the advantage of being born into an economy in which technological

[1] These calculations are based on data in J. Hajnal, 'Aspects of Recent Trends in Marriage in England and Wales', *Population Studies* (1947), Vol. I, and the returns of the 1951 Census.

[2] R. Titmuss, 'The Family as a Social Institution', *The Family: Report of the British National Conference on Social Work* (1953).

[3] Sixteen-year-olds may increase by 31 per cent 1957–63, the age group 15–20 inclusive by 19 per cent. See *The Youth Service in England and Wales* (the 'Albemarle' Report) (1960), Appendix 6, p. 129.

change has brought about widespread upgrading of occupations, the diminution of the proportion of labouring jobs, and an increase in the amount of skilled employment. Georges Friedman has argued that this is not the case: from his broad survey of trends in Western society, he scorns the notion of an imminent 'technicians' Utopia'[1] and claims that, while in the industrially advanced nations the proportion of unskilled labourers has declined, the proportion of semi-skilled, fragmentary, repetitive and mechanized jobs has greatly increased. The French[2] and American[3] statistics which he produces appear to support this contention that since 1910 the proportion of routine, semi-skilled workers in industry has greatly increased, while the proportion of skilled has shown relatively little change. The English statistics supplied by the Census Returns do not fit this picture: with skilled workers two and a half times more numerous than semi-skilled (1951),[4] Friedman is driven to deny the validity of the Registrar-General's data:

> These surprising figures, which may even be regarded as mistaken when compared with the corresponding ones in France or the United States, can only be explained by fundamental differences in the definition and titles given to different occupational categories, partly perhaps also by the traditional policy of British unions, which attempt to maintain the status, and as far as possible the wages, of skilled trades for occupations that have been downgraded by mechanization.

He has less difficulty with American statistics in showing that 'from 1940 on, the proportion of semi-skilled workers is greater than that of either the skilled or the unskilled. Semi-skilled workers now constitute the largest group among the manual workers of American industry.'[5]

There can be little doubt that Friedman's thesis, at least with regard to England, is wrong. Although Erich Fromm[6] and Paul Goodman[7] appear to lend some support to his picture of American employment, their concern is more with the psychological satisfaction of work today, rather than with the level of skill it involves. This, of course, is a quite different question: 'alienated work', socially pointless and trivial work, may require high and rising levels; it may nevertheless fall below the expectations of people who have lived through an age

[1] Cf. P. F. Drucker, *The Practice of Management* (1955) for the argument that mass production and automation mean more highly skilled and trained employees.

[2] Georges Friedman, *The Anatomy of Work* (London, 1961), p. 169.

[3] Ibid., pp. 182–3.

[4] Ibid., p. 172.

[5] Ibid., p. 176.

[6] E. Fromm, *The Sane Society* (London, 1956): 'There is one factor, however, which could mitigate the alienation of work, and that is the skill required in its performance. But here, too, development moves in the direction of decreasing skill requirements . . .' (p. 294). 'To sum up, the vast majority of the population work as employees with little skill required, and with almost no chance to develop any particular talents . . .' (p. 295).

[7] Paul Goodman, *Growing Up Absurd* (London, 1961).

which has seen a revolution of expectation. But when Goodman argues that the status of youth is depressed, and their growing up to adulthood made difficult, because 'there get to be fewer jobs that are necessary or unquestionably useful; that require energy and draw on some of one's best capacities; and that can be done keeping one's honour and dignity',[1] he is, at least in the middle of this portmanteau proposition, stating an argument which is open to statistical verification. (He is forced by his initial assumption to the interesting conclusion that early (middle-class) marriage is today a *substitute* for satisfactory employment.)

There can be little doubt that the entirely contrary view put forward by Talcott Parsons is nearer the truth: 'We feel confident that a careful analysis would reveal that in contemporary organizations not only larger absolute numbers, but larger proportions of those involved are carrying more complex decision-making responsibilities than was true fifty years ago.' 'Now, not only have most of the older unskilled "pick-and-shovel" type jobs been eliminated, but an increasing proportion of the "semi-skilled" machine-tending and assembly-line types of jobs have followed them.'[2] In England the Registrar-General's classification of occupations shows a diminution in the proportion of employed males in unskilled and semi-skilled categories (classes V and IV) between 1931 and 1951: with jobs at both dates categorized on the 1931 classification, the proportion in class V declined from 17·7 to 14·3 per cent, in class IV from 18·2 to 16·0 per cent; on the other hand, the proportion of skilled men (class III) rose from 48·8 to 52·6 per cent.

The expansion and qualitative upgrading of skilled work has meant for the young that during the past quarter of a century they have grown up into a world in which the chances of obtaining skilled employment were steadily increasing. Mark Abrams has estimated that since 1938 the real earnings of 'teenagers' (defined as young people aged 15–24) have increased far more rapidly than adult earnings, by some 50 per cent; and that discretionary spending has increased by 100 per cent.[3] Although only 5 per cent of total consumer expenditure is in the hands of this age group which constitutes 13 per cent of the population over 14 years of age,[4] adolescent poverty may be said to have ended.

Young people have been obliged to enter 'dead-end' jobs far less frequently than thirty years ago: in 1951 they constituted a far smaller proportion of workers in the less skilled occupations than in 1931. The proportion of the employed population under the age of 25 has, of course, declined, from 25 to 18 per cent; but the decline in the proportion employed, for instance, as messengers, roundsmen, bus and tram conductors and lorry drivers' mates has declined much more steeply: from 91 to 35 per cent, 44 to 22 per cent, 27 to 14 per cent and 85 to 67 per cent respectively. Their decline among unskilled workers in miscellaneous

[1] Ibid., p. 17.
[2] Talcott Parsons and Winston White, 'The Link between Character and Society', S. M. Lipset and Leo Lowenthal (eds), *Culture and Social Character* (1961), pp. 110–11.
[3] Mark Abrams, *The Teenage Consumer* (1959), p. 5.
[4] Mark Abrams, *Teenage Consumer Spending in 1959* (1961), p. 4.

trades was from 25 to 16 per cent.[1] The less skilled occupations have become top-heavy with older people.

In consequence, as Abrams has claimed, young people 'Nowadays . . . are increasingly spending their working hours in jobs that require adult, industrial and literary skills, and the capacity to work with adults more or less as equals . . . Thus, in their jobs too, quite apart from their earnings, they have, economically, come much closer to being adults and much further from the subservient roles of the child.'[2] These gains are by no means secure; they have given youth an importance and undoubtedly created an economic climate which favoured their greater reproduction. These very circumstances threaten their position in the future.

[1] *General Report, Census 1951*, Table 63, pp. 136–7. Cf. developments in post-war European industry: younger workers are getting better pay than older men and the general effect has been 'to confer the financial benefit of technical change upon these younger men with formal qualifications'. See *Steel Workers and Technical Progress* (1959): O.E.E.C. Project No. 164, quoted J. B. Mays, *Education and the Urban Child* (1962), pp. 157–8.

[2] *The Teenage Consumer* (1959), p. 13.

4 The Anti-Intellectual Tradition in the West

J. WELLENS

In its struggle with the communist East, the West draws strength from its traditions: devotion to the concept of freedom under the law is perhaps its most powerful silent witness. But not all of these traditions are helpful in the struggle. One of them, a strong anti-intellectual tradition in the social and industrial life of both the United States and the United Kingdom, represents a grave weakness. It is a curious accident of history that this anti-intellectual outlook should afflict both of the two strongest powers in the Western Alliance. In this study I have analysed the origins of this tradition and examined its impact on our industrial situation.

In Great Britain, or, more precisely, in England, the anti-intellectual tradition owes much of its force to the fact that the Industrial Revolution was carried through mainly by pragmatists and artisans at the craft level. At least up to the time of the Great Exhibition of 1851 the Industrial Revolution owed little or nothing to the universities or to men with university training. In the textile trade which sparked off the movement for mechanization Crompton was a typical figure. An impoverished spinner, working entirely on his own, in his own attic and with his own meagre capital, his aim was no more than to provide himself with a more efficient and productive machine, which would give him an advantage over his rivals, from whom the secret was to be withheld. The besieging of Crompton's house by his competitors and the removal of his roofing tiles by these men who were determined that Crompton should not retain his secret, symbolize the brashness of this new movement and give some indication of the powerful social forces behind it. These were the days when an untutored illiterate blacksmith, starting with two or three workmen, could, within twenty-five years, build up an industrial empire employing thousands and live to see his sons enter Parliament. From the rough-and-tumble of this fierce struggle, which was the painful birth of industrial man, the universities remained calmly aloof.

This, too, was the time when industry was building its employment structure

First printed in the British Journal of Educational Studies, *Vol. VIII, No. 1* (*November 1959*), *pp. 22–8.*

and in this structure there was no niche created for the man of learning, if only for the fact that he did not approach industry and offer his services. Thus conditioned to independence, it is small wonder that, as the need for skilled engineers grew, industry created its own avenues for the theoretical training which were quite independent of the universities. Thus was created that estrangement between the worlds of industry and education which persists in some measure to this day and which has had such grievous consequences. As though to emphasize the conflict between the two worlds the industrialist created two myths; the 'hard way man' and the 'man with paper qualifications'. The former he endowed with all the virtues and on the latter he poured his unconcealed scorn. The glorification of the 'hard way man' is one of the two great manifestations of the anti-intellectual tradition in British industry.

How persistent this attitude is proving to be is not generally conceded but in this country it still pervades industry from the management to shop-floor workers, with the possible exception of certain enlightened firms: a few of the biggest ones. This anti-intellectual attitude is least in evidence in the two industries in which we discovered our backwardness at the turn of the century – electrical and chemical engineering. The technical problems posed by these two industries could not be solved by rule-of-thumb methods by men with no background of theoretical knowledge. In our own day as we develop new industries, such as electronics and atomic engineering, we are beginning to see the practical man in a truer perspective and, whether we like it or not, our survival depends upon creating a system which will promote harmony between the practical man and the academic and which will synthesize academic education with practical training. But deep go the roots of this aspect of our anti-intellectual tradition. Thus in February 1958 the Carr Committee, after considering for two years the problem of training young people for industrial employment, found itself able to advise that the educational world should be responsible for academic training and that industry should be responsible for practical training, thereby perpetuating this debilitating division, long since abandoned in other countries.

I have identified one source of the anti-intellectual tradition – one which entered industry from below. But a different anti-intellectual influence, no less powerful, was introduced from above. Its power derives from the fact that it originated within the educational system itself. I shall describe this as the 'public school, colonial ethic', but it must be recognized that, in using this term, I am referring to the origin of the code and not necessarily implying that it is universally accepted in public schools today.

In any educational system it is possible to identify two separate aims, one academic and the other ethical. In our country academic standards stem from the universities: the ethical code was set down by the Public and Proprietary schools and is rooted in our colonial tradition.

The colonizing tradition centres round the code of the frontiersman: of its ideals the most outstanding were courage and endurance, the vital frontiersman virtues. Allied to these were independence, the display of initiative, loyalty to the group and the spirit of competition. The Briton's picture of himself as the embodiment of courage against odds, determined never to show fear or betray his associates, however unworthy (vide 'the sneak'), accorded well with the needs of a colonizing people many of whom would be obliged to live on the frontier. Thus, schoolmasters in England, adopting the classic principle that true education should be a preparation for life, embodied this code of behaviour in their teaching. It is a measure of the importance attached to this code that it grew into such a harmonious system. Games and sports subscribed to the ideal of physical courage and endurance; the residential nature of these schools tended to foster independence, especially of the family; the House system encouraged loyalty within the in-group and the competitive spirit towards the out-group. This was efficient education in the sense that the chosen tools were effective. But if it was efficient, it was also highly specialized: it was education for an aristocracy of leaders and pioneers and it was dominated by the frontier.

Nor were the seeds sown on untilled ground, for the leaders of an earlier age, the Norman barons, had given their sons a practical out-of-doors education, which used sport as a training mechanism and travel to confer a broad outlook; academic knowledge occupied a minor role.

The colonial code has two great weaknesses: it assumes that mankind is mono-sexual and it places little value on academic studies and other things of the mind. Within the colonial code book learning has a very minor part to play, for it is related to the secure home environment. There is no room at the frontier for the man of learning and within this code he has been labelled a 'swot' or, in our own times, a 'boffin' or an 'egg-head'. In the same way there is no room at the frontier for the man of letters, the painter or the musician, occupations which have come to be regarded as slightly cissy because they were pursued only in the soft environment.

So it came about that in an important part of our educational system a code was adopted which had a distinct anti-intellectual bias in the sense that learning and the arts took second place to some attribute called 'character'. It has been fashionable of late to deny that this conflict ever existed but facts have an odd way of asserting themselves. In February 1958 one of the great electrical engineering companies announced its new university scholarship scheme. On that occasion a well-known and distinguished director of that firm said, 'We have been increasingly impressed by the need for intelligence. You want intelligence plus, but you do want intelligence. The old-fashioned combination of brute force and character is not enough.'

The public school, colonial code has had an enormous influence upon our social and industrial life, the more so because it has spread beyond its original boundaries. It was natural that the code should be adopted by the boarding schools and the preparatory schools. It was inevitable that it should, in part, be carried through to the universities which accept recruits at an age at which behaviour patterns are already established. What is less reasonable is that the code found its way into the women's services.

It is interesting that in one important sector of our educational system, the state grammar schools, the seed fell on stony ground. True enough, grammar schools have their house systems, remarkably ill-adjusted to their needs though these are, but the impetus behind the grammar school was more narrowly utilitarian. Parents saw such schools as the key to the material advancement of their children. Whether this aim is worthy is quite immaterial: the fact remains that parents saw academic knowledge as the key to those jobs which they sought for their children and they communicated this idea to their children and the schools. But two other reasons militated against the grammar schools adopting this code. In the first place the grammar school, legalized by the act of 1902, came after the colonial period; in the second place, the grammar school grew out of the elementary school of the nineteenth century and not out of the public school.

The importance of this code can now be seen from the fact that, although half of the managers of British industry are 'hard way men', public school men comprise 33 per cent of top management. What is more, in the hierarchy of management the public school man tends to settle at the top and in the large organizations: only 19 per cent of all managers are public school men.

Thus, from below, the 'hard way man' has brought with him to industrial management an anti-intellectual tradition which sees conflict between the 'practical' man and the 'academic', while the man conditioned by the old colonial ethic has brought with him an anti-intellectual tradition of another kind; that which sees 'character' as a more desirable commodity than brains.

Let us now consider the two factors which have introduced the anti-intellectual tradition in the United States. America had its own frontier period and this produced a central figure with many of the characteristics fundamental to a colonial code. Enterprise, independence, physical courage, endurance, virility and staunchness in the face of danger were just as necessary on the American frontier as they were in the outposts of the British Empire. When Jefferson in 1803, by that brilliant piece of trading known as the Louisiana Purchase, opened up the West to rapid exploitation, he created a situation which placed a premium on this vigorous type of individual and the American go-getter was born.

But the frontier period gave way to another and it did so at that precise moment in time when the school system was undergoing fundamental changes. Which is cause and which effect is not important to the argument. The classic school, transplanted directly from Europe, appeared in Boston as early as 1635 and by 1850 there were hundreds of these essentially middle-class independent schools, the academies. However the state-provided secondary school came earlier in America than it did in England. The famous Kalamazoo test case, which authorized the state secondary school in America, preceded the English Education Act of 1902 by thirty-two years. So that the American High School emerged in that period distinguished by the mass immigrations from Europe and, what is more, the establishment of a system of state secondary schools did not result in a dual system of two types of school running side by side, as in England, but largely replaced the independent academies. The problem of American society at that time had become that of welding into one homogeneous nation a flood of immigrants of divergent culture patterns. The emphasis was on belongingness, togetherness and social adjustment and it was this ethic that was adopted, not only by the schools but by a wider community. The message was spread from the pulpit, by the press, by the cinema and by all the organs of mass-communication in turn. Curiously enough, the message appears from time to time in films and plays in quite unexpected forms, even today, long after the need has passed. Conformity was the supreme virtue. But, just as our colonial code has persisted long after the circumstances which produced it have passed, so the American code of conformity has persisted. It is this code that lays it down that intellectual attainment shall take second place, not to 'character' as in our country but to conformity and social adjustment. 'No geniuses here: just a bunch of average Americans working together' runs the much-quoted sound track of Monsanto's recruiting film.

A second feature of the American school system, similar to that already described, often confused with it but quite distinct from it, is no less powerful in promoting the anti-intellectual tradition. To understand it we must understand the special interpretation of democracy which the American applies to his schools. In England popular education was imposed from above by well-intentioned people and societies devoted to good works and by government action. To the American this is the negation of democracy: it is authoritarianism and he will have none of it. We have already seen that the American academies, in which the authoritarian principle applied, withered in the second half of the nineteenth century in the face of the popular movement. In America today schools are the responsibility of each local community: they grew out of the people, and they are, in consequence, democratic. Surely this use of the word 'democratic' is legitimate: where the British educationist parts company with his American colleague is in the assumption that what is democratic according to this criterion is necessarily the best or the most desirable. Democracy's big problem in this context must always be that of maintaining standards.

How much the schools are a local responsibility is seen from the fact that the Federal Office of Education has very little to do with the nation's schools and provides less than 3 per cent of the revenue for them. Even the State Governments provide a mere 40 per cent of this revenue and the remainder, well over half, is derived from the local taxation which each community voluntarily levies on itself. Schools are controlled by local committees, elected directly and not nominated as in this country. These committees have the power to appoint and dismiss all teachers and the Superintendent of Schools. They decide the building programme and the standard of equipment. If democracy goes so far in school administration little wonder that the curriculum is under democratic influence too. Democracy is taken to mean equality of opportunity for all and this in turn is taken to mean uniform schooling. Uniform schooling, particularly where any form of streaming is frowned upon as undemocratic, tends to become minimal schooling, so that, as one observer has put it, 'In Russia everyone goes to the grammar school while in America everyone goes to the modern school.' According to this conception of democracy 'selective schooling' of the grammar school type is quite abhorrent: it is not democratic. What this means to the outsider not steeped in the American brand of democracy is that the Americans are prepared to sacrifice academic standards to their view of democracy. In fairness we must admit that very few Americans would contest this statement for they see democracy and social adjustment as the greater good, at least as far as schools are concerned. Whether they will continue to do so is another matter. Thus the American school system and the political thought on which it rests have an anti-intellectual bias in so far as intellectual standards are not the primary aim.

It is natural now to turn our attention to the Soviet Union where 'everyone goes to the grammar school'. We are coming, educationists and laymen alike, to recognize that one important measure of a nation's potential is the proportion of its citizens who take higher education and on this assessment we have no reason to be complacent. The advantage enjoyed by the Russians is that they started from scratch twenty-five years ago, relatively unhampered by tradition or preconceived notions. Another advantage is that the government can impose its will and follow through a policy to the end, irrespective of the price, whether this be paid in cash or in human suffering. There can be no doubt that the prospect of grammar school education for all is not a happy one, especially when it is allied, as it is in Russia, to outdated teaching techniques and old-fashioned textbooks. It is interesting to note that the changes announced by Mr Khrushchev on 21 September 1958 seem to suggest that the Russians will be adopting some form of selective education in the near future. One might be excused for thinking that another form of the anti-intellectual tradition exists in Russia: one might imagine that academic standards take second place to political indoctrination but in some curious way the Russians seem to have avoided this pitfall, and they have succeeded in placing intellectual attainment among the virtues.

Basic to any analysis of an educational system are these twin factors of academic content and ethical code. Our own thinking in the field of education is entirely dominated by considerations of academic content and the ethical code which animates and supports it is never held in question. It is reasonable to ask whether our code is outdated. I would say quite definitely that it is. The question then arises, what factors should an up-to-date code contain for education and living in an industrial society? I suggest that there are three main factors. Firstly, there is the academic factor: we must come to recognize the importance of learning and the man of learning. Secondly, there is an industrial factor: we must come to accept continual change as the condition of progress. Thirdly, there is the social factor: we need a new assessment of man's place in the industrial society; we need to adopt a code that will promote co-operation between men working in the same enterprise but which, at the same time, will not result in men sacrificing their personalities and individualities to the organization.

If we can accept these three factors as the cornerstones of the industrial code we can appreciate the anxieties felt in this and other countries.

In Russia the first two items of the code seem to have been accepted already but the third factor is not capable of solution within an authoritarian régime.

In America the acceptance of change as a condition of progress has long been an accomplished fact: it is the air which the industrial American breathes. The fact that they are so concerned about the problems of the 'Organization Man' suggests that they will solve the social factor. But the problem of placing learning in its rightful place is not possible without major adaptations to an education system to which the Americans are passionately devoted.

What of our country? Unfortunately we do not recognize the problem as such. In so far as we are aware of the existence of an ethical code in our educational system this is largely subconscious and even where there is a more acute recognition of it, the existing colonial code is accepted; rarely questioned.

My purpose in this study is to call attention to the nature of the current code and to its anti-intellectual aspect, thereby hoping to promote some informed comment upon it.

5   The Definition of Technical Education, 1860-1910

P. W. MUSGRAVE

The 1944 Education Act gave the first legal definition of 'secondary education', though in effect the definition was a residual after the field of further education had been delineated. 'Further education' was treated in a descriptive manner, and no attempt was made to differentiate technical education.[1] In the empirical atmosphere of English education exact definition has been distrusted, but it is worth examining those definitions that have been made as they should provide some indications of what contemporary opinion saw as the function of the part of the educational system in question. It should, perhaps, be added that, though changes in opinion can be traced in this way, the factors operating to bring about the changes are not discovered.

In the 1860s according to *The Economist* 'the notion of technical education' was 'almost entirely new to the country'.[2] It is true that before this date there had been the Mechanics' Institutes whose aim had been to teach 'useful knowledge', but they had failed in their purpose primarily due to the lack of literacy among those who needed such knowledge. *The Economist* thought that there was a need to arrive at some definite conclusion as to the form technical education should assume in Britain, but was adamant that the workshops and offices of the country were 'its true technical schools'.

These comments were prompted by the appointment in 1867 of the Select Committee on Scientific Instruction with Sir Bernhard Samuelson, the iron-master, as chairman. The main outcome of this Committee was the appointment of the Royal Commission on Scientific Instruction and the Advancement of Science (1870–5) with the Duke of Devonshire as chairman. *The Economist* article showed that practical instruction was to be excluded from technical education. The titles of the two government enquiries indicated quite clearly that it was in theoretical instruction that people sought an answer to the cry for technical education. At this time scientific instruction was almost synonymous

[1] 1944 Act, Section 8 (1) (b) for Secondary and Section 41 for Further Education.
[2] 'What is true technical education?', *The Economist* (25 January 1868), pp. 87–8.

First printed in the Vocational Aspect of Secondary and Further Education, *Vol. XVI, No. 34 (summer, 1964), pp. 105–11.*

with theoretical instruction in chemistry. As Donnelly, then official inspector for science at the Department of Science and Art, put it, 'it would scarcely be too much to say that where science was spoken of it was generally supposed to mean chemistry'.[1] The contemporary view on the content of technical education was put by a witness before the Devonshire Commission, who quoted from a paper written by a Committee of the Royal Society of Arts. The instruction that was needed was '. . . general instruction in those sciences, the principles of which are applicable to various specified employments of life . . . excluding the manual instruction in arts and manufactures which is given in the workshop'.[2]

One of the outstanding figures in the campaign for more scientific instruction was T. H. Huxley. In 1877 he gave an address entitled, 'Technical Education', which he described as 'simply a good education, with more attention to physical science, to drawing, and to modern languages than is common, and there is nothing specially technical about it'. He added, 'The workshop is the only real school for a handicraft.'[3]

In 1877, partly under pressure from Huxley,[4] a committee was formed to investigate how best the City Companies could assist technical education. Written evidence was received from both Huxley and Donnelly. In its report in 1879 it was thought 'unwise to establish any place for teaching the actual carrying out of the different trades', though 'technical education' might be improved by giving 'a knowledge of the scientific and artistic principles upon which the particular manufacture may depend'.[5] It should be noted that the phrase 'technical education' was now becoming more common, and in 1881 A. J. Mundella, then Vice-President of the Committee of Council, took credit in the House 'for being one of the earliest to mention the words "technical education" in this country'.[6]

In the 1880s there was much agitation for further action, and in 1881 a further Royal Commission was appointed. Sir Bernhard Samuelson was chairman and the Commission's title reflected the slight change in point of view in that it was to enquire into 'technical instruction'. Further, the members of the commission, all of whom were dedicated to furthering the cause of technical education,[7] included in their report the instruction of '. . . workpeople, foremen, and proprietors and managers of industrial works'.[8] This implied more specific practical

---

[1] Report of Department of Science and Art (1868–9), p. 63 (Donnelly's Report).
[2] Royal Commission on Scientific Instruction (1872), Q. 7283 (J. G. Greenwood).
[3] T. H. Huxley, Collected Essays, Vol. III (London, 1893), pp. 411–12.
[4] Following two articles in The Economist (17 December 1870, pp. 1515–16, and 14 January 1871, pp. 37–8) Huxley passed a motion in the London School Board pressing for proper use of the City Companies' wealth (The Economist, 3 June 1871, p. 657).
[5] Report quoted by G. T. Millis, Technical Education. Its Development and Aims, p. 56 (London, 1925).
[6] Hansard, 3rd Series, Vol. 260, Col. 537.
[7] M. Argles, 'The Royal Commission on Technical Instruction, 1881–4. Its Inception and Composition', The Vocational Aspect, Vol. XI, No. 23 (1959), pp. 97–104.
[8] Royal Commission on Technical Instruction, 1884, Vol. I, p. 16.

instruction for workpeople as well as instruction in principles for managers.

Between the publication of the report of the Commission in 1884 and the 1889 Technical Instruction Act there were seven attempts to pass a bill on this subject. There was, therefore, much discussion of the topic, and in 1888 a writer discussing 'Technical Education in Board Schools' in *The Contemporary Review* could say that technical education then had 'two distinct meanings – one the teaching of a specific art or trade; the other instruction in elementary science bearing on all arts or trades and the training of hand and eye . . .'[1] This latter instruction was justified since skills could be picked up more easily in after life. Though the quotation refers to an elementary level, it can be seen that the division into practical and theoretical instruction is maintained. The change here is that the practical side is now accepted as 'technical education'. The reference to hand and eye training is interesting; this was only a recent innovation in elementary schools and was viewed with suspicion by the Department of Education.[2] Yet Sir William Hart-Dyke, Vice-President, saw as one aim of the abortive 1887 Technical Instruction Bill: '. . . giving . . . elementary technical instruction, not by any means teaching . . . a trade, but affording . . . training of the hand and eye, either in woodwork or in ironwork, or in other subjects . . .'[3] This double approach was found in 1888 in the Final Report of the Cross Commission on Elementary Education: 'By technical instruction we understand instruction in those scientific and artistic principles which underlie the industrial occupations of the people . . ., as well as instruction in the manual practice involved in the application of these principles.'[4] This new development was questioned by some in that the school was taking over 'that which hitherto lay outside it in the form of apprenticeship'.[5] Industrialists who gave evidence by letter to the Samuelson Commission saw technical instruction as 'no more than a useful adjunct to the system of apprenticing learners for at least three or five years' or reiterated the traditional plea that 'the purely technical part of instruction may be acquired as well, or better, in our workshops'.[6] However Magnus, secretary of the City and Guilds, saw technical teaching as important in modern times in industries where machinery played little part and considered it could take the 'place of that instruction which, in former times, the master gave to his apprentice'.[7] Whether industrialists liked it or not changes were under way, and this was particularly true in London.

[1] Rosamond Davenport-Hill, 'Technical Education in Board Schools', *Contemporary Review* (May 1888).

[2] See an exchange between Samuelson and Playfair (then Vice-President) in 1886, *Hansard*, 3rd Series, Vol. 305, Cols. 1655–6.

[3] *Hansard*, 3rd Series, Vol. 318, Col. 1821.

[4] *Royal Commission into the Elementary Education Act (England & Wales), Final Report* (1888), p. 146.

[5] Idem, Q. 28854 (Alderson).

[6] *Royal Commission on Technical Instruction*, Vol. III, (1884), pp. 645–53, for series of letters.

[7] P. Magnus, *Industrial Education* (London, 1888), p. 26.

An article in *Good Words* in September 1889 described the new London Polytechnic as 'a trade school' where the instruction of artisans and clerks was undertaken 'in principles and to some extent in the practice of their breadwinning pursuits'.[1] Magnus, writing in 1888, saw clearly that 'technical education . . . may include the acquisition of the manual skill which production necessitates'.[2]

It was in 1887 that Huxley made his famous remark that 'at the present moment it passes the wit of man, so far as I know, to give a legal definition of technical education'.[3] Yet two definitions were made by Parliament in 1889. These were in the Technical Instruction Act and the Welsh Intermediate Education Act.[4] The latter is rather similar to the former, which in view of its importance will be quoted at length:

> . . . instruction in the principles of science and art applicable to industries, and in the application of specific branches of science and art to specific industries or employments. It shall not include teaching the practice of any trade or industry or employment, but, save as aforesaid, it shall include instruction in the branches of science and art with respect to which grants for the time being made by the Department of Science and Art, and any other form of institution (including modern languages and commercial and agricultural subjects) which may for the time being be sanctioned by that Department by a minute laid before Parliament and made on the representation of a local authority that such a form of instruction is required by the circumstances of its district . . . manual instruction shall mean instruction in the use of tools, processes of agriculture, and modelling in clay, wood, or any other material.

Two things were clear from this wordy definition. First, every attempt was made to show that it was the theory not the practice that was to be taught, but, secondly, the whole flavour of the passage and more particularly the description of 'manual instruction' indicated that practical instruction would be tolerated. It was useless to shut the door when the horse had already bolted. That this is a true interpretation can be seen from the evidence of Donnelly, by then Director of the Department of Science and Art, when in 1895 he said to the Bryce Commission:

> . . . to be correct, the word used . . . ought to have been 'technology' and not 'technical instruction', only I suppose people would have been frightened at the word 'technology'. 'Technical instruction' has, in some places, been really carried into technical instruction, that is to say into the art itself, which is forbidden by the Act.[5]

[1] Quoted by P. Magnus, *Educational Aims and Efforts* (London, 1910), p. 114.
[2] P. Magnus "Industrial Education", p. 20.
[3] T. H. Huxley, op. cit., p. 440.
[4] See Section 7 of Welsh Intermediate Education Act, 1889 and Section 8 of Technical Instruction Act, 1889.
[5] *Royal Commission on Secondary Education* (1895), Q. 1235.

The Act helped a development that had already begun. It was Donnelly's Department of Science and Art that provided the administrative machinery to accelerate the process. As this Department itself admitted, the effect of the 1889 Act was that 'technical instruction' came to mean the twenty or so subjects already examined by the Department before 1889 together with any other subject sanctioned by the Department in a minute laid before Parliament.[1] Many of these subjects (e.g. iron and steel manufacture) sounded very practical, but the Department still played the game of pretending that 'minuted subjects' did not include the teaching of practice:

> The Department, when giving its sanction to certain subjects (i.e. agricultural processes, such as thatching, hedge-cutting, sheep-shearing), has intimated that the minute is issued on the understanding that the instruction . . . will be confined to . . . the best methods of working and in practising . . . these methods in so far as is necessary for such instruction. Instruction which goes beyond teaching the principles involved . . . is contrary to the Act.[2]

As the Bryce Commission reported in 1895 the Department was 'liberal rather than strict in its interpretation'.[3]

In the 1890s the term 'technical education' rather than technical or scientific instruction had not only become common but had new implications. Samuelson was asked as a witness before the Bryce Commission what meaning he would give to the term 'technical education' and replied, 'I should include everything which prepares a man or a woman for the walk of life which he or she intends to pursue.' Both the breadth of the answer and the inclusion of women are new. Samuelson also differentiated technical secondary education from technical education for adults. The former should be 'combined with general education'; by implication the latter was to be practical.[4] The report of the Bryce Commission saw such secondary education not as 'a substitute for apprenticeship' but 'as distinctly a preparation for it' and therefore stressed a broad general curriculum.[5] The economist, Marshall, writing in 1890, thought that 'according to the best English opinions, technical education for the higher ranks of industry' should be general.[6]

Technical education for the upper levels of the labour force might still be seen as general principles, but at the lower levels to teach the practice was now becoming the custom. In the scheme approved by the Privy Council in 1891 for the use of the City Parochial Charities for founding Polytechnical Institutes in the mould of the Regent Street Polytechnic there was to be instruction in general principles, in 'the practical application of such general rules', and finally in 'details of any

---

[1] *Report of Department of Science and Art* (1891), pp. l–liii.
[2] Idem (1893), p. li.
[3] *Royal Commission on Secondary Education*, Vol. I (1895), p. 28.
[4] Idem, Q's 6243–8.
[5] Idem, Vol. I, pp. 133–4.
[6] A. Marshall, *Principles of Economics*, 1st edn (1890), p. 209.

handicraft, trade or business' which could not easily be learnt in the workshop or place of business, though there was still the saving clause that the instruction was not to be a substitute, but a supplement to practical experience.[1] Such practical instruction based on general principles had become a possibility a generation after the 1870 Education Act, since literacy was now more nearly the rule.

In 1906 a government report dealing with higher technical education was in some doubt as to how to define the relevant terms, since 'the terminology of the whole subject is still, in England, somewhat unsettled', but it wished 'to conform to the best usage'. 'Technical education' was seen as 'education which at least in part has special reference to the actual or prospective occupation of the student'. A new term 'technological education' was defined as 'the branch or branches of technical education which have particular reference to the application of science to industrial processes'.[2] The situation was accepted; the broad field at all levels covered both principles and their detailed application. In 1910 the Report of the Board of Education could write of 'the principles underlying . . . callings in industry, in commerce, in professions or in domestic occupations',[3] while in the same year Magnus, looking back on the growth of the City and Guilds, said, 'it was definitely restricted to the encouragement of the teaching of technology, a term now very generally understood and which was less familiar twenty years ago'.[4] Here can be seen both strands, the principles and the practice.

In the 1860s and 1870s 'technical education' was a rarely used phrase. The commonly used term was 'scientific instruction', by which was meant the teaching of the principles underlying a subject and excluded any teaching of their application to industry. Though in the early 1880s the phrase 'technical education' became more usual, the Samuelson Commission paid homage to the old and the new in that it was to investigate 'technical instruction'. This was the term which passed into the law through the 1889 Act, thereby clearly pointing out the division of opinion of the time. By the late 1880s technical education had come to mean instruction of both a specific and a general nature. Though general technical education could be given in an elementary school to the future worker, on the whole technical education for the lower levels of the labour force had come to be seen as practical, still supposedly backed by general principles. For the higher levels of the labour force technical education was rather considered to be principles. By 1906, however, even at the higher levels the teaching of the practice was permissible.[5] The 1889 Act both accepted the teaching of the practice of trades and also encouraged it, since administrative machinery was set up through the Department of Science and Art by which the teaching of the practice of trades

[1] Quoted in G. T. Millis, op. cit., pp. 78–9.
[2] *Final Report of the Department Committee on the Royal College of Science, etc.* (1906), p. 1.
[3] *Board of Education Report* (1909–10), p. 117.
[4] P. Magnus, *Educational Aims and Efforts* (1910), p. 103.
[5] An interesting commentary on this change can be found in the decline of pupillage in the training of future managers during the period under consideration.

was to be extended. The division of technical education by levels grew stronger in the 1890s and was expressed clearly in the Bryce Report, where technical education was seen either as a broad preparation in secondary schools or as practical instruction for adults; the majority of those in secondary schools were destined for the upper levels of the labour force, whilst most adults undergoing instruction would come from the lower levels of the labour force, having left school at an early age.

In conclusion, the question may be asked, what would be given today as a definition for 'technical education'? The 1956 White Paper on Technical Education made no attempt to define its subject, though it did give useful definitions of technologists and technicians.[1] The Crowther report set out to define 'further education' ('something of a term of art') and commented that 'it is defined by type of institution rather than by type of instruction given'.[2] However, the report thought it would be wrong 'to draw too sharp a distinction between "vocational studies" and "education" ', though some of the former was 'perilously close to the line that separates education from mere instruction'.[3] Here can be seen one of those ironic changes of meaning that take place through time; in 1860 'instruction' meant 'education'.

[1] *Technical Education*, Cmd. 9703 (1956), p. 2.
[2] '15 to 18', Vol. I (1959), p. 318.
[3] Idem, pp. 365–6 and 369.

PART TWO

Education in Society

EDUCATION IS POSSIBLE without writing, but today cultures in which the process of education is purely oral are very rare. In most contemporary societies education, whether considered as a process or an institution, largely depends upon literacy. The coming of literacy brings about general changes other than those that affect education, but one of the crucial determinants of the extent of the changes wrought by literacy and of the rate at which they occur is the status given by any society to the ability to read and write. Historically in Europe, one important event that enabled the status given to literacy to rise was the invention of printing. This brought an end to the scribal culture that had predominated for two or three millennia and allowed the age of mass-produced books to begin. When literacy was defined as valuable and had spread, there was the possibility that education could become a precondition upon which industrialization must rest.

In this part this argument is illustrated by four extracts. In the first Goody and Watt indicate some of the social psychological effects of the coming of literacy. These have important consequences for education. New thought patterns may become available; for example, logical thinking of greater complexity is more easily possible in a written rather than in an oral form. Again, the writing down of one's personal experiences, in the paradigm case in a diary, accentuates the individuality of a member of any society and this in its turn creates the possibility of individual rather than co-operative effort throughout all social institutions including education. There are also important institutional changes. Thus, the system of stratification can change in that new resources for power become available. Eventually the power of the pen may oust that of the sword; hence, those in power may wish to control entry to educational institutions in the hope of keeping their hold on political power.

The invention of printing ensured the possibility of a wider market for reading material. Eisenstein shows how innovation at first influenced the religious institutions that, at the time, completely controlled education in Europe. Although this extract is included here to show the way printing enabled a rise to take place in the status of literacy, Eisenstein also clearly traces the connections that existed between the salient social institutions of the time – namely religion, the economy, the polity and education. Such considerations are clearly relevant to the third part of this Reader. Certainly the rate of literacy rose. There have been few studies of the exact manner in which literacy spreads. In his paper, Kahan has shown one possible mechanism in industrializing societies. He examines the relationship between literacy in rural Russia in the nineteenth century, and the nature of the social positions held by members of the labour force. Kahan substantiates the hypothesis that the nearer persons were to the market, the more chance there was that they would be able to read and write.

The part played by education in the process of industrialization, whether in under-developed or developed societies, is an issue of great controversy. Stone examines here two case studies (namely England and Japan) in the attempt to generate some relevant hypotheses. His paper is a model of comparative historical method in this substantive area of sociology, but it is no disrespect to the author to say that he does little more than show us the probable concepts to use and a possible framework of analysis. At the stage which work in this field has reached, to do this is to achieve much.

I Literate Culture: Some General Considerations

J. GOODY and I. WATT

It is hardly possible, in this brief survey, to determine what importance must be attributed to the alphabet as the cause or as the necessary condition of the seminal intellectual innovations that occurred in the Greek world during the centuries that followed the diffusion of writing; nor, indeed, does the nature of the evidence give much ground for believing that the problem can ever be fully resolved. The present argument must, therefore, confine itself to suggesting that some crucial features of Western culture came into being in Greece soon after the existence, for the first time, of a rich urban society in which a substantial portion of the population was able to read and write; and that, consequently, the overwhelming debt of the whole of contemporary civilization to classical Greece must be regarded as in some measure the result, not so much of the Greek genius, as of the intrinsic differences between non-literate (or proto-literate) and literate societies; the latter being mainly represented by those societies using the Greek alphabet and its derivatives. If this is so, it may help us to take our contrast between the transmission of the cultural heritage in non-literate and alphabetically literate societies a little further.

To begin with, the case of alphabetic reading and writing was probably an important consideration in the development of political democracy in Greece: in the fifth century a majority of the free citizens could apparently read the laws, and take an active part in elections and legislation. Democracy as we know it, then, is from the beginning associated with widespread literacy; and so to a large extent is the notion of the world of knowledge as transcending political units: in the Hellenic world diverse people and countries were given a common administrative system and a unifying cultural heritage through the written word. Greece is therefore considerably closer to being a model for the world-wide intellectual tradition of the contemporary literate world than those earlier civilizations of the Orient which each had its own localized traditions of knowledge: as Oswald Spengler put it, 'Writing is the grand symbol of the Far'.[1]

[1] *Decline of the West*, Vol. II, p.150.

First printed as pp. 332–43 of a paper 'The Consequences of Literacy' in Comparative Studies in Society and History, *Vol. V, No. 3 (1962–3), pp. 304–45.*

Yet although the idea of intellectual, and to some extent political, universalism is historically and substantively linked with literate culture, we too easily forget that this brings with it other features which have quite different implications, and which go some way to explain why the long-cherished and theoretically feasible dream of an 'educated democracy' and a truly egalitarian society has never been realized in practice. One of the basic premises of liberal reform over the last century and a half has been that of James Mill, as it is described in the *Autobiography* of his son, John Stuart Mill:

> So complete was my father's reliance on the influence of reason over the minds of mankind, whenever it is allowed to reach them, that he felt as if all would be gained if the whole population were taught to read, if all sorts of opinions were allowed to be addressed to them by word and in writing, and if, by means of the suffrage they could nominate a legislature to give effect to the opinions they adopted.[1]

All these things have been accomplished since the days of the Mills, but nevertheless 'all' has not been 'gained'; and some of the causes of this may be found in the intrinsic effects of literacy on the transmission of the cultural heritage, effects which can be seen most clearly by contrasting them with their analogues in non-literate society.

The writing down of some of the main elements in the cultural tradition in Greece, we say, brought about an awareness of two things: of the past as different from the present; and of the inherent inconsistencies in the picture of life as it was inherited by the individual from the cultural tradition in its recorded form. These two effects of widespread alphabetic writing, it may be surmised, have continued and multiplied themselves ever since, and at an increasing pace since the development of printing. 'The printers,' Jefferson remarked, 'can never leave us in a state of perfect rest and union of opinion,'[2] and as book follows book and newspaper newspaper, the notion of rational agreement and democratic coherence among men has receded farther and farther away, while Plato's attacks on the venal purveyors of knowledge in the market place have gained increased relevance.

[1] *Autobiography of John Stuart Mill*, John J. Coss (ed.) (New York, 1924), p. 74.

[2] *Cit.* Harold A. Innis, 'Minerva's Owl', *The Bias of Communication* (Toronto, 1951), p. 24. Harold Innis was much occupied with the larger effects of modes of communication, as appears also in his *Empire and Communications* (Oxford, 1950). This direction of investigation has been taken up by the University of Toronto review *Explorations*; and the present authors are also indebted to the as yet unpublished work of Professor E. A. Havelock on the alphabetic revolution in Greece. Among the many previous writers who have been concerned with the Greek aspect of the problem, Nietzsche (*Beyond Good and Evil* (Edinburgh, 1909), p. 247), and José Ortega y Gasset ('The Difficulty of Reading', *Diogenes*, Vol. 28 (1959), pp. 1–17) may be mentioned. Among those who have treated the differences between oral and literate modes of communication in general, David Reisman ('The Oral and Written Traditions', *Explorations*, Vol. 6 (1956), pp. 22–8, and *The Oral Tradition, the Written Word and the Screen Image* (Yellow Springs, Ohio, 1956)) and Robert Park ('Reflections on Communication and Culture', *American J. of Sociology*, Vol. 44 (1938), pp. 187–205) are especially relevant here.

But the inconsistency of the totality of written expression is perhaps less striking than its enormous bulk and its vast historical depth. Both of these have always seemed insuperable obstacles to those seeking to reconstruct society on a more unified and disciplined model: we find the objection in the book-burners of all periods; and it appears in many more respectable thinkers. In Jonathan Swift, for example, whose perfectly rational Houyhnhnms 'have no letters', and whose knowledge, 'consequently . . . is all traditional'.[1] These oral traditions were of a scale, Swift tells us, that enabled 'the historical part' to be 'easily preserved without burthening their memories'. Not so with the literate tradition, for, lacking the resources of unconscious adaptation and omission which exist in the oral transmission, the cultural repertoire can only grow; there are more words than anybody knows the meaning of – some 142,000 vocabulary entries in a college dictionary like the *Webster's New World*. This unlimited proliferation also characterizes the written tradition in general: the mere size of the literate repertoire means that the proportion of the whole which any one individual knows must be infinitesimal in comparison with what obtains in oral culture. Literate society, merely by having no system of elimination, no 'structural amnesia', prevents the individual from participating fully in the total cultural tradition to anything like the extent possible in non-literate society.

One way of looking at this lack of any literate equivalent to the homeostatic organization of the cultural tradition in non-literate society is to see literate society as inevitably committed to an ever-increasing series of culture lags. The content of the cultural tradition grows continually, and in so far as it affects any particular individual he becomes a palimpsest composed of layers of beliefs and attitudes belonging to different stages in historical time. So too, eventually, does society at large, since there is a tendency for each social group to be particularly influenced by systems of ideas belonging to different periods in the nation's development; both to the individual, and to the groups constituting society, the past may mean very different things.

From the standpoint of the individual intellectual, of the literate specialist, the vista of endless choices and discoveries offered by so extensive a past can be a source of great stimulation and interest; but when we consider the social effects of such an orientation, it becomes apparent that the situation fosters the alienation that has characterized so many writers and philosophers of the West since the last century. It was surely, for example, this lack of social amnesia in alphabetic cultures which led Nietzsche to describe 'we moderns' as 'wandering encyclopaedias', unable to live and act in the present and obsessed by a ' "historical sense", that injures and finally destroys the living thing, be it a man or a people or a system of culture'.[2] Even if we dismiss Nietzsche's views as extreme, it is still evident that the literate individual has in practice so large a field of personal

---

[1] *Gulliver's Travels*, Arthur E. Case (ed.), Pt IV, Chap. 9 (New York, 1938), p. 296.
[2] 'The Use and Abuse of History', *Thoughts out of Season*, trans. Adrian Collins (Edinburgh, 1909), pp. 33, 9.

selection from the total cultural repertoire that the odds are strongly against his experiencing the cultural tradition as any sort of patterned whole.

From the point of view of society at large, the enormous complexity and variety of the cultural repertoire obviously creates problems of an unprecedented order of magnitude. It means, for example, that since Western literate societies are characterized by these always increasing layers of cultural tradition, they are incessantly exposed to a more complex version of the kind of culture-conflict that has been held to produce *anomie* in oral societies when they come into contact with European civilization, changes which, for example, have been illustrated with a wealth of absorbing detail by Robert Redfield in his studies of Central America.[1]

Another important consequence of alphabetic culture relates to social stratification. In the proto-literate cultures with their relatively difficult non-alphabetic systems of writing, there existed a strong barrier between the writers and the non-writers; but although the 'democratic' scripts made it possible to break down this particular barrier, they led eventually to a vast proliferation of more or less tangible distinctions based on what people had read. Achievement in handling the tools of reading and writing is obviously one of the most important axes of social differentiation in modern societies; and this differentiation extends on to more minute differences between professional specializations so that even members of the same socio-economic groups of literate specialists may hold little intellectual ground in common.

Nor, of course, are these variations in the degree of participation in the literate tradition, together with their effects on social structure, the only causes of tension. For, even within a literate culture, the oral tradition – the transmission of values and attitudes in face-to-face contact – nevertheless remains the primary mode of cultural orientation, and, to varying degrees, it is out of step with the various literate traditions. In some respects, perhaps, this is fortunate. The tendency of the modern mass-communications industries, for example, to promote ideals of conspicuous consumption which cannot be realized by more than a limited proportion of society, might well have much more radical consequences but for the fact that each individual exposed to such pressures is also a member of one or more primary groups whose oral converse is probably much more realistic and conservative in its ideological tendency; the mass media are not the only, and they are probably not even the main, social influences on the contemporary cultural tradition as a whole.

Primary group values are probably even further removed from those of the 'high' literate culture, except in the case of the literate specialists. This intro-

---

[1] *Chan Kom, a Maya Village* (Washington, D.C., 1934); *The Folk Culture of Yucatan* (Chicago, 1941); *A Village that Chose Progress: Chan Kom Revised* (Chicago, 1950); and for a more general treatment, *The Primitive World and its Transformations* (Ithaca, New York, 1953), pp. 73, 108. See also Peter Worsley, *The Trumpet Shall Sound* (London, 1957). For the concept of *anomie*, see Émile Durkheim, *Le Suicide* (Paris, 1897), Bk II, Chap. V.

duces another kind of culture conflict, and one which is of cardinal significance for Western civilization. If, for example, we return to the reasons for the relative failure of universal compulsory education to bring about the intellectual, social and political results that James Mill expected, we may well lay a major part of the blame on the gap between the public literate tradition of the school, and the very different and indeed often directly contradictory private oral traditions of the pupil's family and peer group. The high degree of differentiation in exposure to the literate tradition sets up a basic division which cannot exist in non-literate society: the division between the various shades of literacy and illiteracy. This conflict, of course, is most dramatically focused in the school, the key institution of society. As Margaret Mead has pointed out, 'Primitive education was a process by which continuity was maintained between parents and children . . . Modern education includes a heavy emphasis upon the function of education to create discontinuities – to turn the child . . . of the illiterate into the literate.'[1] A similar and probably even more acute stress develops in many cases between the school and the peer group; and quite apart from the difficulties arising from the substantive differences between the two orientations, there seem to be factors in the very nature of literate methods which make them ill-suited to bridge the gap between the street-corner society and the blackboard jungle.

First, because although the alphabet, printing and universal free education have combined to make the literate culture freely available to all on a scale never previously approached, the literate mode of communication is such that it does not impose itself as forcefully or as uniformly as is the case with the oral transmission of the cultural tradition. In non-literate society every social situation cannot but bring the individual into contact with the group's patterns of thought, feeling and action: the choice is between the cultural tradition – or solitude. In a literate society, however, and quite apart from the difficulties arising from the scale and complexity of the 'high' literate tradition, the mere fact that reading and writing are normally solitary activities means that in so far as the dominant cultural tradition is a literate one, it is very easy to avoid; as Bertha Phillpotts wrote in her study of Icelandic literature:

> Printing so obviously makes knowledge accessible to all that we are inclined to forget that it also makes knowledge very easy to avoid . . . A shepherd in an Icelandic homestead, on the other hand, could not avoid spending his evenings in listening to the kind of literature which interested the farmer. The result was a degree of really national culture such as no nation of today has been able to achieve.[2]

The literate culture, then, is much more easily avoided than the oral one; and even when it is not avoided its actual effects may be relatively shallow. Not only

---

[1] 'Our Educational Emphases in Primitive Perspective', *American Journal of Sociology*, Vol. 48 (1943), p. 637.
[2] *Edda and Saga* (London, 1931), pp. 162–3.

because, as Plato argued, the effects of reading are intrinsically less deep and permanent than those of oral converse; but also because the abstractness of the syllogism and of the Aristotelian categorizations of knowledge do not correspond very directly with common experience. The abstractness of the syllogism, for example, of its very nature disregards the individual's social experience and immediate personal context; and the compartmentalization of knowledge similarly restricts the kind of connections which the individual can establish and ratify with the natural and social world. The essential way of thinking of the specialist in literate culture is fundamentally at odds with that of daily life and common experience; and the conflict is embodied in the long tradition of jokes about absent-minded professors.

It is, of course, true that contemporary education does not present problems exactly in the forms of Aristotelian logic and taxonomy; but all our literate modes of thought have been profoundly influenced by them. In this, perhaps, we can see a major difference, not only with the transmission of the cultural heritage of oral societies but with those of proto-literate ones. Thus Marcel Granet relates the nature of the Chinese writing system to the 'concreteness' of Chinese thought, and his picture of its primary concentration on social action and traditional norms suggests that the cultural effect of the writing system was in the direction of intensifying the sort of homeostatic conservation found in non-literate cultures; it was indeed conceptualized in the Confucian tao-'tung, or 'orthodox transmission of the way.' In this connection it may be noted that the Chinese attitude to formal logic, and to the categorization of knowledge in general, is an articulate expression of what happens in an oral culture.[1] Mencius, for example, speaks for the non-literate approach in general when he comments: 'Why I dislike holding to one point is that it injures the tao. It takes up one point and disregards a hundred others.'[2]

The social tension between the oral and literate orientations in Western society is, of course, complemented by an intellectual one. In recent times the Enlightenment's attack on myth as irrational superstition has often been replaced by a regressive yearning for some modern equivalent of the unifying function of myth: 'have not,' W. B. Yeats asked, 'all races had their first unity from a mythology that marries them to rock and hill?'[3]

In his nostalgia for the world of myths Plato has had a long line of successors. The Rousseauist cult of the Noble Savage, for instance, paid unwitting tribute to the strength of the homogeneity of oral culture, to the yearning admiration of the educated for the peasant's simple but cohesive view of life, the timelessness of his living in the present, the unanalytic spontaneity that comes with an attitude to the world that is one of absorbed and uncritical participation, a participation

[1] Marcel Granet, *La Pensée chinoise* (Paris, 1934), especially pp. vii–xi, 8–55; see also Hu Shih, *The Development of the Logical Method in Ancient China* (Shanghai, 1922).

[2] *Cit.* I. A. Richards, *Mencius on the Mind* (London, 1932), p. 35.

[3] *Autobiographies* (London, 1955), p. 194.

in which the contradictions between history and legend, for example, or between experience and imagination, are not felt as problems. Such, for example, is the literary tradition of the European peasant from Cervantes' Sancho Panza to Tolstoy's Platon Karataev. Both are illiterate; both are rich in proverbial lore; both are untroubled by intellectual consistency; and both represent many of the values which, it was suggested above, are characteristic of oral culture. In these two works, *Don Quixote* and *War and Peace*, which might well be considered two of the supreme achievements of modern Western literature, an explicit contrast is made between the oral and literate elements of the cultural tradition. Don Quixote himself goes mad by reading books; while, opposed to the peasant Karataev, stands the figure of Pierre, an urban cosmopolitan, and a great reader. Tolstoy writes of Karataev that – in this like Mencius or like Malinowski's Trobrianders – he did not, and could not, understand the meaning of words apart from their context. Every word and every action of his was the manifestation of an activity unknown to him, which was his life. But his life, as he regarded it, had no meaning as a separate thing. It had a meaning only as part of a whole of which he was always conscious.'[1]

Tolstoy, of course, idealizes; but conversely, even in his idealization he suggests one major emphasis of literate culture and one which we immediately associate with the Greeks – the stress upon the individual; Karataev does not regard 'his life . . . as a separate thing'. There are, of course, marked differences in the life-histories of individual members of non-literate societies: the story of Crashing Thunder differs from that of other Winnebago,[2] that of Baba of Karo from other Hausa women;[3] and these differences are often given public recognition by ascribing to individuals a personal tutelary or guardian spirit. But on the whole there is less individualization of personal experience in oral cultures, which tend, in Durkheim's phrase, to be characterized by 'mechanical solidarity'[4] – by the ties between like persons, rather than a more complicated set of complementary relationships between individuals in a variety of roles. Like Durkheim, many sociologists would relate this greater individualization of personal experience in literate societies to the effects of a more extensive division of labour. There is no single explanation; but the techniques of reading and writing are undoubtedly of very great importance. There is, first of all, the formal distinction which alphabetic culture has emphasized between the divine, the natural and the human orders; secondly, there is the social differentiation to which the institutions of literate culture give rise; third, there is the effect of professional intellectual specialization on an unprecedented scale; lastly, there is

---

[1] Leo Tolstoy, *War and Peace*, trans. Louise and Aylmer Maude (New York, 1942), pp. 1078–9.

[2] Paul Radin, *Crashing Thunder: the Autobiography of an American Indian* (New York, 1926), and *Primitive Man as Philosopher* (New York, 1927).

[3] Mary F. Smith, *Baba of Karo, a Woman of the Muslim Hausa* (London, 1954).

[4] Émile Durkheim, *The Division of Labor in Society*, trans. G. Simpson (New York, 1933), p. 130.

the immense variety of choice offered by the whole corpus of recorded literature; and from these four factors there ensures, in any individual case, the highly complex totality deriving from the selection of these literate orientations and from the series of primary groups in which the individual has also been involved.

As for personal awareness of this individualization, other factors doubtless contributed, but writing itself (especially in its simpler, more cursive forms) was of great importance. For writing, by objectifying words, and by making them and their meaning available for much more prolonged and intensive scrutiny than is possible orally, encourages private thought; the diary or the confession enables the individual to objectify his own experience, and gives him some check upon the transmutations of memory under the influences of subsequent events. And then, if the diary is later published, a wider audience can have concrete experience of the differences that exist in the histories of their fellow men from a record of a life which has been partially insulated from the assimilative process of oral transmission.

The diary is, of course, an extreme case; but Plato's dialogues themselves are evidence of the general tendency of writing to increase the awareness of individual differences in behaviour, and in the personality which lies behind them;[1] while the novel, which participates in the autobiographical and confessional direction of such writers as St Augustus, Pepys and Rousseau, and purports to portray the inner as well as the outer life of individuals in the real world, has replaced the collective representations of myth and epic.

From the point of view of the general contrast between oral and alphabetically literate culture, then, there is a certain identity between the spirit of the Platonic dialogues and of the novel:[2] both kinds of writing express what is a characteristic intellectual effort of literate culture, and present the process whereby the individual makes his own more or less conscious, more or less personal selection, rejection and accommodation, among the conflicting ideas and attitudes in his culture. This general kinship between Plato and the characteristic art form of literate culture, the novel, suggests a further contrast between oral and literate societies: in contrast to the homeostatic transmission of the cultural tradition among non-literate peoples, literate society leaves more to its members; less homogeneous in its cultural tradition, it gives more free play to the individual, and particularly to the intellectual, the literate specialist himself; it does so by sacrificing a single, ready-made orientation to life. And, in so far as an individual participates in the literate, as distinct from the oral, culture, such coherence as a person achieves is very largely the result of his personal selection, adjustment and elimination of items from a highly differentiated cultural repertoire; he is, of

[1] In the *Theaetetus*, for example, emphasis is placed on the inner dialogue of the soul in which it perceives ethical ideas 'by comparing within herself things past and present with the future' (186b).

[2] Jaeger, *Paideia*, Vol. II (Oxford, 1944), p. 18, speaks of the dialogues and the memoirs by many members of the circle of Socrates as 'new literary forms invented by the Socratic circle . . . to re-create the incomparable personality of the master'.

course, influenced by all the various social pressures, but they are so numerous that the pattern finally comes out as an individual one.

Much could be added by way of development and qualification on this point, as on much else that has been said above. The contrast could be extended, for example, by bringing it up to date and considering later developments in communication, from the invention of printing and of the power press, to that of radio, cinema and television. All these latter, it may be surmised, derive much of their effectiveness as agencies of social orientation from the fact that their media do not have the abstract and solitary quality of reading and writing, but on the contrary share something of the nature and impact of the direct personal interaction which obtains in oral cultures. It may even be that these new modes of communicating sight and sound without any limit of time or place will lead to a new kind of culture: less inward and individualistic than literate culture, probably, and sharing some of the relative homogeneity, though not the mutuality, of oral society.

To speculate further on such lines would be to go far beyond the purposes of this essay; and it only remains to consider briefly the consequences of the general course of the argument for the problem as it was posed at the outset in terms of the distinction between the disciplines primarily (though not exclusively) concerned in the analysis of non-literate and literate societies, that is, anthropology and sociology.

One aspect of the contrast drawn between non-literate and alphabetic culture would seem to help explain one of the main modern trends in the development of anthropology: for part of the progress which anthropology has made beyond the ethnocentrism of the nineteenth century surely derives from a growing awareness of the implications of one of the matters discussed above: an awareness, that is, of the extent to which, in the culture of oral societies, non-Aristotelian models[1] are implicit in the language, the reasoning and the kinds of connection established between the various spheres of knowledge. The problem has been approached in many ways; particularly illuminating, perhaps, in Dorothy D. Lee's contrast between the 'lineal' codifications of reality in Western culture, and the 'nonlineal' codifications of the Trobriand Islanders; and there, incidentally, although Aristotle is not mentioned, his characteristically analytic, teleological and relational thinking is recognizable in the governing attitudes that Dorothy Lee presents as the typical literate mode of thought in contrast to that of the Trobrianders.[2] Benjamin Lee Whorf makes a similar point in his contrast of Hopi

---

[1] Just as it has been argued that a proper understanding of Homer depends upon a 'non-Aristotelian literary criticism' which is appropriate to oral literature: James A. Notopoulos, 'Parataxis in Homer: a New Approach to Homeric Literary Criticism', *Transactions of the American Philological Association*, Vol. 80 (1949), pp. 1, 6.

[2] 'Codifications of Reality: Lineal and Nonlineal', in *Freedom and Culture* (Englewood Cliffs, New Jersey, 1959), pp. 105–20; see also her 'Conceptual Implications of an Indian Language', *Philosophy of Science*, Vol. 5 (1938), pp. 89–102.

with SAE (standard average European). He sees the 'mechanistic way of think-ing' of Europeans as closely related to the syntax of the languages they speak, 'rigidified and intensified by Aristotle and the latter's medieval and modern followers'.[1] The segmentation of nature is functionally related to grammar; Newtonian space, time and matter, for example, are directly derived from SAE culture and language.[2] He goes on to argue that 'our objectified view of time is . . . favourable to historicity and to everything connected with the keeping of records, while the Hopi view is unfavorable thereto.' And to this fact he links the presence of:

1. Records, diaries, bookkeeping, accounting, mathematics stimulated by accounting.
2. Interest in exact sequences, dating, calendars, chronology, clocks, time wages, time graphs, time as used in physics.
3. Annals, histories, the historical attitude, interest in the past, archaeology, attitudes of introjection towards past periods, e.g. classicism, romanticism.[3]

Many of these features are precisely those which we have mentioned as charac-teristic of societies with easy and widespread systems of writing. But while Whorf and other anthropological linguists have noted these differences between European institutions and categories on the one hand and those of societies like the Trobriands and the Hopi on the other, they have tended to relate these variations to the languages themselves, giving little weight to the influence of the mode of communication as such, to the intrinsic social consequences of literacy.[4]

On the other hand, what has been said about literacy and the consequent developments of Greek thought leading to the logical methods and to the cate-gories of Aristotle may seem to attribute to one individual, and to the civilization to which he belonged, a kind of absolute claim to intellectual validity to which neither the philosopher, the anthropologist nor the historian of ancient civiliza-tion is likely to assent. The currency of such diffuse assumptions in general long ago moved John Locke to an unwonted burst of wintry humour: 'God has not

[1] 'Languages and Logic', *Technological Review*, Vol. 43 (1941), reprinted in *Language, Thought, and Reality, Selected Writings of Benjamin Lee Whorf* (New York, 1956), p. 238.
[2] 'The Relation of Habitual Thought and Behavior to Language', *Language, Culture and Personality, Essays in Memory of Edward Sapir*, Leslie Spier (ed.) (Menasha, Wis., 1941), reprinted in *Language, Thought, and Reality*, p. 153.
[3] Op. cit. p. 153.
[4] For example in his paper 'A linguistic consideration of thinking in primitive com-munities' (*Language, Thought and Reality*, pp. 65–86), Whorf discusses Lévy-Bruhl's account of the thinking of primitive man as characterized by *participation mystique*, and suggests that the differences are related to the structure of language. No mention is made of the role of writing and he seems to see language itself as the independent variable, although in his later paper on 'Habitual thought', he does make a passing reference to writing, as well as to the *interdependence* of language and culture (p. 153). Lévi-Strauss, who is much concerned with the linguistic aspects of the problem, makes no mention of the role of literacy in his analysis of the differences between *la pensée sauvage* and *la pensée domestiquée*, but again the actual process of domestication is peripheral to his study (1962).

been so sparing to men to make them barely two-legged creatures, and left it to Aristotle to make them rational.[1] Nevertheless Locke's own treatment of the 'forms of argumentation' and of 'the division of the sciences' is itself recognizably within the tradition that derives from Aristotle and his time; and so, in some important ways, is the literate culture, not only of the West but of the civilized world today. There is obviously some more or less absolute efficacy in the organization of human knowledge which appears in the thoughtways of the first substantially literate culture, although its definition (which could hardly be more difficult) is well beyond the scope of this paper. Max Weber saw as the essential differentiating factor of Western civilization the 'formal rationality' of its institutions; and this, in turn, he regarded as a more fully developed and more exclusively practised, version of the ordinary human tendency to act reasonably – to behave with 'substantive rationality'. For Weber 'formal rationality' was merely an institutionalized form of this general tendency working through 'rationally established norms, by enactment, decrees, and regulations'[2] rather than through personal, religious, traditional or charismatic allegiances. Weber's differentiation in some respects parallels the differentiation made above between oral and alphabetic culture and in various places he anticipates part of the argument advanced in this paper.[3]

The present study then, is an attempt to approach a very general problem from one particular point of view. In that perspective it suggests one reason for what has been widely remarked upon in the comparison between anthropology and sociology: the relative incompleteness of sociological analyses as compared with those of anthropology, and the tendency for anthropologists studying European societies to limit their observations to village communities or family groups. For, quite apart from differences of scale and complexity of social structure, there are two other dimensions of analysis which can in practice be largely disregarded by the anthropologist but not by the student of literate societies.

First the reifying of the past in written record means that sociology must inevitably be the more deeply concerned with history. The kinds of practical and theoretical issues involved here are numerous, for the great importance of the historical dimension, and its very different kind of impact on various social groups, obviously pose acute methodological problems. At the most general level, the analytic model of the sociologist must take into account the fact that from one point of view his data include materials accumulated from earlier cultures and periods, and that the existence of these records greatly increases the

[1] *Essay Concerning Human Understanding*, Bk IV, Chap. 17, p. 84.

[2] *From Max Weber; Essays in Sociology*, trans. H. H. Gerth and C. Wright Mills (New York, 1946), pp. 298–9. See also *The Theory of Social and Economic Organisation*, trans. A. M. Henderson and Talcott Parsons (New York, 1947), pp. 184–6.

[3] Especially in the 'Author's Introduction' to *The Protestant Ethic*, trans. Talcott Parsons (London, 1930), pp. 13–31, where Weber gives a rapid but comprehensive survey of the problem of 'what combination of circumstances' made some aspects of Western civilization 'lie in a line of development having *universal* significance and value'. See also his lecture 'Science as a Vocation' (*From Max Weber*, especially pp. 138–43).

possible alternative ways of thinking and behaving for the members of the society he is studying, as well as influencing their action in other ways. This added complexity means that certain aspects of the past continue to be relevant (or at least potentially so) for the contemporary scene; and it also means that when functional theoretical models are used, the interconnections can hardly be as direct or immediate as those the anthropologist might expect in non-literate societies.

Secondly, the sociologist must in any case recognize that since in alphabetic society much of the homeostatic function of the oral tradition works at the inward and individual rather than at the overt and public level, sociological descriptions, which inevitably deal primarily with collective life, are considerably less complete than those of anthropology, and consequently provide a less certain guide to understanding the behaviour of the particular individuals of whom the society is composed.

2 The Impact of Printing on European Education

E. L. EISENSTEIN

Before lines were drawn in the sixteenth century, men in Catholic regions appear to have been just as eager to read the Bible in their own tongues as were men in what subsequently became Protestant regions. Similarly, Catholic printers combined humanist scholarship with piety and profit-seeking. They were just as enterprising and industrious as Protestant printers. They also served the most populous, powerful and culturally influential realms of sixteenth-century Europe: Portugal and Spain (with their far-flung empires), Austria, France, southern German principalities and Italian city-states. But they do appear to have been less successful in expanding their markets and in extending and diversifying their operations during the sixteenth and seventeenth centuries.[1] Needless to say, like those of other early capitalist enterprises, the fortunes of printing industries hinged on an exceedingly complex network of multiple interactions. Venetian printers, for example, were affected by a commercial decline that can scarcely be explained by singling out Protestant–Catholic divisions. If we want to understand how these divisions *did* affect an important early capitalist enterprise, however, this can be done better by looking at printing than at metallurgy, mining, textiles, shipbuilding or other such enterprises.

Here the contrast registered on the title-page illustration of Foxe's *Actes and Monuments* – showing devout Protestants with books on their laps and Catholics with prayer beads in their hands[2] – seems to me highly significant. After the

[1] See S. H. Steinberg's remarks (*Five Hundred Years of Printing* (rev. edn, Bristol, 1961), p. 194) about the movement of printing industries from southern to northern Germany after the mid-sixteenth century. 'Type-founding, printing, publishing, book-selling' became 'almost Protestant preserves', in his words. That this oversimplifies and exaggerates a more subtle shift is suggested by R. Hirsch, *Printing, Selling, Reading 1450–1550* (Wiesbaden, 1967), pp. 109–10, and by L. Febvre and H. J. Martin's most useful chapter on the 'geography of the book', Chap. VI in *L'Apparition du livre* (Paris, 1958).

[2] W. Haller, *The Elect Nation: The Meaning and Relevance of Foxe's Book of Martyrs* (New York, 1963), p. 118, and see illustration facing p. 25.

First printed as pp. 36–45 of a paper 'Some Conjectures about the Impact of Printing on Western Society and Thought: A Preliminary Report' in the Journal of Modern History, *Vol. 40, No. 1 (March 1968), pp. 1–56.*

Council of Trent, vernacular Bibles that had been turned out previously in all regions were forbidden to Catholics and made almost compulsory for Protestants. An incentive to learn to read was, thus, eliminated among the former and reinforced among the latter. Book markets were apt to expand at different rates thereafter. Since Bible-printing was a special privilege, its extinction in Catholic centres directly affected only a small group of printers.[1] The entire industry, however, suffered a glancing blow from the suppression of the large potential market represented by a Catholic lay Bible-reading public. Furthermore, vernacular Bibles were by no means the only best sellers that were barred to Catholic readers after the Council of Trent. Erasmus had made a fortune for his printers before Luther outstripped him. Both, along with many other popular authors, were placed on the Index. Being listed as forbidden served as a form of publicity and may have spurred sales. It was, however, more hazardous for Catholic printers than for Protestant ones to profit thereby.[2] To be sure, pastors and printers were often at odds in regions governed by new consistories.[3] But the 'Protestant Rome', despite the spread of Calvinism, was not served by an international clergy controlled from one centre, could not block a free trade in ideas outside its narrow confines, and above all could not 'fix' church policy in a permanent mould in the mid-sixteenth century. Nor did it discourage (quite to the contrary!) the expansion of a vernacular book-reading laity. Cautious Anglicans might temporarily (in 1543) forbid Bible-reading among 'women, apprentices, husbandmen'.[4] Fiery Puritans would never thus abandon the most vital principle of their creed.

[1] The relocation of continental Bible printing centres following its extinction in Venice is described by M. H. Black, 'The Printed Bible' in S. L. Greenslade (ed), *The Cambridge History of the Bible* (Cambridge, 1963), pp. 440–51. H. S. Bennett, *English Books and Readers, 1558 to 1603* (Cambridge, 1965), p. 141, notes how the pace of Bible-printing accelerated under Edward VI and came 'almost to a standstill' under Mary Tudor. Thomas Cromwell's order to place a Bible in every parish church was, incidentally, granted at the bequest of the privileged printer who stood to profit from the order (M. Plant, *The English Book Trade* (London, 1939), p. 50). That certain Catholic privileged printers could and did profit from Tridentine decrees by supplying new breviaries and missals to priests is noted by Kingdon, 'Patronage, Piety, and Printing,' pp. 31–5. The promising French market for vernacular psalters that was closed by Catholic victories at the end of the sixteenth century, is, however, also evident in the same article (pp. 28–30). The crippling effect of French censorship on printers, who could not afford long delays entailed by Sorbonnist debates, is described by D. Pottinger, *The French Book Trade in the Ancien Regime 1500–1791* (Cambridge, Mass., 1958), Chap. IV.

[2] Being listed as forbidden *on the Index*, that is. After the advent of printing, censorship and book-banning were practised in most principalities. Different lists were drawn up by magistrates and princes in accordance with varying policies. Only in Catholic areas, however, was guidance provided by the Index superimposed on these policies.

[3] Examples of conflict are given by Davis, 'Strikes and Salvation at Lyons', *Archiv für Reformations-geschichte*, Vol. LXV (1965), pp. 58–64, and by Kingdon, 'The Business Activities of Printers, Henri and François Estienne', in H. Moylan (ed.), *Aspects de la propagande religieuse* (*Travaux d'humanisme et Renaissance*), Vol. XXVIII (Geneva, 1957), p. 265.

[4] Cited by H. S. Bennett, *English Books and Readers 1475–1557* (Cambridge, 1952), p. 27.

The essential, imperative exercise of religious life, the one thing not to be omitted was for everyone the reading of the Bible. This was what the reformers put in place of the Mass as the decisive high point of spiritual experience – instead of participation in the sacrament of the real presence on one's knees in church, they put encounter with the Holy Spirit in the familiar language of men on the printed page of the sacred text.[1]

That Protestantism was above all a 'book religion' has certainly been noted repeatedly.[2] But this could be more fully exploited in comparative studies if it were related to other unevenly phrased changes set in motion by printing. Given a clearly defined incentive to learn to read that was present among Protestants *qua* Protestants and not among Catholics *qua* Catholics, for example, one might expect to find a deeper social penetration of literacy among the former than among the latter during the second century of printing. Earlier lines dividing literate from unlettered social strata – magistrates, merchants and masters from journeymen artisans and yeomen – might grow fainter in Protestant regions and more indelible in Catholic ones between the 1550s and 1650s. This, in turn, would affect the timing of 'revolutions of rising expectations' and help to account for different patterns of social agitation and mobility, political cleavage and cohesion. We know that the mechanization of most modes of production came much more gradually in France than in England. The effects of the steam press, however, probably came more explosively. Certainly religion had not acted on Bible-reading German Anabaptists or English regicides as an opiate. Many low-born Londoners were already steeped in book-learning, were turning out tracts and proclaiming themselves 'free born', well before Parisian journeymen had mastered letters.[3] One might compare the silent war of words in seventeenth-century England with the efflorescence of chansons and festivals in eighteenth-century France. With regard to morals, the Jacobins were 'puritan'; with regard to oral and visual propaganda, they were not. In brief, literacy rates among revolutionary crowds on both sides of the Channel are worth further thought.

Possibly the most fundamental divergence between Catholic and Protestant cultures may be found closest to home. The absence or presence of family prayers and family Bibles is a matter of some consequence to all social historians. Where functions previously assigned only to priests in the church were also entrusted to parents at home, a patriarchical ethic was probably reinforced. Concepts of the family were probably also transformed where the Holy Spirit was

---

[1] Haller, p. 52.

[2] R. Altick, *The English Common Reader. A Social History of the Mass Reading Public, 1800–1900* (Chicago, 1963), pp. 24–5.

[3] Much useful data on the shaping of an indigenous working-class tradition in seventeenth-century England is given by E. P. Thompson, *The Making of the English Working Class* (New York, 1966), Pt I. In her biography of John Lilburne, Pauline Gregg, *Free-born John* (London, 1961), brings out clearly how much Lilburne's career owed to the printing press. Is there any seventeenth-century French equivalent of 'free-born John'?

domesticated. Of course, family life was sanctified among Protestants by clerical marriage. But boundaries between priesthood and laity, altar and hearthside, were most effectively blurred, I think, by bringing Bibles and prayer books within reach of every God-fearing householder. It might be noted that where Bibles did displace confessors in upper-class Catholic homes, in French Jansenist circles, for example,[1] domestic codes set by Counter-Reformation moralists were also rigorously followed and a so-called bourgeois life-style was manifested, even among nobles of the robe.

Going by the book seems to be somehow related to the formation of a distinctive 'middle-class' or 'secularized Puritan' ethos. To understand this relationship it may be useful to look more closely at what some kinds of early book-learning involved. In particular, we need to think about domestic manuals and household guides while recalling, once again, new features introduced by typography. Like cookbooks and herbals, domestic books were written in the age of scribes. But they were not duplicated uniformly in repeated editions. Reliance on unwritten recipes, here as elsewhere, prevailed. Elizabethans who purchased domestic guides and marriage manuals learned in a new way how family life should be conducted in a well-regulated household.[2] A more limited and standardized repertoire of roles was extended to them than had been extended to householders before. Instead of a cross-fire of gossip conveying random impressions about what was expected or haphazard interpretations of what a sermon meant, books came that set forth (with all the i's dotted and all the t's crossed) precise codes for behaviour that godly householders should observe. These codes were known to others – to relatives and neighbours – as well as to oneself. In so far as they were internalized by silent and solitary readers, the voice of individual conscience was strengthened. But insofar as they were duplicated in a standardized format, conveyed by an impersonal medium to a 'lonely crowd' of many readers, a collective morality was also simultaneously created. Typecasting in printers' workshops thus contributed to role-playing at home.

In dealing with altered concepts of the family and the roles performed within it, we need then to consider the sort of cultural differentiation that came in the wake of the printing press. Early book-learning among Protestants was more homely, perhaps, and less courtly than among Catholics. But we also might note that primers and grammars, arithmetic books and writing manuals became more abundant at the same time in all regions. Both domestic and educational institutions were transformed in a manner that affected well-nurtured youths of all faiths. The sort of changes that affected family life between the fifteenth and eighteenth century have been brilliantly illuminated by Ariès' pioneering study

---

[1] F. J. Crehan, 'The Bible in the Roman Catholic Church from Trent to the Present Day', in S. L. Greenslade (ed.), *The Cambridge History of the Bible* (Cambridge, 1962), p. 222, notes Jansenist insistence on Bible-reading as a layman's duty.

[2] Louis B. Wright, *Middle Class Culture in Elizabethan England* (Chapel Hill, N.C., 1935), pp. 106–10, 206, 211, contains many relevant titles and references. See also p. 203 for the contrast between English domestic books and more aristocratic foreign imports.

of French society.[1] Studies based on other regions are needed to supplement his findings. But new theories are also needed if we wish to understand how and why the changes he describes occurred when they did. 'The family ceased to be simply an institution for the transmission of a name and an estate', it assumed moral and spiritual functions, it 'moulded bodies and souls'. How and why this happened remains to be explored. In setting out to do this, a revival of 'an interest in education' seems to me the wrong place to begin. Why not consider, first of all, how child-rearing and schooling were affected by the printed book?

Possibly no social revolution in European history is as fundamental as that which saw book-learning (previously assigned to old men and monks) gradually become the focus of daily life during childhood, adolescence and early manhood. Ariès has described the early phases of this vast transformation: 'The solicitude of family, Church, moralists and administrators deprived the child of the freedom he had hitherto enjoyed among adults.' The school 'was utterly transformed' into 'an instrument of strict discipline'.[2] I would argue that such changes are probably related to the shift from 'learning by doing' to 'learning by reading'. Surely some sort of new discipline was required to keep healthy youngsters at their desks during daylight hours. Some sort of new profession – that of tutor, schoolmaster or governess – was required to keep them there. And some sort of new attitude on the part of parents was probably also apt to result. A new 'concept of childhood' indeed might owe much to the widened gap between literate and oral cultures. The more adult activities were governed by conscious deliberation and going by the book, the more striking the contrast offered by the spontaneous and impulsive behaviour of young offspring[3] and the more strenuous the effort required to remould young 'bodies and souls'.

The appearance of a stricter domestic discipline, together with new forms of child-rearing, schooling and worship, was probably linked to the inculcation of book-reading habits. But new forms of scurrilous gossip, erotic fantasy, idle pleasure-seeking and freethinking were also linked to such habits. Like piety, pornography assumed new forms. Book-reading did not stop short with guides to godly living or practical manuals and texts any more than printers stopped short with producing them. The same silence, solitude and contemplative attitudes associated formerly with pure spiritual devotion also accompanied the perusal of scandal sheets, 'lewd Ballads', 'merry bookes of Italie' and other 'corrupted tales in Inke and Paper'.[4] Not a desire to withdraw from a worldly society or the city of man but a gregarious curiosity about them could by the eighteenth century be satisfied by silent perusal of journals, gazettes or news-

---

[1] Philippe Ariès, *Centuries of Childhood, A Social History of Family Life*, trans. R. Baldick (New York, 1962). (See this Reader, Part One, No. 2.)

[2] Ibid., pp. 412–13.

[3] This sort of analysis seems relevant also to the problems considered by Michael Foucault, *Madness and Civilization: A History of Insanity in the Age of Reason*, trans. R. Howard (New York, 1965). A redefinition of *la folie* went together with that of *l'enfant*.

[4] Cited by Wright, pp. 232–3.

letters. Increasingly the well-informed man of affairs had to spend part of each day in temporary isolation from his fellow-men.

As communion with the Sunday paper has replaced churchgoing, there is a tendency to forget that sermons had at one time been coupled with news about local and foreign affairs, real estate transactions and other mundane matters. After printing, however, news-gathering and circulation were more efficiently handled under exclusively lay auspices. Such considerations might be noted when thinking about the 'secularization' or 'desacralization' of Western Christendom. For in all regions (to go beyond the eighteenth century for a moment) the pulpit was ultimately displaced by the periodical press and the dictum 'nothing sacred' came to characterize a new career. Pitted against 'the furious itch of novelty' and the 'general thirst after news',[1] efforts by Catholic moralists and Protestant evangelicals, even Sunday schools and other Sabbatarian measures,[2] proved of little avail. The monthly gazette was succeeded by the weekly and finally by the daily paper. Provincial newspapers were founded. By the last century, gossiping churchgoers could often learn more about local affairs by scanning columns of newsprint in silence at home.

In the meantime, however, communal solidarity among parishioners had been dissolved and vicarious participation in more distant events had been enhanced. Indeed, a sharper division between private and public zones of life accompanied the advent of printed publicity. The family, itself, 'advanced in proportion as sociability . . . retreated. . . . It was a movement which was sometimes retarded by geographical or social isolation. It would be quicker in Paris than in other towns, quicker in the middle classes than in the lower classes. Everywhere it reinforced private life at the expense of neighbourly relationships, friendships and traditional contacts.'[3]

But even while social bonds linking parishioners were loosened, the claims of larger collective units also became more compelling. Printed materials encouraged silent adherence to causes whose advocates could not be located in any one parish and who addressed an invisible public from afar. As Ariès himself notes, the 'concept of classes and perhaps . . . the concept of race'[4] appeared alongside a new privacy assigned to family life within the home. Like national consciousness, class consciousness reflected a new form of group identity that displaced an older, more localized nexus of loyalties. Similarly, the amorphous overlapping categories that were assigned different 'ages of man' would later give way to chronologically numbered and segmented age grades. Newly segregated at

[1] Citations from the *British Mercury* of 1712 and Addison in Preserved Smith, *The Enlightenment 1687–1776* (New York, 1934), p. 284.

[2] See Altick, p. 128.

[3] Ariès, p. 406.

[4] Ibid., p. 415. The increasing remoteness and impersonality of political theorizing in the seventeenth century, discussed by Lionel Rothkrug, *Opposition to Louis XIV. The Political and Social Origins of the French Englightenment* (Princeton, N.J., 1965), pp. 458–9, seems relevant to the above analysis.

schools and receiving special printed materials geared to distinct stages of learning, separate 'peer groups' ultimately emerged; a distinctive 'youth culture' that was somewhat incongruous with the 'family' came into being. Such developments, however, did not really crystallize until the last century, after both typography and schooling underwent new transformations.

Public life was none the less profoundly transformed from the sixteenth to the eighteenth centuries, as many historical studies suggest. They say little about the advent of printing. It must have affected traditional governing groups in many ways. The printing of emblems of heraldry and orders of chivalry, for example, probably encouraged class consciousness among hereditary nobles and helped to codify notions about rank, priority and degree.[1] One may learn from Curtis how 'drastic changes introduced by printing' affected undergraduate studies at Oxford and Cambridge and how 'well-born successors to medieval clerks' profited from these changes.[2] Unfortunately, Curtis' approach seems to be exceptional. The effects produced by printing on higher education and academic institutions usually have to be inferred from occasional casual remarks. The same is true of treatments of other pertinent topics. How access to printed materials affected attitudes towards estates of the realm, the cultivation of landed estates, the collection of seigneurial dues, the conduct of courtiers, the strategies of councillors, military and fiscal policies, even the aspirations of would-be gentlemen – all could be usefully explored. Recently some historians have begun to abandon, as fruitless, older debates about the 'rise' of a new class to political power in early modern times. They seek to focus attention instead on the re-education and regroupment of older governing élites – and have, thereby, precipitated new debates. Both lines of enquiry might be reconciled and fruitfully pursued if the consequences of printing received more attention.

According to Hexter, for example, 'a revaluation of our whole conception of social ideas, social structure and social function in Europe in the Age of the Renaissance is long overdue'. We must start 'by thinking in terms not of the decline of the aristocracy but of its reconstruction'. This reconstruction, moreover, was marked by a 'new and radical' suggestion that 'bookish learning' was not 'supererogatory' but indispensable to ruling a commonwealth and by 'a stampede to bookish education' which 'edged the clergy' out of some schools.[3]

---

[1] See the reference to Caxton's *Ordeyne de chevalrie* and other early books on heraldry in E. F. Jacob, *The Fifteenth Century 1399–1485* (Oxford History of England, 1961), p. 665. On the very different form taken by the art of heraldry before printing, see N. Denholm-Young, *History and Heraldry 1254–1310* (Oxford, 1965). The hardening of the concept of 'degree' is treated by Altick, p. 31. The printing of the *Almanach de Gotha* from the eighteenth century on has helped to perpetuate the existence of a hereditary aristocracy despite its political abolition in some regions.

[2] Mark Curtis, *Oxford and Cambridge in Transition 1558–1642* (Oxford, 1959), pp. 89–111.

[3] J. T. Hexter, *Reappraisals in History* (Evanston, Ill., 1961), Chap. IV. See also Lawrence Stone, 'The Educational Revolution in England, 1560–1640', *Past and Present*, No. 28 (July 1964), pp. 41–80.

If Hexter is right, it is also time to start thinking about changes that affected the nature of bookish learning itself. Hereditary nobles were probably forced by these changes to choose between old ways and new ways of training their sons.

> In my day, gentlemen studied only to go into the Church and even then were content with Latin and their prayer book. Those who were trained for court or army service went, as was fitting, to the academy. They learned to ride, to dance, to handle weapons, to play the lute . . . a bit of mathematics and that was all. . . . Montmorency, the late Constable, knew how to hold his own in the provinces and his place at court without knowing how to read.[1]

Once military command required mastering a 'copious flow of books' on weaponry and strategy[2] and royal councillors were called upon 'to think clearly, analyse a situation, draft a minute, know law's technicalities, speak a foreign language',[3] it must have become more difficult to hold one's place in court without knowing how to read. Failure to adopt new ways in some instances probably paved the way for the ascension of new men. Whether we describe it as a 'rise' or 'regrouping' the increasing pre-eminence assigned robe nobles in France, for example, might be examined with this in mind.[4] Officials and magistrates who acquired landed estates and adopted a noble life-style from the sixteenth century on apparently abandoned many of 'their bourgeois ways'.[5] Yet they did not relinquish them all. From the early sixteenth century on, robe nobles were acquiring private libraries that outstripped those of the clergy by the end of the sixteenth century and left those of the *noblesse d'épée* far behind.[6] Was it not largely because learning by reading was becoming as important as learning by doing that the robe took its place alongside the sword? New powers were lodged in the hands of a legal bureaucracy which defined and interpreted rules pertaining to privileges, patents and office-holding while seeking privileges, profits and places itself. Some of these new powers redounded to the benefit of the crown and to the royal officials who served it. But the provincial parliament commanding its own press also became the focal point of resistance to the extension of royal prerogatives; it often played a leading role in the formation of new

[1] Remarks of a seventeenth-century French nobleman, reported by Saint-Evremond and cited by John Lough, *An Introduction to Seventeenth-Century France* (London, 1960; 1st edn, 1954), p. 203. See also the exchange between Richard Pace and a Tudor gentleman in 1514 relating to the same issue, cited by Curtis, p. 58.

[2] John Hale, 'War and Public Opinion in the 15th and 16th Centuries', *Past and Present*, No. 22 (July 1962), pp. 20–2. This whole article contains much relevant material on the effect of printing on military affairs.

[3] Lawrence Stone, *The Crisis of the Aristocracy 1558–1641* (Oxford, 1965), p. 673. See also W. T. MacCaffrey, 'Elizabethan Politics: The First Decade', *Past and Present*, No. 24 (April 1963), pp. 32–3.

[4] See F. Ford, 'Robe and Sword', *Harvard Historical Studies*, Vol. LXIV (Cambridge, Mass., 1953), pp. 246–52.

[5] J. Russel Major, 'Crown and Aristocracy in Renaissance France', *American Historical Review*, Vol. LXIX (April 1964), pp. 631–45.

[6] Febvre and Martin, pp. 398–9.

learned societies and turned out propaganda that mobilized regional loyalties. The issue of literacy is already beginning to appear in discussions of the modernization of privileged status groups, which went hand in hand with the modernization of the royal court.[1] To discuss this issue, however, one must also take cognizance of the activities of printers and booksellers and of how their markets and sources of supply were diversely patterned in different regions. A comparative study of the effects of law-printing in England and in France, for example, might illuminate many issues.

[1] See the contrast between education of robe nobles *vis-à-vis* those of the sword (F. Ford, pp. 217–21).

3 Determinants of the Incidence of Literacy in Rural Nineteenth-century Russia

A. KAHAN

In rural Russia in the middle of the nineteenth century, one of every six boys and one in fourteen girls, at the most, were acquiring literacy to a level that enabled them to retain it. This is judging from data concerning literacy rates among men and women over 60 years of age in the 1890s. By the last decade of the century two fifths of the rural male and one sixth of the rural female youth between the ages of 10 and 19 were literate. Male literacy rates among army recruits, which reflected predominantly rural rates, rose from one fifth in 1874 to two fifths in the mid-1890s and to two thirds in 1913. Among those recruits the rates of literacy at the low extreme (Ufa district) and the high extreme (Lifland district) were as follows: 7 per cent and 95 per cent for 1874–83; 13 per cent and 97 per cent for 1894; and 27 per cent and 99 per cent for 1904. Evidently rural literacy was rising rapidly in Russia during the second half of the nineteenth century, but in a pattern of great diversity. The incidence of literacy both among and within geographic areas varied with the characteristics of subpopulations and with the extent of contacts with markets (rural or urban) and with urban life.

About 1900 the relationship between the various degrees of literacy within the rural population and the levels of income or nature of employment of different groups within that population became the subject of study by economists and statisticians in Russia, giving rise to prolonged controversies. The most widely accepted hypothesis concerning the relationship between literacy and income levels or occupational structures of the rural population was that advanced by Vorobiov and Lositskii, and tested and substantiated by Vikhliaev and others.[1]

---

[1] K. Ia. Vorobiov, *Gramotnost' Sel'skogo Naselenia V. Sviazi s Glavneishymi Faktorami Krest'ianskogo Khoziaistva* (St Petersburg, 1902); A. E. Lositskii, *K. Voprosu ob Izucheniu Gramotnosti Naselenia Rossii* (Chernigov, 1900); P. A. Vikhliaev, *Ekonomicheskie Uslovia Narodnogo Obrazovnia v Moskovskoi Gubernii* (Moscow, 1910).

First printed as pp. 298–302 of Education and Economic Development, *C. A. Anderson and M. J. Bowman (eds.) (Cass, London, 1966).*

In essence Vorobiov *et al.* attempted to prove the following propositions: (1) literacy is positively related to income within the broad income and occupational groups of the rural population; (2) rural residents engaged in non-agricultural activities have a higher literacy rate, regardless of their income position relative to the agricultural population; (3) the relatively higher literacy rate of the non-agricultural rural population varies with the degree of their contact with the market, particularly with urban markets. One should therefore differentiate, within the non-agricultural rural population, among activities connected with the rural markets, activities performed in the rural areas for the urban market, and employment (seasonal and semi-permanent) in urban areas. Literacy increased to the degree that the rural population was exposed to contact with urban areas.

In order to prove his first proposition – that literacy is positively related to income within particular groups of the population – Vorobiov cited a number of studies and surveys. Table I is illustrative. Taking size of farm as a proxy for income, it indicates a quite systematic association between income and literacy in the farm population. In Table II (from the 1920 census in the Russian Socialist Federated Soviet Republic) this relationship is not nearly so neat; literacy actually declined with size of landholding to about the 5-hectare level, stabilized through a middle-size range and then rose again only for farms above 8 or 10 hectares. However, the explanation is clear enough, and supports Vorobiov's second proposition – namely, that individuals engaged at least part-time in non-agricultural activities have on the average a higher literacy rate than the agricultural population, regardless of the income they may derive from agriculture. An even more striking relationship between the degree of literacy within a particular area and the development of non-agricultural activities is suggested by comparing the percentage of workers in non-agricultural seasonal employment with the literacy rate of draftees into military service from the same locality (Table III).

TABLE I

Percentage of Males in Farm Households, Literate or in School*

Size of landholding (in desiatin)	Heads of livestock			
	Less than one	1–2	2–4	4 and over
Below 3	42	50	55	52
3–4·9	49	53	54	59
5–6·9	50	55	56	58
7–9·9	48	54	57	59
10–14·9	55	57	61	62
15 and over	—	—	69	64

* Farm households that possess livestock. These data are derived from an 1897 survey of a typical county (*uyezd*) in Iaroslavl district in which land and livestock are used as a proxy for income.

TABLE II

Percent Literacy in Peasant Farms According to the Agricultural Census of 51 Districts of RSFSR, 1920

Size of landholding (in hectares)	Percentage of literacy		Percentage of farms with non-agricultural incomes
	Males	Females	
0·1– 1	48·1	24·5	25·0
1·1– 2	46·2	21·4	16·0
2·1– 3	42·8	18·6	12·5
3·1– 4	40·7	16·6	10·5
4·1– 5	39·7	15·5	9·6
5·1– 6	39·1	15·1	9·0
6·1– 8	39·1	14·9	8·8
8·1–10	39·6	15·0	8·7
10·1–13	39·7	16·1	7·9
13·1–16	41·2	17·1	7·2
16·1–19	42·1	18·1	7·5
19·1–22	42·9	19·4	7·5
22·1–25	43·4	20·2	7·7
25·1–over	46·6	23·6	7·6

TABLE III

Comparison between the Percentage of Literacy of Draftees during 1887–9 and the Percentage of Passports* Obtained by Peasants in 1887 (some countries of Kostroma District)

Rank by per cent of passports	Counties	Percentage of passports per 100 males in 1887	Percent literacy among draftees
1	Chukhlomsky	29·1	84·0
2	Soligalichski	22·4	69·8
3	Galichski	20·8	64·3
4	Kologrivski	9·2	53·0
5	Buiski	8·9	49·2
—			
—			
—			
12	Vetluzhskii	0·4	33·3

* Passports were documents indicating the permission of the village authorities for the peasant's absence of more than a few weeks.

Source: *Materialy dla Statistiki Kostromskoi Gubernii* (1891), Vypusk 8, pp. 208, 332 and 333.

Having established the relationship between literacy rates and non-agricultural activities, it was logical to expect that extent of contact with the market would be a determining factor in the degree of literacy. The study of Vorobiov on literacy of peasants engaged in non-agricultural activities points both to the relation between income and the literacy level, and to the difference in literacy rates between occupations which can be identified in terms of a degree of contact with rural or urban consumers, middlemen or employers (Table IV).

TABLE IV

Percentage of Literacy among Peasants Employed in Various Non-agricultural Activities (Vorobiov's Sample)

Potters	36	Distillery workers	90
Herdsmen	46	Restaurant service	91
Stevedores	54	Restaurant cooks	94
Tailors, carpenters	57	Meat merchants	96
Day labourers	59	Pastry makers	97
Local coachmen	60	Retail merchants	98
Urban coachmen	84	Dairy merchants	98
Sausage makers	85	Fruit merchants	99
Bakers	86	Textile merchants	100

Source: K. Ia Vorobiov, *Gramotnost Sel'skogo Naselenia v Sviazi s Glavneishymi Faktorami Krest'ianskogo Khoziaistva* (St Petersburg, 1902).

The distinction between village crafts and urban crafts as being important in determining the literacy rate is supported by the evidence from a study of craftsmen. This study, using a sample of 43,575 rural and urban craftsmen, gave for the year 1890 the results shown in Table V. Clearly the village trades are at the lower end of the literacy scale, while urban crafts are marked by a higher degree of literacy. To the extent that literacy represents education, the relationship between education and higher skills becomes established. The influence of urban areas, as centres of industry and trade, in the spread of education on their peripheries was steadily increasing. Given the slow pace of commercialization of Russian peasant agriculture in the nineteenth century, the contact with the urban community through the commodity market or employment triggered for rural population the process of discovering the value of (or return to) education.

Numerous studies and surveys in Russia established the dependency of the literacy rate upon the distance from cities, and the dependency of the frequency of school attendance on the development of rural trades and home industries.

The data assembled in the various surveys seem to suggest that at intermediate levels of income the labour demands of the farm household hindered school attendance. However, even in cases when the increase from small to middle-size landholdings had a detrimental effect upon school attendance of males, this was in part compensated by increased education of females. The process of social and economic differentiation, which weakened subsistence farming and accompanied the commercialization of agriculture, increased the amount of education at both ends of the income scale, and thereby contributed to the rise of the average level of literacy.

TABLE V

Percentage of Literacy Among Rural and Urban Craftsmen, 1890

Toymakers	100	Coopers	33·8
Artist-painters	100	Agricultural implement makers	32·4
Artist-stonecutters	80	Shoemakers	31·4
Carders and reeders	75·4	Weavers and embroiderers	31·2
Leather workers and tanners	72·8	Bristle brushmakers	17·4
Turners	63·3	Carpenters	16·0
Nail makers	44·0	Sieve weavers	15·4
Blacksmiths and locksmiths	42·3	Cart and sledgemakers	5·0
Cabinetmakers	40·2	Wheelwrights	2·4
Basket weavers	39·0		
		Total sample	39·5

Source: F. A. Danilov, 'O Vlianii Gramotnosti, Shkol'nogo Obuchenia i Professional 'nogo Obrazovania na Razvitie Kustarnykh Promyslov,' in *Ekonomicheskaia Otsenka Narodnogo Obrazovania* (St Petersburg, 1896).

The rise in the level of literacy among both the higher income groups of the peasant population and the agricultural labourers becomes the precondition for introduction of machinery and more modern farming methods.[1] The decline of subsistence farming, a type of farming which had not offered visible incentives for education, made it easier to overcome the long-lasting inertia and maintenance of the status quo and to inject an additional impetus to mobility and change in the economy and society.

Against this background one should not overlook the dynamics of the process under way. Two figures might be sufficient to illustrate the relative rapidity of the spread of education despite the various obstacles and short-comings cited above.

The number of pupils in rural elementary schools increased from 1,754,000 in 1885 to over 7,000,000 in 1914. The number of teachers in rural schools increased from 24,389 in 1880 to 109,370 in 1911. What is significant, however, is that during the same period the number of teachers of peasant descent in those schools increased from 7,369 to 44,607. Thus an indigenous group fostering education in this milieu was growing rapidly, a group committed to the task of progress.

[1] In 1895 the Russian Academician Professor Yanzhul' asked the not entirely rhetorical question: 'How will the news about an improvement reach our peasant or rural craftsman while the basic means of communication and transfer of ideas – literacy – is lacking?' I. I. Yanzhul', A. I. Chuprov, I. N. Yanzhul', *Ekonomicheskaia Otsenka Narodnogo Obrazovania* (St Petersburg, 1896), pp. 50–1.

4 Japan and England: A Comparative Study

L. STONE

Two of the most striking success stories in the history of economic development have occurred in two islands lying just off the continents of Europe and Asia respectively. England evolved slowly, and early, and by processes internal to itself; Japan entered into the modern world rapidly and late by selective adoption of concepts and skills developed by others. A comparison of the social structure, educational programme and economic growth of Japan with those of England from the mid-sixteenth century to the early twentieth may nevertheless reveal something of significance. There are three comparisons which can profitably be made here: between late Tudor England and Tokugawa Japan in its prime in the eighteenth century; between mid-seventeenth-century England and mid-nineteenth-century Japan, both on the eve of revolution; and between nineteenth-century England and late nineteenth- and early twentieth-century Japan.

The closest comparison in terms of social structures and educational systems is obviously the first. Both Elizabethan England and Tokugawa Japan were ruled by about 250 noble families (*daimyo*) and a very much larger number of gentry (*samurai*), the remainder of the population being taxed and governed in the interests of this two-stage élite. Both were headed by new authoritarian dynasties, Tudors and Tokugawas, who had recently established themselves by force of arms, had restored order to the countryside, and had secured their power and that of their followers by the confiscation and redistribution of church property, monastic land by the Tudors and, on a lesser scale, Buddhist temple lands by the first three shoguns. Both adapted and developed religious ideologies and institutions for political and dynastic purposes: the Anglican creed and church in England, Chu Hsi Confucianism in Japan. Richard Hooker and Hayashi Razan played a similar role in developing and justifying their respective conformist and deferential creeds by the use of moral and philosophical arguments to prove that

First printed as pp. 219–32 of 'Education and Modernization in Japan and England', Comparative Studies in Society and History, *Vol. IX, No. 2* (1966–7), *208–32.*

the existing social order is ordained by God and Nature.[1] Both ruling families erected elaborate and expensive temples for the worship of the founder of the dynasty: Henry VII's chapel at Westminster, and the great shrine to Ieyasu at Nikkō. The English nobility crammed the parish churches with the ostentatious memorials of their ancestors; the daimyo enshrined their founding ancestors and held yearly services to exalt the prestige of their families. Up to the late seventeenth century in England, and the early nineteenth in Japan, both economies were driven primarily by the demands of the élite for conspicuous consumption. Both developed an exalted sense of national destiny, buttressed by the Anglican religion for the one (it was a Tudor Bishop who opined that God is English), and by Shinto religion, much more gradually and locally, for the other. Both societies were based on the principle of hereditary ascribed status, supported by the legal institution of primogeniture and by strict rules of etiquette. Both societies depended for political and psychological unity in considerable measure on the attractive power of a sophisticated and expensive court life around the Prince in the capital city, Edo or London. Finally it is a remarkable fact that the merchant communities in Tudor England and Tokugawa Japan were both of them extremely traditional and conservative in outlook. In both societies such entrepreneurial initiative and such risk capital as there was seems to have come mostly from the upper landed classes.[2]

There were also, of course, some striking dissimilarities. Though both were ruled by the landed classes, the pattern of relationships was already contractual in the one, still feudal in the other. The encouragement of foreign trade was a prime motive of state policy for the one, the prevention of foreign trade a prime motive for the other. The bourgeoisie played at all times a far greater role in pre-industrial England than it ever did in Tokugawa Japan. Assimilation of a successful bourgeois family into the landed classes was fairly easy in the one (if only in the second generation), fairly difficult until towards the end in the other. In terms both of individual freedom and economic well-being, the condition of the tenantry and rural labourers was far better in the one than in the other, where personal servitude, ascription to the soil, and a crushing burden of taxation were the norm. Both official ideologies served as buttresses of the existing social order, but the English, unlike the Japanese, was under severe and continuous challenge from a potentially subversive variant, Puritanism and Dissent. Part cause and part consequence was that deference and hierarchy were moderately observed in the one, immoderately in the other, and that upper class radicalism was an endemic feature of the one, and very rare in the other until near the end.

At a fairly early stage both societies freed education from the monopoly of priests, England in the sixteenth century, Japan in the seventeenth. Both de-

[1] J. W. Hall, 'The Confucian Scholar in Tokugawa Japan' in *Confucianism in Action*, D. S. Nivison and A. F. Wright (eds) (Stanford, 1959), pp. 270–7.

[2] For England, see L. Stone, *The Crisis of the Aristocracy, 1558–1641*, Chap. VII; for Japan, see J. Hirschmeier, *The Origins of Entrepreneurship in Meiji Japan* (Cambridge, Mass., 1964), Chaps. I, VII.

veloped schools for their élite in which the children could be taught firstly – and most importantly – the virtue of obedience to superiors in order to preserve social stability; secondly, the art of war, which was the original justification of their privileged status; thirdly, the techniques and skills which would equip them for administrative chores in an increasingly bureaucratic society; fourthly, scholarly appreciation of the classics, in which all wisdom was believed to reside; and fifthly, the manners, skills and aesthetic interests that distinguished them from the rest of society.[1] Three advanced thinkers of sixteenth-century England, Thomas Starkey, Nicholas Bacon and Humphrey Gilbert, lobbied unsuccessfully for a state-supported school for the aristocracy; in late eighteenth-century Japan the Bakufu set an example by endowing, supporting and operating a school for samurai, the Shōheikō. Mr Dore's summary of the educational system of Tokugawa Japan reads almost exactly like an account of that of Jacobean England derived from the writings of Tudor educational theorists such as Roger Ascham, Richard Mulcaster and Henry Peacham:

> . . . The means of education were provided by Chinese writings, especially the Confucian classics; its purpose was primarily to develop moral character, both as an absolute human duty and also in order the better to fulfil the samurai's function in society; a secondary purpose was to gain from the classics that knowledge of men and affairs and of the principles of government which was also necessary for the proper performance of the samurai's duties. Certain other technical vocational skills were necessary which could not be gained from classical Chinese study. Also, classical Chinese study itself brought certain legitimate fringe benefits in the form of life-enhancing aesthetic pleasures.[2]

Thus both societies adopted as the basis for their élite education a close, repetitive study of works written long ago in a foreign language – classical Latin in England, classical Chinese in Japan. Both concentrated on the mastery of a limited number of basic texts, which were thought to embody the summum of human wisdom and experience: Cicero, Virgil, Aristotle, Plutarch and the rest in England, the Four Books and the Five Classics in Japan. Just as Machiavelli drew his examples of statecraft from antiquity, so did the Japanese go back to the Chinese classics to learn about military tactics. Both regarded education as a form of physical and mental discipline, a disagreeable penance conspicuously and almost deliberately devoid of nearly all pleasure or intellectual stimulation. The attention of the children was kept focused on the niceties of grammar and syntax by sadistic brutality in England, and by more subtle psychological pressures in Japan. Neither regarded scholarship as a desirable attribute for gentlemen, and the avid pursuit of learning was left to those of lower social status who were seeking a professional career. The purpose of schooling in both societies

---

[1] Cf. Hall, op. cit., p. 297, with Stone, op. cit., p. 680.
[2] R. P. Dore, *Education in Tokugawa Japan* (University of California Press, 1965), p. 59.

was rather the creation of an élite sufficiently well-trained to be of service to the state. Intellectual amateurism was the hallmark of both societies – as it is of all aristocracies. There was one striking difference however: military training continued to bulk large in Japan and martial values continued to be exalted far into the nineteenth century, whereas in England the military component of aristocratic education was already vestigial by the early seventeenth century.

Both systems handled the problem of merit versus rank by giving special privileges to the latter. In Oxford and Cambridge, as in the Japanese fief schools, the sons of high-ranking nobles sat apart, wore distinctive dress and were attended by their personal servants. Since the gentry and nobility rarely took degrees in England, they were hardly ever exposed to direct intellectual competition from their social inferiors. In both systems promotion by merit took second place after ascribed status, and was admitted only so far as was necessary to maintain the efficiency of the administrative system. When they reached manhood, many of the nobles patronized learned scholars and kept them in their entourage for the advice they could offer, for the teaching they could give their children, and for the prestige that such patronage could confer. The function of the *jusha* on a seventeenth-century Japanese fief exactly parallels that of Thomas Hobbes in the service of the Cavendishes, Earls of Devonshire, at Chatsworth. Hobbes' ideas about the need for authority, both in political order and in choice of ideologies, were very similar indeed to those of his contemporary Hayashi Razan, the *jusha* to the Shogun Ieyasu. The activities of the *jusha* in providing a systematic rationalization of the hierarchic social order are precisely those of the religious intellectuals of Tudor England, also working under state or aristocratic patronage.[1]

Below this upper-class educational structure there also grew up in late sixteenth- and early seventeenth-century England and in early nineteenth-century Japan an educational system for commoners, financed by fees and private charity, which provided some technical and book-keeping training for the middle classes. Below this again there developed in both countries a remarkable spread of elementary education which confined itself mainly to basic literacy and moral precepts – particularly, of course, the need for obedience to superiors.

It is worth noting that it was just at this period that England took the technological lead over Europe, not so much by its fertility of invention as by taking over the inventions of others (like Japan under the Meiji). This was a period in which the English showed an intense curiosity about the outside world, travelling far and wide over Europe and America and reporting back what they saw. England copied, and then developed, mining from the Germans, cannon-founding from the French, new textiles from the Dutch, ships and sails from the Portuguese and Spanish. Like the Japanese, most of these advances were the result of government planning rather than private investment, the motive being national security rather than economic growth for its own sake. But this government activity,

[1] Hall, op. cit., *passim.*

plus lower-class technological education, in the end stimulated domestic enterprise and by 1626 a Venetian was remarking that 'English people, to say the truth, are judicious people, and of great intelligence . . . and are very ingenious in their inventions'.[1]

This curiosity about the outside world and this desire to absorb and develop the ideas of others stems from the fact that Elizabethans had little national pride in the English cultural heritage (only towards the end of the sixteenth century did reactive nationalism begin to take hold in Court circles). Compare this with the attitude of the Chinese when first faced with Western superiority in military technology and astronomy in the early seventeenth century. Here the intense cultural pride of the classically trained Chinese mandarin class prevented any assimilation. 'Military defeat was the technical reason why Western knowledge should be acquired, but it was also the psychological reason why it should not be.' The Chinese preferred admitting military defeat to the psychological shock of facing up to the inferiority of their national literary culture when challenged by Western science and engineering.[2]

The second comparison is between England and Japan on the eve of their revolutions, respectively in the mid-seventeenth and the mid-nineteenth centuries. The interest groups and the ideas behind the two revolutions have interesting similarities. Both were in part revolts of dissatisfied gentry, whose education had taught them that they had a duty to rule and how to do so, but whose aspirations for power and responsibility were blocked by a corrupt, inefficient and restricted court élite. Moreover both revolutions occurred at a time when the rate of literacy was somewhere about one third for adult males.[3] Both occurred after a generation of intellectual questioning and debate and after the appearance of many signs of weakening of the old hierarchic social relationships. Both revolutions were the prelude to far-reaching schemes for educational reform, based on the best foreign examples. One of the early steps taken by the Long Parliament was to invite the celebrated educationalist Comenius to pay a visit to England and offer his advice; during the Interregnum Oxford was filled with scientists, and schemes were drawn up for universal elementary education and a third university. Even after the Restoration of Charles II, the largely ineffectual efforts of the Royal Society in its early years to encourage military and industrial technological innovation are very similar in concept to the more thorough and far more successful steps taken in Japan just before and especially after the Meiji Restoration. It was in 1855 that the Shogun established the Yōgakusho, a school of Western learning which within a few years was teaching Western mathematics and science as well as Western languages. Baconian projects for similar scientific institutions in seventeenth-century England remained still-born.

[1] Quoted by C. M. Cipolla, *Guns and Sails* (London, 1965), pp. 41, 87 n. 2.
[2] Cipolla, op. cit., pp. 120–1.
[3] For England, see L. Stone, 'The Educational Revolution in England, 1560–1640', *Past and Present*, Vol. 28 (1964), pp. 41–80.

In Japan revolution was the necessary prelude to a great modernizing drive which a generation later set off a wave of technological innovation and economic growth. The seventeenth-century English revolution, however, had no such dramatic economic and scientific consequences. The reason for the difference lies less in differing aspirations than in differing success. In Japan the revolutionary leaders retained control and imposed their will on their fellow-samurai and the population at large. In England the revolutionary experiment failed, and was followed in 1660 by a restoration of the old order. In any case the road to reform was far less clear to Oliver Cromwell than it was to the Meiji leaders. The former had no model on which to base himself, the latter knew just what a modern society looked like, and how to get to it. And finally the powers of government were very much feebler in the case of Cromwell, despite his military dictatorship; the Meiji reformers had at their disposal a much more sophisticated and efficient bureaucracy. And so in England the drive for educational, social and legal reforms was defeated, technological advance seems to have been halted, and the country went back to the traditional rule by a conservative landed élite trained in the classics. Not only were the numbers passing through the educational system cut back, but the Ancients defeated the Moderns and the curriculum in grammar schools and universities was preserved unaltered into the nineteenth century. There was a reaction in terms both of quantity and quality.

The third comparison is between the two societies in the nineteenth century. Up to the First World War England continued to be ruled mainly by the landed classes, and up to the Second mastery of the classics, with the emphasis on form rather than content, remained the basis of upper-class education. Deliberately revived by the Victorian public schools as a device for teaching the children of the *nouveau riches* the values and culture of the old landed classes, and for training them in self-discipline and public service, this education was perfectly designed to equip an élite with the stern moral qualities needed for the efficient and paternalist administration of a tropical empire. It also provided the instruction which made possible the introduction of a competitive examination system for the rationalized bureaucracy created by the Northcote–Trevelyan reforms of 1855–70, as well as for the scholarship examinations in reformed Oxford and Cambridge. The purpose, and the results, of these arrangements was to perpetuate the rule of the upper classes into the new era, as England's greatest historian, F. W. Maitland, realized only too well. When in 1905 he fought (and of course lost) a battle to remove compulsory Greek as a requirement for entry into Cambridge, he remarked that 'at bottom this is a social question. . . . Having learnt – or what is precisely the same thing – pretended to learn, Greek has become a class distinction which is not to be obliterated'.[1]

[1] Quoted by W. H. Dunham, from *The Letters of F. W. Maitland*, C. S. H. Fifoot (ed.), in *The Yale Law Journal*, Vol. 75 (1965), p. 178.

This combination of restriction to a wealthy élite of access to the higher educational process, of a classical, formalistic, literary, moralistic curriculum, and of competitive entry into the bureaucracy by examination in familiarity with this body of literature, provides a very close parallel indeed to the institutional arrangements of Imperial China.[1] Both were perfect examples of what has been described as 'sponsored mobility'.[2] The social structure and élite standards are preserved intact by a process of deliberate selection by the existing élite of a small minority of children from the lower classes at an early age, for socialization in élite values and training in élite culture. By this means, competition is restricted and hierarchy preserved, while allowing some selective upward mobility to occur so as to replenish élite losses in numbers and talents.

Though the pressures for reform in England were indigenous and based on a wish to preserve the power of the élite and yet provide an efficient administration to run the urbanized society at home and a distant empire overseas, the precise devices adopted to secure this end appear to have been based in no small degree on the Chinese precedents. These were adopted first in India, where the examination system had been in operation as early as 1833 and where Trevelyan had seen it at work.[3] Valuable though the system was in creating better and more honest administration, its functional utility to either England or China in meeting the technological needs of a modern industrial society seems to have been virtually nil.

If we turn from nineteenth-century England to nineteenth-century Japan, some very striking differences become apparent. Between 1750 and 1870 England developed into the first industrialized society in the world, but retained its aristocratic social structure and its dysfunctional élite educational system. Japan began the same process a hundred years later, with other models to choose from. It retained much of its aristocratic power structure, but destroyed the élite education, many élite social privileges and much of the élite anti-bourgeois ideology, in order to break through into the modern world. A ruthlessly modernizing section of the élite seized power in a highly authoritarian society, and deliberately discarded everything which did not contribute to strengthening the resources of the state. Thus both countries retained the traditional pattern of authority throughout the industrializing phase – a fact of some interest to theorists of economic growth. Mr Dore is probably right to argue, with Veblen, that it was the superimposition of rapid industrialization and mobility on a hierarchic and highly deferential social structure ruled by a militarist caste which created the atmosphere and the tensions which provoked the nationalist/imperialist outbreaks of 1890–1914 in England and the 1930s and 1940s in Japan. But late nineteenth-

[1] R. Wilkinson, *Gentlemanly Power* (Oxford, 1964).

[2] Ralph H. Turner, 'Sponsored and Contest Mobility and the School System', *Am. Soc. Rev.*, Vol. XXV (1960), pp. 855–67.

[3] Ssu-Yu Teng, 'Chinese Influence on the Western Examination System', *Harvard Journal of Asiatic Studies*, Vol. 7 (1943); Y. Z. Chang, 'China and the English Civil Service Reform', *Am. Hist. Rev.*, Vol. XLVII (1942).

century Japan rejected the Chinese model of education and administrative recruitment, largely because of its proven military weakness in the face of the Western nations, just at the moment when England adopted some of the model's most essential features. Victorian England was devising an improved version of the past in the education of its élite, both in the clear class divisions that were preserved (and still persist), and in the classics-oriented curriculum, while Japan was proceeding in precisely the opposite direction.

In 1869 there was founded Tokyo University, whose teachings were specifically designed to combine Confucian morality with Western technology, and a decade or so later to foster Japanese nationalism. A year earlier the great educator Fukuzawa Yūkichi founded the first private university, the Keiō Gijuku, with its watchwords of independence and practicality. By his extremely popular writings (he had sold ten million copies by 1897) and by his teaching at the school he did much to effect the fundamental shift of attitudes which turned the Japanese businessman from an object of social contempt to a highly respected and valuable member of the community. The creation among the samurai of this new mentality, and the stress on the need for higher education for business activity, contrasts sharply with the gentlemanly contempt for business prevalent among the classically trained élite of Edwardian England, and with that scarcity of graduates in English business which persist to this day.[1] Finally, in 1872 there was decreed the abandonment in Japan of the two-class educational system, and the introduction, based on a model partly French and partly American, of a unified and universal school system for all. This is a step which England has not yet taken one hundred years later, although compulsory elementary education was introduced in both countries at the same time in 1870.

Why, then, did the Japanese samurai accept this radical transformation of the educational system and the consequent reduction of their prestige and privileges, whereas their Victorian counterparts in England devised new and ingenious ways to retain their position and to defy the values of the economic system upon which the power of their country was based? Mr Dore argues that acquiescence in the changes by the samurai was due firstly to the belief in the efficacy of the educational process in inculcating obedience (they had not been taught, as the English upper classes had learned the hard way in the seventeenth century, to associate widespread lower-class education with political and social radicalism); secondly, to the absence of that class war which was so marked a feature of nineteenth-century England (the 1,200 odd peasant revolts over the two and a half centuries of Tokugawa rule might seem to cast some doubt on this idyllic picture, but Mr Dore dismisses them as the 'sporadic tantrums of irresponsible children, not symptoms of a growing systematic malaise'); thirdly, to their intense desire for national power, which could only be achieved by modernization and all that goes with it; and lastly to a Confucian sense of paternal responsibility. The most compelling reason was surely the third, the realization that mass education

[1] Hirschmeier, op. cit., Chap. V.

was a necessary basis for national power and wealth. The questions put to prominent American educational experts in 1872 by the Japanese Chargé d'Affaires in Washington, and the replies he received, show beyond doubt that it was the overwhelming desire for economic and military predominance which was the driving force behind the educational reforms of the time.[1] That the reforms succeeded in their task is strikingly suggested by the subsequent history of Japan.

If these are the facts of educational policy, and the reasons for them, what effect did they have upon modernization? No one has yet tried to argue that the classical and literary education provided by the eighteenth-century English grammar school, or the conservative and slothful atmosphere of eighteenth-century Oxbridge, had anything to do with England's economic take-off. He would have a hard time if he did, for so many other, more convincing, factors can be adduced to explain it: long experience of technological innovation going back to the late sixteenth century; remarkable scientific progress in the seventeenth century (which took place largely, although not entirely, outside the conventional educational system); ample natural resources of iron and coal in close juxtaposition to good water communications; capital accumulation from colonial trade; and so on, and so on. Education was certainly a factor, but the significant elements here were not the classical curriculum of the landed élite. Firstly, there was a high rate of literacy among the population at large, which may have been up to 50 per cent among young rural males by 1770.[2] Secondly, a more rational and pragmatic educational system flourished in one provincial area – Scotland – whence a steady brain drain supplied eighteenth- and nineteenth-century England with so many of the professional and engineering cadres which she needed. Hardly any of the great Victorian industrial entrepreneurs had been exposed to the classical, gentlemanly English educational process.

If we turn to Japan, the first question is how Tokogawa education made possible the Meiji reforms and so prepared the way for the astonishing economic growth a generation later. The very high rate of literacy in the mid-nineteenth century clearly put Japan in a class by itself compared with any other non-Western country, and this must be a factor of the greatest importance. Mr Dore rightly argues that it had four effects. It ensured 'a positive attitude towards the process of deliberately acquiring new knowledge'; it is evidence of growing mobility aspirations that could finally be realized after the crust of social conservatism was broken by the Meiji Restoration: the idea of progress had already been implanted in Japanese minds; it widened the net of potential talent whence the future leaders of modernizing Japan could be drawn, as is shown by the fact that about a quarter of the leading entrepreneurs of the early Meiji era came

[1] H. Passin, *Society and Education in Japan* (Teachers College, Columbia University, 1965), pp. 212–25.

[2] J. D. Chambers, 'Three Essays on the Population and Economy of the Midlands', in D. V. Glass and D. E. C. Eversley (eds), *Population in History* (London, 1965), p. 330 n. 13.

from the peasantry;[1] lastly it accustomed the population to being governed by the written word.

But what of the training of the élite, the samurai? As we have seen, their education, like that of their counterparts in England, was ethical in objective, repetitive and unquestioning in method, and classical in content. According to Mr Dore, however, this backward-looking education also played its part.[2] The most persuasive arguments depend on the quantity of education rather than the quality, in that the mere fact of being given some kind of mental training, whatever its content, accustoms men to the idea that education is normal and desirable in itself. It is more difficult, however, to explain the beneficial effects of this particular type of education. Mr. Dore's first argument is based on a Darwinian – or Toynbeean – theory of the survival of the fittest, namely that *some* survived the system with their intellectual curiosity not only unimpaired but positively stimulated by the challenge (just as *some* survived, and survive, a classical education at an English public school). Secondly, Mr Jansen has emphasized that a very strong competitive instinct developed in these schools – much stronger than in their English counterparts, where competition was largely confined to the playing fields – and this was an important factor in creating the atmosphere of an 'Achieving Society'. The world view of Confucianism was basically rational, and therefore well adapted, in Weberian terms, for the modern world. There were, as Mr Albert Craig has recently shown, few theological obstacles in neo-Confucianism to the reception of modern science, and the type of religious opposition which Galileo or Darwin encountered in Christian Europe did not occur in Confucian Japan.[3]

This argument makes very good sense, although it is an observed fact that modernization is not dependent on a *uniformly* rational viewpoint. In Japan the modernizing process was accompanied by a rapid growth in Shintoism deliberately fostered as an ideal tool for developing a national consciousness and national unity. Although its functional utility is beyond question, the fact remains that Emperor-worship was essentially irrational and primitive in outlook and played an important part in the outburst of nationalist excess and reckless military aggression of the early twentieth century. What needs explaining, moreover, is why Confucianism aided assimilation of Western ideas in Japan, but in China acted as a mental block.

If nationalism, the lust for imperial military greatness, was the driving force for educational change, a further question is what it was that induced the samurai to study and to imitate Western technology with such astonishing assiduity and lack of xenophobic jealousy. Twelve per cent of the first educational budget of the Meiji era, and 2 per cent of the total budget, was spent on sending Japanese

---

[1] Hirschmeier, op. cit., p. 249.

[2] Mr. Dore's arguments are more clearly developed in his article in M. B. Jansen (ed), *Changing Japanese Attitudes toward Modernization* (Princeton, 1965).

[3] A. Craig, 'Science and Confucianism in Tokugawa Japan', in Jansen (ed), op. cit.

students abroad to pick the brains of the West. Another 10 per cent of the Ministry of Education's budget went on salaries to foreign teachers of languages, medicine, science and even philosophy and the law. Thus when the Ministry of Public Works set up a technical training department in 1871, it was entirely staffed by Englishmen and it was not until the 1880s that the number of foreign educators in Japan began to decline. One suggestion is that it was the very subservience and humility induced by the practice of unquestioning rote-learning in the educational process which made it psychologically easy for the Japanese to copy so enthusiastically the ideas and inventions of others. Just as it was the Tokugawa 'training to be trained' which prepared the way for educational expansion, so it was the respect for knowledge, whatever its sources, which was responsible for the inclusion among the five articles of the Meiji Charter Oath of the objective of seeking knowledge throughout the world as a means of strengthening the Imperial throne.

If we turn to Victorian England we find that it had a ruling class with similar national aspirations, encouraged by a very similar educational process, but one which lacked the zeal for technological education and the willingness to learn by the experience of other nations which characterized the Japanese leaders. Even the introduction of examinations for the home civil service was resisted for fifteen years on the simple grounds that 'the plan is Chinese', an objection which would have been utterly incomprehensible to the Japanese.[1] This resistance to alien ideas derived from the self-evident fact that mid-Victorian England had indeed very little to learn from foreigners about anything, from constitutions to locomotives. The memory of this remarkable era of intellectual, political and technical supremacy survived in the minds of Englishmen long after the reality had fled, whereas the Japanese had no such period of undoubted superiority to look back to, and were prepared to go to any lengths to maintain and strengthen their national independence and strength. Furthermore, this English memory of past supremacy was strongly reinforced by the self-conscious amateurism and insular nationalism induced by a public school classical education, to which every successful late Victorian entrepreneur inevitably subjected the heirs to his fortune and his business. It was just at the peak of England's imperial expansion, at the end of the nineteenth century, that English industrial growth began to lag, that conservatism and inertia began to be the hallmark of the English entrepreneurial class. Whereas the reforming Japanese samurai launched a massive drive for university expansion and technological education copied from the various nations of the West, the English public-school-trained leaders retained the élitist view of higher education as a preserve of the few, and their traditional snobbish contempt for base mechanic arts (now reinforced by the anti-materialist ideas of Matthew Arnold). By 1900 English university education was quantitatively beginning to fall behind those of America, France and Germany, and it was turning out far fewer chemists and engineers than its main economic rivals.

[1] Ssu-Yu Teng, op. cit., p. 304.

Such was the cult of the amateur and the domination of classical studies in English universities that even in the humane field of history the lead had passed to Germany, where the professional training of the Ph.D. was now in full swing. As a result, entrepreneurship still existed in late-Victorian England, but it took the form of organizational innovations in mass production and distribution, introduced by lower-middle-class men like Lipton, Guinness, Boot or Courtauld, men who had not been stamped in the classical public school and Oxbridge mould. It was the older businesses which stagnated, as the children of their creators absorbed the upper-class ethic and turned their energies to social climbing, philanthropy and politics.[1]

A final question is why the Japanese samurai found it relatively easy to shed their classical educational system, whereas the English upper classes have clung to it with such extraordinary persistence. Here one can do little more than speculate, but it may be that it was the sheer arcaneness of classical Chinese scholarship, its utter remoteness from Japanese past history and contemporary experience which created that extraordinary compartmentalization which is such a feature of the modern Japanese mind. This habit of keeping different areas of knowledge and ideas quite distinct from one another may have helped samurai trained in the traditional way to grasp for the technology of the West, however alien it might be to them, and to copy without shame or embarrassment the inventions and institutions of other cultures as a means to the end of their own rampant nationalism.

The two other societies with a classical educational tradition were far less conscious of the arcaneness of their studies, and so were under less pressure to compartmentalize. To the Chinese, the classics were a vital and living part of their own historical tradition, and for centuries cultural pride prevented them from assimilating Western ideas. To the English the classics were in fact foreign, but they contrived to identify themselves with the classical world by various devices. In the sixteenth century, when the curriculum was first introduced, they did it (or some of them did) by developing the twelfth-century legend of the descent of the royal dynasty from Brutus, a Trojan fleeing from the doomed city after the Homeric siege. The Arthurian legend was dragged in to provide a Romano-British link, and in no time at all Queen Elizabeth found herself supplied with a coat of arms displaying her distinguished classical ancestry – including a quartering with the letters S.P.Q.R. [*Senatus Populusque Romanus*] on a diagonal bar.[2]

At the end of the nineteenth century the late Victorians and Edwardians could, and did, identify their society with that of Periclean Athens in its ideals and its constitutional arrangements, and with Augustan Rome in its sense of imperial

---

[1] D. H. Aldcroft, 'The Entrepreneur and the British Economy, 1870–1914', *Econ. Hist. Rev.*, 2nd series, Vol. XVII, No. 1 (1964); C. H. Wilson, 'Economy and Society in Late Victorian England', loc. cit., Vol. XVIII, No. 1 (1965).

[2] T. D. Kendrick, *British Antiquity* (London, 1950), pl. XIb.

mission. Both political parties found what they wanted in the classics. Fifth-century Greece appealed particularly to young Liberals like Richard Livingstone and Alfred Zimmern, the former going so far as to declare: 'Trust in the people, tempered by caution, was Mr Gladstone's definition of Liberalism. Leave out the three last words and you have the principles of Pericles'. The role of slavery in Greek society was explained away by the assertion that 'the difference between our industrial classes and the Greek slave is spiritual rather than material'. Imperial Rome was naturally more attractive to Tories, and both scholars and pro-consuls – Lords Bryce and Cromer and Sir Charles Lucas – busied them-selves with reinterpreting the Roman Empire in the light of the problems and aspirations of the British nearly 2,000 years later. Moreover, both groups could appreciate the sense of natural superiority over other peoples that runs through the Periclean funeral oration, and much of Roman literature. Thus the Edward-ian ruling class responded immediately to the ideas which they thought they could extract from a reading of the classics: the cult of the amateur, the contempt for bourgeois activities, values and persons, the sense of national superiority and imperial responsibility, the idealization of such wholly masculine com-munities as the public school, the university and the army. Although even the defenders of the system were critical of the emphasis in the curriculum on form rather than content, a defect which if anything got worse as the twentieth century wore on, they were nevertheless firmly convinced that there was no incompatibility between a classical education and a modern, competitive, scienti-fic and industrial nation.[1]

Apart from this highly speculative hypothesis, it is difficult to see, on the basis of the evidence supplied by Mr Dore, that the character of traditional samurai education can have had any effect in creating this far-reaching difference of attitudes of English and Japanese élites towards industry and technology. And so it looks very much as if, in Japan as in England, technical innovation and entrepreneurial initiative occurred in spite of rather than because of the élite educational system, and under the leadership either of men trained outside the system altogether, as in England, or partly of outsiders and partly of men in open rebellion against their background and education, as in post-1868 Japan. Indeed, other writers have pointed not to the survival but to the breakdown of the old educational system in the mid-nineteenth century and to the introduction of Japanese and Western studies as key factors in the new situation. This certainly seems a more reasonable hypothesis and one which conforms more closely with

---

[1] R. W. Livingstone, *The Greek Genius and its Meaning to Us* (London, 1912), p. 68 (see also pp. 239–50); *A Defence of Classical Education* (London, 1916), p. 187; A. E. Zimmern, *The Greek Commonwealth* (Oxford, 1911); P. A. Brunt, 'Reflections on British and Roman Imperialism', *Comparative Studies in Society and History*, Vol. VII (1965), p. 227. The remark by Livingstone should be compared with the line taken by aristocratic apologists for the Southern Way of Life in the United States over the last hundred years (e.g. George Fitzhugh, *Sociology for the South, or the Failure of Free Society*, Richmond, 1854).

the observed facts.[1] Mr Dore himself concludes his more recent article with these apologetic words about the training of the élite: 'It was a type of education which had to go in a modernizing country, but at least it had the honour to carry the seeds of its own destruction.' It was England's misfortune that the seeds of destruction of a similar type of education, if seeds there were, should have fallen upon such stony ground.

[1] Hall, op. cit.; Hirschmeier, op. cit., Chaps. V, VII.

PART THREE

The relationship between Education and Other Social Institutions

ONE IMPORTANT WAY of seeing education is as a social institution within which certain processes occur. The focus is put upon the institution rather than the processes. This part contains six papers that concern education as an institution, while in the fourth and final section emphasis is given to the processes that take place within this institution. Whenever sociologists examine societies in an institutional framework they tend to be concerned with the relationships between the various parts of the social system. Here we are interested in the way in which education interrelates with certain other social institutions that, in Britain (and these papers on the whole are concerned with Britain), have had, and still have, salience for education. These are the family, the system of social stratification, the economy and religion.

There has been a tendency through time for the process of education to be defined as no longer the total responsibility of the family. Musgrove shows how this movement of education from family to school affected the middle class during the century from 1780 to 1880. In a static society each social stratum recruits the next generation to its own ranks and the family is an important agency in this process. But in a more mobile society movement is possible from one stratum upward to another and such mobility is often achieved through the educational system.[1]

The upper stratum of any society has often used the schools to prepare the next generation to succeed its members as the political élite. In his paper Wilkinson compares the ways in which the English public school in the late Victorian era, and the Confucian educational system were used for this purpose. One

[1] Two papers relevant to this process are W. M. Mathew, 'The Origin and Occupations of Glasgow Students, 1740–1839', *Past and Present*, Vol. 33 (July 1966), pp. 74–94; and L. Stone, 'The Educational Revolution in England, 1560–1640', *Past and Present*, Vol. 28 (July 1964), especially pp. 57–68.

method was to define industry as having low status. This had implications for the growth of technical education, which Musgrave traces for the period from 1860 to 1960. This sector of education is shown to interlink with other social institutions in much the same way as the more often considered schools and universities. Thus links are obviously seen with the economy, but also are found with political institutions and with the system of stratification. In this last connection, for centuries apprenticeship played an important part in allowing upward social mobility. Bowman's paper indicates this, and also describes the educational and familial functions that apprenticeship served. But the most important lesson of this paper is that Bowman shows the way in which one institution can keep the same name over a long period of time and even be thought by a majority of people to be fulfilling the same functions, while, in fact, closer analysis indicates that the social functions played by apprenticeship changed greatly over the period here considered; more particularly the function of general education largely lapsed and that of social welfare grew in importance.

Throughout the history of education in Britain, religion has played a crucial part. Cannon shows that even when, or, in her view, because religion came to have less social salience, it still exercised immense power over the legal definition of education which was made in 1944, and which largely rules the educational system today, at the start of the 1970s.

I   Middle-class Families and Schools, 1780-1880: Interaction and Exchange of Function between Institutions

F. MUSGROVE

Many middle-class families of the later eighteenth century undertook instruction of their children and adolescents which a century later was regarded as the proper concern of schools. Domestic education was by no means new: among the aristocracy and gentry it had a long Renaissance and even medieval background. What was new from the 1770s and 1780s was the vigour with which domestic education was advocated, and the extent to which it spread among the professional middle classes. This type of education, conducted either by parents or by a resident tutor, served middle-class society well for half a century. But by the 1830s new middle-class needs were felt, products of a rapidly changing economy and society, which the family alone could not meet. The needs of an increasingly mobile society, of individuals who were moving into occupations and social positions for which their family traditions and experience provided little appropriate training, were met by middle-class proprietary schools.

The late eighteenth-century expansion of domestic education was a self-conscious attempt to revive the ideal of domestic education and to integrate the child more closely in the adult world. The consequences were intellectual, religious and social precocity, an early maturity and adult standing which those who remembered an earlier tradition of parental aloofness lamented,[1] and which prolonged schooling and training for the professions in the mid-nineteenth century effectively undermined. Locke had reproved the gentry and middle-class families of the late seventeenth century for the rigid segregation of children, for 'a constant stiffness, and a mien of authority to them all their lives'.[2] These child–parent relationships did not change quickly in response to Locke's exhortations. A century later David Williams was making similar complaints in his

---

[1] See V. Knox: *Liberal Education*, Vol. II (1795), 'On Knowing the World at an Early Age'. Cf. J. Priestley, *Observations on Education* (1788), p. 57.
[2] *Thoughts Concerning Education* (1693), Sec. 96.

First printed in Sociological Review, *New Series, Vol. 7, No. 2 (December 1959), pp. 169–78.*

Lectures on Education (1789).[1] Susan Sibbald and Mary Butt (later Mrs Sherwood) have left vivid accounts of the separation of child and adult spheres in middle-class eighteenth-century households.[2] But Locke gathered an influential following. James Whitchurch championed Locke's views in his *Essay upon Education* (1772),[3] and R. L. Edgeworth put him to the test. Paradoxically the unsociable Rousseau, who would have Emile not only isolated but with a tutor as nearly his coeval as possible, and who inveighed against premature attainments, did more than our own indigenous authors to encourage the short-lived domestic experiment with its inevitable consequence of precocious intellectual development – well known in the case of John Stuart Mill, but amply documented in innumerable other cases.[4]

The domestic experiment lasted in full vigour and with considerable success for half a century, from the 1770s to the 1830s. Its main advocates were Locke, *Some Thoughts Concerning Education* (1693), Rousseau, *Emile* (1762), Lord Kames,[5] *Loose Hints on Education* (1781), R. Shepherd,[6] *Essay on Education* (1782), David Williams,[7] *Treatise on Education* (1774), William Cobbett, *Advice to Young Men*, and M. and R. L. Edgeworth, *Practical Education* (1789). Domestic education had its critics and the severest were: Father Gerdil,[8] *Reflections on Education* (1765), Helvétius, *Treatise on Man* (1772), Vicesimus Knox, *Liberal Education* (1781), George Chapman,[9] *Treatise on Education* (1790), Mary Wollstonecraft, *Vindications of the Rights of Women* (1796), and M. D. Hill, *Public Education* (1822). Others sought a compromise between public and private education – typically an association of friendly families sharing tutors: James Barclay,[10] *Treatise on Education* (1743), Thomas Sheridan,[11] *Plan of Education for the Young Nobility and Gentry* (1769), Joseph Priestley, *Observations on Education* (1788), David Williams after further reflection in *Lectures on Education* (1789) and William Barrow,[12] *Essay on Education* (1802). Numerous handbooks and manuals on domestic education, in addition to these more theoretical and

[1] See Vol. II, p. 291.
[2] F. P. Hett, *Memoirs of Susan Sibbald* (1783–1812), p. 6, and S. Kelly (ed.), *The Life of Mrs Sherwood* (1854), p. 38.
[3] See pp. 70–1.
[4] See, for example, R. Southey, *The Life of Wesley* (1820), pp. 429–30; J. Bonar, *Malthus and his Works* (1885); F. E. Kingsley, *Charles Kingsley* (1891); *A Memoir of John Keble* (1808); S. P. Thompson, *The Life of William Thomson* (1910); J. Ruskin, *Praeterita*.
[5] Henry Home (1696–1782), Scottish judge.
[6] 1732–1809; son of a Lincolnshire clergyman; educated at Corpus Christi College, Oxford.
[7] 1738–1816; Dissenting minister and private tutor.
[8] 1718–1802; Savoyard; Cardinal 1777.
[9] 1723–1806; educated Banff and Aberdeen; schoolmaster and private tutor.
[10] fl. 1743–74; curate and schoolmaster.
[11] 1719–88; actor and manager.
[12] 1754–1836; headmaster of the Academy, Soho Square, London.
For earlier doubts on domestic education and advocacy of the school, see Comenius, *The Great Didactic*.

polemical treatises, were produced. Of these may be mentioned Mrs Chapone, *Letters on the Improvement of the Mind* (1773), Thomas Day, *Sandford and Merton* (1783), Mrs Sherwood, *The Fairchild Family* (1818), E. W. Benson, *Education at Home* (1824), and Isaac Taylor, *Home Education* (1838). These books gave guidance to the parent–teacher through imaginary dialogue between parents and children, and described in story form the routine of the ideal educative family.

Tuition in the home was by no means new in the late eighteenth century: what was novel was its increasing extent and, in many instances, its greater effectiveness. Locke's unflattering views on the Public Schools were widely shared by his contemporaries among the gentry, but tutors of his day, and later, in general fell short of the high standards he prescribed and were hampered in their work by undue parental interference. Defoe regarded private tutors as 'murtherers of a child's morals',[1] and Fielding's portraits of domestic tutors in *Joseph Andrews* (1742) and *Tom Jones* (1749) are probably representative of their kind. Their type certainly survived into the late eighteenth century and Maria Edgeworth, in her novel *Ennui*, provided her noble hero with a tutor who was of the opinion that 'everything which the young Earl of Glenthorn did not know by instinct of genius, was not worth learning'.[2]

The declining eighteenth-century reputation of the Public and grammar schools, occasioned by their inadequate supervision of their charges, their inflexible curriculum and methods, and, in the case of the latter, by their social promiscuity[3], gave rise to the extension of the domestic alternative. Defoe complained in the early eighteenth century that it was mainly eldest sons who were kept at home and given (inadequate) domestic tuition: 'Of thirty thousand families of noblemen and gentlemen of estate which may be reckoned up in the kingdom, I venture to say that there is not two hundred of their eldest sons at a time to be found in both our universities. At the same time you will find ten times that number of their younger sons.'[4]

Although the growing commercial class of the late eighteenth century enabled the Public Schools to maintain their numbers and even in some cases to increase them,[5] domestic education certainly gained in both quantity and quality in the closing decades of the century. Dilatory and episodic home teaching was still common enough,[6] but so was pre-Public School education in formal schools[7] until Prep Schools were widely established in the second half of the nineteenth

---

[1] See *The Compleat English Gentleman*, p. 71.
[2] See *Tales of Fashionable Life*, Vol. I, p. 2.
[3] See Defoe, op. cit., p. 7.
[4] Ibid.
[5] Eton, Harrow, Charterhouse, Rugby and Shrewsbury increased in numbers 1780–1830; only Westminster suffered a decline. See E. C. Mack, *Public Schools and British Opinion* (1938), p. 73.
[6] See Jane Austen, *Emma* (1816), Chap. 5; *Life of Geo. Crabbe* (1834), pp. 135–6.
[7] See, for example, the variety of educational experience of Gibbon and Southey before going on to a Public School: E. Gibbon, *Autobiography*, and *Life and Correspondence of R. Southey* (1849).

century. Even the Public School headmaster and author of Public School stories, F. W. Farrar, held high the ideal of domestic education for children under Public School age.[1]

Although the inadequate and harassed governess[2] was often the main instrument of domestic education, particularly for younger children and girls, until the middle decades of the nineteenth century, men of high ability were turning to private tutoring in the late eighteenth century. Frequently they were men of high scientific attainment – Joseph Priestley, Colin Milne, the botanist, Charles Hutton and John Bonnycastle, mathematicians whose talents had as yet but little scope in industry or public institutions. But leisured middle-class parents took increasingly to the task of educating their own children. Rousseau's advice ('Poverty, pressure of business, mistaken social prejudice, none of them can excuse a man from his duty, which is to support and educate his own children') was widely heeded. Charlotte Mason has gone so far as to make the following claim:

> No other educationalist has had a tithe of the influence exercised by Rousseau. Under the spell of his teaching, people in the fashionable world, like that Russian Princess Galitzin, forsook society, and went off with their children to some quiet corner where they could devote every hour of the day, and every power they had, to the fulfilment of the duties which devolve upon parents. Courtly mothers retired from the world, sometimes even left their husbands, to work hard at the classics, mathematics, sciences, that they might with their own lips instruct their children . . . (Rousseau) had chanced to touch a spring that opened many hearts. He was one of the few educationalists who made his appeal to the parental instincts.[3]

It was for such devoted – but often bewildered – parents that Edgeworth wrote *Practical Education*. He was familiar with the parent who asked: 'What is to be done? How do we begin? What experiments are suited to children? If we knew our children could try them.' It was to meet this demand that parents' manuals multiplied, but even these were not always sufficient for the extensive requirements of the day,[4] and more fathers than William Cobbett were driven to writing their own textbooks.

Vicesimus Knox, headmaster of Tonbridge School, opposed as he was to domestic tuition, was driven to recognize its increasing popularity in the late eighteenth century, and also its boldly experimental nature.[5] When he republished

[1] See *St Winifred's or The World of School* (1862), pp. 10–12.
[2] See Anne Brontë, *Agnes Grey* (1847), Chap. 7.
[3] See *Parents and Children* (1907 edn), p. 2.
[4] Isaac Taylor complained of the lack of such manuals in the 1830s: see *Home Education* (1838).
[5] V. Knox: op. cit., Vol. II, p. 260 n: 'Almost every private tutor . . . pretends to some nostrum, or new and expeditious method of teaching; which proves infallibly, that all the masters that have presided at Eton, Westminster, Winchester, the Chater-House, Merchant

his *Liberal Education* (first published in 1781) in 1795, he included a chapter 'On Private Tuition' to cater for this growing practice and interest. 'I have observed that private tuition seems lately to have prevailed in this country more than ever.' He decided to come to terms with it.

Dr Nicholas Hans examined a sample of 3,500 eighteenth-century men (1685–1785) in the *Dictionary of National Biography* and found that 28·5 per cent were domestically educated. A quarter of the peers' sons and a third of the gentry's were educated at home.[1] These proportions almost certainly increased around the turn of the century. When M. D. Hill wrote his *Public Education* in 1822 to champion the school against the home, he was fighting an apparently failing cause and realized that desperate remedies were necessary in public education. The strictures on Public School education in the *Edinburgh Review* were a symptom of a massive decline in public confidence. 'By 1835 it had become clear that if no reforms were to occur the middle classes would desert the schools entirely.'[2] The family was still, as fifty years before, the key educational institution.

The defeat of the domestic ideal

The domestic experiment perished in the fifty years 1830–80. It had previously flourished because public education was in low repute, because society was as yet changing but slowly and the traditional outlook and knowledge of the family were still relevant to the uprising generation, because the structure and circumstances of the leisured, extended middle-class family, which could usually draw for aid upon a wide range of uncles and aunts as tutors, made it practicable, and because the family was becoming increasingly child-centred: the children of the late eighteenth-century household were displacing the male seniors of the household as the focus of attention.

The child-centred middle-class family of the late eighteenth century jealously guarded and enfolded the child, insulating him from undesirable contacts and often altogether from his age-peers.[3] Contemporaries often attributed the rise of the filiocentric family to the ideas of freedom and equality which were abroad at the time of the French Revolution.[4] William Barrow asserted that 'The wishes

---

Taylors and St Paul's were fools and blockheads, in comparison with the redoubtable and self-important innovator or empiric.'

[1] N. Hans, *New Trends in Eighteenth Century Education* (1951).

[2] Mack, op. cit., p. 192.

[3] For ideal pictures of withdrawn domesticity, see Benson, *Education at Home*, pp. 5–6, and Mrs Sherwood, *The Fairchild Family*. The rise of the doctrine and practice of 'hardening', based on the recommendations of Locke and Rousseau, championed by Thomas Day, George Chapman and Whitchurch is no refutation but a further expression of increased concern for child welfare. With its basis in medicine as well as morals, it appealed to the age which discovered vaccination as the most effective means of ensuring children's health at a time of ravaging child diseases and high infant mortality.

[4] See Hannah More, *Strictures on the Modern System of Female Education* (1801 edn), Vol. II, p. 320.

of the child are always consulted, and generally adopted. Parental authority is universally relaxed and in many instances nearly relinquished . . . Thus is too often begun and completed the character known amongst us by the appellation of a Jacobin or a Democratist.'[1]

But the change in family attitudes can be traced in innumerable family chronicles before the writings associated with the French Revolution appeared.[2] It coincided with growing family size, as infant mortality rates declined, but escapes any easy demographic explanation. It cannot be accounted for in terms of the balance of age-groups in the population. It did not arise – as similar twentieth-century attitudes are sometimes held to have done – from the growing scarcity-value of children, for child-centred attitudes went along with the increasing number of children in proportion to total population, their ever greater expense both for middle-class parents concerned to educate and display them according to their rank (or the rank above them), and for working-class parents who were progressively prevented by benevolent legislation from putting them to industrial employment.[3] The heightened evaluation of children is probably most satisfactorily related to the economic potential and consequent social power of the young in an industrial system which was increasingly automatic and depended ever less on training and experience. Prolonged tutelage was less and less necessary for the maintenance of the economic system, as the Taunton Commission concluded from its enquiries in Yorkshire in the 1860s.[4] (Even the date at which prolonged training for middle-class professions became general can be considerably ante-dated.[5] But the attitude of adults was ambivalent. Precocity was a threat which extended education and unpaid training effectively met in all classes of society as the nineteenth century progressed. An elaborate system of schools prolonged the dependence of the young and redressed the balance of power between the age-groups.)[6]

Parents collaborated after the thirties in their own usurpation by age-peers who, relegated to schools, formed themselves in defensive solidarity against their seniors and elaborated their own juvenile sub-culture.[7] The changing organiza-

[1] See *Essay on Education* (1802), Vol. II, p. 320.

[2] See J. H. Plumb, 'The Walpoles: Father and Son', *Studies in Social History* (1953); *Life of William Hutton* (1817), pp. 29–30; E. Gibbon, *Autobiography*, p. 112; W. Jones, *Letters from a Tutor to his Pupils* (1775), p. 8; G. M. Trevelyan, *English Social History* (1946), p. 309.

[3] See C. Booth, 'Occupations of People in the United Kingdom, 1801–1881', *Journal of the Statistical Society* (1886).

[4] See Vol. IX, pp. 222–3.

[5] See R. L. Edgeworth, *Professional Education*.

[6] It was one of William Cobbett's main objections to school education that it kept the young in subservience and dependence longer than the economic system justified. See *Advice to Young Men* ('Where in all creation, is there so helpless a mortal as a boy who has been always at school?').

[7] The typical child's story of the mid-nineteenth century was a school story and no longer a tale of family life. Peer-group morality was the subject of *Tom Brown's Schooldays* (1856), *Eric, or Little by Little* (1858), *Boys' Own Paper* (from 1879), *Stalky & Co.* (1903). Cf. the concern with child–parent relationships in the late eighteenth-century stories:

tion of the family itself, the increased tempo of social change, and the social relevance of refashioned middle-class schools, made obsolete the family as a comprehensive educational institution.

The revival of confidence in public education can be explained only in terms of the interaction between family and school. Mack's attempt to explain it in terms of the influence of great headmasters and abstract social 'forces', 'liberalism', 'conservatism', 'reaction' and 'liberal conservatism'[1] lacks reality: only an analysis in concrete terms of interacting social institutions and exchange of function can transform description into explanation.

Domestic education was the *technique par excellence* of a relatively static society: it ensured the maximum transmission of parental *mores* and occupations. The squires who speak in Defoe's *Compleat English Gentleman* are staunch for home education for this reason; the late eighteenth-century theorists who defended domestic education frequently did so on these grounds.[2]

The needs of socially mobile groups which were produced by the Agrarian Revolution, the French Wars and the Industrial Revolution, could not be met by domestic tuition. A newly enriched family could not easily enter the superior class culture on wealth alone: the children needed an educational institution which would conceal rather than reinforce the family's traditions.[3] Wealthy eighteenth-century farmers, concerned for unbroken succession in farm-ownership and management tended to express their social aspirations through their daughters rather than their sons: the former were sent away to boarding schools.[4] The nineteenth-century proprietary schools arose on urban industrial wealth, they did not arise because there were more opportunities for lucrative professional employment to which they provided an entrée:[5] such opportunities lagged far behind educational expansion. Boys in mid-nineteenth-century Public Schools were not, for the most part, groomed for well-paid employment but handicapped in their search for it by an irrelevant education and the outward signs of genteel status. (Few could be expected to face their predicament with the ultimate realism of Ernest Pontifex.) The great expansion in well-paid employment was in 'industrial management'[6] for which the Public Schools were no preparation. The Empire was necessary as a form of out-relief. The new Public Schools make

---

The Happy Family . . . Intended to Shew the Delightful Effects of Filial Obedience (1786), *The Happy Family at Eason House, Exhibited in the Aimiable Conduct of the Little Nelsons and their Parents* (1799), *History of the Daveport Family* (1800).

[1] See E. C. Mack, op. cit., pp. 400–1.

[2] See Clara Reeve, *Plans of Education* (1792), and J. W. Whitchurch, op. cit., pp. 103 and 115.

[3] See *Schools Inquiry Commission* (1868), for the reports of Mr Stanton (Vol. XIII, p. 43) and Mr Bryce (Vol. IX, pp. 589 and 724).

[4] Clara Reeve, op. cit., pp. 134–5.

[5] For evidence of lack of professional opportunity at the time of Public School expansion, see J. C. Hudson, *The Parent's Handbook* (1842); F. Davenant, *What Shall My Son Be?* (1870).

[6] See C. Booth, loc. cit.

sense only because a family was already wealthy and because unpaid or ill-paid careers in Parliament, the Army, Church, or at the Bar, brought not a livelihood but a valued status.

The schools offered to meet these new social needs more effectively than the family. They developed a new exclusiveness that guarded the child from social promiscuity and contamination as effectively as the most jealous parental surveillance, and more effectively than the *nouveau riche* parent could manage. Those proprietary schools flourished which reinforced the solidarity of social and socio-religious groups.[1] Grammar and Public Schools regained a lost vitality when they evaded their founders' democratic intentions and catered for discrete social grades. Those which failed to do so declined into elementary schools.[2]

The middle-class family was turning outwards to satisfy many of its basic needs: it had lost its former measure of self-sufficiency. The strains of social mobility and the atrophy of the wider functions of the extended family caused it to eject its young into the care of auxiliary educational agencies. Le Play commented in the early nineteenth century on this outward turning of English sons, compared with French sons of similar social level, their retreat from the parental roof until the death of the father or the departure of the widow.[3] But what was more significant in the evolving nuclear family of the nineteenth century was the outward turning of daughters: the burden of unmarried daughters was probably the severest strain on the Victorian family and did most to make it widen its horizons. The decreasingly domestic Victorian age[4] could not absorb its middle-class women in marriage; it was ever less willing to support them in idleness. The extreme solutions of female emigration and even Protestant Convents for surplus spinsters[5] were canvassed. The feminist movement of the nineteenth century was born not of increased opportunities for employment and independence for women but of frustrations within the home, not least the custom, in a household of daughters, of marriage by seniority. The women created their own opportunities: they forced themselves into a reluctant economic system.[6] The all-embracing family was burst asunder by the intolerable burden of unmarried daughters.

By the 1870s and 1880s the family had abdicated from its front-line position in education. Its auxiliaries had taken over. Dr Arnold supported the domestic ideal at Laleham but defeated it at Rugby. The thirties were the watershed. When Isaac Taylor wrote his *Home Education* in 1838, on the eve of the founding of Marlborough, Cheltenham and Wellington, he realized that he was advocating a type of education which could be enjoyed by a dwindling and even esoteric

---

[1] E.g. Quaker, Woodard and Wesleyan boarding schools. See *Schools Inquiry Commission*, Vol. IX, p. 231.

[2] Ibid., Vol. III, p. 45, Vol. IX, p. 151, Vol. XII, p. 35, Vol. XIV, p. 123.

[3] See *Les Ouvriers Européens* (1855).

[4] See C. Ansell, *Statistics and Families* (1874), for increasing average age at marriage of professional men.

[5] See Clara Reeve, op. cit., pp. 119–20.

[6] See Bessie Parkes, 'A Year's Experience of Women's Work,' *Trans.*, *N.A.P.S.Sc.* (1860).

minority. He could only fight a rearguard action, hoping to keep the practice alive in devoted circles. Between the publication of his book and the writings and activities of Charlotte Mason forty years later, there occurred the renaissance of the English Public School. Charlotte Mason still hankered after the domestic ideal,[1] but when she founded the Parents' National Educational Union at Ambleside in 1877 she realized that she had to come to terms with the now self-confident school. Hers was an anachronistic experiment in restoring the authority of the dethroned parent.

[1] See *Home Education* (1899).

2 The Gentleman Ideal and the Maintenance of a Political Élite

Two Case Studies: Confucian Education in the
Tang, Sung, Ming and Ching Dynasties; and the
Late Victorian Public Schools (1870–1914)[1]

R. H. WILKINSON

'*The stock exchange is a poor substitute for the Holy Grail. . . .*

'*The bourgeoisie produced individuals who made a success at political leadership upon
entering a political class of non-bourgeois origin, but it did not produce a successful
political stratum of its own although, so one should think, the third generations of the
industrial families had all the opportunity to form one.*'

JOSEPH SCHUMPETER[2]

Leaders are not all governors, for government survives by magic as well as by
reason, by dignity as well as by its decisions. 'Rationalist and unheroic', the
bourgeois lacks 'the mystical glamor and the lordly attitude' which made the
medieval lord respected as a ruler of men.

So runs Schumpeter's argument. It is an argument that stresses *aptitude* –
political aptitude – rather more heavily than it does *motivation*. The bourgeois,
contends Schumpeter, often 'wants to be left alone and to leave politics alone'
for the very reason that he senses his inadequacies in the political sphere.[3] What
Schumpeter does not really detail are the positive factors – the attitudes and
motivations – that directed the landed classes, rather than the bourgeoisie,
towards public service. The purpose of this paper is to examine these factors, and
to suggest that they were all part and parcel of a 'gentleman ideal'. I am going to
argue that this ideal was a sort of controlling link in a two-way relationship

---

[1] Read before the Fifth World Congress of Sociology, Washington, D.C., August 1962.
[2] Joseph Schumpeter, *Capitalism, Socialism & Democracy* (Harper, New York, 1942),
pp. 137, 298.
[3] Joseph Schumpeter, ibid., pp. 137–8.

First printed in Sociology of Education, *Vol. 37, No. 1 (Fall 1963), pp. 9–26.*

between government and a political élite. On the one hand, it aided government recruitment by making public service a gentlemanly obligation. On the other hand, it defended the identity, the political power and the social prestige of an élite group by inspiring that group to retain their grip on public affairs.

In both Imperial China and Victorian England, the gentleman ideal was promoted by education systems whose values were those of the landlord rather than those of the urban businessman. As with values, so with power: Confucian education and the Victorian Public School both conferred career advantages on the gentry, on the group whose living came from rents – and from certain professional but non-entrepreneurial functions.[1] Through education the gentry retained prime access to high positions in government.[2] Not only did the classical curriculum – tailored to civil service examinations – favour the cultural background of the landed family, but the whole education system actually made gentlemen by the same indoctrination that made rulers. Students from non-gentry origins were stamped with the gentry's traditional outlook. It was, as one English historian described it, the manufacture of 'synthetic gentility'.[3]

The definition of a gentleman

At this point, we should define the word 'gentleman', and establish more clearly the relation between the gentleman ideal and a way of life connected with land. In *The Concise Oxford Dictionary*, a gentleman is defined as (1) a man 'entitled to bear arms' but not of the nobility, (2) a man with 'chivalrous instincts, fine feelings and good breeding', (3) 'a man of good social position, a man of wealth and leisure'.[4] Let us for the moment, ignore the first part of this definition: the 'entitled to bear arms' phrase stems from feudal concerns with soldiering – a subject beyond the scope of this essay. What should first be noted is the overtone of moral superiority that the definition carries. The very word 'gentleman', in fact, displays the same character, and Reinhold Niebuhr points out that this is also true of both 'gentleman' and 'nobleman' in other European tongues.[5] In China, likewise, the nearest equivalent to 'gentleman', *juin-tze*, meant literally 'superior man'; the superiority it referred to was first and foremost moral.

[1] The Chinese gentry were perhaps subject to more social mobility than the English gentry; their social status depended directly on membership in, or kinship with, the degree-holder group. *Shen-shih*, the Chinese word commonly translated as 'gentry' literally means 'degree-holders'. When I talk of the Chinese gentry, I mean those families enjoying social prestige and a respected standard of culture, non-commercial but not necessarily large landowners. They shared status and values in common rather than great wealth.

[2] W. L. Guttsman, 'Aristocracy and the Middle Class in the British Political Élite, 1886–1916', *British Journal of Sociology* (London, March 1954). Robert Marsh, *The Mandarins: The Circulation of Élites in China* (Free Press, Glencoe, U.S.A., 1961), pp. 78–82.

[3] E. Wingfield-Stratford, *The Squire and His Relations* (Cassells, London, 1956), p. 389.

[4] *Concise Oxford Dictionary* (Oxford University Press, 1958).

[5] Reinhold Niebuhr, *Moral Man and Immoral Society* (Scribners, New York, 1932), p. 126.

Now, there are two secondary characteristics of the gentleman concept that are particularly important for our study. The first is classical learning and the second is the possession of leisure.[1] Both were concerned with an aesthetic ideal of elegant ease – or at least a *posture* of ease.[2] In China, as in eighteenth- and nineteenth-century England, this ideal was defended by families who possessed or wanted to possess landed wealth; and it supported a moral premium on moderation, self-restraint and social harmony.

To the gentleman, and those who respected him, classical culture was supposed to confer moral advantage by providing select access to past wisdoms. Confucian doctrine stated quite explicitly that great virtue could only come through learning. In England, the moral claims of the classicist – to be truly 'civilized', etc. – were fainter, but in tacit form they existed.

Both societies, however, made familiarity with a classical body of knowledge a matter of aesthetic, as well as moral, advantage. 'Puns, euphemisms, allusions to classical quotations, and a refined and purely literary intellectuality were considered the conversational ideal of the genteel man,' commented Max Weber on gentlemanly society in Imperial China.[3] To a lesser extent, the power of the apt and witty classical allusion carried advantage in England. Certainly it did in the (old-style) Houses of Parliament.

Classical culture, in short, contributed to the differentiated style that gave the gentleman élite its magical aura. In both societies, respect for classical education was linked with the agrarian traditions of the ruling group. Gentry classes, compared with urban and business classes, seem to venerate tradition above the uncertain promises of change. In 'classic' literature and art, the gentleman finds his preferences fulfilled. For, by definition, a classic only becomes a classic when it gains a measure of antiquity; when it appears to conform to a well-ordered structure; and when it follows absolute and unquestionable rules.[4]

Despite this common theme, the connection between classics and leisure, and the relation of both to public service, was not precisely the same for Confucian China as it was for Public School England. In each case, it is true, classical knowledge was a prerequisite for passing civil service examinations. (Although Latin and Greek by no means monopolized British Civil Service examinations, they dominated Public School entrance tests, and the Public Schools in turn provided the best access to high government office.) In England, however, the factor of leisure counted for more than it did in China.[5] The gentlemanly figure was one

---

[1] It is interesting here to note that in the *Oxford Dictionary* the subsidiary *legal* definition of the gentleman contains the factor of leisure: a man 'who has no occupation'.

[2] '. . . moderate in his words but ardent in his actions'. Confucius, *Lun Yu*, Pt XIV, Chap. 29.

[3] From *Max Weber: Essays*, translated by H. Gerth and C. W. Mills (Kegan Paul, London, 1947).

[4] *Concise Oxford Dictionary:* see under 'classic', 'classical' and, by contrast, 'romantic'.

[5] The Chinese official, it is true, enjoyed leisure in which to pursue prestige-conferring cultural pastimes. But his public post made leisure possible, not vice versa. cf. Jacques

who didn't have to work too exclusively or too obviously for a living; he had leisure and means both to pursue culture and to seek relatively unremunerative public office. This, at any rate, was the image that the British gentleman élite presented. It linked an amateur ideal to the spirit of public service. I do not here imply that English gentlemen did not seek culture for its own sake. By the end of the nineteenth century, indeed, the moral propagandist Samuel Smiles had convinced even gentlemen that work was good in itself. Be that as it may, public service and classical attainment were useful adornments for the man who wished to feel himself a leisured gentleman, free of the need to view work solely for the bread it won.

In China economic factors dictated a somewhat different role for the concept of leisure. According to Chang Chungi-li's estimate, the largest source of income for the Ch'ing Dynasty's *literati* élite was official, professional and 'gentry' services (including local government and teaching). This accounted for 46 per cent of the élite's income, compared with 32 per cent from land rents and 22 per cent from commercial activity.[1] Since the official, both at local and Imperial level, commonly made a comfortable living, he did not depend on private means as did the British M.P. and the unpaid Justice of the Peace. Consequently, it is doubtful whether the Chinese *literati* sought public office as a symbol of gentlemanly leisure. In China the factor of leisure operated more as an attitude of mind: both in government policy and in gentlemanly manners, it was leisureli*ness* that counted. On the personal plane, leisureliness went with the *juin-tze*'s attention to gracefulness, formal dignity and etiquette. On the official plane, it appeared from time to time in a *wu-wei* (do-nothing) policy of governing. Just as Sir William Gilbert's aristocracy 'did nothing in particular and did it very well', so many Imperial bureaucracies followed a course of elegant inaction. Such a course Confucian wisdom had appeared to sanction by claiming that rulers could induce a measure of social harmony through the sheer weight of personal, moral example.

If the Chinese did not really seek office as a symbol of leisure, he did seek it as a symbol of classical culture. This was true at least, Levenson argues, by the late *Ming* dynasty. Chinese educators used both amateurism and a brand of careerism to produce a public service élite. It was careerist in the sense that schools and tutors concentrated mainly on preparing their students for government examinations that would qualify them for public office. Yet, the system was amateurist in the sense that the classical curriculum was itself 'non-vocational' and that office was sought as the highest symbol of a generally cultured man.[2]

Susceptibility to appeal by symbol – that is the key link between the gentleman ideal and the formation of a public service élite. On the one hand, duty symbolized

---

Gernet, *Daily Life in China on the Eve of the Mongol Invasion* (Allen & Unwin, London, 1962), p. 183.

[1] Robert Marsh, op. cit., p. 65.

[2] John K. Fairbank (ed.), *Chinese Thought & Institutions*, p. 321 (Chap. by Levenson).

privilege: public service certified membership in a social élite.[1] On the other hand, and conversely, the education system made privilege a reminder of moral duty.

This mutual interaction of privilege and duty, of group status and group service, was the way by which gentlemanly education wrought cohesion out of man's egoism. True, the school of Confucian ethics, like that of Thomas Arnold, made direct appeals to altruism. But, tacitly at any rate, both systems recognized that appeals to altruism were not enough. As Reinhold Niebuhr wrote in *Moral Man and Immoral Society*, egoism, especially 'group egoism', is too strong a force to be combated simply by educational appeals to selflessness. Niebuhr's prescription was to use moral restraints to reduce egoism, but also to rely on coercion, balancing group power against group power.[2]

The two education systems under review had a somewhat different approach to the problem of egoism. What they in fact did was to couch appeals to egoism *within* an appeal to altruistic public service. They posed public service as a moral status-symbol, as a credential of membership in an élite which enjoyed moral prestige as well as political power. To implement the beliefs that this involved, two factors were necessary. First, the social climate had to be such that the notion of an élite group setting a moral example to the non-élite could win general acceptance throughout the society as a whole. This factor obtained in Confucian China as it did in the subsiding Evangelicanism of late-Victorian England. Both societies displayed clear-cut class differences; and in both the ruling class could enhance its authority by appearing an Institute of Good Works, a moral elect.

The second factor applied to attitudes within the élite itself. To perpetuate the élite, gentlemanly education[3] had to see to it that the student perceived self-interest largely in terms of moral prestige, and that he identified himself closely with the public service élite. It had, in short, to make him see privilege and duty as two faces of the same thing. The way that the education system instilled such an attitude was to play on *aesthetic* emotion. It made the individual seek public leadership because to do so was tasteful, beautiful. This tendency to confuse beauty and virtue, manners and morals, is a major characteristic of the gentleman. 'Manners makyth man,' said the fourteenth-century founder of a famous Public School,[4] and over the course of years, 'manners' came to mean a host of aesthetic devices that moulded the gentleman to his political role. The same pattern of devices also emerged in China, where it was a strong tenet that outer propriety

[1] Robert Marsh shows how local leadership *functions*, rather than *wealth*, gave the Chinese landowner and even merchant the most prestige: op. cit., p. 38.
In Victorian England, similarly, the *nouveau riche* industrialist raised his social prestige by taking on the style and duties of the country squire.
[2] Reinhold Niebuhr, op. cit., especially pp. 20–1.
[3] Here I include family upbringing under gentlemanly education. In China, of course, Confucian education was closely linked to family upbringing: there was no dominant system of private boarding schools. It should also be noted that clan rules (codes of behaviour for family members) were most elaborate, by and large, in gentry families.
[4] William of Wykeham, Bishop of Winchester, who founded the sister institutions, Winchester College (the Public School) and New College, Oxford.

could affect inner virtue. The way in which these devices worked should be examined in some detail.

The mechanism

Both education systems transmitted values through etiquette, a code of behaviour sanctioned by mystical tradition and group standards of good taste. It was a code, therefore, whose enforcement depended less on coercion than on the subtle pressures of majority opinion. Most important, the same body of etiquette which instilled intense communal loyalties also created the differentiated style of the élite: it inculcated distinctive manners and bearing, and it accustomed the individual to colourful privileges of status. In other words, etiquette mirrored perfectly the role of the gentleman ideal that we referred to at the beginning – the ideal's function as a two-way link between duty and status, between the spirit of public service and the identity of an élite.

The etiquette of Confucian education was called *li*, and it is significant that originally this word referred only to rules of religious worship. As such, *li* ordered the rituals which fanned communal loyalties. Not only did it govern ancestor-veneration and other ceremonies exalting the clan but it was applied to Imperial court ritual as well. The symbolic message of ceremonial *li* was that the individual should subordinate himself to the community, be it the family or the nation, whose historic continuity denoted a group immortality.

It was perhaps inevitable that *li* should also come to confer privilege on those who headed the community. Family elders and government officials alike were marked out by *li* for special acts of deference, modes of address, etc., by others. At one end, indeed, the ethical sanctions of *li* merged with the sumptuary laws that enforced privileges of degree-holders and officials. Even these exclusive legal privileges, however, included many that were aesthetic rather than utilitarian, perquisites of dress and ornamentation.

Unlike Public School etiquette, much of *li* existed in writing and was taught as an academic subject. The more learned a man was, the more propriety he was expected to show.[1]

> He'd a lordly look and natural dignity. A man like that, if not a god, must be at least a high official or a ruler of men.[2]

So wrote a story-teller of the Tang dynasty. In fact, 'natural dignity' was supposed to be acquired through learning, for not only did Confucian thought blur the distinction between manners and morals, but it declared that scholarship was a

[1] Again it is here relevant that clan rules of propriety were most elaborate in the families of the *shen-shih* – degree-holding gentry. Cf. D. S. Nivison and M. Wright, *Confucianism in Action* (Stanford University Press, 1959).

[2] 'Foxes' Revenge', a *T'ang* story in *The Courtesan's Jewel Box* (Foreign Language Press, Peking, 1957), p. 96, quoted by Robert Marsh, op. cit., p. 2.

prerequisite for moral superiority.[1] And since a degree – or kinship with a degree-holder – was the main qualification for membership in the gentleman élite (*shen-shih*), it followed that scholarship awarded social status at the same time that it conferred moral prestige.

Whereas Chinese etiquette focused loyalties first and foremost on the family, Public School etiquette focused on the school community and its sub-unit, the House. Both systems, therefore, confronted the individual with a community small and immediate enough to appear as a vivid entity. And in each case, the community dwarfed the individual against an awe-inspiring array of historical tradition. Public School etiquette, like its Chinese counterpart, constantly invoked 'School tradition' to demand group-directed behaviour. Tradition was the silent arbiter of 'good form', endorsing 'House spirit' and 'teamwork', decreeing what habits were 'done' and what were 'not done'.[2] At many Public Schools unwritten rules set out initiation rites which made the entering 'new boy' perform exercises of deference to the school community and its proud traditions.[3] Other rules inspired deference to the school community by ordaining a student hierarchy of rank and privilege. Many of the privileges were aesthetic in value, referring to details of dress; and naturally the most prized emblems were reserved for the community leader – the prefect, the football captain. In addition, a myriad train of sartorial 'colours' went out to the athletic heroes who won public victory for their house or school.

From the above it can be seen that the same etiquette which accustomed the student to style-differences based on rank-differences also enlisted hierarchy as a creator of deference to the community. It wasn't simply that the system awarded most prestige to those who performed distinguished public functions for the community as a whole. It was also that the whole ethos of Public School hierarchy, like that of the Chinese clan, tended to keep the individual, especially the more junior individual, 'in his place'. Conceit above one's station seems to have been counted a prime offence at many Public Schools. At Harrow, for instance, it was 'swagger' for a junior boy to roll up his umbrella out of doors, or to enter another house than his own uninvited. And at Haileybury, a junior who showed hair under his cap would be told by prefects or others 'to take *side* off'.[4] (Note that words like 'swagger' and 'side' all carry pejorative connotations of aggressive, individualist behaviour.) Aesthetic requirements, indeed, demanded some moderation from the prefect himself. Public School notions of leadership emphasized a style that

[1] 'No virtue can remain untainted without learning' – Confucius, *Li Ki* (Book of Rituals), Sec. I. But, of course, careerism affected many scholars' pursuit of culture. Cf. 'The Bookworm', a satirical short story of the *Ching* dynasty, by P'u Sung-ling, in *Famous Chinese Short Stories*, retold by Lin Yutang (Pocket Library, New York, 1954).

[2] Vivian Ogilvie, *The English Public School* (Batsford, London, 1957), pp. 181–3. Cf. C. E. Pasco, *Everyday Life in Our Public Schools* (Griffith & Farran, London, 1881).

[3] Ogilvie, ibid., pp. 181–3, and G. F. Lamb, *The Happiest Days* (Joseph, London, 1959), pp. 19–26.

[4] E. H. Pitcairn, *Unwritten Laws & Ideals of Active Careers* (Smith Elder, London, 1899), pp. 286–9.

Cyril Connolly called 'prettiness': an effortless grace, a casual assurance, the light touch in command.[1]

At this point some general reflections should be made on the style that dignified and differentiated the gentleman élite. First, it could claim to be the only national style, and this enhanced its magical aura. In both societies, most of the non-élite had mannerisms and speech which varied sharply between geographic regions. By contrast with these differences, the style of the gentleman had a cosmopolitan flavour. In nineteenth-century England, the development of transport facilities increased the number of Public Schools which could boast a national clientele. (Most Public Schools, it will be remembered, were boarding schools.) A Public School accent and manner sprang up, cutting across regional differences. In China, likewise, a central, mandarin dialect and bearing existed, but the most important national feature of the élite style was the ability to write – and write elegantly. The Imperial examinations, drawing candidates from all over the Empire, maintained the unifying influence of Chinese writing and calligraphy. If and when he became an official, the Confucian scholar was expected to be able to write government memorials in a beautiful style that betrayed no trace of his regional origins.

The national style of the élite was well-suited to the amateur ideal, the gentlemanly concept of the whole man. The gentleman was taught to consider himself above specialization, whether in the sense of regional style or that of technical know-how. Both of the latter were reserved for his social inferiors, since specialization in any form was deemed narrowing. With regard to technical specialization, furthermore, such expertise was the mark of one who had to use knowledge to earn a living and not for the leisured pursuit of wisdom and beauty. In any event, thought the gentleman, effective leadership depended on general qualities of mind, on moral stature and on mannerly self-assurance: endowments like these far outweighed any amount of specialized skill. Such a non-technical bias was well in tune with the credentials and aptitudes of these who presided over gentlemanly education. In Public School England, the archetype educator was the classically trained Churchman; his counterpart in Confucian China was the scholar who, very often, had failed to win a government post and had turned to teaching as the nearest substitute. Neither sort of educator was likely to give much place to technical expertise in his overall concern for moral education.

The second major point about the style of the élite was the psychological effect it had on the élitist individual. A prime assumption of the gentleman was the notion that outer actions could strengthen inner faith. It was an assumption that seems to have contained some truth; by all accounts the style of effortlessness did bolster self-assurance, and attention to prescribed courtesies did enhance moral self-esteem. What is more, the following of a set etiquette, ordained not by the individual but by community tradition and group standards of good taste, gave

[1] Cyril Connolly, *Enemies of Promise* (Macmillan, New York, 1948), pp. 174, 214.

the individual a sense of social belonging. As Erich Fromm has pointed out, the lone Englishman in the jungle who still 'dressed for dinner' could, by so doing, feel at one with his home community.[1] And when the etiquette followed was that of a traditionally superior class – in this case, the gentry – so much the better for the individual's self-assurance.

Related to the above was another psychological effect of gentlemanly style. It was an effect described by the reporter, James Morris, who applied it to the entire English character. 'In their *private affairs,*' wrote Morris, 'the English try to be *undemonstrative* but in *public manners they do what the drill sergeant says*. They march down the years to the twirl of the bandmaster's silver stick and with bags and bags of swank.'[2] Morris was referring mainly to the British love of pomp and pageantry, but his observation is equally applicable to the gentleman's concern for elegant and courteous manners. For like public ceremonial, manners tend to substitute formal channels of expression for spontaneous demonstrativeness.[3] Equally like public ceremonial, manners encourage the individual to seek emotional outlet in an elaboration of aesthetic form. It can be seen, therefore, that manners tend to collectivize feeling. Not only is it their role to harmonize individual egoisms, but the criteria of good manners depend, almost by definition, on group standards of good taste.

The whole tenor, in short, of gentlemanly manners was to stress social harmony and co-operation by the same token that it inhibited private demonstrations. The courtesies that the gentleman performed were courtesies of duty and command; in the final analysis they were not courtesies of intimate friendliness and emotional warmth. If the gentleman's behaviour was group-directed, class-directed, community-directed, his motivation was not 'other-directed' (to use David Riesman's term). The gentleman practised manners less to win the approval of others than because his manners were both the obligation and the distinction of the public service élite.

This brings us to a third point about gentlemanly style – the social significance of the word 'harmony'. In that word lies one of the reasons why the gentleman tended to identify beautiful manners with superior moral character. For 'harmony' has a moral as well as aesthetic connotation, and to the gentleman it represented a prime value in itself. On the personal plane, it meant gentleness, or what the Chinese called *ching*: the curbing of base and selfish passions. It was a quality very much bound up with the amateur ideal of the well-rounded man, for it sought to secure moderation by *balancing* virtues and aptitudes against one another. Behind the value of personal harmony there rests a certain belief that faults are but virtues pushed too far, to the exclusion of other virtues. 'Respect-

[1] Erich Fromm, *Fear of Freedom* (Routledge & Kegan Paul, London, 1960), p. 15.

[2] James Morris, in *New York Times Magazine*, 13 November 1960. Italics added.

[3] In China, the prominence awarded writing as a gentleman's means of expression itself tended to dampen spontaneity. 'Phantasy and ardour fled from the formalistic intellectualism of the spoken word into the quiet beauty of the written symbol.' – Max Weber, op. cit., p. 430.

fulness, without the rules of propriety, becomes laborious bustle,' wrote a Chinese sage, '. . . carefulness [becomes] timidity; straightforwardness [becomes] rudeness.'[1]

On the social plane, the gentleman's concern with harmony led to an emphasis on moderation and compromise. This was particularly true of Public School England where the sportsman's ethic of the 'good loser' reigned. But it also characterized Imperial China. If Confucian morality added an ideological note of bitterness to bureaucratic faction fights, it also induced the losing party to promote its views by mere advice-giving or by protest resignations rather than by violence. Applied to political thought, the gentlemanly ideal of social harmony befitted best a minimal concept of government, an outlook which saw the ruler as guardian rather than innovator. New ideas and methods nearly always appear to disrupt, however much they may serve the long-run interests of social harmony. In Chinese society, moreover, we have already seen that classical precepts supported the *wu-wei* (minimal) notion of central government by declaring that a ruler could induce social harmony purely through personal, moral example. It is also likely that an executive authority will be tempted into a relatively passive role whenever it lays great stress on the magical properties of government. Preoccupation with a style of graceful ease, a style betokening mastery of life's struggles, may encourage the ruler to avoid those struggles in the first place. The more a ruler enters into the day-to-day affairs of his subjects, the less easy he will find it to maintain that mysterious aura of differentness and infallibility which gives a government magic dignity. As studies of primitive societies seem to indicate, there is a certain relationship between mystic ritual and requirements of physical cleanliness.[2] On the political level, accordingly, the ritual aspect of government may demand 'cleanliness' from human squalor and strife.

The Context

As I have constantly suggested, gentlemanly values were nurtured by a landed way of life. The premium on social harmony, after all, was best suited to a relatively stable agrarian society, especially one cushioned by geography from the disruptive effects of outside influences. In both societies under review, a rentier group had found the leisure in which to elaborate an elegant style and to pursue classical learning for reasons not directly utilitarian. Above all, they had been able to develop the political uses of etiquette, securing social harmony by ethical obligation and by manners as much as by legal coercion. For the élite, duty and responsibility were matters more of class honour and obligation than of individual, rational decision. Similarly, the gentleman commanded deference from his social inferiors not for what he did but rather for what he was – a member of a certain class.

[1] *Lun Yu*, Pt XIV, Chap. 29.
[2] Lucy Mair, *Primitive Government* (Penguin, London, 1962), p. 225.

From this it follows that the value of social harmony included the conservative notion that social inequality, tempered by inter-class obligation, was in accord with the laws of nature.

> The rich man in his castle,
> The poor man at his gate,
> God made them, high or lowly,
> And ordered their estate.[1]

So wrote Mrs Alexander, that most prolific of Victorian hymn-writers, and it is significant that the above verse comes in a much-loved children's hymn praising the divine beauties of nature. (Equally significantly, the verse has now been dropped from most hymn-books.) The same assumption, that a natural hierarchy characterized society and universe alike, marked the dominant Confucian tradition during our period of review, the *Chu Hsi school*.

It is widely recognized, of course, that in both societies a structure of well-defined classes did not preclude social mobility. And it was here that education had a major part to play, reconciling social mobility with clearly marked class distinctions. Both Confucian education and the Victorian Public Schools absorbed into the gentleman élite individuals from families below the élite. By perpetuating an attractive gentry style and manners, and by associating such style with moral status, the education systems played on the ambitions of the social climber. They gave him gentlemanly status, and by the same process indoctrinated him with gentlemanly attitudes.

High among these attitudes, as we have already stated, was a strong leaning towards the public service professions. The whole ethos of both education systems was far better suited to government leadership than it was to the pursuit of business profit. In the first place, government – and in England, the Church – had far more need of the gentleman's magic style than did the textile mill or the trading firm. Not until the twentieth century and the development of Public Relations, have business firms rivalled governments in their systematic attempts to win power by emotional appeal, by magic display of a group image as well as by rational persuasion.[2] Compared with the commercial expansion and enterprise that characterized both Imperial China and Victorian England, government was

---

[1] 'All Things Bright & Beautiful', *Hymns Ancient & Modern* (Clowes and Son, London).
[2] It is my private hypothesis that the rising fashionability of the advertising and public relations occupations in Britain is due to this very fact. For what are advertising and public relations but the professionalized practice of manners, far from the greasy wheels of technology. Further, the commercial exploitation of hostmanship introduces a note of leisure – or the posture of leisure – into office hours.

In connection with my discussion of the *professions* and *élitism* (see below) one should note the steady attempts of advertising to make itself into a profession, with formal examinations and such titles as 'Practitioners in Advertising'.

Before advertising, however, could become fashionable, the gentleman had to say good-bye to his disdain for the commercial middleman. Long before this, though, another commercial occupation had attained some gentlemanly acceptance: namely, banking.

a *relatively* static affair.[1] The ruler's main task, like that of the Public School prefect, was to consolidate rather than innovate, to harmonize different interests and to keep order. Where change was required it was a matter of gradual adjustment rather than of dynamic invention. Under these conditions of leadership, a respect-incurring *manner* of command was indispensable.

What I have just stated is really the corollary to Schumpeter's description of the apolitical bourgeois. If the bourgeois felt a greater aptitude for the world of business, the gentleman felt a corresponding confidence in the world of government, whether as a local magistrate or as a national bureaucrat. Accordingly, one effect of the gentleman's going into public service was to sharpen the distinctive appearance of the gentleman élite; by emphasizing the value of dignity and magical style, political experience strengthened those qualities in the class that possessed them.

The second way in which the education systems oriented their members towards government occupations was to make the educational community – the Chinese clan, the Public School – a symbol for other communities which would later claim the individual's loyalty. When the educational community played on aesthetic emotion, it was really forging a *nationalism*; through the pressures of etiquette and tradition, the community induced the individual to identify himself with it 'voluntarily'. What conerns us here, however, is that the individual was expected to relate to other groups as he related to his educational community. In China, this principle, the inculcation of loyalty by analogy, was reflected in the terms *fu ma kuan*, 'parent officials', and *tzu min* 'children people'.[2]

It could be argued, of course, that the ethos of gentlemanly education should have promoted loyalty to any group, including the private business firm. Assuming the gentleman went into business in the first place, such an argument might possibly be true. A Far Eastern businessman once told me that in his experience British executives were far more apt than Americans to remain with one 'House' during their entire careers. But gentlemanly education encouraged its youth to identify most readily with those groups which, like the educational community itself, enjoyed hallowed traditions, a strong *esprit de corps*, and a magic sort of personality. These traits characterized a formally-organized civil service and the nation as a whole far more than they did the rationalist business firm. Certainly this was, for the most part, the case in an individualist, entrepreneurial stage of economic activity, before the 'professionalization' of management, the growth of giant corporations and the rise of the 'organization man'.

In Public School England, the traits of the educational community, with its monastic barrack-room living, were also those of the military regiment. The same resemblance between education and military service did not obtain in Confucian

---

[1] Admittedly, the Chinese central government entered into many industrial pursuits, e.g. the salt and iron monopolies. But civil servants were not recruited as potential entrepreneurs.

[2] C. K. Yang, *The Chinese Family in the Communist Revolution* (M.I.T., Cambridge, Mass.), pp. 5–6.

China. There virtue was sought through scholarship rather than athleticism; and moral suasion was preferred to muscular evangelism. Not surprisingly, the Chinese held professional soldiering in low regard, and Imperial defence suffered accordingly.[1]

The third way in which the education systems directed their members towards government service was to act as a sounding-board for the landed gentry's traditional prejudices about careers. This was particularly true of China, where merchants were officially excluded from degree-examinations, and Confucian thought identified private profit-seeking with *li* – roughly defined as selfish greed. To a lesser extent, anti-trade prejudices marked Public School opinion in the Victorian era, despite the constant intermarrying between Money and Birth. Ideally, the gentleman viewed money as a mere *provider*, a guarantor of leisure and culture. He could not view money as a *score*, the measure of industrial creativity, because he was brought up to seek honour in community leadership rather than in private enterprise-building. Behind these attitudes there probably lay a fear, the fear of rising commercial power and its threat to the traditional order of a gentry-dominated world. Economic factors aside, the gentleman could not help but distrust the businessman. Where the latter was individualist in his striving, the other respected public service as the duty of a close-knit class. Where the businessman hailed energy and efficiency before all else, the gentleman placed equal weight on dignity and custom. Where one, in short, was mainly rationalist, the other was traditionalist.

The position, in Victorian England, of the private 'professions' affords a further perspective on gentlemanly attitudes towards public service. By and large, the Church, the Law, Teaching ('at the right place') and to a lesser extent Medicine seem to have occupied a middle ground of prestige between government occupations and most forms of commercial activity. There is some evidence, though inconclusive, to suggest that the more famous Public Schools admitted with complete readiness the sons of professional men at an earlier date than they generally did the sons of businessmen.[2]

Reflection about the comparative prestige of the professions is instructive, because it reveals further the relationship between attitudes towards employment and the maintenance of a political élite. Within the hierarchy of professions themselves, T. H. S. Escott, the Victorian commentator, observed that G.P.s and solicitors had lower occupational status than had barristers and clergy. This phenomenon Escott traced to two factors which fit fairly well into our description of the gentlemanly outlook. In the first place, Escott argued, the lower profes-

---

[1] Cf. J. K. Fairbank and Edwin Reischauer, *East Asia – The Great Tradition*, Vol. I, *A History of East Asian Civilization* (Houghton Mifflin, Boston, 1960), pp. 189–91.

[2] T. C. Worsley, *Barbarians & Philistines* (Hale, London, 1940), pp. 97–8. T. W. Bamford, 'Public Schools & Social Class, 1801–1850', *British Journal of Sociology* (September 1961). This article indicates that in the period preceding that under review, the most famous Public Schools admitted considerably more boys from professional families than they did from business families.

sions appeared to have a narrow *expertise*, whereas the activity of the barrister and the bishop could make a *general* impact on the public mind. Secondly, doctors and solicitors had to undergo the vulgar commercial process of receiving money directly from their clients.[1] Hypothetical as these arguments are, the fact that a distinguished Victorian could write them is significant in itself.

Taking all the major professions together, one characteristic they held in common was an outward contempt for aggressive salesmanship. As T. H. Pear points out, a private profession has clients, whereas a trade has customers. What is healthy competition to the second is client-stealing for the first.[2] In other words, a profession possesses a group spirit which mutes any competitive individualism that occurs within it.

If the profession has a group spirit, it also has an élite spirit. To cite Pear again – the professions have often been described by their critics as 'conspiracies against the public'.[3] Like a bureaucratic civil service, a profession derives some of its élitist *esprit de corps* from formal methods of recruitment. These, in fact, form an integral part of what constitutes a profession. Thus, quite recently, the editor of the *Princeton Alumni Bulletin* could define the professions as 'those vocations which rest upon a systematic body of knowledge of substantial intellectual content and which are entered by advanced degrees, i.e. examinations demonstrating minimum standards of education and competence'.[4]

Now, to the extent that this definition stresses specialized and theoretical expertise, it is unfriendly to the amateur ideal of the gentleman. On the other hand, the professional examination, like its civil service counterpart and like the various Public School initiation rites, invests a group with a mystique. By confronting new members with a traditional body of knowledge to be rigorously learned, the profession acquires the aura of historic continuity; it appears as a group which is more than the sum of present members. Recruitment by formal examination, moreover, gives the profession the image of a community not lightly entered nor easily understood by the outsider. It should also be noted that, until the rise of the American business school, this professional mystique was largely withheld from the businessman who learned his job more by individual experience than from a clearly recognized, communal body of knowledge.[5]

[1] T. H. S. Escott, *England: Its People, Polity, & Pursuits* (Chapman & Hall, London, 1885), pp. 355–6.

T. H. Pear points out that the practice of selling medicine for profit around 1800 lowered the prestige of G.P.s – *English Social Differences* (Allen & Unwin, London, 1955). It was ungentlemanly, perhaps, to make a great deal of money very obviously from a humane service.

[2] T. H. Pear, ibid., 22.   [3] T. H. Pear, ibid., 37–8.

[4] John P. Davies, writing in the *Harvard Alumni Bulletin* (Cambridge, Mass., 17 March 1962).

[5] Élitism in the professions suggests that, ironically enough, democracy may encourage the growth of its own brand of élitism, by demanding formal criteria for the entering of many occupations. In the same way, the Chinese bureaucracy set tests which increased the exclusivist aura of government, although the tests were designed to call forth talent and reduce family influence in recruitment.

From the foregoing it can be seen that the ideals and requirements of the private profession were fairly similar to those of the political élite. Both groups appeared to imbue their members with properties that did not originate with the individual but belonged to the group as a whole. Among such properties, in the case of the private profession, was the possession of esoteric knowledge; like the classical culture of the Chinese degree-holders, professional knowledge bore the image of an immortal entity conferred upon the individual by the élite group, whose trust that knowledge was.[1] On a somewhat vaguer note, the Public School treated wisdom in the same way – as the property of a status-group and external to the individual. It was on just this point that in 1924 Sir James Barrie made a speech twitting the schools. Apparently, he said, they claimed to possess a 'mysterious something' that 'oozes out of the historic old walls'. By way of reply *The Times* claimed solemnly that the 'something' came from outside the individual; it was 'non-analysable' and non-intellectual, and it induced boys to distrust their individual intellects and do an unselfish job.[2]

Social mobility and hereditary privilege

The *Times*–Barrie exchange, however comic its tone, has a meaning which is central to our understanding of the gentleman élite. For the gentleman's distinctive aura depended, at least in part, on a tacit claim to qualities derived mystically from outside the individual. From this point of view a hereditary ruling class enjoys advantages of prestige over a purely merit-selected ruling class. The latter must base its leadership qualifications on an aggregate of individuals still alive, on the character they have shown, the efforts they have made, and the training they have received during their own lifetimes. By contrast, an aristocracy can attribute its leadership qualities to a long line of ancestors, including famous men whose glory is intimately linked with that of the historic community. Moreover, the person who claims that he is *born* to rule bases his claim on a far more mysterious process than the person who claims that he has tangibly proved himself worthy to rule.[3]

Biologically, of course, the above is nonsense. There is little evidence to suppose that leadership qualities, even qualities of style and manner, can be inherited. When men claim that the aristocrat is born to rule, they really mean that he is

[1] This is not to deny a great difference between the Confucian concept of knowledge and the Victorian professional one. Unlike the latter, Confucian knowledge was absolutist, discouraging further additions, to a known body of principles, and accordingly opposed to inductive thinking. It might be said, however, that one characteristic of professional examinations is their tendency to stress memory-work, the learning of fact and generally accepted principles.

[2] Edward Mack, *Public Schools & British Opinion Since 1860* (Methuen, London, 1938), p. 401.

[3] Lucy Mair, op. cit., p. 218.

brought up to rule. Family traditions and home influence are just another form of education.

This does not alter the fact that a political élite with a hereditary core can claim a glamour that a 'meritocracy' will find it hard to equal. Mythical as the basis of that glamour may be, it will none the less exist in the eyes of the non-élite, provided social values are not actively hostile to the notion of hereditary privilege. And if the hereditary ruling class can match its aristocratic aura with claims to reward merit, it will have unusual power to inspire deference in the non-élite and attract new blood into its ranks. Against the material inducements of private profit-making, the political élite will be able to offer its *nouveau* recruits the honour of association with the aristocrat – and with the latter's public service tradition.

It was on these lines that the social composition of the gentleman élite in both societies was formed. On one hand, the education system conferred prime advantages on well-to-do families, especially among the landed, and this group formed the nucleus of the political élite. By adjusting its curriculum to the requirements of civil service examinations, the education system harnessed the public service traditions of the gentry to the recruitment needs of bureaucracy. On the other hand, the political élite absorbed a limited number of the non-élite. Furthermore, government recruitment stressed merit criteria in selection; although it must be said that the very criteria themselves, emphasizing classical knowledge and a certain set style, favoured the gentry individual.

What the political élite really did was to compromise between hereditary privilege and the reward of merit. Confucius himself appears to have supported this ambivalence; he favoured government recruitment based on merit, but he would have allowed the nobility certain ritual privileges.[1] The same compromise appears in the British honours system, where hereditary titles coexist with a hierarchy of earned knighthoods and orders. Behind the compromise lay a rationale, however unarticulated, that every critic of élitist education should consider. In terms of effective leadership, the gentleman élite stands or falls on the assumption that before one talks of selecting political ability one must talk of producing political motivation, of inducing men to take on public responsibility in the first place. And the most potent way to produce political motivation – so runs the élitist argument – is to secure 'a social stratum . . . that takes to politics as a matter of course.'[2]

Conclusion

By its very nature, the gentleman élite paid an intellectual price for its self-perpetuation. Social mobility or no, to the extent that it indulged hereditary

---

[1] *Analects*, Bk III, Chap. 22.
[2] Joseph Schumpeter, op. cit., p. 298.

privilege, it inevitably lost some 'village Hampden' his opportunity.[1] The very process, moreover, of making political gentlemen displayed weaknesses: loyalty-indoctrination by aesthetic device inhibited rigorous questioning; and the amateur figure showed little sympathy for technological innovation and expert method. Gentlemanly education, like society itself, faced an age-old dilemma: the fact that loyalty-training and intelligence are not easy companions.

In judging the productivity of gentlemanly education, however, one should not simply ask how much national intelligence it produced and whether a less élitist system could have produced a greater aggregate of skills and ability. These questions are important, but to meet the champions of the political élite one must meet them on their own ground. And to do this one must ask other questions. Did gentlemanly education make up for its intellectual deficiencies by supporting a spirit of public service, by ensuring that enough men of some raw ability and integrity preferred government responsibility to private profit? Could a more democratic system of education have poured the same flow of talent into relatively unremunerative government posts? On the other hand, at what point does such a flow defeat its own ends by starving industry, science and other key occupations that nourish the state? These questions are barely within the scope of this paper but they are worth the asking.

[1] Full many a gem of purest ray serene
   The dark unfathom'd caves of ocean bear;
   Full many a flower is born to blush unseen,
   And waste its sweetness on the desert air.
   Some village Hampden that with dauntless breast,
   The little tyrant of his fields withstood;
   Some mute inglorious Milton here may rest,
   Some Cromwell guiltless of his country's blood.
                    – Thomas Gray, *Elegy Written in a Country Churchyard*

3 Constant Factors in the Demand for Technical Education, 1860–1960[1]

P. W. MUSGRAVE

During the last century there have been several constant factors in the demand for technical education. These have been present throughout the period, despite the emergence of new demands and the disappearance of old ones. The category of new demands is illustrated by the growth of the demand for clerical education, for technical education for women, and in the years since 1945 by the introduction of training schemes for foremen and of Day Release on a countrywide scale. Demands that have disappeared are more rare, but a good example was the demand up to about 1890 for evening classes to eliminate illiteracy.

It will be shown that throughout the period there have been two main constant stimuli to the demand for technical education. Firstly, there has been the pressure of foreign competition and the recognition that one of the ways to meet and overcome it was through the better organization of technical education. Secondly, there have been key figures who have spoken up for technical education, thus keeping it in the public eye, when but for them it might have been forgotten. Some of these individuals have been the leaders of either technical education or scientific instruction movements.

The nature of these two stimuli will be considered before passing on to an examination of the constant demands for technical education to serve those social functions which an educational system can perform. These functions will be described under five headings. Firstly, there is the economic function; here the demand is for education to permit the economic system to function well. Secondly, there is the mobility function; here the demand is that the educational system may sort out the more able from the population. Thirdly, there is the political function; here it is demanded that the educational system help to preserve the present system of government. Fourthly, there is the function of providing innovators; here the demand is that productive invention may be encouraged. Lastly, there is the function of transmitting the culture of the society; here the

[1] I wish to thank Dr G. Baron of London University and Mrs J. E. Floud of Nuffield College, Oxford, for their criticisms of this paper.

First printed in British Journal of Educational Studies, Vol. XIV, No. 2 (May 1966), pp. 173–87.

demand is basically the conservative one of passing on through the schools the main patterns of society.

Two of these functions may be dismissed briefly, namely the cultural and innovatory functions. The demand for transmitting a society's culture through technical education as such is almost non-existent. Such transmission is latent in technical education. Thus, unconsciously, part-time instructors drawn from industry pass on the culture patterns of industry to the new generation of workers. The function of providing innovators through technical education is not one that has been constant through the period. Before the foundation of what is now the Department of Scientific and Industrial Research in 1916 and its sponsorship of the Ph.D. degree there was very little emphasis on research in industry in this country, or indeed much interest by industry in pure research within the universities. So, because in the first case the demand for technical education to serve that function was latent, and because in the second case the demand was not constant, only the three remaining functions (economic, mobility and political) will be examined here.

These demands led to opposition (negative demands) and throughout the period there was constant hindrance to the advancement of technical education from the following causes. The low status of science itself led to difficulties; employers always preferred 'practical' to 'college-trained' men; manufacturers were keen to keep technical processes secret; the Trade Unions were never wholeheartedly in favour of technical education; lastly, the ever-present desire for cheapness in education did not help.

I

To those who saw Britain's industrial might displayed at the 1851 Exhibition it seemed impossible that she should ever be other than the foremost industrial nation. There were, however, some murmurings that all was not well, and by 1867 at the Paris Exhibition these had become shouts. Dr Lyon Playfair, a juror at the Exhibition, wrote to the Taunton Commission, which was then examining secondary education, to draw its notice to the implications for its enquiry of the rise of foreign industries. The commission, deeming the subject of 'scientific instruction' to be outside its terms of reference, passed the letter to the government. There was already pressure for improvements in technical instruction, and the government appointed a Select Committee to investigate the matter under the iron-master, Sir Bernhard Samuelson. This Committee reported in 1869. *The Economist*, at this time a strong supporter of *laissez-faire* in education as in all else, commenting on the report said:

Our danger from foreigners in regard to scientific instruction and superior education generally is more apprehended than real, though few will doubt that apprehension is well founded. There is abundant evidence at the same time that manufactures and workmen are alike aware to the want and necessity of supplying it.[1]

This would seem an optimistic conclusion in view of evidence in the report that foreigners had now caught up with us in, among other industries, dyeing, lace-making and engineering. Yet it does show that foreign competition had forced manufacturers to realize that technical education was an aid to greater efficiency, thus would yield greater profits, and this was the main criterion. It is rather ironic that the French came to the same conclusion; one of the reports of the French jurors stated, 'The upward movement is visible, above all, among the English. The whole world has been struck with the progress which they have made since the last Exhibition, in design . . .'[2]

In 1869 the Iron and Steel Institute was founded, and in his opening address the Duke of Devonshire alluded to strong foreign competition. The Duke was chairman of the Royal Commission on Scientific Instruction. The successive reports of this body published in the early seventies again stressed the connection between foreign competition and technical education. The Royal Commission on Technical Instruction reporting in 1884 under Samuelson's chairmanship once more emphasized this same point.[3]

Despite the great advances brought about by the Technical Instruction Act of 1889 it was still possible for Lord Haldane in 1901, when speaking on the Finance Bill, to say that we have 'got to train the minds of our people so that they may be able to hold their own against the competition which is coming forward at such an alarming rate'.[4] In 1906 a committee initially under Haldane's chairmanship reported on the South Kensington Science Institutions; their first conclusion was 'That the position of this country makes further provision for advanced technological education essential.'[5]

The 1914 war was a great jolt to many industries in this country, as it was discovered that many vital supplies came from Germany. The government committee, which eventually led to the Department of Scientific and Industrial Research, commented, 'It is impossible to contemplate without considerable apprehension the situation which will arise at the end of the war . . . unless our scientific resources have previously been enlarged and organized to meet it.'[6] Yet in 1925 a well-known Principal of a Technical Institute discussing the part played by foreign competition in stimulating the demand for technical education could write, 'Today there is the same industrial problem.'[7]

[1] *The Economist* (19 September 1868), p. 1079.
[2] *Hansard*, 3rd series, Vol. 191, col. 176 (Lord Robert Montague, 1868).
[3] The *Royal Commission on Scientific Instruction* contains constant questions on foreign conditions; see also *Royal Commission on Technical Instruction*, Vol. I, p. 508.
[4] *Hansard*, 4th series, Vol. 94, col. 655.
[5] *Final Report of the Dptl. Ctee. on the R. Coll. of Science*, etc., Vol. I (1906), p. 23.
[6] *Scheme for the Organization and Development of Scientific and Industrial Research* (1915), p. 2.
[7] C. T. Millis, *Technical Education: Its Development and Aims* (London, 1925), p. 11.

Since the 1939 war the export drive has concentrated attention on national productive efficiency and the way that technical education can aid this. The 1956 White Paper on 'Technical Education' made much of international comparisons in output at the various levels of technical education. In 1958 the Carr Committee published its report 'Training for Skill'. This covered the problems of apprenticeship training during 'the bulge'; in its conclusions it speaks of the need for a high quality of training 'to enable us to maintain our place as one of the great manufacturing and trading nations of the world'.[1] In 1962 the government made proposals to expand industrial training and after comparing our system with that of our competitors commented that, 'We must be quite sure that our own arrangements do not fall behind.'[2]

Throughout this same period not only has there been the stimulus of foreign competition to goad manufacturers to demand technical education; there have also been many outstanding individuals who have spoken up in a disinterested way for the same cause. Such men played a big part in making public opinion realize that there was an unrecognized need for such instruction. They educated public opinion and brought about much of importance.

In 1867 Dr Lyon Playfair, who had been keen on technical instruction for some years, caused the Select Committee to be appointed as described above. This Committee was under Sir Bernhard Samuelson, another advocate of the same cause, who was to be Chairman of the Royal Commission on Technical Instruction in the early eighties. The need for leadership in this country at the time can be seen from the circumstances of the appointment of this commission. The members offered themselves for service and undertook to pay their own expenses providing their report was published as a Royal Commission.[3] The report of this commission indirectly led to the Technical Instruction Act of 1889. In the debate on this bill the member for Finsbury E., speaking in opposition, mentioned that 'a certain number of Gentlemen constitute themselves the guardians of technical instruction'.[4] It is impossible not to mention the work of T. H. Huxley for scientific and technological education, both as a publicist and through the South Kensington group of institutions. It was, too, in the eighties that the City and Guilds Institute of London was started. The outstanding individual here was its director Philip Magnus (later Sir Philip). Throughout the eighties and nineties he addressed meetings, opened schools, gave prizes; he was a missionary for technical education.

In the inter-war years economic conditions were such that little money was spared for the needed expansion of technical education. In fact, expenditure on all further education as a percentage of total educational expenditure fell from 6 per cent in 1920 to 5·2 per cent in 1932 and rose to 5·5 per cent in 1938,

---

[1] *Training for Skill* (1958), p. 32.
[2] *Industrial Training: Government Proposals* (1962), p. 3.
[3] See M. Argles, 'The Royal Commission on Technical Instruction, 1881–4: Its Inception and Composition', *Vocational Aspect* (Autumn, 1959).
[4] *Hansard*, 3rd series, Vol. 339, col. 1253 (Mr Rowlands).

though much of this movement was related to changes in age structure and the decline in the number of apprentices.[1] Yet throughout the period Lord Eustace Percy, at one time President of the Board of Education, spoke up for technical education. Much of what he wished to do was rendered impossible by the financial stringency of the government at the time. However, under him the Board published a series of pamphlets on individual industries and asked industries to let the Board know what they needed. He initiated a report by H.M.I.s enquiring into the provision of further education in Yorkshire. This report led to the establishment of a regional committee with representatives of industry and local authorities; this arrangement was subsequently imitated elsewhere, as for instance in the West Midlands.[2] These were wise measures and cost little.

However, it was not until Lord Percy was appointed chairman of the committee that reported in 1945 on 'Higher Technological Education' that circumstances were more favourable. This report gave impetus to the great expansion in technical education since the war. During the same period the iron and steel industry has built up a remarkable system of education and training under the leadership of its Federation.[3] It may be that corporate leadership has taken the place of outstanding individuals, though in the case of the steel industry it is possible to identify individuals as important within the committee responsible.

It can thus be seen that in view of the work and the leadership of outstanding individuals, often outside industry, there is a strong case for disagreeing with the Crowther report's general conclusion on technical education 'that virtually everything that exists . . . has come into existence as the conscious answer to a demand arising from industry or from individual workers'.[4]

II

These two stimuli, namely the presence of foreign competition and of outstanding individuals, have been constant in creating the demand for technical education which was wanted, however, to serve various social functions. Firstly the economic function will be examined. As might be expected in the case of the demand for technical education, there has been a much greater stress on this function than on the mobility or political functions.

The early demand for education for workers to aid them in industry was for elementary education purely to eliminate illiteracy. However, even in the sixties there was a demand for more precise scientific attainments. In 1868 *The Economist* wrote of the extremely elaborate machinery coming into industrial use as

[1] J. Vaizey, *The Costs of Education* (London, 1958), pp. 73–4.
[2] See, for examples, Board of Education Pamphlet No. 74, *The West Midlands Metal Working Area* (1929), and Hansard, 5th series, Vol. 209, cols 548–9 and 1068, Vol. 217, cols 1105–6.
[3] See P. W. Musgrave, 'The Growth in the Demand for Training in the Iron and Steel Industry, 1945–64', *Vocational Aspect* (Spring, 1966).
[4] '15 to 18', Vol. I (1959), p. 333.

'the strongest possible evidence in favour of a good scientific education for the artisan even before he enters the workshop'.[1] It was in the sixties that the Department of Science and Art founded its examinations in scientific subjects which were to form the basis of technical education until about 1900. After the 1880s these examinations were taken both by schools and technical classes; the numbers from both these categories grew almost without break until 1900.

Letters from manufacturers published by the Royal Commission on Technical Instruction of 1881–4 spoke of the need for more practical classes.[2] These classes became available in the eighties. The City and Guilds' courses grew in numbers. The London Polytechnics began their trades courses. Also under the 1889 Act it became possible for subjects of a technological nature to be authorized through the Department of Science and Art. There was an instant rush of authorizations, after which the nineties saw a steady growth in this type of practical training.

In the 1914 war the Board of Education went much farther than it had done before when it introduced training courses for munition workers, which eventually were in much demand. After the war there was the growth of the London Trades Schools which were strictly vocational in aim. At the same time and more particularly in the provinces, the Junior Technical Schools had a broader-based curriculum, but were usually expected to supply pupils with some vocational attainments.

Since 1945 there has been a great increase in Day Release from industry. This has covered all levels of workers; there are both apprentices, who very often receive vocational training at Technical Schools during their day's release, and also a growing number of operatives. For the latter group, however, the curriculum is usually of a liberal nature, though some relevant vocational element is retained. It is only on such terms that employers will release their workers.

It should be noticed that there was a demand for practical attainments at all levels of the labour force throughout the period. From 1864 to 1868 the Schools Inquiry Commission (Taunton) sat to investigate provision of what would now be called secondary education. *The Economist* headed the review of its findings 'The Middle Class Schools Commission'[3] and pointed out that a good academic education had a vocational relevance. In the same year the chairman of the trustees of Owens College, Manchester wrote to *The Economist* stressing that there was a need for scientific education for directors as well as artisans.[4]

This middle-class demand for useful attainments at the higher levels of education found expression in the growth of the civic universities during the last part of the nineteenth century. Thus we find Firth College, Sheffield, endowed by the steelmasters and supplying training to metallurgists. In 1901 an H.M.I. (Northern Division) quoted the following from a newspaper, 'The most

---

[1] *The Economist* (7 November 1868), p. 1273.
[2] *R.C. on T.I.*, Vol. III (1884), pp. 645–53, especially Nos. 5 and 9.
[3] *The Economist* (14 March 1868), pp. 292–4.
[4] Ibid. (8 February 1868), p. 153.

pressing problem now, even in the interests of the rank and file of industry, is the education of the prospective captains of industry.'[1] Magnus, writing in 1903, stressed that such education was an essential link in communicating pure scientific discoveries to industry.[2] Since the 1920s, at first slowly, industry itself has begun to provide managerial education, and since 1945 no large company without training schemes of this sort could hope to recruit men of a good quality.

One of the remarkable things about the demand for technical education over the last century has been the constant emphasis that it should be in principles, not in practice. The examinations of the Department of Science and Art on the whole were in pure, not applied, science. In the 1860s and 1870s technical instruction really meant pure scientific instruction, as can be seen from the fact that both the Select Committee of 1868 and the Royal (Devonshire) Commission of 1870-5 were appointed to enquire into 'Scientific Instruction'.[3] In 1879 the Executive Committee that helped to start the City and Guilds Institute reported that 'it would be unwise to establish any place for teaching the actual carrying out of the different trades', but they advised giving 'the knowledge of the scientific and artistic principles upon which the particular manufacture may depend.'[4] It is worth notice too that the 1889 Technical Instruction Act was to aid 'instruction in the principles of Science and Art applicable to industry', though it also made possible the teaching of practice.

This demand for principles extended backwards to the newly developing system of secondary schools. Several of the members of the Royal Commission on Technical Instruction were practical men of business, yet they laid emphasis on a broadly based secondary education as the best grounding for industrial managers. In 1894 Organized Science Schools were required to make provision for 'a good general education'. Under Morant at the Board of Education this influence was strengthened by the 1904 Secondary School Regulations.

Michael Sadler writing in 1903 emphasized this point: 'A well-planned course of liberal secondary education, lasting up to 16 years at least, has been found elsewhere to be the best preparation for technical training and for the practical tasks of business life.' He quotes a Sheffield engineer as demanding mathematics, English, French, 'general notions of science', drawing, geography, and Latin.[5] But this breadth was not only wanted in schools.

There can . . . be little doubt that the general trend of recent educational policy has been to emphasize two important ideas: (i) that vocational instruction must be based on a foundation of general education, (ii) that this vocational

[1] B. of E. Rep. (1901), Vol. II, pp. 285-6.
[2] Sir Philip Magnus, Educational Aims and Efforts (London, 1910), pp. 267-8.
[3] For some discussion on the contemporary definitions of technical education, see the author's 'The Definition of Technical Education: 1860-1910', Vocational Aspect, (May 1964). (Included in this Reader, Part One, No. 5.)
[4] Quoted by C. T. Millis, op. cit., p. 56.
[5] M. E. Sadler, Report on Secondary and Higher Education, Sheffield Education Committee (1903), pp. 5 and 17.

work should as far as possible include instruction in the scientific principles on which industrial processes are based.[1]

This was written in 1918. Millis writing of the principles of good technical education in 1925 stressed the same point.[2] In 1944 a Joint Committee of the Association of Technical Institutes and of Principals of Technical Institutes pleaded that 'the curriculum of the secondary technical schools should be as liberal in conception and treatment as that of the secondary grammar school'.[3]

It is of interest to speculate why practical businessmen while throughout the period stressing the importance of workshop training should yet have considered organized technical education as instruction in principles. In 1877 Siemens proclaimed, 'Let technical schools confine themselves to teaching those natural sciences which bear upon practice; but let practice itself be taught in the workshop . . .'[4] In the last part of the nineteenth century various reasons were given for this. Thus, technical schools lacked or could not afford adequate machinery, or it was not up-to-date. The workshop was the best place to learn – a common belief. The need for keeping processes secret was also mentioned. The tenets of *laissez-faire* doctrine in the 1860s and 1870s demanded that no help be given to particular trades, though by then there was realization that some aid could be given to industry in general. In the field of technical education this implied that instruction in the general principles of chemistry might be given, but that to teach the technology of dyestuffs was a hidden subsidy to the textile industry. More recently and especially since 1945 a common reason given is that education must ensure flexibility in a rapidly changing era and that early specialization will not achieve this. 'Early' here can mean up to first degree standard. It can be seen that a demand constant throughout the period has been backed by different reasons at different dates.

A demand for education of an economic nature which has been found throughout the century has been to assist in safety measures. In 1874 Robert Applegarth, the trade unionist, giving evidence before the Devonshire Commission, compared accident rates on the continent and in England and went on to refer to the need for technical education.[5] The Master Cutler, speaking before the Samuelson Commission, said accidents were common, 'many of these are caused from the workman's ignorance of weights and want of knowledge of that description'.[6] In 1950 at the British Iron and Steel Trades Training Conference Professor Dent quoted a firm whose accident rate had dropped as a result of Day Release, and in the same conference a delegate told how his firm was now supplying training

[1] *Report of the Prime Minister's Committee on Natural Science* (1918), p. 40.
[2] C. T. Millis, op. cit., p. 134.
[3] Quoted O. Banks, *Parity and Prestige in English Secondary Education* (London, 1955), p. 156.
[4] *Journal of the Iron and Steel Institute*, Vol. I (1877), pp. 8–9, Siemens' Presidential Address.
[5] *R.C. on S.I.* (1872), Q. 1970.
[6] *R.C. on T.I.* (1884), Q. 7765.

courses for workers with the result that accidents were fewer and less damage was done to plant.[1]

Throughout the period one form of industrial training has been in constant demand, namely apprenticeship. In the eighties opinion had it that the apprenticeship system had broken down. In the debate which led to the appointment of the Samuelson Commission this is mentioned by several members, including A. J. Mundella, the Nottingham hosiery manufacturer, who was then Vice-President of the Education Department.[2] Samuelson himself was keen on the apprenticeship system and, according to Magnus, in editing the Royal Commission's Report brought into 'prominence the advantages of the apprenticeship system and workshop training, wherever any of us ascribed, in his opinion, too much influence to technical instruction'.[3] By 1908 Sadler could say that apprenticeship was 'practically a dead letter'.[4] The 1914 war did not improve the position, so that in the 1920s the Ministry of Labour instituted a full-scale enquiry into the subject.

Since 1945, however, apprenticeship seems to have taken a new life, and, although the demand for craftsmen is much reduced, yet employers expect them to be supplied in the traditional way. But a new function has been given the system in training higher grades of skilled labour. 'The apprenticeship system now embraces future technicians and technologists, even some scientists, and various managerial specialists.'[5] It is almost as if employers are transferring their demands that the apprenticeship system function as a training mechanism and now require its aid in sorting out the labour force, that is in the mobility function.

The demand for technical education to assist in the mobility function has been constant throughout the last century. The Select Committee of 1868 in its conclusions stated that the acquisition of scientific knowledge was 'only one of the elements of industrial education and industrial progress' and mentioned also the 'enlarging of the area from which the foremen and managers may be drawn'.[6] They backed this with evidence from a Birmingham glass and chemicals manufacturer; there is mention of the same purpose by a Yorkshire ironmaster.[7] Magnus put forward the same view in evidence before the Cross Commission, 'Higher instruction would facilitate the selection of foremen from the mass of workmen.'[8] This demand did not only come from the employer but also from the worker. In the mid-eighties Millis began teaching in Technical Institutes and in commenting on the students who took Science and Art classes mentioned that

[1] *Report of 3rd Training Conference*, B.I.S.F. (London, 1950), pp. 37 and 43.
[2] *Hansard*, 3rd series, Vol. 260, cols 528 (Anderson) and 538 (Mundella).
[3] P. Magnus, op. cit., p. 93.
[4] M. E. Sadler, *Continuation Schools in England and Elsewhere* (Manchester, 1908), 2nd edn, p. 382.
[5] K. Liepmann, *Apprenticeship* (London, 1960), p. 20.
[6] *Select Committee on Scientific Instruction* (1868), p. iii.
[7] Idem, Qs. 4920 (J. Kitson of Leeds) and 6635 (J. Chance of Birmingham).
[8] *R.C. on Elementary Education Acts, England and Wales, 2nd Report* (1887), Q. 28,747.

they were mainly more skilled workmen in Engineering and Building Trades who hoped to qualify for better positions.[1]

Since 1945 the same point has been made, sometimes with the rider that no talent must be allowed to go to waste in this competitive age. Thus a speaker at an Iron and Steel Industry Conference in 1949 spoke of 'the importance of sifting the material' for best placing and for the future, by which was meant the future needs for foremen.[2] Again Liepmann writes, 'There are firms with a high proportion of semi-skilled workers: the apprentices they train are intended to provide foremen for the semi-skilled departments in addition to craftsmen working on the shopfloor.'[3]

Finally, there has been a constant demand for education to serve the political function of preserving social discipline. This ultimately assists the employer in the field of labour relations and in productivity. Professor Judges quotes Mr William Williams, M.P., who told the House in 1846 after the Rebecca riots that 'an ill-educated and undisciplined population, like that existing among the miners in South Wales, is one that may be found most dangerous to the neighbourhood in which it dwells, and that a band of efficient schoolmasters is kept up at a much less expense than a body of police or soldiery'.[4] In 1866 Ruskin speaking to an audience of Bradford businessmen of their ideal mill said, 'In this mill are to be in constant employment from eight hundred to a thousand workers, who never drink, never strike, always go to church on Sundays and always express themselves in respectful language.'[5] Many witnesses before the commissions of the late nineteenth century speak of education as improving either 'social habits' (usually thinking of drunkenness) or 'the spirit of reasonableness' (usually thinking of strikes).

During the middle of the 1914 war there was much unrest in industry, and Lloyd George set up a Commission of Enquiry into Social Unrest in the summer of 1917. The reports of both the Welsh and Scottish Divisions spoke of the help education, more particularly adult education, could give in removing the basic causes of such social difficulties. In 1925 Millis was demanding that 'employers take a keener interest in the training of their young workpeople and recognize the value of education in the Institutes in promoting the moral and intellectual welfare of their young workers'.[6] Since 1945 some have seen Day Release as a way of promoting this purpose. A spokesman from one of the largest British iron and steel companies said in 1949 that their young workers 'had been taught discipline at the county college'.[7]

---

[1] C. T. Millis, op. cit., p. 30.
[2] *Report of 1st Training Conference*, B.I.S.F. (London, 1949), p. 19.
[3] K. Liepmann, op. cit., p. 63.
[4] A. V. Judges, 'Education in a Changing Society', in *Yearbook of Education* (London, 1950), p. 132.
[5] J. Ruskin, *The Crown of Wild Olive* (1886), G. Allen (ed.) (London, 1916), p. 106.
[6] C. T. Millis, op. cit., p. 121.
[7] *Report of 1st Training Conference*, B.I.S.F. (London, 1949), p. 22.

III

Throughout the last century these demands for technical education have met constant opposition (or negative demands). One of the main hindrances to the development of technical education has been the low regard in which industry was held. In 1862 Ruskin gave some indication of this when he wrote

> the tact, foresight, decision, and other mental powers, required for the successful management of a large mercantile concern, if not such as could be compared with those of a great lawyer, general, or divine, would at least match the general conditions of mind required in the subordinate officers of a ship, or of a regiment, or in the curate of a country parish.[1]

In 1872 in evidence to the Royal Commission on Scientific Instruction the Principal of Owens College said that the 'great branches of manufacturing industry which rest, in a greater or lesser degree, on a scientific basis, have been (as was to be expected) much more slowly recognized as liberal professions in England than on the Continent'.[2] This low status was shared by science. Matthew Arnold wrote that 'our great intellectual fault' was 'indisposition' to 'science' and 'systematic thought'. 'The result is that we have to meet the calls of a modern epoch . . . with the idea of science absent from the whole course and design of our education.'[3] Ten years later the Royal Commission on Technical Instruction recommended the establishing of secondary schools in large towns which were to teach no classics and more mathematics and science; Magnus comments that this was 'then regarded as the very radical opinion' and 'essentially revolutionary'.[4]

The low status accorded to science and industry was diagnosed as the main cause of the slow application of advances in pure or applied science to industry. In 1917 one writer commented that 'during the past fifty years hardly any English public man of affairs possessing any knowledge of scientific principles has arisen, and no Government Department having the faintest interest in scientific industry has existed'.[5] That this is still a difficulty can be seen by the following extract written in 1950, 'it is a common belief in this country that a career in applied science or industry is in some way inferior to that of other professions'.[6] It is often claimed that this low status steers able boys away from industry and

---

[1] J. Ruskin, *Unto This Last* (1862), G. Allen (ed.) (London, 1910), p. 28.
[2] *R.C. on S.I.*, 1872, Q. 7283.
[3] M. Arnold, *Higher Schools and Universities in Germany*, 2nd edn. (London, 1874), p. 207, and pp. 217–19.
[4] P. Magnus, op. cit., p. 28.
[5] W. J. Pope (Prof. of Chemistry, Cambridge) in *Science and the Nation*, A. C. Seward (ed.) (Cambridge, 1917), p. 11.
[6] Sir Ewart Smith, 'The Critical Importance of Higher Technological Education in relation to Productivity', *The Advancement of Science*, Vol. VII, No. 27 (December 1950), p. 305.

applied science into arts and pure science.[1] The very persistence of this claim shows that the status of applied science, industry, and thus of technical education, remains low.

The distrust for the theoretical had a paradoxical result. Though the demand for technical education was for principles, yet there was still an intense and persistent demand for practical men. In 1868 a Leeds ironmaster reported that he did 'not know of a single manager of ironworks in Yorkshire who understands the simple elements of chemistry'.[2] He had himself brought a man from France to manage his works. That his course was not followed by many must have been due to this distrust. The same spirit can be seen in a Board of Trade witness to the Devonshire Commission, 'No experiments that any scientific persons can make are equal in number or importance to those which a practical trade or business makes for itself.'[3] In 1881 it was said of one of the greatest of steelmasters, Menelaus, the manager of Dowlais, 'He made the best guess he could as to the strength there should be, then multiplied by four and the things never broke.'[4] Menelaus himself was, however, pained by the weight of his creations.

This attitude did not alter much with the turn of the century, and in 1909 the Board of Education could say, 'There still exists amongst the generality of employers a strong preference for the man trained from an early age in the works, and a prejudice against the so-called "college-trained man",'[5] though they did think this a dying view. Yet in discussing the period from 1905 to the early thirties a recent survey of a large steel company says 'that it is probable that the vast majority (of departmental managers and their immediate assistants) continued to be promoted from the works, and that their qualifications were limited to the experience which they gained on various jobs within the firm'.[6] In 1927 the Balfour Committee on Industry and Trade had already criticized the Iron and Steel Industry for its small number of technically trained men.

As late as 1949 a director of one of our largest steel works could say, 'There is a lurking fear in many manufacturers' minds that these highly qualified men with certificates, degrees and diplomas, are "booksie" boys, very high falutin', and with not a vestige of a foot on terra firma.'[7] In case it should be thought that this evidence only covers one industry, a recently published Pelican book by a successful British industrialist contains these words, 'The British . . . have a profound and well-tested respect for the "practical man", and a distrust for what

---

[1] For a recent investigation of this problem, see *Technology and the Sixth Form Boy*, Oxford Dept. of Education, (1963), especially pp. 14–16.

[2] *R.C. on S.I.* (1868), Q. 4997 (J. Kitson).

[3] *R.C. on S.I.*, Vol. II (1874), Q. 12,637.

[4] *Journal of the Iron and Steel Institute*, Vol. I (1881), p. 161.

[5] *Board of Education Report* (1908–9), p. 90.

[6] W. H. Scott and others, *Technical Change and Industrial Relations* (Liverpool, 1956), p. 72.

[7] *Report on 1st Training Conference*, B.I.S.F. (London, 1949), pp. 39–40.

seems over-logical or smacking of theory.'[1] This desire for practical men from his own workshop has not made the British employer over-keen to call on the services supplied by technical education.

A further restraint has been the constant desire for secrecy. In 1872 the Royal Society of Arts founded the first strictly technological examinations. Students did not come forward due to fear by employers of losing trade secrets. For the same reason when Lt. Col. J. F. D. Donnelly from the Science and Art Department (in 1874 to become its Director of Science) travelled through the North to aid this scheme, manufacturers said that they would do all possible to stop it. Opposition to the creation of the City and Guilds was expressed on similar grounds by a member of the founding committee.[2] One of the reasons given for lack of support to Sheffield Technical College was fear of losing trade secrets. In the early nineties Professor Arnold, the metallurgist of Sheffield University, was allowed to visit all local works, but, as part of his conditions of service, was under an interdict that he would not write a textbook. In this case it was not only that the manufacturers of Sheffield did not want their English rivals to know their processes, but they were also afraid of imitation by the Germans and Americans.[3]

It was, however, not just in Sheffield nor in the steel industry alone that secrecy was a hindrance. The Senior Science and Art Inspector in the N.W. Division wrote in 1895, 'In some instances manufacturers are perfectly antagonistic, as they say that they are afraid of trade secrets being revealed.'[4] In 1901 the Senior H.M.I. for the N. Division wrote of the lack of demand for the trained man, 'He might, if employed, become familiar with the trade processes peculiar to his employers and, having improved upon them, might sell his information to rival firms in the neighbourhood.'[5] Yet it is remarkable that in an article on training in small steel firms written in 1952 the same point is again made, 'the secrecy which surrounds certain techniques in some corners of industry will still deter some from backing free interchange'.[6] It may perhaps be objected that trade secrecy is economically justifiable. What is important for this analysis is that such secrecy has been found to correlate directly with unprogressive firms who have a low interest in science and hence little demand for technical education.[7]

Very little support has come from Trade Unions for technical education. In evidence before the Devonshire Commission in 1872 Applegarth told what the

[1] Sir F. Hooper, *Management Survey* (London, 1960), p. 14. On this point, see J. Wellens, 'The Anti-Intellectual Tradition in the West', *B.J.E.S.* (November 1959). (Included in this Reader, Part One, No. 4.)

[2] *R.C. on T.I.* (1884), Q. 4410 (evidence of representatives of City and Guilds).

[3] *Final Report of Departmental Committee on the Royal College of Science, etc.*, Vol. II (1906), Qs. 1954–8 (J. Arnold).

[4] *Report of Department of Science and Art* (1895), p. 29.

[5] *Board of Education Report*, Vol. II (1901), p. 285.

[6] 'Training in the Smaller Steel Firms: II', *T.E.S.* (4 April 1952), p. 289.

[7] C. F. Carter and B. R. Williams, *Industry and Technical Progress* (London, 1957), p. 179.

Amalgamated Society of Woodworkers, his own union, was doing for technical education, but knew of no other union doing anything, not even the engineers.[1] It is important to appreciate that only craft unions existed at this time and that even by 1914 the General unions were not really developed as today.

In 1887 Hart Dyke, speaking on the abortive Technical Instruction Bill, said that the working class were determined that, whatever else it might be, the bill was not going to be 'a trade-teaching Bill'. In the nineties Magnus gave frequent addresses 'to trade unions which, at that time, were by no means active supporters of technical education'.[2] Sadler in 1908 wrote, 'The Trade Union Movement, as such, has had until late years no direct connection with educational movements'. He gave as the reason for this that their main objects had been very definite, namely work for status and wages.[3]

The unions might perhaps have been expected to realize the educational implications of apprenticeship. In 1927, however, the Balfour Committee pointed out that whatever interest the Unions took in apprenticeship was with regard to such matters as age of entry, wages and ratios of apprentices to journeymen.[4] This is the crux of the matter. The unions traditionally have viewed their responsibility with regard to apprentices as merely controlling the supply of that particular type of skill, since in this way the level of wages could be influenced.

In the steel industry training at operative level has traditionally been by experience and promotion by seniority. The attempt since the war to introduce a nationwide Junior Operative training scheme and make promotion dependent upon success in a City and Guilds' examination has met with opposition from the Unions. Thus in 1950 a discussion group at a training conference stressed 'that . . . the Trade Unions too should be educated into helping and not hindering the promotion of keen young workers'.[5] As Liepmann said in 1960, 'Trade unions have by no means been a driving force in the development of technical education for apprentices.'[6]

Finally, there has been the constant pressure to spend less on education throughout the period. In an era when the ideals of Gladstonian finance were still strong Hart Dyke argued for the Technical Instruction Bill in 1887 by quoting costs of training per head per annum calculated to the last penny.[7] This too was the era of Payment by Result and Robert Lowe.

One of the difficulties in gaining the acceptance of Engineering in the universities was the great cost of apparatus. The Royal School of Mines, later part of Imperial College, was always short of funds to equip itself with metallurgical

[1] R.C. on S.I. (1872), Qs. 2007–8.
[2] P. Magnus, op. cit., p. 111.
[3] M. E. Sadler, Continuation Schools, pp. 371–2.
[4] Factors in Industrial and Commercial Efficiency, Vol. I (1927), p. 147.
[5] Report of 3rd Training Conference, B.I.S.F. (London, 1950), p. 43.
[6] K. Liepmann, op. cit., p. 155.
[7] Hansard, 3rd series, Vol. 318, col. 1823.

machinery and was much criticized because what plant it had was on so small a scale as to be unrealistic.

In the inter-war years education suffered cuts in allocations after the Geddes Committee of 1922 and the May Committee of 1931. Since 1945 education has rarely had a high priority when cuts in the capital investment programme have been necessary. The fate of the county colleges envisaged in the 1944 Act is a further example of the way this force has affected the education of young workers. Demand for education, like other economic commodities, to be effective must be backed by money.

IV

This study of the constituents in the demand for technical education which have remained constant over the last century can best be concluded by quoting a recent writer (1958):

> Despite the long history of pressures to encourage the greater use of science in industry in Britain, contemporary writers still normally write on this with the freshness of discovery, not the burden of repetition, or surprise at this type of continuity. It might be more fruitful if more effort was made to assimilate the long historical retrospect.[1]

[1] D. L. Burn (ed.), *The Structure of British Industry*, Vol. II (London, 1958), pp. 438–9, fn. 4.

4 The Evolving Economics of Pre-Industrial Apprenticeship[1]

M. J. BOWMAN

Under serfdom the labour of children was 'contracted out' between villein and lord, and the sons of the villeins were placed to work in 'manufactures'. This practice grew, especially in the towns. It was common among the London guilds by 1300, it prevailed in most towns by the mid-fifteenth century, and was made national by statute in 1562. Contractual apprenticeship had developed from a private custom to a public institution. Initially only one of the ways of gaining entry to a guild or obtaining the freedom of a borough, by the mid-sixteenth century it had become the usual way to both. Meanwhile, entry was becoming more restricted; the poor and the servile were largely excluded from the preferred occupations. Thus apprenticeship became both a pervasive training agency and a device for rationing access to preferred occupations and to rights of fuller civic participation. The training included personal habits and morality as well as skills, and the system was even regarded as a strategy of birth control.

This complexity of functions shows up clearly in the 1562 act and the 1601 poor law. The statute required a term of seven years training and forbade practice before the age of 24; the restriction on marriage and various other London guild rules were adopted nationally. A special clause reserved the wealthiest trades to sons of propertied persons. Farmers with half a tilled ploughland might take apprentices and compel service from artisans and labourers during harvests, and writs could be required of servants before moving. (Note the numerous parallels to Soviet policies of a few years ago.) The poor law of 1601 reaffirmed earlier statutes permitting compulsory apprenticing of pauper children, and stipulated long terms; most of these were only pseudo-apprenticeships in which little skill

---

[1] For its historical evidence this section relies wholly upon O. J. Dunlop, *English Apprenticeship and Child Labour: A History* (Unwin, London, 1912). Since what is included here is telescoped from an entire book and is the mere bones of what recurs on many pages, no specific citations are given. Except as explicitly attributed to Dunlop, the interpretations are mine.

First printed as pp. 106–9 of Chapter 6, 'From Guilds to Infant Training Industries', in Education and Economic Development, *C. A. Anderson and M. J. Bowman (eds.) (Cass, London, 1966).*

was learned. Their aim was to insure that poor children contributed to their own support, to restrict vagrancy, and to improve the morals of the 'degraded' classes. In an age when education was not yet a mass aspiration and there were few free schools, there was undoubtedly an essentially moral basis for these provisions, in addition to their convenience as a method of poor relief, but the outcome was extensive exploitation of child labour.

To assess adequately how far early apprenticeship contributed to social and economic mobility and how far it restrained mobility would require a better historian. The age believed in status, but it was not monolithic on this issue. Beginning as early as 1437, a series of acts tried to bring guild rules under scrutiny and approval in order to prevent monopoly. The steady stream of complaints about evasion suggests that mobility exceeded what the sponsors of the regulations anticipated. Meanwhile, restrictions were coming to be 'justified' on grounds of raising and controlling quality; in this the guilds received support from a government that believed expansion of sales depended upon raising quality rather than reducing prices. This was not inconsistent with sumptuary legislation, since policy focused on foreign sales. Dunlop cites five methods used in the sixteenth century to preserve and promote industrial skills: (1) specialization, enforced by prohibiting intrusion into other crafts; (2) detailed stipulations of standards; (3) requirement of apprenticeship for practice of a craft; (4) use of marks on work done; and (5) powers of search for guild masters within cities and for Crown officers elsewhere.[1]

The stirrings that had been reflected in the mixture of mobility and restriction in apprenticeship were but part of the broader currents that led to the Civil War (1660); the war brought disorganization and weakened the guilds. There had earlier been attrition of many regulations, accompanied by weakening belief in minute regulation of trade. Then in 1669 the courts ruled that the apprenticeship act applied only in the towns. But for some years the guilds became increasingly exclusive; consequently evasions multiplied and the courts progressively withdrew their support. Practice and training in crafts grew outside the towns, free of guild rules; the hold of masters over apprentices weakened. Apprenticeship was inching towards the freedom and flexibility of modern times. When, in 1756, a guild sued a man for trading without having been an apprentice, the court ruled that every man had a natural and legal right to exercise whatever trade he pleased. Before the end of the eighteenth century the guild system had largely broken down, less because of factories themselves than because of the growing spirit of capitalist commercialism and the pre-factory victory of freedom over regulation. Picking up the thread at this point, Smelser demonstrates how factories completed the transformation – almost.[2] But this is a later time, to be referred to below.

[1] Dunlop, op. cit., Chap. 3.
[2] Neil J. Smelser, *Social Change in the Industrial Revolution* (University of Chicago Press, Chicago, 1959).

Apprenticeship was an institution for the formation of skills, and we may gain considerable insight by viewing it as 'investment in human capital'. This view is obviously appropriate for the era in which apprenticeship entailed onerous servitude, albeit for only a seven-year term. Apprentices were indeed treated as property from the early sixteenth century, and their services could be sold by the master (though this came to be subject to a tax and approval of the guild). At an early date the guilds found it necessary to introduce regulations to prevent pirating.

The seven-year contract enabled the master to reap a rich reward from the outlays for maintenance and training he made during the earlier part of the term, but he wanted to protect this investment. So long as he could do so, apprentices were in demand, and the boy did not have to pay directly for his training; rather sold himself into indenture. As this firm grip on the apprentice weakened, the market changed. By the early seventeenth century a complex system of premium payments had emerged. These were scaled according to both the father's trade and status and the standing of the trade to which a boy was apprenticed. (It should be remembered that apprenticeship was not restricted to manual occupations.) Lower-status fathers paid premiums to get their sons into better occupations. This practice of paying premiums continued to spread, though it was never part of formal guild policy. By the end of the seventeenth century it was common in London and Manchester, and the sums required were growing. By the eighteenth century, premiums might run to several hundred pounds, and now better (or more alert) families paid higher fees to place their sons with the better masters. Meanwhile, the amount of genuine training under apprenticeship had increased, the more extreme forms of exploitation by masters were curbed, and the security of the master's investment had sharply declined. Accordingly there was a change in the way in which the apprentice paid, for he had always paid.

My reading of this chapter in economic history suggests several points that may be relevant for less-developed countries today. But let me first summarize. The groundwork for English economic development was laid not by a free, wide-open system but by one embracing rigid controls, including compulsory training and consequent compulsion in choice of vocation. The system fostered limited mobility from rural areas to towns, but only when a stable, job-training place was available. (Others escaped the meshes in the legal net and drifted townward, though in moderate numbers.) Geographic and occupational mobility expanded with the widening market economy. Apprenticeship was not only training in manual skills; it provided participant education on a broad front. This no doubt fostered ingenuity. It also gave apprentices from lower levels of society an introduction to the ways of living of their betters.[1] Meanwhile, the whole system

[1] We might draw parallels here with the 'apprenticeships' of the household domestics in contrast to the field hands in the American ante-bellum South, as with the learning of the African 'boy' in the colonies and ex-colonies of that continent. Further from this, and yet related, is part of the rationale of the secondary boarding school in Africa, as a total environment.

provided the capital for investment in training by contracts based upon private returns, but – and this is important – these arrangements were enforced first by monopolistic groups and then also by the state.

Today developing countries face a very different world. Usually human freedoms are supposed to be respected and no one may sell himself into indenture. (However, indenture is used for some rare skills, such as teaching. And there was a legitimatized alternative for doing this more broadly inherent in Stalinist patterns of industrialization, which in practice amounted to widespread slavery to the state.) In the less industrialized economies there is still a large subsistence sector, but migration to towns is largely uncontrolled. In contrast to sixteenth- and seventeenth-century England, training does not follow in the wake of the demand for skills. Instead many countries today are trying to create skills in a massive way in the hope that these supplies will generate their own demand. They are trying to do this with little in the way of participant observation, either at home or with a master. Add the greater speed of change today, and the facts that many countries are in a hurry and would jump several centuries, that the artisan is likely to have a small place in these new economies, that an immense cultural leap must be made by the masses, and we begin to appreciate the task the schools are being asked to shoulder.

5 The Influence of Religion on Educational Policy, 1902–1944

C. CANNON

The popularly phrased 'decline of religion' which has accompanied the growth of industrialized Britain, is a far from simple phenomenon. Religion is a source of norms and values, but on the other hand its rites may continue to be practised because they retain social significance without religious meaning. There are also religious institutions, and these are interrelated with secular institutions in such a way that a considerable amount of religious influence may be discovered at the institutional level in an apparently secular society. During a period of rapid social change, accompanying changes in the role of religion in society can only be clarified by taking into account all these elements, and paying particular attention to the relationship between religious and secular institutions.

The aim of this article is to stress one aspect of this relationship, by showing how the influence on education has been maintained, and in some ways increased, during the twentieth century, in a period of steady decline in popular support for the churches.

But this dichotomy in itself is too simple, for the decline in religious support has not been a unified one. Some forms of religious behaviour have become minimally practised while others are still widespread; also, measures of religious behaviour must not necessarily be taken as measures of religious beliefs, which are much less susceptible to sociological analysis. Similarly, the relationship between religion and education is of several kinds. First, there is the policy making relationship, involving analysis of the religious pressures behind legislative action; second, there is the existence of both religious and secular educational institutions; and third, there is the influence of religion in the schools themselves.

It is at the first level that religion has retained the greatest influence, though the nature of this influence has altered since the beginning of the century as a result of a shift in majority religious policy[1] towards the diffusion of influence

[1] The exception to this is the Catholics' policy for separate denominational schools, which has changed very little since the nineteenth century.

First printed in British Journal of Educational Studies, *Vol. XII, No. 2 (May 1964),* pp. 143–60.

throughout the state system rather than the retention of separate schools. This change is the churches' adaptation to the growth of the secular system; it may be interpreted as the reaction of a long-standing institution to a newly expanding one which presents a threat to one of its customary functions.

The change in religious policy is obviously related to changes at the institutional level, where the proportion of religious schools has dwindled steadily since 1900 [1] in spite of increasing government aid. This decline has to some extent been counter-balanced by the increasing penetration of religion in the state schools, but finally the success of the churches in the realm of policy depends on its interpretation by the teachers to the children. As the teachers are products of a secular society there exists a difference between the legal norms expressed in the 1944 Act and the situation in the schools. A Marxist analysis, in terms of the imposition of an ideology by the governing classes, is not apt in an industrial democracy because there are so many sources of values and conflicting interest groups. A minimum condition of success would be ideological control of those who interpret religious policy; [2] but even in such a case, the teacher of religion or the religious school would have to counter the whole force of secular influence in the rest of society. Thus, during the 1944 Act debates, several speakers expressed misgivings as to the convictions of the teachers who would have to operate it, and the investigations in 1954 [3] into the working of the Act suggested that its operation in the schools did not fulfil the expectations with which it was framed.

The present aim is to demonstrate the continuation of religious influence at the first level – that of legislative action – since the beginning of the century. This can be shown by a comparison of the religious provisions of the two major Education Acts in 1902 and 1944, and a content analysis of the Parliamentary debates on the two acts, which reveals the continued religious preoccupations of the speakers in 1944, in spite of the very different social and political context in which the debate was conducted.

A comparison of the religious provisions of the 1902 and 1944 Education Acts

During the debates on the 1944 Education Bill, Mr Ede, the Parliamentary Secretary, claims that denominational schools will be in a better position as a result

---

[1] Number of Public Elementary and Voluntary Recognized Schools, England and Wales.

	Public elementary	Voluntary recognized
1903	6,145	14,082
1938	10,363	10,553

from Board of Education Statistics of Public Education General Tables.

[2] This is what church school managers demand when they ask for control of the appointment of teachers of religion.

[3] *Religion in Schools.* Report of an Enquiry into the working of the 1944 Act. Research Committee of the Institute of Christian Education, S.P.C.K. (1954).

of it than after the 1902 Act.[1] A comparison of the religious provisions of the two acts supports this claim. In a period of forty-two years, during which it is possible to document a steady decline in religious influence in general, religion has become an integral part of the educational system. This happens in two ways: the position of the voluntary schools is more firmly established, and religious influence is given a statutory place in the state educational system.

I. THE POSITION OF THE VOLUNTARY SCHOOLS

The financial aid granted by the government is more generous in 1944. In 1902, the managers of voluntary schools were responsible for the provision of schools and for all alterations and repairs, except those due to 'wear and tear'.[2] In 1944, while they still provide the building, the managers' responsibility for alterations and repairs is reduced to half the cost, and excludes entirely certain essential facilities, and repairs to the inside of the buildings.[3] In 1902 the exclusion of 'wear and tear' from the managers' liabilities caused much Nonconformist bitterness,[4] whereas in 1944 the more generous provisions were accepted with little protest in the House.

In both 1902 and 1944, the actual expansion of the voluntary system is more or less precluded by the absence of any grant towards the provision of new schools. In 1944, however, several concessions were made in this direction, largely because of pressure from High Anglican and Roman Catholic representatives; these result from continuation of a policy initiated in 1936 when the category of 'Special Agreement' Schools was established. These schools formed a new category, half-way between voluntary and state schools: they submitted to more public control in exchange for a 50–75 per cent grant towards the provision of new buildings for children of secondary school age, and the retention of limited facilities for denominational religious teaching. This provision was made to allow voluntary schools to undertake 'Hadow reorganization', and it is revived in the 1944 Act. A further concession is the allowance of government loans on easy terms to voluntary schools wishing to make alterations or transfer to new buildings.[5] The provisions of 50 per cent grants towards new schools made necessary

---

[1] House of Commons Debates, Vol. 396, col. 493. Mr Butler makes the same point on introducing the bill, col. 229.

[2] Part III, Clause 7(1)d, 1902 Bill.

[3] Part II, Clause 15(3), 1944 Bill.

[4] This was not only because the amendment was considered 'more loot for the Bishops', Lloyd George, Vol. 116, col. 1352, but also because it was the result of a Lords' amendment although it was strictly a financial measure and thus should not have been discussed in the House of Lords; the amendment was worded in such a way as to make it in order, with instructions to the Commons to delete certain words – see the heated discussion on the unconstitutional nature of this, in the debate on the House of Lords Amendments, Vol. 116, cols. 1366–415.

[5] Part IV, Clause 105, 1944 Bill. This clause was passed after the insertion of a safeguard against its use in 'single school' areas. A 'single school' area is one in which the only state-maintained school is a voluntary one.

by population movements or replacement of out-of-date buildings completes the
the Act's concessions to the Catholic agitation for complete state support for their
schools.

Thus in 1944 considerable assistance is given towards the provision of voluntary school buildings, under certain conditions, whereas in 1902 the managers
had in all cases to 'provide the school building free of charge'.[1]

2. RELIGIOUS INFLUENCE IN THE STATE SYSTEM

The most important increase in religious influence, however, is that the provision
of Agreed Syllabus[2] religious worship and instruction is made compulsory in
state provided schools.[3] Also, provision is made for the establishment of advisory
committees on religion by local education authorities, and for teachers to qualify
in religion as part of their training course. Efficient teaching of religion is considered more important than ease of withdrawal from the lesson, for the 'Time
Table' clause is dropped, making it possible to give a religious lesson at any
period in the day. Religious influence in the state system is further increased by
the new category of 'controlled' school, which enables a voluntary school to
transfer all its liabilities to the local authority, while retaining a minority representation on the management and facilities for a limited amount of denominational
religious education.

In 1902 the issue of compulsory religious education was raised as an amendment in the Commons and the Lords, but dropped without extensive discussion,
being considered to present too many problems of definition besides undesirable
compulsion.[4] Similar conceptions to the 'Controlled school' were also discussed
but never came near to becoming part of the Bill. But in 1944, in an irreligious
age, religious education becomes the only compulsorily provided subject in
English state schools; and denominational religion is for the first time accepted
in a category of school which is virtually a part of the state system.

3. Other clauses in the 1944 Act make legally possible the provision of religious
education of a type other than that normally given, in both voluntary and state-
provided schools;[5] the religious exclusiveness of different types of school thus
becomes of secondary importance to the need for every child to receive appropriate religious education.

Two further provisions illustrate the religious conception of education behind
the 1944 Bill. The clause that children should be educated, where possible,

[1] Part III, Clause 7(1)d, 1902 Bill. The trend described has been continued in the 1957
and 1959 Acts which increased the grant to 75 per cent and made it available for the provision of aided secondary schools to supplement existing aided primary schools.

[2] 'Agreed Syllabus' religious instruction is given according to a syllabus agreed by a
committee including representatives of the various churches.

[3] Part II, Clause 25, 1944 Bill.

[4] *Hansard*, House of Commons, Vol. 113, col. 361, and House of Lords, Vol. 116,
col. 567.

[5] Part II, Clause 25, 1944 Bill.

'according to their parents' wishes'[1] although also carrying secular implications, was inserted largely on the basis of the argument that it would ensure the right of a parent to send a child to a denominational school even if this was not the most convenient one:[2] Catholic convictions on the rights of parents over the religious education of their children carried some weight here. The other provision is the inclusion of the word 'spiritual', among the purposes of education, in the statement at the beginning of the Bill: 'and it shall be the duty of the local education authority . . . to contribute towards the spiritual, moral, mental and physical development of the community by securing that efficient education . . . shall be available'.[3] The final form of this phrase has an interesting history; it results from an amendment raised in the Lords[4] expressing the view that the inclusion of the word 'moral' does not go far enough, and is only decided upon after considering whether 'spiritual' or 'religious' is the more appropriate word. This discussion is typical of the religious preoccupations of the speakers in the Lords debates.

The increased religious influence outlined above is accompanied as might be expected, by a certain increase in public control over the voluntary system, but this increase does not satisfy the principle of 'public control proportionate to state aid', which in 1902 was the chief issue upon which the Nonconformist opposition attacked the Bill; for instance the new controlled schools abrogated all financial responsibilities while retaining some religious independence and representation on the board of managers.[5]

All other arrangements for dual control remain, with minor concessions, substantially the same in both Acts.

This comparison of the two Acts shows that financial assistance to voluntary schools is considerably increased in 1944, and there is less, rather than greater, unity of control since two intermediate categories of school are established; in particular, the voluntary schools are safeguarded against disappearance by the 'controlled school', which does away with the need for impecunious managers to transfer their schools entirely to the state system, and thus lose all religious interest. The 1944 Act was passed in a far more 'secular' period than the 1902 Act; and yet its provisions, when compared point for point, are more favourable to the religious interest; and it established, for the first time, the legal obligation of every state school in this country to provide a religious education.

[1] Part IV, Clause 76, 1944 Bill.
[2] House of Lords Debates, Vol. 132, col. 864.
[3] Part II, Clause 7, 1944 Bill.
[4] House of Lords Debates, Vol. 132, cols 271 and 773.
[5] Part II, Clause 30, 1944 Bill.

A comparison of the opinions on religion expressed during the passage of the 1902 and 1944 Education Acts

Not only are the religious provisions of the 1944 Act favourable, but a great deal of time is taken in discussion of the religious clauses, in comparison with the important secular innovations also before the House. There is however a change in the emphasis of these discussions which illustrates the determination of the denominations to sink their differences as far as possible in the interests of the religious influence in general.

I. FROM SECTARIANISM TO RELIGIOUS AGREEMENT

The 1902 Education Bill took up more parliamentary time than any bill previously before the House;[1] during its passage it was held up chiefly by Opposition attempts to reject it or alter its religious character by pressing many amendments to a division. The 1944 Act, on the other hand, passed smoothly and with very few amendments taken to a division.

Most of the obstructions in 1902 were caused because, as Herbert Samuel said, the Bill was 'saturated through and through with the very spirit of sectarianism'.[2] During the Committee stage the debates read like those of a theological rather than an educational Bill; in Lloyd George's words, 'for hours this House swirled round and round in the vortex of a mad frenzy of theological controversy'.[3]

The issue which caused more controversy than any other was that surrounding the 'Kenyon–Slaney' amendment. This stated that religious instruction in voluntary schools should be given according to the trust deeds if any, and under the control of the managers, and it was introduced to safeguard the schools against 'Romish practices';[4] the storm of opposition to it from the Catholics and High Anglicans reflected the current controversies over 'ritualism', and the rights of laity and clergy in the Church of England. Denominational issues also permeated the discussions on the *kind* of religious education to be taught in state schools, and the whole House of Lords debate is devoted to the securing of further Church of England concessions and is dominated by the Bishops. A final example illustrates the close link between politics and religion in 1902. Opposition speakers refer again and again to 'the bargain' made behind the scenes between the Church of England and the government. This is 'not an Education Bill, it is a Convocation Bill. It is in that nest the egg was laid, and it has been brought here for us to hatch it' (Harcourt).[5]

[1] The Committee Stage lasted thirty-eight days before the Closure Motion which brought the Report Stage to a conclusion. See House of Commons Debates, Vol. 114, cols 607–50.
[2] House of Commons Debates, Vol. 115, col. 977.
[3] House of Commons Debates, Vol. 115, col. 1118.
[4] House of Commons Debates, Vol. 113, col. 1316.
[5] House of Commons Debates, Vol. 107, col. 986. There are many other similar accusa-

By 1944 suspicion of Church of England pressure has become suspicion of 'the Churches', for religion has drawn uneasily together to defend its causes. But such suspicions are only voiced at all by a tiny minority. Mr Bevan believes that, as the tradition of compromise with religious organizations outside Parliament prevents the government accepting amendments, it is a waste of time discussing them;[1] but he is supported only by Mr Gallacher and Sir H. Williams.[2] This reduction in suspicion of ecclesiastical pressure occurs in spite of the fact that the negotiations with the Churches before and during the passage of the 1944 Bill were prolonged and intensive, and the delicate balance of interests achieved did in fact make alterations in the House less possible than in 1902.[3]

The harmony of the 1944 discussions was nicely prophesied in the course of the 1902 debates by the Secretary to the Board of Education: 'Some day we shall realize that religion is and always must be an integral part of education', and then we shall see religion 'set to education like perfect music unto noble words, and at last in the fullness of time there will descend upon our schools the blessing of peace'.[4]

The 1944 'blessing of peace' might be more accurately described as an armed truce, for many of the old sectarian issues were revived during the debates. The Catholic view, for example, remained unchanged, and occupies more time than any other issue: it is given the attention of fourteen speakers during the second reading, and wide discussion in the committee stage. The increase in concord is, however, shown in several ways, and the need to avoid controversy prefaces the remarks of ten speakers during the Commons second reading of the Bill. There are also references by Lords with long memories to the controversies of 1902 and 1906. Thus Lord Mottistone, who remembers Birrell's Bill, congratulates Mr Butler on having 'cut the gordian knot' and got 'Christians, Protestants and Nonconformists to lie down together'.[5]

2. THE MAIN THEMES OF THE 1944 DEBATES

The most noticeable result of this increase in unity is the change in the *emphasis* of the religious discussions, away from claims for the support of their own schools (except from the Catholics) and towards the introduction of religious education into all state schools. This emphasis allows the development of three related themes which are repeated in various forms throughout the passage of the

---

tions: e.g. Vol. 112, col. 189; Vol. 115, cols. 518 and 1152. Harcourt supported Education League principles.

[1] House of Commons Debates, Vol. 397, col. 1084.
[2] House of Commons Debates, Vol. 397, cols 2444–9.
[3] For an account of these negotiations which reveals the precarious nature of the religious agreement, see M. Travis *Dual System Reform in England and Wales 1941–44* (M.A. University of London, 1949).
[4] House of Commons Debates, Vol. 115, cols 1042–3.
[5] House of Lords Debates, Vol. 132, col. 155.

Bill and the educational debates which preceded it. The argument runs as follows:

(a) There has been a decline in religion in England and the world since the beginning of the century, to which can be attributed juvenile delinquency, declining morals and the present war. This decline is the result not merely of materialism, but also of past disputes among the Churches and the consequent inadequacy of religious education in the schools.

(b) In spite of this decline, Britain remains fundamentally a Christian country; the present war is seen in terms of Christian morality fighting paganism, and the hope of the future lies in this 'ingrained' Christianity of the British people being retained and fostered. Because they are basically religious, British people desire that their children should be given a religious education, even if they do not themselves attend church.

(c) It is thus possible for members to assert a large demand for religious education for young people and also to see it as a potent influence towards the raising of moral standards and the prevention of future war.

All these themes are seen in embryo in 1902, and many sentiments expressed in the two Bills could be plausibly transposed. But in 1902 the frequency of their expression is much less in relation to the length of the debate because so much time is taken up with denominational issues.

Some comparative quotations will illustrate these themes:

(a) The pagan state of the world is responsible for present evils

In 1902 Heally (R.C.) looks abroad and sees that 'these anarchist movements which have led to the assassination of the Presidents of the United States and the French Republic have been due to the expulsion of God from the schools'.[1] Materialism at home is also responsible for much. 'We see a growing love of material well-being, a growing indifference to the non-material welfare of the country' (Lord Hugh Cecil).[2]

As one would expect from its war-time setting, in 1944 the references to world paganism have increased. Thus in the Lords debate, such opinions as this are prominent: the real enemy is 'naked materialistic paganism which has reared its head in Europe to a height unknown for a thousand years, and which threatens Christendom today and with it our civilization, our homes, our people.'[3] But irreligion is also noted at home: it has been said that there 'is something like a landslide from organized religion. It is asked whether by Church standards the nation is becoming pagan.'[4] These phrases are repeated in similar forms in

[1] House of Commons Debates, Vol. 114, col. 686.
[2] House of Commons Debates, Vol. 115, col. 849. For many other assertions of the religious indifference of people and its consequences, see House of Commons Debates, Vol. 115, cols 1000 and 1270; Vol. 112, col. 1061, etc.
[3] Earl of Selborne, House of Lords Debates, col. 970. See also Lord Samuel, col. 28.
[4] Viscount Sankey, House of Lords Debates, Vol. 132, col. 85.

numerous speeches,[1] often with particular reference to the irreligion found among evacuees.

(b) Nevertheless, Britain is basically Christian, and this is shown in the demand for religious education by parents throughout the land

Most speakers are convinced of this in 1902,[2] and just as certain in 1944, the only difference being that in 1902 most speeches are couched in denominational terms. The people want religion but they want denominational or undenominational religion, according to the adherence of the speaker.

The following is typical of the 1902 attitude: 'ninety-nine out of every hundred English lay-parents preferred, or at any rate were well-satisfied that their children should receive undogmatic instruction under the Cowper Temple Clause'.[3] In contrast '. . . a large proportion of the people of the country demanded and desired to have for their children a denominational education'.[4]

The two kinds of religious education are supported by speakers who claim specially favourable results from one form or the other. For instance, Mellar in the House of Commons claims a startling moral improvement in towns where non-sectarian instruction is given. Before, the people were little better than savages, now they are industrious and law-abiding.[5] On the other hand, the Bishop of London in the Lords 'proves' the inadequacy of mere Board School religion by asserting that 80 per cent of Bethnal Green boys attend no place of worship after they leave school.[6]

In 1944, belief in the basic Christianity of the British is constantly aired in the House of Commons: 'a vast body of persons', 'millions of humble people', desire that 'Christian morality should be an integral and honoured part of the citizens' education'.[7] In spite of the much discussed religious ignorance of evacuees, Viscountess Astor states at every opportunity her conviction that Britain is 'the most Christian country in the world',[8] while Colegate thinks that 'if you would have a plebiscite of parents over 95 per cent would vote for compulsory worship'.[9]

---

[1] For example, House of Commons Debates, Vol. 396, col. 290; House of Commons Debates, Vol. 397, col. 1072; House of Lords Debates, Vol. 132, col. 190; col. 385; col. 973.

[2] Roberts, House of Commons Debates, Vol. 113, col. 371. 'The prevailing sentiment of the country was in favour of some form of religious instruction in every school.'

[3] Bryce, House of Commons Debates, Vol. 113, col. 1428.

[4] Sir Griffith Boscawen, House of Commons Debates, Vol. 111, col. 172.

[5] House of Commons Debates, Vol. 111, cols 200–1.

[6] House of Lords Debates, Vol. 116, col. 63.

[7] House of Commons Debates: Butler, Vol. 397, col. 2402. Lindsay; Vol. 396, col. 442; Ede, Vol. 396, cols 488 and 492.

[8] Vol. 397, col. 2423. She makes the same point during the debate on Educational Reconstruction. Vol. 291, col. 1965.

[9] Vol. 397, cols 2410–1.

(c) The cure for all our troubles is religious education in the schools

In 1902, as we have seen, belief in this is tempered by the belief that only *the right* kind of religious education will have the desired effects. But in 1944, speaker after speaker welcomes the introduction of non-denominational religious education and worship in state schools. Documents such as the Spens and Norwood Reports are used to buttress this view,[1] whereas the McNair Report is severely criticized by the Archbishop of Canterbury for its neglect of religious issues.[2]

The following are typical of the views expressed. 'The evils which exist in our midst could not possibly exist if the population were brought up on a religious rather than a secular basis'.[3] It is a 'revolutionary Bill . . . the answer to the secularism of the century'.[4] These are the optimistic expectations from universal religious education.

The religious tone of the 1944 education debates

Perhaps the most striking fact about the 1944 Bill is the general religious tone of the debates. In 1902 preoccupation with religious issues was inevitable because the legislation passed in 1902 really marks the transition from a mainly church-administered to a mainly state-administered system. In 1944, however, there was no such inevitability; when one considers the background of religious indiffer-ence, and the far-reaching changes in the organization of secondary education which the Bill introduced, the concentration on religious aspects is the more remarkable.[5]

This religious emphasis can be illustrated in several ways. First it is not un-expected that in 1902 nearly all the speakers in the House of Commons second reading, and all the speakers in the House of Lords, refer to religious matters. But in 1944 the proportions are not much lower. In the Commons second reading, 24 out of 31 speakers refer to religion, 18 of them substantially; in the House of Lords, 22 out of 28 speakers give a large part of their speeches to it.

It may be argued that this emphasis is the result of the apathy of non-religious members. There is some evidence of this in the small attendance at the Debate on Religion in Education in 1941, which only produced five speakers, all of whom were ardent supporters of the cause.[6] There is also a feeling that justification is needed if a speaker omits the subject of religion.[7] Nevertheless the time given to religious topics is indicative of more than lip-service; a noticeable aspect is that

---

[1] Vol. 396, col. 439.
[2] House of Lords, Vol. 132, col. 38.
[3] House of Commons, Vol. 397, col. 1157.
[4] House of Commons, Vol. 397, col. 2252.
[5] See House of Commons, Vol. 398, col. 2200, for a comment on this lack of balance in discussion.
[6] House of Commons, Vol. 376, November 1941.
[7] House of Lords, Vol. 132, col. 160.

expression of a secular or agnostic view is nearly as limited in 1944 as it is in 1902. In 1902 two speakers claimed that there should be no religious education in schools.[1] In 1944, only Mr Gallacher and Mr Bevan present the view that education has nothing to do with the next world and that therefore the Church should have nothing to do with the schools; according to them the religious clauses are 'a plot to foist religion on the state'.[2] But they receive little support for these opinions and the general impression is that those Members interested enough to speak on education are also those who are interested in religion. In fact some of the most vocal represent specific religious interests.

Of one thing there is no doubt, and that is the strong religious conviction of those who are responsible for piloting the Bill through both Houses. The religious tone of the whole Commons debate is set by Mr Butler, who gives it a central place in his opening speech, by quoting both the Prayer Book and a hymn. It is continued by Mr Ede, Parliamentary Secretary for Education, who closes the second reading with a hymn he sang in church as a child. The same spirit is shown in all the speeches of Lord Selborne, who pilots the bill through the Lords. He believes that Anglo-Saxon democracy would perish without the Christian ethic, and that unless we are brought up to be a God-fearing, practising Christian nation 'all our vaunted progress in other directions will crumble into dust'.[3]

Perhaps the focus of interest is best summed by Mr Cove's speech on the Committee stage:

> The Bill's main purpose . . . is to give answer to secularism and neutral religious opinion . . . For the first time in British history, the State comes in and decrees that there shall be in every elementary school throughout the length and breadth of the land a collective set of worship . . . 20 or 30 years ago it would have been a first-class political issue. . . . But it has been accepted and I am sure the Bill will be regarded as one which will have effected, as far as religious teaching is concerned, a completely revolutionary change.[4]

Conclusion

Although the optimism of Mr Cove and others about the religious effects of the 1944 Act are not borne out by subsequent practice, this analysis shows clearly the continuation of religious influence on educational legislation, in a period of continuous decline in religious practice; for the 1944 Act is the successful culmination of efforts by the Churches and religiously interested Members of Parliament to increase the impact of religion on education, which can be traced

[1] Parliamentary Debates, Vol. 110, cols 561–3.
[2] House of Commons: Gallacher, Vol. 397, cols 1072–3 and 1155; Bevan, Vol. 397, col. 1086. See also col. 2137 for the opinion that the majority of the people are agnostic and none the worse for that.
[3] House of Lords, Vol. 132, cols 199 and 970. on moving that the bill do now pass.
[4] House of Commons, Vol. 397, cols 2251–2.

through previous Education Acts, efforts which have continued in the post-war period. It only remains to discuss tentatively, some of the possible reasons why this culmination was possible.

An immediate factor which was of course partly responsible, is the political situation in which it was discussed; one of total war, and with a Coalition Government, as against the intensely divided House in 1902. Such a situation was conducive both to idealism about the future and to protestations of unity against a common foe.

Apart from this immediate factor however, the hypothesis is that the course of religious decline since the beginning of the century has in itself produced factors which have helped to maintain religious influence on educational legislation. This hypothesis can be illustrated by an examination of both religious and secular aspects of social change.

I. CHANGES IN POLITICAL AND OCCUPATIONAL INSTITUTIONS

In the political sphere, the decline in the power of the House of Lords to oppose Commons Bills, and the changes in its political composition, at first sight appear to point to a decline in an important source of religious influence. Between 1902 and 1914 attempts to secularize education failed because of Lords' opposition;[1] in the modern period, the power of the Upper House to prevent such legislation would be much less, though it is significant that such attempts are no longer made. Similarly, the growth of the Labour Party has broadened the social composition of the House of Commons by drawing on those sections of the population in which religious influence is weakest.

Outside the House, the increase of secular pressure groups, both from the trade union movement and from the teachers' and educational administrators' occupational organizations, means that policy-makers must take into account many secular opinions from groups some of which have a strong interest in equality of opportunity.[2] This change takes place in a period when the growth of administrative bureaucracy has taken decision-making a step back from open combat in the House to discreet consultation behind the scenes.[3]

However, a closer look at these political and occupational changes shows that they contain elements which may not be so unfavourable to religious influence. Although the power of the House of Lords has declined, it still retains the full representation of the Church of England through the Bishops; a privilege not shared by any other interest group in the controversy. It also continues to draw its members substantially from the élite section of the population in which the power of the 'Establishment' remains strongest.

[1] E.g. Birrell's Bill in 1906.
[2] The expansion of the teaching profession since 1902, involving training in L.E.A. training colleges, has produced a heterogeneous body, less likely to be imbued with religious traditions than the early elementary school teachers.
[3] See J. D. Stewart's account of this process, in *British Pressure Groups*, 1958.

Similarly, the growth of the Labour movement and the teaching profession are not necessarily inimical to religious influence on legislation. Although many studies show how the increasing secularization of left-wing politics in the twentieth century, even in such religious strongholds as Wales,[1] there has remained a thread of religious motivation in parts of the Labour leadership, and there has certainly been no great increase in anti-religious feeling. Analysis might show the same to be true in teachers' organizations and the trade union movement. Further, the increasing influences of pressure groups in the period, while encouraging the hearing of secular views, has also enabled the Churches to express their attitude more effectively. Between 1902 and 1944 they assumed the role of pressure groups with a recognized right to be consulted about educational legislation, and their influence was made the greater by their increasing determination to sink what differences they could in the face of growing religious indifference. In addition, the period sees the decline of a pressure group which between 1902 and 1910 promoted with some success, a specific secular alternative to religious education in schools.[2]

2. DEVELOPMENTS IN EDUCATIONAL IDEOLOGY DURING THE 20TH CENTURY

There are two trends which may have relevance.

(a) The concept of 'equality of opportunity' motivated some left-wing politicians to attack the dual system as a source of potential inequalities for both pupils and teachers. While this has led some to campaign for the abolition of dual control, it has also been interpreted in terms of the right of parents to have their children educated in religious schools. And, once the impracticability of abolishing the dual system has been conceded, 'equality of opportunity' demands increased financial aid in order to overcome the material inadequacies of church schools. In fact these schools have always benefited from the fact that they were in receipt of state aid long before the state education system existed.[3]

(b) There has been a broadening of the whole conception of education during the twentieth century; while the growth of technical and further education has

[1] George How comments on this trend in 1904. Labour and the churches, are 'drifting farther apart from each other every year. Labour feels . . . the Church is a capitalist organization. The churchgoing employer and the stay-away trade-unionist are alike suspicious of each other.' In Mudie-Smith (ed.), *The Religious Life of London* (1904), p. 243.
  See also Brennan, Cooney and Pollins, *Social Change in South West Wales*, pp. 138–9.
[2] The Moral Instruction League founded in 1896. Its activities culminated in the International Inquiry into Moral Instruction and Training in Schools in 1908. For an account, see Spiller, *The Ethical Movement in Great Britain* (1934), and F. H. Hilliard 'The Moral Instruction League 1897–1919', in *Durham Research Review*, Vol. III (12 September 1961).
[3] Since the first Committee of Council grants to Church schools in 1833.

been largely outside the religious influence,[1] in less specialized schools the concept of 'the education of the whole child' has involved spiritual aspects to be fed on religion. Such a concept however, has developed in a period when sectarianism is declining, and this may be a further factor encouraging the expansion of non-denominational Christianity, rather than the retention of separate denominational establishments.

3. THE SOCIAL PATTERN OF RELIGIOUS DECLINE SINCE 1900

The suggestions outlined above would need further research to verify or modify them. There is, however, ample evidence about the nature and distribution of the decline in religious practice since the turn of the century. Although this evidence is mostly of a small-scale regional kind, its cumulative effect is clear.

The trends most significant to the present discussion are the following: the social class pattern of allegiance, the nature of surviving religious practice, and the relationship between religion and youth.

(a) The social class pattern of allegiance

The irreligion of the urban proletariat has been noted since Horace Mann wrote in 1851 'more especially in cities and large towns it is observable how absolutely insignificant a proportion of the population of the congregation is composed of artisans'.[2] However, certain sections of working-class leaders received their only education through the Churches, particularly through some Nonconformist sects. Even this link becomes more tenuous at the turn of the century,[3] so that the twentieth-century decline in religious observance probably affected all classes equally. Although there are few detailed class breakdowns of church attendance at the turn of the century, Booth makes clear that the class pattern in London,[4]

[1] This is partly because they developed at a period when it was possible for the churches only to try to preserve their existing stake in the system. By 1944 Mr Moelwyn Hughes considers the idea of a religious technical school to be quite outlandish. 'It is impossible to imagine,' he says, 'an aided technical school. Imagination boggles at the idea.' House of Commons Debates, Vol. 397, col. 2357. Unfortunately for Mr Hughes' imagination the aided technical school exists. There were two Catholic technical schools in Manchester in 1962; see *Catholic Education Handbook 1962–3*, pp. 171–4.

There is also some evidence however, that religious influence has not been considered necessary in these branches of the education system. For example, the need for religious education in 'Young People's Colleges' is discussed in the Lords debate in 1944, at both the second reading and committee stages; but Lord Selborne piloting the bill for the Government does not consider it appropriate to require it in either further education, or technical colleges; the religious purpose of education applies only to children below school leaving age or those older ones who attend grammar or independent schools. House of Lords Debates, Vol. 116, col. 63.

[2] 1851 Religious Census. p. clviii.

[3] E. R. Wickham, *Church and People in an Industrial City*, analyses this estrangement. Pp. 199–202.

[4] 'Where the streets are "red" we find a vigorous middle-class religious development combined with active social life. Where "pink" there is as regards organized religion a comparative blank. Where "blue" we have the missions, and step by step as it deepens

and Rowntree estimates that the class proportions of church attendance in York, were roughly the same in 1935 as in 1901.[1]

Thus the religious practices of today, of church attendance, membership and particularly the leadership of local parishes,[2] remain as in the days of Booth and Mudie Smith predominantly middle and upper class, among all main denominations except the Catholic.[3] This reflects the social significance of religious practice, and confirms the likelihood of religious convictions remaining strongest among those in positions of leadership in other spheres.[4]

(b) The nature of remaining religious practices

Examination of different indices of religious practice shows that socially significant practices such as marriage and baptism have retained comparative popularity, while those demanding personal effort and conviction, such as regular attendance or church membership, have suffered the greatest falling away. Thus regular church attendance between 1900 and 1944 seems to have fallen from about 30 to 10 per cent of the population.[5] On the other hand, baptism in the Church of England remains at about 60–70 per cent of all live births in England throughout the twentieth century,[6] and although religious marriage ceremonies have been declining since the introduction of civil marriage in 1836, they still account for 69 per cent of all marriages.[7]

This retention of the occasional 'social' rituals probably reflects the spread of an attitude of vague indifference and goodwill towards religion, tempered by an unwillingness to commit oneself against it, in case there is 'something in it'. In 1909 Masterman comments that the 'drift is towards a non-dogmatic affirmation of general kindliness and good fellowship',[8] and other surveys from the beginning of the century make the same point, mostly in connection with the working class. It is probable that this vagueness, which is also commented on in many modern

---

to "black" the more hopeless becomes the task.' Charles Booth, *The Life and Labour of the People in London*, Vol. 16 (1903 edn), p. 424. The colouring of the streets represents his estimate of the wealth of an area.

[1] R. S. Rowntree, *Poverty and Progress*, p. 423. But his criterion of class is subjective.

[2] For evidence on parish leadership, see R. H. T. Thompson, *The Church's Understanding of Itself* (1957), p. 58; and W. S. F. Pickering, Ph.D., *The Place of Religion in the Social Structure of Two English Industrial Towns*, Vol. VII (London, 1958), p. 24.

[3] For the class distribution of church attendance in the modern period, see Gorer, *Exploring English Character*, p. 241; Pons, Ph.D., *Social Structure of a Hertfordshire Parish* (London, 1955), p. 201; and Caradoc Jones, *A Social Survey of Merseyside* (1934), pp. 337 and 340.

[4] Cauter and Downham, *The Communication of Ideas* (1954), p. 255.

[5] This is a cumulative picture from a number of local surveys. E.g. Rowntree, *English Life & Leisure*, p. 341; Pickering, op. cit., p. 36. For a comparison of several modern surveys, see Carr Saunders, Jones and Moser; *The Social Condition of Modern Britain* (1958), Chap. 18.

[6] *Facts and Figures about the Church of England*, Church Information Office (1959), p. 24, Table 25.

[7] *Registrar General's Statistical Review*, Civil Tables (1952), Table 5, Appendix B.

[8] G. K. F. Masterman, *The Condition of England* (1909), pp. 79 and 221.

studies,[1] had by 1944 also affected that section of the middle class which at the beginning of the century was intensely involved in inter-denominational disputes; this change in attitude towards a more general devotion to the Christian ideal is directly reflected in the tenor of the debates on religious education in 1902 and 1944.

Further evidence of the growth of indifference and vague identification is the lack of increase in atheism during the century. Mudie-Smith in 1903 reports that the workers are indifferent rather than atheist,[2] and in 1954 Cauter and Downham report nominal allegiance to a denomination among all but 2 per cent of their 1,200 subjects.[3] The majority of those holding such vague attitudes identify themselves with the Church of England; and although the Established Church cannot claim to be the 'church of the people' from statistics of church attendance and membership, it still maintains contact with more than half the population through the rituals of birth, marriage and death.

This growth of vague goodwill makes an active public opinion about religious legislation increasingly unlikely; and in Parliament, as we have seen, those who care enough to speak on the subject are those who remain positively committed.

(c) The relationship between religion and youth

Related to the attitude described above, is the persistence and spread of the tendency to see religion as something useful for others; chiefly the weak, the aged and the young. The association of youth and religion is shown not only in the high figures for baptism and confirmations compared with other religious practices,[4] but in surveys of religious behaviour from the beginning of the century until today.

'The children are everywhere persuaded to attend the centres of religious teaching, everywhere as they struggle to manhood and womanhood in a world of such doubtful certainties they exhibit a large falling away.'[5]

The picture is the same in the mid-twentieth century; there is no doubt that Sunday School attendance is a 'national custom'[6] which involves about half the children of a town on an average Sunday,[7] and is unrelated to the church-going habits of the parents. Religious practice does not become a matter of personal decision, however, until a child becomes a member of an adult congregation, and

---

[1] E.g. Mass Observation, *Puzzled People* (1947), p. 104. Pickering, op. cit. (1958), Chap. VI, p. 91: 'They persist bravely and boldly in practice and doctrine they find hard to justify, but this in itself seldom causes them alarm or frustration.'

[2] Mudie-Smith, op. cit., pp. 28 and 39.

[3] Cauter and Downham, op. cit. (1954), p. 50. This very low percentage may be the result of the interview situation. See also Mass Observation, op. cit., p. 24.

[4] *Facts and Figures about the Church of England*, op. cit., p. 25. Table 26 gives figures for confirmation and shows a total decline of only 5 per cent between 1891 and 1950.

[5] Masterman, op. cit. (1906), p. 221. See also Booth, op. cit., Vol. 16, pp. 423 and 403, Mudie-Smith, op. cit., p. 324.

[6] Gorer, op. cit., pp. 245–7.

[7] Pickering, op. cit., Appendix 6. Cauter and Downham, op. cit., p. 52.

the evidence is that church attendance falls away in later adolescence or the early twenties; two surveys which studied youth and the churches in particular found levels of weekly attendance of about 25 per cent,[1] which is higher than that found in surveys of adults.

This higher level of religious activity among the young reflects the attitudes of parents and others in authority, rather than anything about the religious life of children. Many besides the politicians are of the opinion that religion will keep children 'from bad ways' and give them ethical standards.[2]

This belief seems to be unchanged from the time when Booth was writing and religious education was being fought for in the House of Commons in 1902. As our analysis shows, in 1944 when the familiar revelations were rediscovered – that youth in spite of its higher church attendance is mostly 'religiously almost il-literate'[3] – the answer as before is thought to be to improve religious education in schools: and with decline of religious practice in the interval the urgency of the remedy is that much greater. This is in spite of the evidence that school or Sunday School religion has proved a very temporary influence when set against the background of an indifferent home.

There are, of course, denominational variations in the trends outlined here. The groups suffering least from them are certain small sects and the Catholics, who still retain more overall cultural and religious significance for their numbers. Cumulative evidence makes it clear that the Catholics have an unusual class distribution, a more representative age distribution, and a higher proportionate church attendance than other major denominations. These factors are obviously related to the greater consistency of their educational policy throughout the period under discussion.[4]

To summarize: this analysis of the pattern of religious change since the turn of the century shows the inadequacy of such a simple concept as 'the decline of re-ligion'. One must distinguish different aspects of religious life, and denominational variations; of greatest relevance to the present theme is that declining religious enthusiasm has led to the spread of indifference rather than antagonism, thus favouring acquiescence in religious legislative proposals. Religious interest probably remains strongest among those in positions of leadership, including

[1] B. D. H. Reed *80,000 Adolescents* (1948), p. 42, Table XXII. Also I. C. Cannon, Ph.D., *The Social Situation of the Skilled Worker: a study of the Compositor in London* (London, 1961), Chap. 6, p. 26. Twenty-five per cent of first-year apprentices 'go to church regularly', but 55 per cent had been to Sunday School. Both these studies are biased towards skilled workers; they may also be over-estimates.

[2] See Hoggart, *The Uses of Literacy*, p. 98 and *Puzzled People*, Mass Observation, pp. 87–8.

[3] See B. H. D. Reed, op. cit., p. 187. Also *The Church and Youth*, Report of the Church of England Youth Council, pp. 11 and 947.

[4] In spite of increasing isolation as the Church of England became less interested in the maintenance of separate schools, the Catholics have continued to pursue their policy. For example, they staged a large-scale pre-election constituency campaign in 1950, through the Catholic Electors' and Parents' Associations. See A. C. F. Beales, 'The Struggle for the Schools', p. 402, in S. A. Beck (ed.), *The English Catholics* (1950).

political leadership; and the religious education of children is still seen by such leaders as the panacea of the nation's social ills. Consequently, as evidence of indifference grows, religiously committed political leaders press this panacea the more strongly and meet less opposition from denominational or secular opinion, either in Parliament or outside it. So it is not merely the 'inertia of institutions' which is at work to maintain religious influence on education, but certain favourable elements arising from the pattern of religious and social change.

PART FOUR

The Organization of Education

THE STATUS AND DEFINITION given to education in any society govern the nature of the educational system that is set up. Thus, the status with which education is viewed, when balanced against that given to other social institutions, will play a large part in the decisions that are made about the allocation of resources for establishing and maintaining the schools and other educational organizations. In addition, the contemporary definitions specific to each sector of education will influence the way in which those in power work upon the historically determined educational system to decide how the resources allocated to it shall be used in each respective sector. In this way the expectations of behaviour in such positions as headmaster or teacher will be determined. Methods of teaching, the subjects to be taught and modes of examining will be similarly influenced. And finally, the educational organizations established, which have so far been seen as dependent variables, may come to exercise an autonomous influence on their environment, so that methodologically we should best consider them at this focal point as independent variables.

The status given to education rubs off on those who teach. In his contribution to this final section, Tropp analyses the changing status of the elementary teacher in England, contrasting it with the rather more highly regarded secondary schoolmaster, and relates the growth of esteem given to education (and hence to the teacher) to the gradual development of a teaching profession. This is a topic that is still of great practical concern and that cannot be considered without some understanding of its historical setting. The nineteenth century was an age of charismatic headmasters and, in the social circumstances of the time, there evolved a definition of their role that, as Baron shows, had a crucial influence on the expected behaviour, particularly of headmasters but also of teachers, at all levels of the educational system during the period when the British state system of schools developed. Hence, this definition still exerts a powerful force on how our schools are run today. The behavioural expectations of teachers, however, have always varied by such categories as sex, type of school and age of teacher. In her paper Charmian Cannon analyses the determinants of the role expectations of one such category, namely the teacher of physical education in selective secondary schools for girls.

Sociologists have only recently begun serious examination of the process of teaching and of the curriculum. Little relevant historical work exists. The first paper included here is about the seminar as a mode of teaching. Watt clearly relates this method of university teaching to 'the ideas of [the] times' and compares the ways in which the seminar developed in Germany and the United States and briefly contrasts England, where a lesser emphasis on postgraduate training led to the evolution of a different form of seminar. At the centre of the curriculum, throughout most of the historical period with which we have been concerned in this book, was the teaching of the classics. However, the consequences of teaching this subject and the reasons used to justify it have varied. Father Ong indicates that even by the time of the Renaissance the teaching of Latin had latent consequences in that it tended to act as a male puberty rite helping to toughen the adolescent for his anticipated future role as an adult. It was mainly those who would form the élite who underwent this rite and Campbell shows how, through time, the content of the justifications for teaching classics changed, but that there has always been present an élitist tradition in the way in which the case was argued. Since the middle of the last century, curricula have been much influenced by the widespread growth of examinations. Little is known of the processes whereby the syllabuses for examinations are set and changed. In a brief case study Musgrave looks at the development of a higher-level technological examination in an endeavour to isolate where power lies in such a process of educational decision-making.

Educational organizations develop a life of their own and come to affect their surrounding environment. The nature and extent of such influence changes through the history of any one educational organization. Here Bamford gives some indication of the extent and variety of the influence of Rugby School on Rugby town during much of the nineteenth century.

I Some Aspects of the 'Headmaster Tradition'[1]

G. BARON

It is a tradition of English life [wrote Norwood in 1909] that the headmaster is an autocrat of autocrats, and the very mention of the title conjures up in the minds of most people a figure before which they trembled in their youth, and with which they have never felt quite comfortable even in mature life. The headmaster, in most English schools, certainly holds a position of absolute power, for which no analogy can be found in any other profession whatever, a position, further, of authority and in influence far surpassing all that is exercised by those of the same rank in other countries.[2]

The assessment is no longer generally valid,[3] but the position of the headmaster, both in old-established Public and grammar schools and even in the 'new' secondary schools, still continues to be a distinctive feature of English education and attracts, as it has always done, the attention and surprise of foreign visitors. While he can no longer, without arousing opposition or ridicule, exert the auto-cratic powers which made his Victorian predecessors legendary figures, he is still, in a very real sense, the pivot and focus of his school, whether it is con-trolled by an independent governing body or by a local education authority. A headmaster is expected, if not to rule, certainly to lead, both by staff and pupils alike and one who is 'weak', in that he fails to protect his colleagues from outside interference, or who cannot make decisions and enforce them within his school, is little esteemed, no matter what qualities of personal charm, sympathetic understanding or academic distinction he may possess. Moreover, he is expected to have sufficient acquaintance with each of the hundreds of pupils in his school

[1] Although much of what follows might apply, with slight variations, to the office of the headmistress in girls' schools and, with much greater variations, to the office of head-teacher in the superseded elementary school, attention in this study is limited to the main body of tradition evoked by the term 'Headmaster'.

[2] C. Norwood and A. H. Hope, *The Higher Education of Boys in England* (1909), p. 213.

[3] Its relevance until recent days is suggested by the literature of schoolmastering in the present century, from Walpole's *Mr Perrin and Mr Trail* through Bernard Henderson's *Schoolmasters All; or Thirty Years Hard* and H. S. Shelton's *Thoughts of a Schoolmaster* to *Chalk in my Hair* by 'Balaam'.

First printed in Leeds Researches and Studies, *No. 14 (June 1956), pp. 7–16.*

to satisfy parents who wish to discuss details of their children's education with him. Indeed, a major popular criticism made of the comprehensive schools now being opened in London is that no head could conceivably know personally two thousand children and the suggestion that this particular responsibility should be assumed by his colleagues does not give widespread satisfaction.[1]

In spite of the importance attached to his office, little examination has been made of the evolution of this concept of the 'Headmaster'. At most, it is ascribed to the respect for 'tradition' usually considered characteristic of the English approach to social institutions. But this is merely to note that what exists now has existed for an appreciable span of years and furnishes no explanation as to why a particular institution has survived, nor what successive and diverse influences have sustained and modified its original form and later growth. Close examination of such influences may, however, show that what is termed 'tradition' is in reality not merely due to inertia and an aversion to change, but to a delicate counterpoise resulting from a series of dissimilar but compensating, social factors.

In the case of the headmaster the tradition is not one distantly seated in our history. Until the beginning of the nineteenth century the 'Headmaster', as distinct from the 'Master', hardly existed, save in a few of the larger and better known schools. A school consisted of one man and his pupils. Even when an 'Usher' was appointed it was not unusual for him to be quite independent of the Master and to be responsible to the trustees of the foundation alone. Only exceptionally, when numbers rose and when the Master wished to lighten his duties, did he engage personal assistants at his own expense.

The rapid development of the more famous Public Schools in the first half of the nineteenth century, however, resulted in the Master being obliged to engage a number of assistants, whose numbers rose or fell with the fortunes of the school. In some cases their position was little better than that of the ill-paid and half-literate teachers in some of the private schools of the time; in others they enjoyed profits earned from boarding pupils in their own houses or augmented their stipends by fees received for private tuition. In the newer schools, such as the City of London School and University College School, founded to meet rising middle-class demands, the need for a 'staff' in the modern sense of the term was apparent from the earliest days and the number of assistant masters and their conditions of service were determined by energetic governing bodies.

At this stage in the development of secondary education the position of the headmaster was by no means as stable as it was later to become. At Eton, Westminster and Winchester he was 'an officer and subordinate member of the Foundation or College, and subject to the superintendence of its head, the Provost, Warden or Dean';[2] and at the newly founded Liverpool Institute School his

---

[1] This aspect of the headmaster's role probably derives from Thring, who declared that 'as long as the Headmaster knows each boy, he is a Headmaster; the moment he does not, the man who does is so far Headmaster'.

[2] *Report of the Public Schools Commission*, Vol. I (1864), p. 4.

office hardly existed at all, in that its powers were shared in turn, on the Scottish pattern,[1] by a number of masters of equal status. It was, indeed, by no means certain how a large school should be organized and especially where the centre of power should lie. Had it not been for the appointment of Arnold to Rugby the issue might conceivably have been a major one.

The originality of Arnold lay in his regarding his school first and foremost as a community which shaped the characters of his boys as well as their minds. Moreover, because of his sense of pastoral mission, which expressed and was supported by the liberal evangelism of his time, he was convinced that he must be the centre of that community and exercise his influence on every individual member of it. Thus he developed his well-known prefect system through which he enlisted, though not without difficulties, the aid of older boys to discipline and guide the younger and placed his carefully chosen assistant masters in charge of the 'Houses' hitherto run by 'Dames'. Throughout, to parents, old boys and his many friends and correspondents, he never tired of showing how his work at Rugby was a vocation.

It is understandable that the example of Arnold spread to other boarding schools of similar status and importance: the conditions under which boys were taught, the absence of effective organization, the misuse of endowments and, above all, the low moral tone of school life became increasingly repugnant to the awakening conscience of early Victorian England. It was not inevitable, however, that it should exert the profound influence that it did on the wide range of endowed grammar schools, both boarding and day, which were so drastically reformed in the middle of the century, nor that it should be adopted in the many new foundations which came into being. That this was the case resulted from other factors, including the determination of the rising industrial and commercial interests to break down institutions based upon privilege and patronage and to apply, in their reconstruction, the lessons learnt in the business firm and the factory in which rewards, and, indeed, security depended upon day-to-day performance. What took place, then, was an 'organizational' as well as an industrial revolution, which produced the Civil Service, the Army of the Cardwell reforms and later the organs of local government which we know today. In educational matters the Public Schools Commissions of 1864 and the subsequent Public Schools Act of 1868, though by no means root and branch in their approach, firmly remodelled the government of the major Public Schools and made their headmasters responsible to, and dismissible by, the governing bodies of their schools, whilst at the same time affirming their control over internal organization.

Four years later, the members of the Schools Inquiry Commission, in the

---

[1] In Scotland, according to H. M. Knox, as the range of subjects studied in secondary schools grew during the nineteenth century, there was a 'tendency for the virtually independent heads of the separate departments to form a council of masters, sometimes presided over by each in turn, to manage the internal affairs of the school in republican fashion'. H. M. Knox, *Two Hundred and Fifty Years of Scottish Education, 1696–1946* (1953), p. 40.

course of their thorough and detailed examination of all other schools providing secondary education in some form, found many extraordinary instances of gross mismanagement and neglect. They recommended, therefore, that in all cases a Master should be dismissible by his governing body and that, furthermore, his emoluments should be 'largely and intimately connected with his success'. It was indeed urged by Sir John Coleridge with the formidable backing of Mr John Stuart Mill and Mr Morley that the Master should be guaranteed nothing save house and grounds rent free. Beyond this he should receive a fixed sum for each boy admitted to his school. Other Commissioners felt, however, that a small regular income should also be guaranteed in order to give new Masters time to build up their schools.[1]

This approach, the counterpart in secondary education of 'payment by results' in the elementary field, reflected the current belief that the methods which had proved so successful in the industrial field would be similarly beneficial elsewhere.

W. E. Forster certainly espoused it wholeheartedly.

We had [he said in the House of Commons, when introducing the Endowed Schools Bill of 1869] to consider carefully this question – whether it is desirable that masters should have any payment out of the endowment or should entirely depend upon school fees. I confess that I formed my opinion on this point in a great measure from my trade experience. I looked upon masters as persons employed by the trustees to do certain work and – I hope that they will not feel the comparison a disparaging one – I thought it would be right to treat them as I should treat persons whom I employed to do any commercial work. Now, I have found that the way to get the best service in such cases is to give a small fixed income, which makes a man independent of great want and calamity and then make the remainder of his income depend, fairly and generously, upon the success of the undertaking in which he is engaged. I believe that will be the system by which we can best regulate the payments to the masters of these schools whereas very frequently their income is entirely independent of the success of the school and in those cases the school does not succeed.[2]

In the revision of school schemes which followed the passage of the Endowed Schools Act the recommendations of Forster and his colleagues were substantially accepted and the personal fortunes of headmasters intimately linked with those of their schools. More important still, the staffing of the schools was, in the great majority of cases, placed wholly in the hands of the headmasters. They were given full powers to appoint and dismiss their assistants and, provided that the total expediture did not exceed a fixed sum, to pay them whatever salaries they considered advisable. The supremacy of the nineteenth-century headmaster

[1] *Report of the Schools Inquiry Commission*, Vol. I (1868), p. 599.
[2] *Hansard* House of Commons, 3rd Series, Vol. CXCIV (18 February 1869), cols 1364–5.

in his school was thus based upon his possessing all the powers of the nineteenth-century employer.[1]

Many consequences followed. Since the emoluments of a headmaster depended upon his success in increasing the numbers in his school, he had not only to make a show of efficiency, but he had to bow to the increasing pressure to bring scientific subjects, modern languages and geography into the curriculum. Similarly, he had to respond to the demands of parents and employers for visible results and hence sought to enter as many pupils as possible for examinations such as the Oxford and Cambridge 'Locals', the London Matriculation and those of the College of Preceptors. Another important result of the widening of the curriculum and the development of new specialisms was that the prestige of a headmaster came to be based less upon his scholarship, although this might on occasion be considerable, but upon his organizational powers; his capacity for maintaining and developing the 'tone' of his school and for fostering its corporate life through athletics and out-of-school activities; his sense of occasion as expressed through morning assemblies and speech days; and the personal links which he established with parents, old boys and civic leaders.

The Schools Inquiry Commission had reported adversely on the virtual monopoly of headmasterships by clergymen. 'It is said,' they wrote, 'and we think with justice, that the profession suffers from the frequent restriction of valuable masterships to men in Holy Orders – and we believe those of our witnesses are right, who consider that their abolition would go a long way to give the profession of teaching a position and importance of its own.'[2]

Despite the subsequent removal from many schemes of clauses requiring headmasters to be in Orders, the replacement of clerics by laymen proceeded slowly. The evidence submitted to the Royal Commission on Secondary Education in 1895 by the Assistant Masters' Association showed that of the 596 headmasters of the public secondary schools of which details had been obtained, as many as 283 were clerics.[3] It was not until local education authorities, influenced by their nonconformist voters, began to be represented on governing bodies after 1902 that the possession of Holy Orders ceased to be an important qualification for a headmastership of an endowed grammar school. Moreover, the long continuance of the clerical headmaster tradition could not fail to influence the attitudes of those who were laymen. They assumed, and were expected to assume, something of the moral purpose of their predecessors and often paid particular atten-

[1] In some cases the new governing bodies set up by the Endowed Schools Commissioners signally failed to show the zeal expected of them and resorted to 'farming' their schools to the headmaster. That is, they made over to him the income of the trust and let him keep whatever fees he could obtain. In return he shouldered all financial responsibility for the running of the school. *Royal Commission on Secondary Education*, Vol. I (1895), pp. 45–6. This system persisted in remote rural grammar schools until the early years of the present century.

[2] *Report of the Schools Inquiry Commission*, Vol. I (1868), pp. 611–12.

[3] *Report of the Royal Commission on Secondary Education*, Vol. IV (1895). Minutes of Evidence No. 13,099.

tion to religious training. Indeed, even at the present day, the headmaster, because he conducts the 'daily act of worship' and not infrequently takes upon himself the religious education of his senior boys, is linked with the older order.

From the point of view of the consolidation of the 'idea of the headmaster' an important factor was the influence of reform in creating a community of understanding among those so clearly responsible for the well-being of their schools. The Headmasters' Conference brought together the leaders of the most prominent schools from 1869 onwards, while by the end of the century the Headmasters' Association, set up in 1890, had enrolled practically every headmaster of a secondary school of note. Through the latter body in particular, the man working in some obscure country grammar school or some newly founded municipal secondary school was brought into touch with the great figures of the day, heard them declare with passion their determination to defend their independence against the central authority and local authorities proposed by the Royal Commission on Secondary Education and was strengthened in his own resolve to assert his authority over his school and its destiny. The headmaster remained no longer an isolated figure, dependent only upon his school and his personal qualities for his status, but was a member of a well-organized body of vigorous and active men, who, through the Conference and the Association, constantly voiced their disapproval of any infringement of their authority and their autonomy. Thus when the Board of Education and the local education authorities eventually came into being they entered an area in which the chief vantage points had already been seized by well-organized and determined forces.

By comparison with the headmasters, their employees, the assistant masters, were slow in developing a sense of identity and common purpose. This was largely because of the very great diversity of men staffing the schools. They ranged from graduates of Oxford and Cambridge, whiling away a few years before entering upon a good 'living', to youths who remained at their schools for two or three years as underpaid drudges. Between these two extremes there were ex-elementary school teachers, who had, in some cases, secured degrees of London University by part-time study; athletic young men prepared to 'look upon cricket not only as their pleasure but as their duty';[1] and a motley and changing assembly of others who had failed to make good in a recognized profession. Tenure, even for well-qualified men, was insecure and not infrequently a change of headmaster meant the dismissal of the entire existing staff of the school.[2]

---

[1] 'Schoolmastering as a Profession' (by an unnamed author), *The Journal of Education* (January 1886), p. 21.

[2] A notable case occurred at Grantham School in 1899, when a retiring headmaster dismissed his three assistants at short notice and his successor told them, a few days before a new term began, that he had appointed his own men and did not wish to re-engage them. (*The Journal of Education* (September 1899), pp. 549 *et seq.*). That this was not an isolated instance is borne out by the evidence of one of the witnesses before the Royal Commission on Secondary Education, who stated that 'when you dismiss the headmaster you dismiss every man in the school'. Questioned further he maintained that 'unless the new headmaster cares to take them on, they must all go'. These statements were ac-

Salaries, too, were low, even by the standards of the day, and there could be little hope of increments for length of service. Finally, nothing in the way of superannuation existed, save in the most well-endowed schools.

Nevertheless, the expansion of the older Universities following the reforms of the mid-century and, more particularly, the increasing number of graduates produced by London, Wales and Victoria, meant that the core of well-qualified men serving as assistant masters was growing. It was not until 1891, however, that their frustration first expressed itself in an organized form through the Assistant Masters' Association. It is significant that the earliest energies of the latter were not devoted to campaigns for adequate salaries or pensions, but to securing that its members should no longer be regarded as the employees of their headmasters and should be accorded equal status with them as employees of the same governing bodies.

This first objective was attained with the passing of the Endowed Schools (Masters) Act of 1908 and the assistant masters in grammar schools ceased to be the paid servants of their headmasters.[1] From this time their position was closer to that of teachers in elementary schools and secondary schools maintained by local education authorities in which head-teachers and staff alike were employed by the latter or by appropriate governing bodies.

As has been suggested, there was, during the last decade of the nineteenth century, considerable nervousness among the well-established headmasters of existing grammar schools lest the proposed Board of Education and local education authorities would bring about the loss of their independence and oblige them to conform to rigid codes and regulations of the kind associated with the elementary school world.

In the event, the Board proved to be their ally and lost no opportunity for emphasizing that all secondary schools should, through the institution of individual governing bodies, enjoy a wide measure of independence and that headmasters and headmistresses alike should retain the pre-eminence which they had attained during the preceding century.[2]

---

cepted without challenge. *Report of the Royal Commission on Secondary Education*, Vol. IV (1895), Minutes of Evidence No. 13,223.

[1] The Act provided that, in an endowed school, 'any master in the school, by whomsoever appointed, and whether appointed before or after the passing of this Act, shall be deemed to be in the employment of the governing body for the time being of the school.' The Endowed Schools (Masters) Act (1908), Sec. I (1) and (3).

[2] This was stressed with particular insistence in the Prefatory Memorandum to the 1905–6 Regulations for Secondary Schools. '. . . experience proves that in a school of the Secondary type full efficiency can be secured and the best teaching and organizational power attracted, only where the Head Master or Head Mistress is entrusted with a large amount of responsibility for and control over teaching, organization and discipline. In particular the appointment and dismissal of Assistant Staff is a matter in which a voice ought to be secured to the Head Master. In the majority of Secondary Schools of the highest grade the appointment and dismissal of the Staff is entirely in his hands, subject to the obligation to report his action to the Governors and his liability to dismissal for improper exercise of his powers. In other cases he exercises these powers subject to the

Some of the new local education authorities, however, were not always of this mind. They, and particularly their Secretaries and Directors of Education, were striving to establish their position in respect of schools which had hitherto held them at a distance and in respect also of their own higher grade and day technical schools which, in some cases at least, were seeking to secure something of the independence of the secondary schools proper. Hence they were anxious to acquire or retain control of staffing and tended to treat headmasters with scant respect. Close local control was, nevertheless, strongly resisted by the Board. Its officials were men educated in schools of national status and prestige and they viewed secondary education as a vehicle for the cultural life and traditions of the nation as a whole rather than for local and sectional interests. It was, therefore, to protect the headmaster against undue interference that they stressed the importance of every secondary school having its own governing body, composed not only of members of the local education committee but also of men and women with special knowledge and interests in educational matters. It is interesting to note that, from this time, governing bodies were intended to become the protectors of the independence of the headmasters of the new secondary schools rather than, as envisaged by the nineteenth-century reformers, the means for checking their excess.

During the vital formative years between 1902 and 1914, moreover, the influence of the Board made itself insistently felt through its indefatigable teams of inspectors. They did not hesitate to recommend the removal of an inefficient headmaster, but they emphasized the importance of his office by the detailed attention which they paid to it during full inspections and by the support which they strove to give to men who could bring the spirit of the established grammar schools and of the older Universities into the new county and municipal schools. In many areas local authorities began to think on similar lines and show a preference for men with distinguished educational antecedents.

To some extent, the years following the First World War saw a shift in what might be termed the 'centre of gravity' of secondary education. The rapid increase in the number of secondary schools maintained or controlled by local education authorities meant that their staffs, benefiting from the activities of the National Union of Teachers in the elementary school field, secured a standard salary scale through the Burnham settlement, a nationwide superannuation scheme and, as a result of stubbornly fought battles with individual local authorities, a vastly increased security of tenure. In that headmasters in such schools were now dealing with men independent of them as regards their salaries and tenure, they were in a far less autocratic position than before. Similarly, in independent

approval of the Governors. In any case, it is important that he should have formally secured to him the right to be consulted by the Governing Body and to submit his proposals to the Governors and have them fully considered, both as regards staff appointments and on all points relating to the conduct of the school as an educational organization' (Cd. 2492 of 1905, *Regulations for Secondary Schools*, p. xv).

and direct-grant schools, while headmasters retained their powers to appoint and, with the approval of their governing bodies, to dismiss their assistant masters and while salaries and pensions depended upon the custom of each individual school, the ability of any school to attract able and well-qualified masters depended upon it offering them conditions of service at least as favourable as those available to them if they joined the service of a local education authority.

Yet despite these factors and despite also the changed social atmosphere of the post-war years, the headmaster, both in maintained and in less closely regulated schools, still continued to enjoy a distinctive position. Paradoxically enough, a major reason for this was the freedom which the Board of Education sought to give to each school and indeed to each assistant master in his actual work in the classroom. Since the duties of the latter were not defined and still less the precise content of his teaching or the methods he should use, he had, within the school itself, no clearly formulated professional rights. He could be required by his headmaster, who alone was responsible for internal organization, to teach subjects for which he had little liking, or to accept what he considered an undue proportion of difficult or backward forms. Furthermore, although his headmaster could not bring about his dismissal, save after a hard-fought and wearing struggle with his professional association, he could exercise an often decisive influence through the open testimonial or the confidential reference. On the other hand, the increasing uniformity of the academic and professional background of headmasters and assistant masters, combined with the revolt in the twenties and the thirties against the authoritarianism prevalent in many occupations in Victorian and Edwardian times, made the confident exercise of such powers less attractive to headmasters themselves.

It remains to be seen how far the greatly expanded conception of secondary education resulting from the Act of 1944 will bring new elements into the situation. There has been a reversion, as regards the basis of the headmaster's salary, to the principle of it being closely linked to the number of pupils in his school, but the motive has not been to encourage headmasters to attract more pupils but to ensure that salaries roughly correspond to existing responsibilities. The former inflexibility of the Burnham scales has also been modified, so that headmasters can exercise decisive influence over the allocation of allowances for advanced work to assistant masters. On the other hand, the difficulty of finding men to staff the schools, at least in science subjects, restricts any tendency towards arbitrary and capricious action in any side of school organization. Furthermore, the interlinking of all forms of school with the agencies of the welfare state brings constant pressure on a headmaster to think in terms of immediate administrative necessity, of compromise to meet the wishes of the many bodies and individuals concerned with his school and of quick and effective response to the social situation in which he works.

So far, however, there are few signs of any significant change, on a scale commensurate with that which took place in the last century, in fundamental thinking concerning the headmaster's office. It might perhaps be expected that, just as the prevailing industrial philosophy of a hundred years ago affirmed his autonomy and his personal responsibility, so might the present-day development of managerial training lead to attempts to analyse and assess his position in a world of increasingly complex interrelationships. But, despite the vast scope of secondary education and the incorporation within it of secondary modern schools and secondary technical schools, some of the roots of which lie deep in the old traditions of elementary education, very little has yet been said or written bearing on the subject. In particular, no thought appears to have been given to examining how assistant masters might, before entering upon headmasterships, prepare themselves through organized and intensive study for their new duties.[1] There is, of course, no intention here to suggest that the headmaster is less sensitive to changing circumstances than the business man or the civil servant. The reverse is frequently true. What is argued is that serious thinking and consequently popular speculation about his role and about school structure is dogged by recollections of earlier stereotypes derived from the time-hardened images of the great Victorian individualists and hence difficult to assess within the close-knit patterns of shared responsibility characteristic of present-day enterprise. As a result the demands made by rapid social change and by the vast network of welfare services linked with the school tend to be regarded as extraneous, or at most peripheral, to the main task of leadership within the school itself.

It has been seen that, quite apart from considerations of social philosophy, the increase in the size of schools and their staffs was a major factor in the growth of the 'Headmaster Tradition' in the nineteenth century. It seems more than likely that the stimulus to remodel it will come from the new comprehensive schools which, by reason of their complexity as well as, in some cases, their size, will make the distribution of authority essential. If this is so, it is to be hoped that its basis, though widened, will remain within the school itself and not be imperceptibly transferred, owing to the weight of administrative considerations and outside influences, to the 'community' or its representatives. A stand on this issue, which will only be successful if based on careful thought by those concerned, will preserve the essence of the position taken up by those who, like Thring and many others, fought for the independence of the school from directed political and social pressures and who, in their day, could only achieve their ends by stressing their own personal privileges and authority.

[1] Save by W. O. Lester Smith, who has tentatively suggested that teachers of experience should be able to follow courses designed to illuminate in a liberal way problems of educational organization and administration. He envisages that 'such courses should serve education much as the Staff College serves the Army as a preparation for leadership'. W. O. Lester Smith, *The Teacher and the Community*: Studies in Education No. 3: Evans Bros. for University of London Institute of Education (1950), pp. 13–15.

2 The Changing Status of the Teacher in England and Wales

A. TROPP

For the importance of the teacher in educational policy, and for many of the factors determining his status, we must look to the history of the profession.

As a first step we can divide the history of the elementary teaching profession into four periods. Until 1846 there was a period of chaos, when the general stereotype of the teacher was that of a person inefficient, illiterate and good for nothing else. From 1846 to 1862, with government intervention, there was a sharp rise in the status of the teacher. This sharp rise came up against an educational reaction which generated the stereotype of the teacher as over-educated and conceited and led to a deliberate lowering of the teacher's status. From 1862 to about 1920 the teachers' associations struggled for the improvement of the teacher's status. This struggle led to a stereotype of the teachers being politically unscrupulous in the pursuit of their professional ends. Added to this, from 1895 onwards the desire to better the schools led to a belief that the existing teachers were under-educated and uncultured. By 1920 the elementary teachers had succeeded in gaining their main ends and in securing the objective basis for an increase in status. From then to the present day the stereotype we discussed earlier has been gradually building up.

The secondary teachers have had three 'status periods'. Until 1902 their profession was, in the main, in its original chaotic state. From 1902 until about 1911 their status increased sharply, both absolutely and in relation to that of the elementary teachers. The growing unification of elementary and secondary education which culminated in the Education Act of 1944 has brought the two sides of the profession together and led to a relative (although perhaps not an absolute) decrease in the status of the secondary grammar school teacher.

First printed as pp. 147–70 of Section II, *Chapter 3,* The Yearbook of Education, 1953 *(Evan Bros. Ltd, London).*

Foundation of the elementary teaching profession

In spite of abortive attempts by charitable persons to found an educational system in the eighteenth and early nineteenth centuries, no organized provision for the education of the lower orders and no organized profession of educators existed in England and Wales before the second half of the nineteenth century. The children of the poor, if they were educated at all, received their education either at their parents' knees or else at the scattered private or charity schools which catered for the children of the relatively prosperous working-class parents who were able to forgo their child's earnings and pay the small fees demanded by the teacher.

The main forces which have shaped the nature and problems of the elementary teaching profession can already be seen in these first attempts to create a system of mass education. Education for the poor had its origin as a charitable service conferred by the rich or, as some would put it, as a ransom paid to placate the forces of social revolution.

Unlike the medical and legal professions, there was no slow 'spread-down' of the services of skilled professionals. Since middle-class education was in only slightly better state than education for the poor, there were in fact no skilled professional teachers in existence. The new profession of 'teacher of the poor' was bound to be independent in origin.

Under any known method of education, the salaries of the teachers constitute the major part of current expenditure. Even after the intervention of the state, money for the education of the poor was extremely scarce, and if education was to reach many children the salary that could be offered to the teacher was of necessity low. That teachers were obtained at all was due fundamentally to the fact that there was no recognized skill or technique to be acquired, and no reliable criteria of success or failure. Such a position is not unique to the teaching profession. But in the case of the other professions which deal in intangible services (e.g. medicine, law), the profession itself has managed to lay down standards of skills to be acquired by entrants and criteria of success and failure. As a result of the small economic reward that was offered to teachers in the eighteenth and early nineteenth centuries, few recruits could be attracted from the relatively educated middle classes. Since the entrants to the profession came almost entirely from the poor or from the failures of the middle class, it was not possible for them, unaided, to afford the lengthy period of education and training which was necessary to make up their deficiencies. The early attempts to extend education to the poor came up against this problem. The charity school movement of the eighteenth century was forced to take untrained and semi-literate teachers. The monitorial system of the first three decades of the nineteenth century promised a cheap and easily applied solution by setting the older children to teach the younger. Not only did the system economize in the use of adult teachers but the function of the adult teachers themselves was greatly simplified. All that was required of them was 'an aptitude for enforcing discipline, an acquaintance with mechanical details for the preservation of order, and that sort of ascendancy in his school which a sergeant-major is required to exercise over a batch of raw recruits before they can pass muster on parade'.[1]

These attempts to perform the function of the teacher by semi-illiterate tellers of Bible stories and adult drill-masters contributed to the low opinion that was generally held of the profession. The 'stereotype' of the teacher as a man 'good for nothing else' persisted even after the new teachers commenced entering the schools from 1846 onwards. As one of the new teachers was to complain in 1860:

A short time ago, not so far back as the days of our grandfathers, scarcely even as far as those of our fathers, the children of the poorer classes of this country derived all the education it was thought necessary to give them from men, the generality of whom were incompetent to fulfil the ordinary business of every-day life, men who, having been crippled in the wars or become physically disabled for manual labour, were promoted by the officers of the parish to the office of schoolmaster. In many cases they were like the schoolmaster of Waldbach, who was found in a little dirty room with a crowd of children around him, and who when asked what his qualifications for the office were, naïvely answered that he had been keeper of the Waldbach pigs, and was thought to be the best fitted to look after the children. That there were exceptions is certain: but, generally speaking, the amount of knowledge possessed by these elementary teachers was very small. We cannot wonder, then, that our parents, and the world at large, grew up with such peculiar opinions as to what an elementary teacher was. The poor fellow was patronized, and snubbed by the squire and his lady, and looked upon by most as at best a genteel pauper. Perhaps the poor pedagogue did not feel the degradation of his position. Let us hope he did not. Things have changed now in respect to the position of the teacher. Half a century of gradual improvement – the last fifteen years of which have shown a greater advance than all that went before – has given a different standing to the pedagogue; but how slow is the change in public opinion. The opinions and habits of thought of many have never altered; they think as lightly of the modern teacher as of the one they knew in their youthful days. They think him a man to be patronized and snubbed like the one of old; and if he resents such treatment their surprise is unbounded.[2]

By the 1830s it was obvious that the monitorial system had failed. It was not that the monitors were incapable of performing the task for which they had been recruited. The purpose of the monitorial system was to teach the three Rs, and it was believed that morality would emerge as a by-product. The new emphasis (in large part due to the social discontent of the time) was on the direct moral

[1] *Educational Expositor* (March 1853).
[2] T. Ward, 'The Teacher's Duties in the Present State of Education', *The Educational Guardian* (January 1861).

elevation of the masses, and for this purpose the contact of adult moral minds was necessary.

Given the necessity for extending education to the poor, it became plain that the main requisite was a supply of efficient, trained, religious and humble teachers. In the reports of the voluntary educational societies, the Parliamentary Select Committees and the Committee of Council, there appears statement after statement that education was being crippled because salaries were too low to obtain properly qualified masters. The Reverend Derwent Coleridge was to describe the ferment of that time as follows:

> Somewhat more than twenty years ago – it was felt by all the more zealous, and shall we not admit, by all the wiser friends of popular education, that to elevate the social position – the 'status' as it was called – of the men through whose instrumentality the social regeneration of the largest class of the community was to be effected, was the one thing needful. It was seen that the day had come that the same process by which a few ages before the clergy themselves had been rescued from a like degradation must be repeated in the case of their humble coadjutors. The same process. The men must be fitted for a better position, and a better position must be found for the men. They must be better educated and better paid.[1]

The religious societies themselves were powerless to better the situation, for their resources were strained to the utmost in constructing schools and training teachers. Influenced in large part by Kay-Shuttleworth's experiment at Battersea, they made a series of attempts to secure more efficient teachers through the founding of training colleges, but these attempts had been only partially successful. It was difficult to secure entrants with more than the scantiest education, and the schools could not afford to institute a pupil-teacher system which might close the gap between the age at which poor children left school and the age at which it was possible for them to enter the training colleges. Moreover, even if suitable entrants were obtained and trained, the training was often used as a stepping-stone to more lucrative employment. For while the teacher was grossly underpaid and schools were grossly understaffed, no sense of vocation would keep the teacher at his work. Until conditions inside the schools were improved, improved training would only mean that 'our normal institutions may turn out nurseries for railway clerks'.[2] Again, while all schools were woefully short of funds, the cheapest teachers were sought, and trained masters were sometimes regarded as expensive luxuries beyond the reach of the average schools.

This complex of problems, which stultified educational growth and the organization of the teaching profession, was finally solved by government action. Sir James Kay-Shuttleworth (Secretary of the Committee of Privy Council from 1839 to 1849) had been the foremost of those who had realized the true nature of

[1] Derwent Coleridge, *The Teachers of the People* (1862), pp. 21–5.
[2] *Quarterly Review* (September 1846), pp. 420–1.

the 'educational difficulty'. It was obvious that only government intervention and assistance could solve the educational problem, and under the conditions of the time this assistance would be acceptable only if it left the authority of the existing religious bodies virtually supreme. His method of reconciling these difficulties consisted in promoting a pupil-teacher system (1846), which was intended to serve the double purpose of improving the instruction given in the elementary schools, and of providing for the training colleges a succession of capable pupils whose fees and expenses would be paid from government funds.

It was under this system, modified in detail on several occasions, that the majority of entrants to the profession were recruited until the first decade of the twentieth century.

After 1846, the standard of professional ability, the 'licence to teach' (or rather the licence to secure public money towards one's salary) was the possession of a government certificate awarded on the results of an examination supervised by government inspectors. While the government did not directly employ the teachers, and refused to treat them as civil servants, it effectively controlled the means of entrance and the standard of entrance to the profession. Not only was the certificate a licence to teach – it also gave to the teacher the right to have apprentices bound to him (for which he was paid), and an augmentation of salary of from £10 to £30 a year.

Under the regulations of 1846, the elementary school world was meant to constitute a closed system. The most intelligent and worthy pupils in the elementary schools were to be apprenticed as 'pupil-teachers' at the age of 13. They were to assist in the school for five years, and were to receive in return an annual stipend of from £10 to £20, and one and a half hours of advanced instruction a day from the master. The master had to be approved by the H.M.I. (Her Majesty's Inspector) as a suitable person to be in charge of pupil-teachers, and was to receive a special grant for training them. Each year the pupil-teachers were to be examined by an H.M.I. on a set syllabus, and were also required to present certificates of good conduct from the managers of the school, and of punctuality, diligence, obedience and attention from the master or mistress.

At the end of five satisfactory years of service the pupil-teachers were to enter for a competitive examination for a 'Queen's Scholarship' to a training college. Those successful were to stay at the college for two years. After leaving college the certificated teacher (providing he taught in a school under government inspection), would receive an augmentation grant, and finally there was a provision for retiring pensions to teachers with long and efficient service. 'To a precarious and frequently make-shift occupation he [Kay-Shuttleworth] brought the stability and prestige of Government support, to an easily entered and indifferently practised calling he brought rigid selection by examination and inspection.'

The new profession

The system was an immediate educational success. By 1860 there were 6,433 certificated teachers and 13,237 pupil-teachers in the schools of England and Wales. In spite of the slowness of the change in the popular stereotype, the status of the certificated teacher was obviously improving. The latter was not as amenable to the orders of his superiors as the old teachers had been. In spite of their rise from the 'respectable working class' to the lower middle class, the new teachers showed signs of being discontented with their status and their conditions of work.

An examination of the various educational periodicals of the period,[1] and of the activities of the various teachers' associations,[2] reveals a series of frictions arising out of the nature of the teacher's life and work and his relations with his 'employers' and the state. By far the most important in the teacher's mind was his demand for a higher 'social position'. From 1853 onwards, article after article deals with the social position of the schoolmaster – what it was and what it should be.[3]

The complaint usually followed the line that the teacher's training and qualifications led him to deserve a higher social position in society than he occupied at the time. There was a feeling that the teacher should be ranked with the other learned professions, not merely on his own account but because it was necessary for the interests of elementary education. Raising the schoolmaster's position was to be accomplished by giving him better remuneration and by treating him in all respects as a professional person. Another aspect of the teacher's 'status anxiety' was his complaint of his 'social isolation'. He considered himself superior to the mass of 'honest hard-working clowns' among whom he laboured, and yet he was not accepted as an equal by the independent professionals and the middle classes.

Opinions as to how the teachers themselves could help to raise their own status and cure their social isolation varies from belief in agitation to 'patient perseverance in well-doing'. Many teachers believed that 'next to incompetence and

[1] *The English Journal of Education*, 1843–64; *Papers for the Schoolmaster*, 1851–71; *The Educational Expositor*, 1853–5; *The School and the Teacher*, 1854–61; *The Educational Guardian*, 1859–63; *The Pupil Teacher*, 1857–63; *The Literarium*, 1854–7; *The National Society's Monthly Paper*, 1847 ff.; *The Educational Record of the British and Foreign Bible Society*, 1848 ff.; *The Quarterly Magazine and Record of the Home and Colonial Society*, 1848–9; *The Educational Paper*, 1859–63; *The Educator*, 1851–4.

[2] There were numerous district associations (the most important being the 'Metropolitan Church Schoolmasters' Association', founded in 1838) and two 'National' associations both founded in 1853, the 'Associated Body of Church Schoolmasters' and the 'United Association of Schoolmasters'.

[3] There is an enormous literature on this subject. For a typical example, see *The Educational Expositor* (March 1853), 'On the Social Condition of the Schoolmaster' and the resultant discussion in *Papers for the Schoolmaster* (April 1853); *Educational Expositor* (June, July, September 1853).

shortcomings, nothing can more surely retard the elevation of the craft than querulous impatience for it', but others were not so patient.

There were many outside the profession, particularly among the clergy, with whom the teachers tended to compare themselves, who did not believe that the teacher could ever reach the status of the learned professions for, 'however much I may esteem them as friends and fellow-labourers, till they are taken from the same rank of society and have undergone the intellectual training and the social discipline which it is absolutely necessary the doctor, the lawyer, and the clergy-man should undergo, I must confess myself to be one of those interested and prejudiced persons who cannot accede to the national schoolmaster a rank on the level with the learned professions'.[1]

The other complaints of the teachers were in the main associated with their desire for a higher social position. They complained of their low salaries (although in truth their salaries had risen steadily since 1846), and of the lack of possibili-ties of promotion. They demanded the opening of the inspectorate to teachers as a means of raising the status of the whole profession, but this demand was refused because elementary teachers were not 'fitted by previous training and social position to communicate and associate upon terms of equality with the managers of schools and the clergy of different denominations'.[2]

They complained of the goverment's refusal to carry out its pledge to grant teachers a pension, of the compulsory extraneous duties demanded by many employers and of their insecurity of tenure.[3]

These complaints were to be expected, and were an inevitable and healthy reaction of a new and growing profession. The increasing independence of the teacher was shown by the publication of teachers' periodicals and the founding of local and national associations. In the main, the friends of popular education encourage this growing independence, although many of them felt called upon to warn the teachers against excessive clamour. It is difficult to say how deep was this feeling, for only a small minority of teachers were members of the national associations,[4] and while the latter were active in campaigning for teachers' rights, they took great care to reassure the authorities that they were not trade unions bent on subverting the social order, and that the motives of teachers were higher than 'mere self-advancement'. Their attempts[5] to reassure the authorities

[1] The Rev. William Rogers, in the *Educational Expositor* (June 1853).

[2] Report of the Newcastle Commission, *B.P.P.*, Vol. XXI, Pt 1 (1861), p. 160.

[3] Although the *Minutes* of 1846 had contained promises of pensions for teachers, the language of the *Minutes* was ambiguous, and after Kay-Shuttleworth's resignation in 1849 the Committee of Council refused to grant pensions. It was not until 1875 that the claims of teachers to pensions under the terms of the 1846 *Minutes* were admitted. A general pension scheme was not sanctioned by Parliament until 1898.

[4] The number of teachers who were members of the national associations in 1860 was about 800. The 'Associated Body of Church Schoolmasters' had about 660 members in that year, and the 'United Association of Schoolmasters' about 150. In that year there were about 6,500 certificated teachers in England and Wales.

[5] See details of the First Annual Meeting of the Associated Body of Church School-masters in *The School and the Teacher* (January–May 1854).

were, however, in vain, and the growing independence of the teachers was used as a critical argument to destroy the 1846 system.

Educational reaction and the teacher's status

From the inauguration of the 1846 system a barrage of objections had been directed against it by various interested parties. There were constant complaints from the dissenters that the church was being favoured at their expense, and from some Liberals that a teacher-army was being called into existence which would either control the government or else act as the tool of an unscrupulous government. There were attacks on the 1846 system by those who saw it as hindering the development of a full, compulsory, and non-sectarian system. But the bitterest and most persistent complaints came from those middle-class parents who said that they were forced to pay for the education of the poor while the government did nothing for middle-class education. There were constant complaints that working-class children were receiving a better education than middle-class children, and were using that education to compete with middle-class children in the job market. More directly, there were complaints at the growing 'burden' of the government grant for education.[1]

Accompanying these direct attacks on popular education was an even more bitter attack on the educator of the poor. The main attack was on the so-called 'over-education' of the teacher. This over-education was said to make the teacher conceited and ambitious, to lead him (or her) to ape his betters in dress, and to press for a higher social position. This discontent with his position led him to move constantly from school to school and finally to desert the profession and compete with the children of the middle classes in the new white-collar occupations. Once again these actions were made more difficult to bear because the teacher was said to owe his education, training and position to the charity of the middle classes.

The 'over-education' of the teacher led to two other evil results. In the first place, it led him to neglect the groundwork of education and the less intelligent children in his school. This, it was said, was the reason why many children left school unable to read or write. In the second place, the teacher was led to over-educate his more intelligent pupils and make them unfit for their position.[2]

It is true that the self-assertive attitude of many of the younger teachers fresh from colleges was in some measure responsible for the widespread hostility towards the profession as a whole. It is also true that one hears many criticisms of teachers for devoting too much attention to their older and brighter scholars and

---

[1] Which had risen between 1851 and 1859 from £150,000 to £836,920.

[2] This summary is based on extensive readings in the periodical and pamphlet literature of the time. For examples of this criticism, see Rev. Richard Burgess, *National Schools and National School Teachers* (London, 1848); *Quarterly Educational Magazine* (October 1848); Rev. J. C. Wigram, *Present Aspects of Popular Education* (London, 1849); *English Churchmen* (28 September 1854): Correspondence.

neglecting the younger and backward. But as Frank Smith has put it, 'the problem before the head-teacher was whether to give his energy to the older children who stayed on till they reached the top class, and showed a satisfactory return for his labour, or to this migratory and unteachable group at the lower end of the school.'

By 1858 the discontent of the middle and upper classes with the educational system had reached such a pitch that the government appointed a Royal Commission 'to enquire into the present state of popular education'. The commissioners in turn appointed ten assistant commissioners, who were each sent to a specimen district to gather facts bearing, *inter alia*, on the over-education, conceit and neglect of duty of the teachers.

The Report of this 'Newcastle Commission' was published in 1861. The evidence of the assistant commissioners tended to show that the 'over-education', 'dissatisfaction' and 'conceit' of the certificated teacher had been much exaggerated. The commissioners were sufficiently impressed by this to dismiss these charges as groundless, though in other places their report seems to have been prepared with disregard to the evidence before them. For example, on the basis of evidence that was later shown to rest on an arithmetical error,[1] they concluded that a large proportion of the children in the schools were not being satisfactorily taught and attributed this to 'the difficulty which superior teachers found in heartily devoting themselves to the drudgery of elementary teaching'. They proposed a system of 'payment by results' (against the advice of most of their witnesses), to force the teachers to attend to their younger and less able pupils.

The Press and the periodicals made even more biased selections from the biased selections in the report. The kind of impression which the literate public gained from all this was that 'we were over-teaching our masters and under-teaching our children',[2] that 'the Privy Council have been long manufacturing razors for the purpose of cutting blocks, and in future the instrument must be better adapted for its purpose'.[3]

A torrent of abuse was launched at the luckless teachers, who held meetings, wrote letters and signed petitions defending the educational system and their own reputations. This feeble show of resistance still further infuriated the op-

---

[1] The commissioners based a great deal of their argument on a Report by H. M. I. Norris (*Minutes*, 1859–60, pp. 103–13, quoted in *Report of Newcastle Commission*, pp. 244–5), that in his district only 25 per cent of the children were receiving an adequate elementary education. This much-quoted statement (repeated four times by the commissioners and innumerable times in the controversy around their report) was the fundamental argument on which the opponents of the 1846 system rested their case, and is still to be found in educational histories. The whole basis for Norris's calculation was, however, shown by the Rev. T. R. Birks, M.A., to rest on a mathematical error (in *The Great Fact*, etc. (London, 1862)). Norris admitted his error (see *B.P.P.*, Vol. XLIII (1862), pp. 161–7, and *Hansard* (20 March 1862), Sec. 1862, speech of Earl Granville), and attempted to undo the damage he had done. The tide of hostility towards the 1846 system was, however, too strong to be much influenced by facts.

[2] *The Economist* (21 September 1861).

[3] *Quarterly Review*, No. 220 (1861), p. 506.

ponents of education. It was in this atmosphere of dislike and distrust of the teacher and education and of religious tensions between Nonconformists and Anglicans that Robert Lowe (then Vice-President of the Council) conceived his 'Revised Code' in 1861.

This Code abolished augmentation grants and pensions for schoolmasters. A capitation grant was to be paid to the managers on a system of 'payment by results' in reading, writing and arithmetic. For purposes of examination, the children were to be grouped by age, and no grant was to be given for children above the age of 11 years. The training college course was to be ruthlessly cut down as well as the number of pupil-teachers and the amount of instruction they were to receive. Thus the direct connection between teachers or pupil-teachers and the state was cut and they were thrown on the mercy of school managers.

From August 1861 until May 1862 a violent battle was waged in Parliament and in the country at large on the Revised Code. An overwhelming flood of pamphlets, letters, memorials, petitions and resolutions condemned the proposed changes either as a whole or in part. It was shown that the Revised Code was based on a wrong view of the state of education, that it neglected the real problems facing the educational system, and that it was a gross breach of faith with the teachers, managers and educational societies. It was pointed out that all the existing cer-tificated teachers had been tempted into the profession by promises of augmen-tation grants and pensions. Almost every petition condemned these breaches of faith, and the condemnation was supported even by many who agreed with the main principles of the Revised Code.

All opposition was, however, in vain. While, under pressure, the Revised Code was altered in minor respects, its main principles became operative in 1862.

A great deal has been made of the Newcastle Commission in this article because it had such a tremendous effect on the future of the teaching profession. Until 1861 the path of professional improvement, of increase in status and self-respect, had moved steadily upwards. The signs of 'dissatisfaction' must be regarded as healthy symbols of growing professional spirit. But in the years between 1858 and 1862 the growing feeling of discontent inside the ranks of the Nonconformists and middle classes, using as its excuse a real (although exag-gerated) weakness in the educational system, succeeded in forcing the elementary teaching profession into a new path. The Revised Code lowered the status of the teacher, gave the profession a grievance which was to shape its ideology for the next fifty years, and reduced the whole level of instruction both of the teacher and of the children he taught. The teachers were now at the mercy of the managers and of the new inspectors, who had power to break their careers without their having any rights of appeal whatsoever. In sheer self-defence the elementary teachers were forced to organize, and in 1870 (by which time the first paralysing effects of the Revised Code had worn off) they formed the 'National Union of Elementary Teachers'.[1]

[1] Now the National Union of Teachers or N.U.T.

The struggle for status

The N.U.E.T. was conceived in protest and grew in an atmosphere of conflict. From its foundation it had the double function of advancing the interests of teachers and of reforming and improving the educational system. To achieve these aims it had to fight government departments and public authorities. Now, teachers in England have never been civil servants, and this has given them the advantage of being free to use political pressure in Parliament or in the municipalities.

In its early years, the union strove to achieve three major objectives: control of entry into the profession, making it possible for elementary teachers to be promoted to the inspectorate, and obtaining a comprehensive scheme of pensions. It had little success in its first aim: by the end of the century nearly half the teachers were uncertificated. With regard to the second, it was more successful: in 1893 a handful of ex-elementary teachers were admitted to the inspectorate, and after 1880 the authorities also promised that no teacher's certificate would be cancelled or suspended without full enquiry and without allowing the teacher concerned to meet the charges made against him. Lastly, in 1898, a scheme of pensions was introduced. Another major triumph, largely due to the union, was the abolition of the 'payments by results' system which had done much to lower the status of the profession and to debase its outlook.

The methods used by the N.U.T. to achieve these ends are partly but not wholly to be explained by the nature of the relations between the state, the employers and the teachers. But we should also note the disinclination to use trade-union methods and the desire of teachers to distinguish their position from that of manual workers.

What it did, in fact, was to send deputations and memorials to public and government departments and to 'lobby' in Parliament. By 1890 it was freely recognized that no major measure of educational policy could be passed against the opposition of the N.U.T.

Teachers were elected to school boards in 1870 and, when this was forbidden in 1875, ex-teachers and union officials were elected to them. Besides this, the union used ruthless and efficient legal action to increase the freedom of teachers where this was threatened; it did its utmost to prevent employers from getting anyone to replace a wrongfully dismissed teacher; and it was even ready to interfere as an organized body in school-board elections.

During these years (1870–95), important changes were taking place in the methods of educating and training pupil-teachers. Central classes were set up for collective instruction by specially selected teachers, the system spread to all main towns, and more and more were the young boys and girls looked upon as pupils rather than teachers. Many began to look forward to the day when a reorganized secondary system would be integrated with the training colleges, and when elementary teachers would be recruited freely from the middle classes. In 1890 an important step was taken when provincial universities established 'day training colleges': evidence that universities were awakening to the needs of the teaching profession.

The attitude of the teachers themselves to these changes was almost uniformly favourable. A few teachers disliked losing the instruction of their pupil-teachers, and felt that the higher academic standard of the pupil-teachers from the centres was no substitute for the practical knowledge gained through early teaching experience. Majority opinion, however, was favourable to any change which would raise educational standards and hence the status of the profession.

The affiliation of training colleges to the universities, and the alteration of the course of study so as to lead to a university degree, had long been among the ideals of the N.U.T. It was felt that these changes would raise the teachers' status and efficiency and aid in breaking the stranglehold of the government on the profession.

Combined with these motives was a longing for 'culture'. James Blacker, in his Presidential Address to the N.U.T. Annual Conference in 1901, represented the feelings of the profession when he said: 'The organized thousands of the National Union of Teachers have aspirations towards that high intellectual plane which has come to be embodied in one word: "culture".'[1]

The elementary teachers were bitterly aware that in spite of their certificates and long and arduous training they still had not been received into the ranks of the 'cultured' middle classes. In the stereotype of the teacher as we find it at the turn of the century, certain elements are familiar, for example 'that the teacher owed his position to the charity of others', 'that the teacher's work required no special abilities, that his hours of work were short, and his holidays were long', 'that the teachers as public servants had no right to any opinions of their own on educational politics'. There were, however, two rather important elements that had been generated in the period between 1870 and 1895.

The first was that, owing to the low social class from which the teachers were recruited, they were necessarily uncultured and narrow. One quotation must serve to make this point:

> The elementary school teacher is not likely to be a person of superior type. He is, in truth, a small middle-class person – with all the usual intellectual restrictions of his class. He is, in other words, unintellectual, knowing hardly anything well, parochial in sympathies, vulgar in the accent and style of his talking, with a low standard of manners. He is withal extremely respectable, correct morally, with a high sense of duty, as he understands it, and competent in the technique of his calling – What we want is educated ladies and gentlemen as teachers.[2]

[1] National Union of Teachers' Annual Report (1901), p. xl.
[2] Harold Hodge, 'The Teacher Problem', *Fortnightly Review* (May 1899).

There was enough truth in statements of this kind to make teachers squirm mentally, and enough falsehood and misrepresentation to make us wary of accepting them as completely accurate versions of the state of the teaching profession. Among the elementary teachers of this period were men like Sir James Yoxall, Sir Ernest Gray, T. J. Macnamara, James Runciman, Mrs Burgwin, G. A. Christian, F. H. Spencer and countless others. Looking back on that generation we can now see that there was no need for any teacher to be ashamed of his profession.

The second element in the stereotype of the teacher was an attack on the N.U.T. Here accusation and rebuttal can be given in one apt quotation by an anonymous writer.

Some observers resent its [i.e. the N.U.T.'s] activities, dub it a trade union, and charge it with narrowness and party spirit. But, whatever may be the dangers of the situation, there is no doubt that the position which the Union now enjoys has been earned by unceasing effort and devoted labour. To it, and almost to it alone, the country owes the destruction of vicious theories about state interference with the work of the elementary schools which were rampant twenty years ago, and are still cherished in a sneaking kind of way by many people who ought to know better. But victories of this kind are not bought for nothing. Fighters have not the virtues of students, and are apt, indeed, to lose perceptions which are necessary to the most far-seeing statesmanship. 'Every country,' says the proverb, 'has the foe it deserves,' and when a critic dwells on the failings of the N.U.T. it is well to remind him of the kind of policy against which the Union had so long to protest.[1]

The ideology of the elementary teachers in the late decades of the nineteenth century and the early decades of the twentieth century is the most important clue to their reactions to educational and social change. The factors of 'social isolation' and 'status anxiety', which we have noted in the 1850s, were still present. Added to this was the contribution of the Revised Code – the feeling that in the past the teaching profession had been 'betrayed'. The identification with working-class education had led to a working partnership between the N.U.T. and the working-class movement, although the individual teacher tended to keep himself aloof from the working class.

Much of the bitterness and frustration which existed in the profession at this period was due to the teacher's feeling that in his rise from the working class he had come up against 'caste' lines, that he could rise 'so far and no farther'. Much more was due to the very real frustration which teachers experienced in their work, which was a product of the gap between what their training and conscience told them 'could be' and the actual state of the schools.

It is in these terms that we can understand much of the confused skirmishing

[1] 'Movements in English Education', *The Citizen* (March 1897).

which preceded the passing of the Education Act of 1902, and the kind of pressures which led to the expulsion of Sir Robert Morant from his office of Permanent Secretary of the Education Department in 1911 (see p. 209).

The secondary school teacher

So far in this article we have concentrated our discussion on the 'elementary' school teacher. The profession of 'secondary' school teacher did not fully emerge until after the 1902 Act, although the previous history of teachers in secondary schools is of importance in sketching the various forces that have influenced the changing status of the teacher.

As early as 1846 the teachers in private middle-class schools had formed 'The Royal College of Preceptors',[1] the leading idea behind the formation of the College being to constitute a diploma-granting authority with eventual monopoly of teaching in middle-class schools.

Throughout the period from 1846 onwards the relationship between the middle-class secondary teachers and the elementary teachers was a watchful and hostile one. In 1858 a suggestion that certificated teachers should be admitted to the Royal College of Preceptors was turned down because 'the status of the certificated master is far beneath that of the independent middle-class educators'.[2]

The two sides of the profession came together from 1862 to 1867 in the first serious campaign for scholastic registration.[3]

The coalition, however, was an uneasy one, for the two sides wanted different things from scholastic registration. In general, the secondary teachers wanted it in order to found a Certificate of Competence and through it a profession, while the elementary teachers wanted it in order to safeguard their certificates and free themselves from government control. The elementary teachers also hoped to raise their status by associating themselves with the higher-status middle-class teachers. The secondary teachers were always willing to break the alliance if they thought they could obtain from Parliament a separate bill from which elementary teachers were excluded; but the N.U.T. was soon strong enough to block any measure which 'set up a line of separation between the certificated teachers and all other parts of the scholastic profession'. The state, meantime, showed no signs

---

[1] The Association was formed 'by a number of the principals of schools, who felt that the position of the private teachers was endangered by the rapid improvements which were being made in the training and education of the masters of schools of a lower grade, supported, in part at least, by the state' (*Museum*, April 1861).

[2] For this incident, see *The Literarium* (August–November 1857); *The School and the Teacher* (February–March 1858).

[3] The part the elementary teachers played in this campaign has tended to be ignored. See *Educational Guardian* (January–March 1863); *English Journal of Education* (1863); *Papers for the Schoolmaster* (May 1863; December 1867); *Museum*, (November 1864; October 1868); *The Academia* (8 January, 11 April 1869).

of being willing to relinquish any measure of its control over the elementary teaching profession.[1]

The second object of the College of Preceptors was the establishment of an institution for the training of secondary school teachers. Here again the College was unsuccessful, and until the twentieth century only a handful of secondary teachers were actually trained.

During the period in which the N.U.T. was growing in influence and numbers, the secondary teachers set up various organizations to represent their interests. Unlike the elementary teachers with their one comprehensive union, the secondary teachers were organized in separate associations of head masters, head mistresses, assistant masters and assistant mistresses.[2]

The secondary teachers (and in particular the assistant masters), like the elementary teachers, devoted a great deal of their attention to matters like security of tenure, pensions, salaries and extraneous duties. But again, like the elementary teachers, they were very much concerned with educational matters. This meant that they were increasingly drawn into the clash of educational, political and religious forces which from 1888 to 1902 prevented the passing of any effective legislation.

There is no doubt that, in spite of their lack of training, the status of the secondary school teachers was higher than that of the elementary teachers. They were recruited from a higher class in society (they had often 'come down' in the world), and they were assumed to possess the elements of 'culture'. There was a persistent hostility between the secondary teachers and the elementary teachers which still affects relations between the two sides of the profession to the present day. Each side had a stereotyped view of the other – the elementary teacher was thought of as 'uncultured', a drill-master using tyrannical methods to enforce learning, while the elementary teacher thought of the secondary teacher as a 'snob' who was incapable of teaching his limited store of knowledge.

These stereotypes may have had some justification in the past, but have long since ceased to have any basis in reality.

The 1902 Act and Sir Robert Morant

From 1880 onwards, with the gradual lifting of the revised code, there was a tendency for children to stay longer at school: by 1895 there were in elementary schools more than a quarter of a million over the age of 13. In some districts, they were gathered in separate schools and were receiving an education superior to that of the local secondary school. The system, in fact, was breaking its bounds.

[1] For the story of the secondary teachers, see Beatrice Webb, Special Supplement on 'English Teachers and their Professional Organization', *New Statesman*, Vol. V, No. 129 (25 September 1915), pp. 11–18, and also (2 October 1915), pp. 14–24.

[2] There were strong sectional antagonisms among the elementary teachers, but these sectional antagonisms tended to be limited to caucuses and pressure-group manoeuvring inside the N.U.T.

This aroused anxiety among those who feared the competition of working-class children with their own and, a more worthy objection, many felt that the so-called 'higher-grade schools' and 'pupil-teacher centres' were cramming their pupils for examinations without caring for their health or general education. It was urged that an integrated system of secondary education, staffed by cultured secondary teachers, would serve the nation better.

It was against this background that the Education Act of 1902 was passed, amidst unprecedented religious bitterness. It said little about a basic social issue: the demarcation between the elementary and the secondary school,[1] which necessarily involved the related issue of 'one profession or two'. On this matter, the direction of movement was laid down not by Parliament but by officials of the Board of Education. And between 1902 and 1911 this meant, in fact, by Sir Robert Morant, then Permanent Secretary. During these years it can truly be said that his will almost alone was effective in British education. His personality and influence were such that even forty years after his resignation it is difficult to see his actions clearly and without prejudice. There has recently been a tendency among writers on education to blame Morant for many of the weaknesses of English education, and in particular for the neglect of technical education. This does not seem to be a valuable criticism: a more fruitful approach is to see Morant's actions as stemming from a deeply rooted belief in 'education for leadership', a view he held in common with the secondary teachers, the Conservative Party and the majority of educationists of his time.

Running throughout the educational policy of the Board (and of the majority of the local education authorities) was one primary conception. This was that the main task of the educational system was to select an 'aristocracy of brains' wherever they might be found and ensure them the best education it was possible to give. This best education was primarily the type of education given in the older public schools and universities. This conception was in no way a 'caste' conception. The fact that it involved a comparative neglect of elementary and technical education was primarily due to the shortage of money for education. As it seemed necessary to concentrate on one thing at a time, it was thought that the most pressing needs were to raise the standards of secondary education, to raise the standards of training of teachers for elementary schools, and to provide as lavish a scholarship scheme as possible to enable working-class children to proceed to secondary schools. This conception of education was essentially hierarchical. A clear distinction was to be made between elementary education (for the

---

[1] The 'elementary school interests' can be said to have included the N.U.T., the School Boards and much of the Liberal Party. The 'secondary school interests' can be said to have included the secondary teachers' associations, the county councils and the Conservative Party. On all this, B. Webb, ibid. (25 September 1915), pp. 18–22, is the most reliable source. It is important to realize that the conflict between the two 'interests' reflected the conflict between 'education for leadership' and 'secondary education for all', which is so important in twentieth-century educational thought. This conflict in turn rests upon a dispute on the meaning of 'equality' in a democratic society.

majority of the population), and secondary education (for the élite). The only points of contact between the two types of education were that a number of elementary school children were to be selected at the earliest possible age for transfer to the secondary schools, that elementary school teachers were to be recruited from the products of the secondary schools, and that the most successful secondary scholars would proceed to the older universities and from these would be recruited the administrators and inspectors of the whole system, as well as the teachers in the secondary schools.

While this was to be the final state of the system, in the process of building it up the administrators and inspectors would have to be recruited mainly from the existing 'products of the older universities', and this would involve the virtual exclusion of ex-elementary teachers from the inspectorate. This method of recruitment was also to hold for as many as possible of the secondary school teachers and of the inspectors of the local education authorities. Thus the elementary school teachers, who had struggled to win promotion to the inspectorate and a united profession, would find themselves once more excluded.

As this policy was put into effect, there was a growing tension between the N.U.T. and the Board of Education. The elementary teachers resented the Board's preoccupation with secondary education, the 'freezing-out' of ex-elementary teachers from the secondary schools, the inspectorate and the staff of training colleges, the statutory limitation of the instruction to be given in training colleges, the limitation of facilities for secondary education to a few and the Board's support for the abortive 'two-column' register.[1]

They felt that the Board's policy was 'undemocratic' and 'caste-ridden'.[2]

Early in 1911, details of a confidential circular issued by the Board of Education began to appear in the newspapers. In this circular, elementary teachers were referred to as 'uncultured and imperfectly educated' and as 'creatures of routine'. Local education authorities were to be encouraged to replace the ex-elementary teachers in their inspectorate with men of the 'varsity type'. Taking advantage of a favourable political climate, the N.U.T. launched a ferocious campaign which eventually succeeded in driving Morant from office. Whether Morant was in fact mainly responsible for the issue of the *Holmes Circular* is doubtful. The circular was used by the N.U.T. as a 'lance-head, a point of a spear, directed against a system which has lasted for many generations and is supported by many interests'.[3]

---

[1] On all this, see the Annual Reports of the N.U.T. and *The Schoolmaster* (1902–11).

[2] While there were many sources of tension, it is doubtful if the conflict, when it came in 1911, would have been waged with such bitterness had it not been for the personality of Sir Robert Morant. He has been described by his biographer, B. M. Allen, as 'ready to sweep aside ruthlessly . . . any particular individual that hindered . . . the achievement of his end'. It is extremely probable that Morant felt the N.U.T. and its officials to be among those that hindered the achievement of his end. Only violent personal hostility can explain the bitterness with which the N.U.T. officials attacked Morant over the *Holmes Circular*.

[3] *The Schoolmaster* (27 May 1911).

After the downfall of Morant no education official, however exalted, could ignore the N.U.T.[1]

The 'general improvement'

While the N.U.T. was settling its account with Sir Robert Morant, it was attempting to come to some satisfactory arrangement with the local education authorities set up under the 1902 Act. The older problems of compulsory extraneous duties and insecurity of tenure tended to become less important, while the salary question grew more and more important. Before 1902 the Union had found it almost impossible to influence salaries directly except in the case of the larger school boards. Now (stimulated in large part by a rise in the cost of living) the Union was able to launch a salaries campaign and use the strike weapon for the first time to secure its demands.[2]

By 1914 the N.U.T., in co-operation with the secondary teachers' associations, was preparing to launch a full-scale campaign to raise the salaries and status of the teachers. The 'campaign' from 1910 to 1914 had succeeded in improving teachers' salaries in 149 out of 321 districts. Apart from this direct effect it had succeeded in leading public opinion to a knowledge of the inadequate salaries received by teachers. Immediately following the outbreak of war the executive of the N.U.T. decided to suspend the national campaign on salaries. As the war progressed the salaries of other occupations rose rapidly, in step with the rising cost of living, while the teachers' salaries remained stationary. In 1916 the campaign was recommenced and strike action was threatened in many areas.

In their campaign for higher salaries the teachers were aided by two factors. The first was that the whole educational system was threatened with collapse due to a serious shortage of entrants to the teaching profession.[3] During the administration of Sir Robert Morant a series of administrative measures destroyed the pupil-teacher system and instituted instead the system under which teachers were recruited from the secondary (now secondary grammar) schools. While the transition was eased by the establishment of special grants or 'bursarships' to aid children staying at secondary schools till 17 or 18, the total effect of the change was to make it more difficult for working-class children to enter the profession. At the same time, the profession was still not attractive enough to bring in any sizeable body of recruits from the middle classes.

The second factor which aided the pressure of the teachers for an increase in salaries was the war-stimulated desire for educational advance and for an increase in the length of school life and a reduction in the size of classes. It was realized

[1] George Tomlinson (then Minister of Education) is reported to have said, perhaps whimsically, in 1950, 'I would never dare to issue a circular without the approval of the N.U.T.' H. C. Dent, *Change in English Education* (1952), p. 51.

[2] For example, in Herefordshire (1910).

[3] The number of entrants to the profession had fallen from 11,018 in 1906–7, to 4,703 in 1913–14: *B.P.P.* Vol. XXV (1914), p. 148, and *B.P.P.*, Vol. XVIII (1914–16), p. 59.

that any educational advance was dependent upon an increase in the supply of teachers, and this in turn depended upon 'a general improvement in the prospects of the teaching profession'.[1]

The pressure of the teachers for a higher status thus met with a favourable response from the government. From 1917 onwards, the government actively intervened in the 'salaries problem', and in 1919 set up the 'Burnham Committees', composed of equal numbers of representatives of the teachers' associations and the local education authorities. These were charged with the task of securing 'the orderly and progressive solution of the salary problem . . . by agreement', and the agreements that were made were enforced by a series of minor teachers' strikes (sometimes with the support of the Board of Education). The effect of the recommendations of the Burnham Committees was to more than double the average salaries of the teachers, although in real terms the teachers were perhaps no better off than they had been before the war. Of greater importance in increasing the attractions of the teaching profession was Mr Fisher's Superannuation Act of 1918, which offered the teachers a generous non-contributory scheme.

The year 1920, in effect, marks a peak year for the profession. While it had still not gained control over the means of entrance, untrained teachers were slowly disappearing. After 1913, promotion to the elementary school inspectorate was mainly from the ranks of experienced elementary school teachers. The Burnham Committees and the Superannuation Act of 1918 had given the teachers assured salaries and pensions. From the viewpoint of the profession itself, the new atmosphere created many problems: it had to accustom itself to new responsibilities of co-operation. Unfortunately, the fifteen years of economic crisis and educational economy from 1921 to 1936 made the transition more difficult than it would otherwise have been. For teachers were forced to defend their hard-won salary and pension gains against a series of attempts to curtail them by thrifty Chancellors of the Exchequer. At times it seemed as if the existence of the Burnham Committees themselves was at stake. The defence of their gains by the teachers led to some attacks on the profession which are oddly reminiscent of the atmosphere during the Revised Code controversy. Thus, the Report of the Third Committee on Public Expenditure stated:

> It must be borne in mind that 'certificated teachers' who receive the highest salaries and who form the majority of the profession, have generally spent two years in a training college largely at the expense of the public.

A statement which might be compared with that of *The Times* newspaper (1 April 1861):

> Certificated teachers should . . . remember that they have been raised to their present position of affluence and comfort from poverty by the expenditure of public money. The capital employed in teaching them their profession has not been their own.

[1] *B.P.P.*, Vol. XI (1917–18), p. 51.

On several occasions the teachers' salaries and pensions were cut, with or without their consent. The unions were also forced into some of the most bitter strikes in their history by the attempts of a few local education authorities to cut salaries further than the national minimum.

On the whole, however, the teachers succeeded in stabilizing their salaries during a period of falling cost of living at a level which represented a substantial increase in their standard of living. This is the first and primary factor in the increase in status of the profession between the wars. It is certain that during the years of the depression the teachers had a higher standard of living than they had ever previously possessed. The profession as a whole was also spared the horrors of mass unemployment, although there was much unemployment among newly trained teachers.

The second factor responsible for improving the status of the profession was the change in the background of the majority of the profession, as the older teachers, who had entered the profession through pupil-teachership, were replaced by the products of the secondary schools. Although the social origins of the new entrants were similar to those of the old, the new entrants possessed more of the valued 'culture'. Under this heading must also be mentioned the increasing proportion of trained teachers and graduates in the profession. During the twenties and thirties, graduates had been forced into the elementary schools (at elementary school rates of pay). While this had increased the status of the elementary teacher, it may have lowered the status of the graduate teacher as such.

The third factor lay in the after-effects of the success of the teachers' associations (and in particular the N.U.T.) in ridding the life of the teacher of the humiliating insecurities of tenure, extraneous duties and confinement to the lower ranks of the educational system. Associated with this was the growing political influence of the teachers' associations in Parliament, on the local education authorities, and in the country as a whole.

The fourth and last factor to be mentioned was the increase in the status of education itself. The realization of the importance of education, both to the nation and to the individual child (if only in helping him to secure a good position in life), meant realization of the importance of the work of the teacher.

The last war contributed to the improved status of the teachers. Their heroic part in the mass evacuation of children captured public imagination, and a more sympathetic attitude towards the teaching profession was discernible. Indirectly, the war, like previous wars, was the cause of a wave of interest in education which in turn was to alter the status and conditions of the teacher.

The history of English education in the twentieth century can be viewed in large as a return to the ideals of 'one educational system and one profession', which we found as a slogan of the N.U.T. in the later years of the last century. The 'growing together' of elementary and secondary education which culminated in the 1944 Education Act necessarily led to a 'growing together' of the two sections of the profession.

The McNair Committee proposed an integrated system of training for graduates and non-graduates alike, and an increase in the salaries and conditions of both sections of the profession. Following the 1944 Act, 'Area Training Organizations' were set up to complete the process by which control of the teacher's training was relinquished by the state and taken over by the universities.[1]

The full unification of the profession has been prevented by traditional rivalries which have little relevance in the contemporary school world. The obscuring of the boundary between elementary and secondary teachers has also led to some complaints from secondary grammar school teachers (the old 'secondary' teachers), that they have lost status in comparison with the primary school and secondary modern school teachers (the old 'elementary' teachers).

In the last few years, Britain's sombre economic position and the slowing down of educational advance have led to fears among the teachers that the existing educational system was in danger. More immediately, the 'baby boom' has led to a shortage of teachers and to demands from some quarters that the standard of entry into the profession should be lowered in order to staff the schools. The teachers' associations have been condemned for opposing this dilution and for making their opposition effective through their representatives on the Area Training Organizations. The teachers have been accused of self-seeking, but have replied that only further educational advance and improved qualifications of teachers would benefit the country in the long run.

Conclusion

It is now possible to bring together the threads of the argument on the status of teachers. The theory has been proposed that 'in general those positions convey the best reward, and hence have the highest rank, which (a) have the greatest importance for the society, and (b) require the greatest training or talent'.[2] This theory is far too general to be of value in helping us to understand the factors affecting the status of the teaching profession. We have here to demonstrate the interrelationships of the following five determining factors:

(1) The esteem in which education is held, i.e. in hard terms, the amount of money the public (or its effective representatives) is ready to spend on education.

(2) The qualifications demanded of the teacher.

(3) The salary and general working conditions of the teacher.

(4) The amount of aid offered to recruits to the profession.

(5) The influence of the organized teachers.

[1] Until 1926, the final examination of students in training was carried out entirely by H.M. Inspectors. For changes in teacher training in the twentieth century, see *Education, 1900–1950: The Report of the Ministry of Education for the year 1950*, Cmd. 8244, Chap. VII, pp. 79–92.

[2] K. Davis and W. E. Moore, 'Some Principles of Social Stratification', *American Sociological Review*, Vol. X (April 1945), p. 243.

An increased public interest in education leads to a demand for more and better teachers. These teachers can in general be obtained only by increasing the attractions of the profession, and the amount of aid offered to recruits. The relative emphasis accorded to increases in salaries, improved working conditions and the amount of aid offered to recruits varies from time to time. It might be possible to obtain more and better teachers solely by increasing the attractions of the profession, without offering any new aid to recruits. In general, however, the educational authorities have relied on a combination of both policies to bring in recruits.

The status of the teacher tends to improve in so far as there is enhanced public esteem for education, higher qualifications are demanded of teachers, and salaries and working conditions are improved. Increased aid to recruits may, however, produce an unfavourable reaction. The influence of the organized teachers has been used to secure that any demand for more teachers is not met by lowering the qualifications required of teachers or by increasing aid to recruits alone, but rather by improving salaries and working conditions.

In general, we can say that the improved status of the teacher from 1800 onwards can be attributed to the dual influence of an increase in the publicly acknowledged importance of education, and the influence of the organized teaching profession.

We have noticed that the 'status anxiety' and 'social isolation' of the teacher were important features of the profession in the nineteenth century. The 'social isolation' has lessened with increasing urbanization and the growth of other 'new middle-class' occupations. The 'status anxiety' has returned in the post-war years as a common complaint of all the white-collar occupations. It has arisen from the increasing cost of living and the decreasing differential advantage of the white-collar occupations over the manual workers. In the case of the teachers it is also reinforced by fear of dilution.

If one is to hazard a prediction about the future of the teacher in England and Wales, one must take into account that, given that Britain is to solve her long-run economic problems, she will do so only by making more effective use of her human resources. This necessarily means paying increased attention to education. Any attempt at dilution of the teaching profession, even if the resistance to such policy by the organized teachers is overcome, will thus prove self-defeating and a costly failure. If this is realized, it is likely that the attractions of the teaching profession will be increased and the conditions under which the teacher works will be bettered. One cannot conclude from this, however, that his 'status' will increase in proportion. 'Status' is essentially a relative concept, and it is probable that the future will see a continuation of past trends whereby the statuses of various occupations are brought nearer to equality.

3 Some Variations on the Teacher's Role

C. CANNON

Introduction

The role of the teacher revolves round the transmission of knowledge and the transmission of values; particularly by virtue of the second function, teachers play a part in the socialization of the child. This analysis is not, however, very helpful in understanding the role of a particular teacher in modern industrial Britain. Not only is the role becoming equivocal in a society in transition to an economy of affluence, it is also differently conceived by different sections of society, and by the school pupils, the headmaster and the parents.[1]

Leaving aside the personal factor, and the broad influence of social and economic change, the emphasis laid on the two basic functions will differ according to the teacher's specialist knowledge and the age, sex and status of his pupils. For example, the infant teacher must be a socializer rather than a transmitter of knowledge, fulfilling a partly maternal function, but at the same time expanding the child's conception of the feminine role beyond that of the maternal, and providing a source of values beyond those of the home.[2] Similarly, the socializing function may be dominant in a non-selective secondary school, specially where a large cultural gap exists between the teacher and the taught. The teacher who accepts this role whole-heartedly becomes more of a social worker (the modern equivalent of the missionary role of the nineteenth-century elementary school teacher),[3] than a 'man of knowledge'.[4] Many teachers, however, do not accept this role in the secondary school, partly because the academic role

[1] See Jean Floud, 'Teaching in the Affluent Society,' *British Journal of Sociology* (December 1962); and Bryan Wilson, 'The Role of the Teacher', *British Journal of Sociology* (June 1963), for discussion of the teacher's role in modern Britain.

[2] See Talcott Parsons, 'The School Class as a Social System; some of its functions in American Society,' *Harvard Educational Review*, Vol. XXIX (1959), pp. 297–318, for an analysis of the role of the infant teacher in American schools.

[3] See Jean Floud, op. cit.

[4] See F. Znaniecki's analysis of the role of 'the man of knowledge' in 'The Social Role of the Man of Knowledge'; an accessible account is in the review by R. K. Merton, *American Sociological Review*, Vol. VI, No. 1 (1941), pp. 111–15.

First printed in Education for Teaching, *No. 64 (May 1964), pp. 29–36.*

may be more in accordance with their interests, but also because it is evidently more likely to lead to the attainment of high professional status. Within an occupation as stratified as teaching, the one with higher prestige is the teacher whose role is most akin to that of a university lecturer – the sixth-form teacher, whose charges are treated as intellectuals less far along the same academic road, to whom he is a guide rather than an instructor.

A further source of role variation lies in the specialist function of the secondary school teacher. This is most evident in a large school carrying a variety of courses, academic, technical, remedial, general; but it may also be seen interestingly in a selective school in which every teacher has a specialist qualification and teaches one subject only throughout the school.

The role of the academic teacher in a selective secondary school

This social situation emphasizes the academic function of the teacher. He stands as the representative of his discipline, and may be identified with it to such an extent that he sees children merely in terms of their ability in his subject.[1] So-and-so is 'no good', meaning not responsive to this particular teacher's presentation of his specialism. The subject becomes not merely a body of knowledge but a way of life which must seek disciples; thus the teachers compete, not merely for facilities, rooms and time on the time-table, but for the most able pupils. Their aim becomes to 'scoop' certain wavering but intelligent children as adherents to their subject, to read it to specialist level in the sixth form, and graduate in it at the university.

Although in a selective secondary school, the dominant tone is academic, the academic role is not the only one found in such a school. The honours graduate who takes charge of a class performs a socializing function: responsibility for the induction of thirty children into the school culture. If a particular class is unruly or nonconformist the image of their form teacher suffers accordingly for he is judged not merely by his examination results or the noise coming from his class-room but by the collective behaviour of his form even when it is not directly under his supervision. Similarly, the academic role may be broadened by informal responsibility for extra-curricular activities such as drama and debating.

[1] F. Stevens, *The Living Tradition: The Social and Educational Assumptions of the Grammar School*, p. 57 '. . . the curriculum of the grammar school is highly fragmented, and staffs reflect this fragmentation not only by regarding themselves very much as specialists but also by distinguishing children according to their ability to "do" certain subjects. Some teachers think in terms of highly specific aptitudes, as when a mathematics master says that 7 per cent of the pupils will never learn anything in his subject, or a geography mistress confidently asserts that as some people are born without a sense of space, maps are meaningless to them.' (1960).

The role of the non-academic teacher in a selective secondary school

There will also be specialists in the school whose chief role is not an academic one. The university graduates are surrounded by a 'fringe' of specialists in music, art, physical education, woodwork, domestic science, whose central business is not the central business of the school. The art and music specialists may be part-time teachers, concerned with practising their own art while teaching it for their bread-and-butter. This gives them a relative detachment from the total life of the school, and the liberty to interpret their role with more individual variations. The art teacher, for instance, is often permitted an eccentricity of dress and demeanour which is associated by his academic colleagues with the artistic temperament and may be cultivated by the artist as a smoke-screen behind which to play his role as he likes.

Because girls' schools have usually been modelled on boys' schools, and have inherited the conception of the school as a community with functions beyond those of mere tuition, both will have their share of these specialists, designed to cater for the development of the aesthetic and physical aspects of the child's nature,[1] and the need to produce leading citizens. In girls' schools however, the future citizen, or at least the less able one, is pictured as a home-maker, and trained in domestic science; and the physical education specialist has a wider role to play than in the boys' school because of the different patterns of development of the physical education professions for men and women. The latter was an important career for the pioneers of women's emancipation, while the former has tended to be split between the drill sergeant and the rugger blue.[2]

The rest of this article analyses the role of the teacher of physical education in the girls' selective secondary school, as this is highly specific, and provides an interesting example of the complexity of the role analysis of teachers. Two concepts will be mainly discussed: status, in the sense of prestige in the separate culture of the school; and role, or the social behaviour expected of one holding a particular occupational position, by virtue of the duties of that position. These two are closely interrelated; prestige depends partly on factors such as age, recruitment and training, and these help to shape the way in which the role will be played. They are however, also partly a function of that role; and the nature of his duties is the most important factor in determining the social standing of a

---

[1] This aim is written into the 1944 Act: 'and it shall be the duty of the local education authority . . . to contribute towards the spiritual, moral, mental, and physical development of the community', Pt II, Clause 7.

[2] The historical literature concerned with the profession contains many references to the difference in training of men and women physical education teachers: e.g. 'We have been struck by the complete absence of any provision for the training of men teachers of Physical Exercise comparable with that made in several institutions for training women teachers.' Departmental Committee's Report on Salaries in Secondary Schools, 1918. Reported in the *Ling Leaflet* (October 1918).

teacher. For example one would expect lower prestige to be accorded to a role such as the one under review which is seen as peripheral to the main purpose of the school.

This discussion will therefore examine the following variables: the sources of recruitment, and conditions of training and employment which confront the physical education teacher; the demographic structure of the profession; the duties which compose the role and their relation to the duties of others in the school system; and finally the type of relationship with pupils and colleagues resulting from the foregoing factors.

The main themes will be illustrated from historical sources; some of these are taken from the early days of the profession, for many of the traditional functions of an occupation are laid down in its formative years. It is then that members seek to build up an image of themselves and their duties, and are forced to formulate these explicitly. They then strive to maintain in changing conditions the role they have carved out for themselves, and which others expect them to perform.

The physical education teacher in a girls' selective secondary school

The demographic pattern of the physical education profession is markedly different from that of the academic teacher, showing a definite bias towards youth and lack of responsibility. In a recent sample,[1] 66 per cent of them were found to be under 30 compared with 36 per cent of History teachers who are representative of graduates. This picture is partly the result of the fact that, whereas graduate teachers drop in numbers on marriage, there is an increase again between the ages of 50 and 60, representing partly the unmarried of an earlier generation, and partly married 'returners'. This trend is absent among physical education teachers many of whom leave teaching by the time they are 30 and either do not return at all or do so in a more sedentary capacity.

Not only are physical education teachers markedly younger than their colleagues; they hold fewer posts of responsibility. In the same samples 51 per cent were found to be in non-graded posts, compared with 22 per cent of History teachers and 32 per cent of English teachers. It is not clear how far this is a function of youth and how far a matter of policy.

These factors contribute to a relationship with the graduate staff which on the whole lacks the dignity of age and seniority. Further factors contributing to the same result are discussed below.

There are two characteristics shared by physical education and domestic science teachers, which help to determine their relations with the graduate staff: their source of recruitment, and their working conditions.

[1] These figures were made available to me by the Association of Assistant Mistresses who conducted a survey in 1960 into the supply of teachers for girls' grammar schools.

Recruits to these branches of teaching tend to be drawn from among those girls in a grammar school who are personable, with practical ability, and a reasonable academic competence. They are not however, usually the same pupils who are considered to be potential university candidates, but are drawn from the same academic 'belt' as seen by their teachers, as the general training college entrants. The following description was given in the early days of the profession of the type of girl considered a suitable recruit: 'For girls who have not an overdose of brain, but are intelligent and obliged to earn their own living, there are few openings which lead up to so attractive a calling as that of Physical and Health Mistress in a school.'[1]

Within the grammar school range of ability, the same expectation would hold today: the extremely able girl who also excels physically is more likely to enter university and play games in her spare time.

Domestic science and physical education teachers share one other characteristic: isolation. They are usually trained in specialist colleges where they meet only other potential domestic science or physical education teachers.[2] In the case of the latter, they have probably been at one of a few major colleges, which are often situated in large grounds and away from urban centres.[3] This means that during training they have little opportunity to consider themselves as teachers in general terms, or to discuss their academic work with those in different fields.

Training in isolation is followed by geographical isolation in the school. The domestic science teacher will have her specially equipped room, in which she will be isolated with her pupils for comparatively long periods. The physical education specialist will have her gymnasium or even a whole wing of the school.[4] Otherwise she is outdoors on a field, or travelling in a coach to a swimming bath. In her free time she is supervising the allocation of equipment or talking to her fellow-specialists in a room devoted to changing facilities and sports gear. Opportunities to meet her academic colleagues are further limited by the fact

[1] Arthur Montefiore, 'The Physical Education of Girls', *Educational Review* (1892).
[2] The training of Physical Education teachers is as stratified as that of other teachers. It is shared between the general training colleges, where until the three-year training started, a girl could add a third year's Physical Education training to her two years' general course, and the specialist colleges which give a three-year course entirely devoted to P.E. The former training has usually supplied secondary modern schools and the latter most selective secondary schools and all independent or direct grant girls' secondary schools. The exception to this pattern is a degree course at Birmingham University started in 1946, which includes Physical Education among its subjects. It should be added that this stratification is likely to break down somewhat now that all teachers have a three-year training. The specialist colleges are also tending to move away from the earlier pattern by introducing the possibility of a second, more academic teaching subject.
[3] There are seven Physical Education colleges in England, of which two are very isolated and one relatively so. The time-consuming nature of the curriculum makes contact with other students difficult in all of them.
[4] This isolation is increased by the architectural planning of the new schools. Some of the large ones have a Physical Education wing with a separate room for the staff, situated so far away from the main staff room that the games staff have to make a real effort to go there.

that her role often includes attending to sick and injured children during breaks in the school day.

This geographical and social isolation may reinforce the mutual suspicion which started in school as girls tended to develop images of themselves as the 'studious' or 'outdoor' type. It is reinforced further by the occupational disease already mentioned, of thinking of pupils in terms of subject ability. This may segment the assessment of the children by the different academic specialists, but they at least all see them in terms of their minds. The physical education teacher on the other hand is concerned with their bodies; she sees them as useful in the school team, participants in a dancing display or organizers of games. Her interests thus cut across those of the academics so that they make competing claims on the time and energy of the same child.

The physical education teacher has a somewhat ambivalent status in the eyes of the rest of the staff: their attitude is compounded of envy and disdain, with a dash of affection. On the one hand she tends to have low status because she is seen as 'anti-academic', an image resulting from the conditions of recruitment and isolation mentioned above, and the fact that she is non-graduate[1] and represents the physical as against the mental life. In accordance with the image of the practical but empty-headed which has not changed since its classic formulation in the Norwood Report,[2] the physical education teacher is not expected to be verbally articulate or interested in ideas.[3] This may be partly, however, because she would then be encroaching on the territory of the academic staff; and already by her youthfulness and the popularity of her activities she has a way to the hearts of her pupils.

It is here that the envy lies; the physical education teacher seems to flaunt her youth and health; and it is evident that her job is a soft option, for she does not have to struggle with nights of marking books, and days of keeping children's noses to them. Evident also, that because she enjoys jumping about in short clothes she has not fully grown up; and thus she may be treated with affectionate patronage as if she were a kind of staff 'mascot'.

To her pupils too, the physical education teacher is the antithesis of book-learning. They see her as symbolizing activity; she drags them out of the warm corners of libraries on to freezing fields, or releases them from drudgery to joyful

[1] The lack of prestige (and pay) resulting from non-graduate status has been a source of grievance to physical education specialists for many years, e.g. 'Gymnastic Teachers under the Burnham Scale', by M. Muncaster, B.A., deplores the fact that the training is not recognized by the Burnham Committee as being a graduate equivalent; 'this reflects the unsatisfactory position of Physical Education in the educational system. The only solution would be a graduate training.' See Report of the 26th Annual Holiday Course, 1925.

[2] *Report on Curriculum and Examinations in Secondary Schools*, H.M.S.O. (1943), pp. 2–4.

[3] This idea is borne out to some extent: women physical education teachers rarely express themselves in professional articles. In the last three issues of the *Journal of Physical Education*, the journal of the profession, *all* the articles were by men, though they form a small minority of the membership of the Physical Education Association. It has been suggested to me, however, that this is characteristic of women teachers in general.

exercise, according to the side of the academic fence from which they view her. Because she usually makes herself heard and seen in large spaces she appears out of place in a classroom supervising preparation, or taking an academic lesson; the room is too small for her and the quietness oppressive.

The role of the physical education teacher is thus strictly circumscribed by the expectations of her 'social circle',[1] but within these limits she has a fairly wide range of functions, which may be summed up in the phrase which has long been the motto of her professional association, 'a healthy mind in a healthy body'.

These functions are as follows:

(1) the nurse and medical auxiliary
(2) the promotor of positive physical and mental health
(3) the skilled physical performer and coach
(4) the organizer;

there is also a fifth function, the aesthetic, in schools in which dance is taken seriously for its artistic value rather than as a useful means of occupying the masses on wet days.[2]

The care and maintenance of the healthy body has both prophylactic and remedial aspects; it partakes of the role of the health educator and the nurse. Both these aspects are illustrated in these early statements of the purpose of training, and the duties of the 'physical mistress' in a girls' school:

> They study all matters affecting drainage, ventilation and light . . . they learn to diagnose deformities . . . students in fact are not only trained to be teachers of a system of Physical Education but also to fulfil . . . the duties of a health mistress.[3]

> The Physical Mistress must be more than a mere teacher of drilling and gymnastics. She must judge the suitability of desks to special cases, test eyesight, judge the effect of any particular clothing. She must co-operate with the medical inspectress in cases of existing or possible defects, and provide and carry through remedial measures.[4]

Although the urgency of the remedial aspect has declined, these expectations would still be apt in the post-1945 period. Because of this combination of functions the physical education teacher is to the physically awkward or ailing child, not only the embodiment of positive health but the means of comfort and help. She may however, by virtue of the dual role, reinforce feelings of inadequacy in such

[1] The 'social circle' describes the set of people who participate in the performance of a given social role, grant the player of the role certain rights, and expect from him certain functions which supposedly satisfy their needs. For an analysis of this concept, see Znaniecki, op. cit. (1940), pp. 13–19.

[2] The role analysis which follows represents an 'ideal type' of the physical education teacher, upon which there are many variations. Obviously no teacher fulfils all these functions with equal success, although in a small school she may be expected to.

[3] Montefiore, op. cit. (1892).

[4] *Ling Leaflet* (1906).

children: the young nurse by her robustness makes the patient even more aware of frailty, but when she is also the witness of unsuccessful attempts at physical prowess, the effect is likely to be redoubled.

The third element in the role of P.E. teacher is that of the games and athletic coach. She is the expert at physical techniques; responsible for general levels of physical education in the school, but particularly for the advanced training of the most able, so that they may compete with other schools and bring home glory. Because English schools are communities and competitive games have an important identification function, pride in athletic achievement is simulated by the whole staff or at the very least by the headmistress. The results of games are read out in assembly, and the teams rise, or are otherwise acknowledged.[1] Academic staff may feel their successes to be more hardly won; but the cup or shield on Prize Day are spectacular symbols of achievement, and the fact that they are more loudly applauded than the University scholarship reinforces the ambivalent relationship between the physical education and academic staff discussed earlier.[2]

Fourthly, the physical education teacher's role involves organizational aspects. The manoeuvring of children in swimming baths and sports fields is accompanied in many schools by responsibility for manoeuvring them in assembly and fire-drill. There seem two possible influences behind this extension of function; one is part of the practical-academic dichotomy mentioned earlier. The practical ability needed for organization is thought to be linked to other practical abilities. The expected relationship is stressed in the following description by a headmistress of the qualities of a physical education teacher:

> The practical abilities she invariably possesses, and her organizing powers make her a most valuable member of staff . . . a most valuable adjutant to the headmistress . . . [1943][3]

[1] In one girls' school the practice has been for the whole team to file over the platform and shake hands with the headmistress whether the match was won or lost. This ceremony emphasizes both their collective service to the school, and the sentiment that it is the game and not the result that matters.

[2] For the value put on athletic prowess by the pupils of American high schools, see Coleman, *The Adolescent Society* (Free Press, 1962); and 'Academic Achievement and the Structure of Competition', *Harvard Educational Review*, Vol. XXIX, p. 367. There is an absence of studies of the English school which one suspects might show similar results, at least in middle-class selective schools.

[3] L. E. Charlesworth, Headmistress of Sutton High School for Girls, 'Physical Education in a Girls' Secondary School', in *Physical Education and School Hygiene*, Vol. XXXV (1943), p. 139.

4 The Seminar[1]

I. WATT

I

Methods of teaching obviously reflect the ideas of their time, and reflect them not only as regards intellectual attitudes to the knowledge purveyed but as regards the social attitudes between teachers and taught. (One obvious analogy is the way religious attitudes are formalized in the seating plans of church architecture.)

In the Middle Ages, the lecture system was the main form of teaching. The authority of the Doctors was symbolized by the pomp of their academic garb, which separated them from the laity by a conspicuous sartorial distinction which is still oddly popular among some denizens of the academy today. Very summarily one can say that the doctors of Salermo, Montpelier, Paris, Boulogne and Salamanca in the twelfth and thirteenth centuries were considered to be, like priests, the unique repositories of unchanging and unchallenged knowledge, whether of religion, of medicine or of law. The rediscovery of Aristotle and the development of Scholasticism combined to bestow upon the teacher in the medieval university a dominance which has never been surpassed, and which was associated with a remarkable degree of doctrinal uniformity.

In addition to lectures, the medieval university also found it necessary to institutionalize other forms of teaching which employed dialectic and discussion. Hence the disputation, where the application of accepted dogma to particular practical points was debated. The disputations were of two main types: one, where the doctor maintained his thesis against all comers; another, much less lofty, which was for students, and which developed greatly in the thirteenth century for arts students. In one of its early forms a Master of Arts would propound a thesis, which was attacked by another Master; the Bachelors of Arts defended the original thesis; the scholars mutely watched and listened, and a

---

[1] This article is based on a paper given on 21 November 1963, in a series on 'Objectives and Methods in Higher Education' sponsored by the School of Education, University of Manchester.

First printed as pp. 369–78 of 'The Seminar', Universities Quarterly, Vol. XVIII, No. 4 (September 1964), pp. 369–89.

Doctor presided. Later the student disputation took a much humbler form with students disputing under the surveillance of a mere Bachelor.[1]

There is a great distance, of course, between the seminar and the medieval disputation. The knowledge in a disputation consisted of a fixed body of principles and knowledge; and secondly, discussion was aimed not at acquiring new knowledge or upsetting old ideas, but only at giving practice in the techniques of oral exposition and debate.

Both printing and the seminar are generally agreed to be German inventions. It was in Germany that the invention of printing made the large lecture unnecessary in so far as it was merely a means of disseminating established information. The ending of this professional academic monopoly no doubt explains why many universities were hostile to printing in its early days; the chief learned supporters of printing tended to come from outside the universities, whether among the patrons of the New Learning, or among the humbler brethren of Germany and the Low Countries who wanted to read the Bible for themselves.

Luther was the greatest champion of the printing press, and of vernacular literacy, and it was in the Lutheran states of Germany that new educational ideas became most influential. The contrast with other countries in the sixteenth and seventeenth centuries is striking. Wherever the established churches were strong, as in France and Italy, the universities, closely tied to traditional ideas, continued with the old curricula and teaching methods; and the same is true of Oxford and Cambridge, though to a lesser degree. As a result, most of the great scientists, philosophers, and other men of learning were not formally associated with the universities at all in the seventeenth century. But in Germany there was no strongly entrenched central church, and so both the syllabus and the teaching methods of the universities were freer to change.

Literally, 'seminar' derives from *seminarium*, a seed-bed. Livy speaks of *equites seminarium senatus*; Luther called schools *seminaria ecclesiae*; and Comenius insisted on the literal application of the term to schools. The term 'seminary' or *seminarium*, meaning an institution for training priests, was well established in the seventeenth century; and the secularized form of this, the training college for teachers, is still the primary denotation of *das seminar* in German. This is no doubt one reason why it is so difficult to trace the first usage of the term 'seminar' to denote a special kind of university teaching in which discussion and research, rather than lecture and recitation of lessons, are the characteristic forms of instruction. But if it is impossible to recover the details of the earliest appearances of this seminar form of teaching, there seems to be no doubt that it is closely associated with Lutheranism, with its dual emphasis on the individual quest for truth, and on the democratic dissemination of literacy; and it seems likely that it was the coming together of these forces within the relative freedom of the University of Halle that led to the institutionalization of the academic seminar.

[1] Hastings Rashdall, *The University of Europe in the Middle Ages*, F. M. Powicke and A. B. Emden (eds), Vol. I (Oxford, 1936), pp. 219, 445–52, 492–4.

It was, for example, with the University of Halle, founded in 1694, that the pietist scholar Augustus Herman Franke was associated as Professor of Greek and Oriental languages from 1692 onwards till his death in 1727.[1] Franke's primary achievements were in the field of popular education, and in promoting Bible reading and missionary activity; but to train a superior religious ministry he set up a *Collegium Orientale*, composed of twelve students who lived in close association with Franke, and whose training, in addition to attendance at lectures, included frequent informal conversations and disputations. There seems to have been a similar kind of teaching in the larger *collegia biblica*, groups of students who held weekly discussions with Franke on biblical subjects. Halle was advanced in other ways: it is said to have been the first university to offer instruction in the vernacular and not in Latin; and it was also at Halle that the great Christian von Wolff (1679–1754) laid the intellectual foundations of the modern idea of a university. In his *Reasonable Thoughts on God, the World and the Souls of Men* (1719), Wolff asked for an end to the authority of Aristotle and of any transcendental authority in the domain of law and morals; in its place he demanded an unprejudiced and open-minded search for truth. It was also at Halle, and during Wolff's teaching career, that another essential feature of the modern university came into being, when in 1711 Jacob Gundling formulated the principle of 'Lehrfreiheit and Lernfreiheit': the student was to be free to choose what he would be taught, and the professor to teach according to his own intellectual interests.

Although the term seminar in its general sense of 'training institution' was already current at Halle and elsewhere, it is not until two generations later, though again at Halle, that one discovers the historical prototype for the academic seminar. J. M. Gesner's seminars at Göttingen may be somewhat earlier, but it is the Philological Seminar which Friedrich August Wolf began at Halle in 1786 which is generally considered to have been the most influential. There may seem to be little opportunity for revolutionary innovation in the field of classical philology; but it was Wolf's development of textual criticism which opened up the whole question of the authorship of the Homeric poems and later led to the Higher Criticism of the Bible in the nineteenth century; while the concomitant rediscovery of popular culture and folk-lore by Herder and others had very wide social and political implications. As to teaching method, Wolf was apparently content to guide the discussions of his students, each of whom prepared written or oral theses on topics set beforehand, and usually involving some form of specialized research.[2] Out of this no doubt derived another sense of the term seminar in German, meaning a specialized research department or institute; for the texts and manuscripts collections used by the class were often collected in a

[1] H. E. F. Guerike, *The Life of Augustus Herman Franke*, trans. Samuel Jackson (London, 1837), pp. 87–8, 142–9.

[2] See Matthew Arnold, *Higher Schools and Universities in Germany* (London, 1874), pp. 77–83, and the works cited in the next note.

special room, which became the main focus of the work of a group of students, working under several seminar directors.

In nineteenth-century Germany the teaching seminar became the main means whereby a university élite was trained, mainly in classics. Normally, admission to seminars only required evidence of sufficient knowledge of that particular subject; every member was obliged to perform regular written and oral work; and the system became a unique demonstration of the idea of the free collective pursuit of knowledge. There was very wide variation from university to university, and from period to period, as regards teaching methods: one common pattern was for the director to give a theme or a textual problem to an individual student; the student wrote an exercise, and then handed it to some other students for their criticism; and finally this exercise, together with a report embodying the criticisms of the other students, were discussed at a general meeting of the seminar under the guidance of the director.

The mutual interdependence of reading, writing and general discussion under the direction of an expert in the particular topic studied, seems to me to be the most valuable element in the seminar; but there are also drawbacks, which appeared very early.

First, the early seminars depended upon research, mainly philological; obviously not all academic subjects offer the same opportunities for new discoveries, and they tend to do so less as they develop. Secondly, less advanced or the less gifted students tend to find themselves left out. A minimum prior knowledge is obviously necessary to make participation in a seminar possible. In Germany in the nineteenth century it sometimes took two years after admission before a student was ready, and as university numbers increased an *Aufnahmeprüfung*, or qualifying examination, became necessary in some universities before admission to seminars was allowed. In others a more elementary class, the pro-seminar, was developed so that students could get some preliminary guidance and training in the subject, before being admitted to the seminar proper.[1] Again *Lernfreiheit* meant the student's freedom to choose; and paradoxically this often led to subordination of the mass of the students to the favoured few, because although all were free to come to the seminar, not all were equally gifted or well-prepared.

In recent years various methods of rectifying these difficulties have been attempted: classifying seminars from lower or elementary (*Proseminare*) to higher or advanced (*Hauptseminare*), sometimes with further subdivisions (*Mittelseminare, Oberseminare*); requiring a *Seminarschein*, or entrance qualification for the more advanced seminars, which is based on a successful report or *Referat* in the less advanced seminar; or dividing the attendance at a seminar into a small panel

[1] See especially Friedrich Paulson, *The German Universities: Their Character and Historical Development*, trans. E. D. Perry (New York and London, 1895), and *The German Universities and University Study*, trans. F. Tilly and W. W. Elwang (London, 1906); also Gunnar Thiele, *Geschichte der Preussischen Lehrerseminare* (Berlin, 1938), pp. 314–68.

of active participants in the front rows with the other students, colleagues and members of the public behind them, commenting on the reports of the panel, or asking questions. But with the great expansion of university education, the problem of numbers has now become virtually insoluble; the present situation in Germany, where many hundreds, and in some cases over a thousand, students attend what is still called a seminar, obviously makes its proper functioning impossible, and thus reminds us that its survival under conditions of mass higher education is problematic.

Especially problematic, of course, where a small professoriate clings to its virtual monopoly of teaching, for an egalitarian attitude is necessary not only for the general health of the academy but also for that of the seminar. In Germany *Lehrfreiheit* gave the professor an autonomy both inside and outside the academy which assisted the creation of a special caste, the *Gelehrtenstand*. This meant that the numbers of people allowed to conduct university lectures or seminars were very restricted; and it also implied a very esoteric conception of freedom – it is worth remembering that the professor's freedom to teach whatever subject he chose became the banner under which other freedoms and duties were disregarded and lost.

II

In America higher education developed when the old universities, such as Yale and Harvard, were still largely undergraduate institutions, and when Germany was virtually the only place to go for research.[1] The seminar, or what was then known as the 'seminary method' of teaching, was brought back by scholars who had done most or all of their graduate training in Germany. Its beginning in America is usually held to have occurred at the University of Michigan. In 1869 the historian Charles Kendall Adams returned from Europe, and, we are told in B. A. Hinsdale's *History of the University of Michigan*, he soon 'introduced the Seminar method of instruction into his advanced classes, which method met with much favour and was afterwards taken up by other professors'.

The terms of Hinsdale's comments on the innovation make clear the reasons for its enthusiastic reception:

That the teachers of the academical youth should be investigators and discoverers of truth is the first of the twin ideas relating to instruction that Germany has done so much to propagate; the other is that students also should engage in investigation. From the two ideas . . . a third one naturally follows: namely, that teachers should teach their pupils to conduct research work. This is the origin of the well-known German invention, the *Seminar*.

[1] C. K. Thwing, *The American and the German Universities* (New York, 1928), pp. 68–71; J. S. Brubacher and Willis Rudy, *Higher Education in Transition: An American History, 1636–1956* (New York, 1958), pp. 171–195.

Professor Charles K. Adams was the head of the Department of History, but his example was soon followed by Professor Moses Coit Tyler, of the English Department, and thence spread to other departments and universities. The fullest description of an early seminar in America is probably that of Henry Adams at Harvard in the 1870s, which he describes in *The Education of Henry Adams*. Adams began with radical doubt:

... In essence incoherent and immoral, history had either to be taught as such – or falsified.

Adams wanted to do neither. He had no theory of evolution to teach, and could not make the facts fit one. He had no fancy for telling agreeable tales to amuse sluggish-minded boys, in order to publish them afterwards as lectures. He could still less compel his students to learn the Anglo-Saxon Chronicle and the Venerable Bede by heart ... The college expected him to pass at least half his time in teaching the boys a few elementary dates and relations, that they might not be a disgrace to the university. This was formal; and he could frankly tell the boys that provided they passed their examinations, they might get their facts where they liked, and use the teacher only for questions. The only privilege a student had that was worth his claiming, was that of talking to the professor, and the professor was bound to encourage it. His only difficulty on that side was to get them to talk at all. He had to devise schemes to find what they were thinking about, and induce them to risk criticism from their fellows. Any large body of students stifles the student. No man can instruct more than half a dozen students at once. The whole problem of education is one of its cost in money.

The lecture system to classes of hundreds, which was very much that of the twelfth century, suited Adams not at all. Barred from philosophy and bored by facts, he wanted to teach his students something not wholly useless. The number of students whose minds were of an order above the average was, in his experience, barely one in ten; the rest could not be much stimulated by any inducements a teacher could suggest. All were respectable, and in seven years of contact, Adams never had cause to complain of one: but nine minds out of ten take polish passively, like a hard surface; only the tenth sensibly reacts.

Adams thought that, as no one seemed to care what he did, he would try to cultivate this tenth mind, though necessarily at the expense of the other nine. He frankly acted on the rule that a teacher, who knew nothing of his subject, should not pretend to teach his scholars what he did not know, but should join them in trying to find the best ways of learning it. The rather pretentious name of historical method was sometimes given to this process of instruction, but the name smacked of German pedagogy, and a young professor who respected neither history nor method, and whose sole object of interest was his students' minds, fell into trouble enough without adding to it a German parentage (pp. 300–6).

Adams ran his seminar by choosing specially interested and specially qualified students. He introduced the students to the original sources of information which meant that they had a relatively narrow range of study, and he encouraged them to tackle their subject independently by providing the widest possible choice of books:

> The course began with the beginning, as far as the books showed a beginning in primitive man, and came down through the Salic Franks to the Norman English. Since no textbooks existed, the professor refused to profess, knowing no more than his students, and the students read what they pleased and compared their results. As pedagogy, nothing could be more triumphant. The boys worked like rabbits, and dug holes all over the field of archaic society; no difficulty stopped them, unknown languages yielded before their attack, and customary law became familiar as the police court; undoubtedly they learned, after a fashion, to chase an idea, like a hare, through as dense a thicket of obscure facts as they were likely to meet at the bar . . .

So much did Henry Adams want to disclaim the authority of the 'professor' that he even decided in 1877 that a rival history course should be set up by a conservative professor, Henry Cabot Lodge, to offset his own democratic and radical views:

> He wanted to help the boys to a career, but not one of his many devices to stimulate the intellectual reaction of the student's mind satisfied either him or the students. For himself he was clear that the fault lay in the system, which could lead only to inertia. Such little knowledge of himself as he possessed warranted him in affirming that his mind required conflict, competition, contradiction even more than that of the student. He too wanted a rank-list to set his name upon. His reform of the system would have begun in the lecture room at his own desk. He would have seated a rival assistant professor opposite him, whose business should be strictly limited to expressing opposite views. Nothing short of this would ever interest the professor or the student; but of all university freaks, no irregularity shocked the intellectual atmosphere so much as contradiction or competition between teachers. In that respect the thirteenth-century university system was worth the whole teaching of the modern school.

We meet here one of the further difficulties of seminar teaching. Quite apart from the fact that the very specialized researches which Adams's students conducted had little conceivable relation to their future lives, unless they also were to become university teachers, it was also unlikely that many students would combine sufficient knowledge, training and courage to give their teacher any thorough criticism.

This is a general difficulty with seminar teaching. It can more easily produce the egalitarian form than its substance, and the authority of the teacher can be more crippling to the student in the seminar than in the lecture, where there is no obligation to respond. This danger is illustrated in a report of the seminars given by A. S. Cook, Professor of English at Yale:

> His teaching was to the last degree exacting and remorseless. He did not lecture, but conducted his classes by Socratic questioning, never if he could help it divulging a fact himself but forcing each student to expose his ignorance, and then invariably examining him the next time to see if he had corrected it. There were no rules of fair play in his quest of truth. He even tried to correct faults of character . . . at least a third of every class hated this man who always hurt them . . .[1]

The problems of the autocratic temperament will no doubt always be with us, but it seems clear that the rapid spread of seminar teaching in the United States was mainly due to the way that the pursuit of knowledge was vitalized by its being made a part of a joint effort by students and teachers. This appears in the account made by a visitor[2] to Johns Hopkins in 1911:

> Everywhere I could see students entering professors' rooms, stopping them in the Hall. Even more disconcerting was the fact that after a meeting of the Journal Club, several students adjourned with members of the faculty to an oyster bar . . . where the discussion continued vividly and informally. How different it was, not only from the Sorbonne University, to conduct the seminary in economics in this way. The meetings are not in the nature of class meetings. They are announced publicly (in the *University Gazette*) and are open to all . . .

We still of course meet the difficulty of the unprepared student. Thus the visitor to Johns Hopkins continues:

> A young man who had incautiously enrolled for graduate English without being aware of its strong linguistic colouring was asked late in October if he was ready to go to the class of historical grammar. 'Is that what you call it?' he replied. 'I've been sitting in the back row for three weeks without the least idea what it's all about. The professor puts a couple of words on the blackboard and says something about them. The Fellow disagrees. Then they and one or two others argue about it for the rest of the period. It's all over my head.'
>
> It was over his head and the only way he could hope to profit by the course was to bone up the fundamentals for himself in the library.

It cannot be claimed that such experiences are unique; the problem of how to classify seminars, and regulate admission to them, is always difficult; and there is

---

[1] G. W. Pierson, *Yale College: An Educational History, 1871–1921* (New Haven, 1952), pp. 284–6.
[2] Gilbert Chinard. See J. G. French, *A History of the University Founded by Johns Hopkins* (Baltimore, 1946), pp. 333–5.

a particular difficulty in the specialized research seminar, where both the subjects and the scholarship are relatively remote. But the research seminar has become the essential basis of the American system of graduate teaching, which is highly effective, and which compares very favourably with any other system, except perhaps for the few exceptional students who are capable of working entirely on their own.

In England, however, the question of postgraduate training is of secondary importance, and it is therefore the less advanced forms of teaching which are inspired by the general method and spirit of the seminar that are of most immediate relevance to our present needs. In the United States few undergraduate classes are actually called seminars; but the staple undergraduate courses contain its essential elements: they combine common class-readings, regular written assignments, and a basically conversational and dialectical method of teaching and discussion. For this kind of teaching there seems no better word than seminar, however vague the term, and however different its meaning from its established German and American usages.

5 Latin Language Study as a Renaissance Puberty Rite

W. J. ONG

I

The reasons why any particular society follows the educational curriculum which it does follow are always exceedingly complex. Because, in being a preparation for the future, it is inevitably a communication of what is available from past experience, education is always primarily a traffic in this experience and only secondarily a matter of theory. The theories concerning the handling of this experience never quite compass the actuality and totality of the experience itself. They are generally rationalizations, after-thoughts, however valuable or venturesome they may be under certain of their aspects.

This is true of education today, and it was true of education during the Renaissance. To be sure, no one bristled with educational theory more than Renaissance man. He had often very definite ideas as to what should be done to produce the proper sort of courtier or soldier or scholar or even ordinary bourgeois. Yet his theories never quite came to grips with everything in the pedagogical heritage.

Such is the case particularly with the Renaissance teaching of Latin. Depending on how much or how little he was influenced by the humanist tradition, the Renaissance educator thought of Latin as bringing students into contact with the ancients, whom Erasmus had declared to be the sources of practically all human knowledge. But quite independently of this theory, the Renaissance educator was also compelled to teach Latin because the books in use, contemporary as well as ancient, were books written in Latin or translated into Latin. These included the books on language and literature, on 'philosophy' (which meant, besides logic, physics and what we might best style general science, inextricably interwoven with psychology and snatches of metaphysics), books on medicine, law and theology, not to mention books on military science, botany, alchemy, physiognomy, geography, and on every other more or less learned subject. This unacknowledged reason for teaching the language – the fact that pupils had to be able to read it, write it, and think in it – in actuality outweighed all other reasons through the Renaissance period.

First printed in Studies in Philology, *Vol. LVI, No. 2 (April 1959), pp. 103–24.*

This fact also made the teaching of Latin inevitably different from the teaching of Greek or Hebrew, although in the upper reaches of humanist theory these two languages were recommended for study at least as urgently as Latin. The humanists' own encomia of Greek and Hebrew, from Erasmus to Ramus and beyond, together with institutions such as the nominally trilingual colleges of Louvain, Salamanca and Alcalá, attest the existence of this equal theoretical esteem for Greek and Hebrew and of a desire to implement the theory. Yet Renaissance Greek and Hebrew are sorry failures compared to Renaissance Latin. They produce no perceptible literature at all. When someone, such as Poliziano, writes epigrams in Greek, this achievement – or, perhaps better, this tour de force – is completely overshadowed by the bulk of the same author's Latin writings. And the currency of Hebrew never even remotely approximated the extremely limited currency of Greek.

As compared with the other 'classical' languages, the Latin of the time thus has a viability which is not at all accounted for by humanist theories and attitudes regarding the ancient world. To understand the practices of the Renaissance educator we must look beneath his theories for other things, for the psychological and social drives, for the complex of psychological and social stresses and strains and compulsions to which he is heir and which register in his performance. Here I should like to single out for attention some patterns in the Renaissance teaching of Latin which manifest certain of these complexes and suggest that the Renaissance teaching of Latin involved a survival, or an echo, devious and vague but unmistakably real, of what anthropologists, treating of more primitive peoples, call puberty rites.

II

There is a vast literature on puberty rites, but a brief summary of some of their features will suffice to make the necessary points about Renaissance Latin language teaching and study.[1] Peoples of simpler culture have, virtually universally, a systematic ceremonial induction of adolescent youths into full participation in tribal, as opposed to family and clan, life. These rites have certain more or less

[1] See Hutton Webster, *Primitive Secret Societies* 2nd edn rev. (Macmillan Co., New York, 1932), pp. 20–73; A. E. Jensen, *Beschneidung und Reifezeremonien bei Naturvölkern* (Stuttgart, 1933); Arnold van Gennep, *Les rites de passage* (E. Noury, Paris, 1909), pp. 93–164; Goblet d'Alviella, 'Initiation (Introductory and Primitive)', *Encyclopedia of Religion and Ethics*, James Hastings (ed), Vol. VII (T. and T. Clark, Edinburgh, 1914), pp. 314–19; Charles W. M. Hart, 'Contrasts between Prepubertal and Postpubertal Education', in *Education and Anthropology*, George D. Spindler (ed.) (Stanford University Press, Stanford, California, 1955), pp. 127–45, and the discussion by various persons which follows, pp. 145–62, etc. See also Hutton Webster, *Taboo, a Sociological Study* (Stanford University Press, Stanford University, California, 1942), p. 109 n. For a brilliant, if somewhat precious and erratic, extrapolation on a theme relevant to puberty rites, see José Ortega y Gasset, 'The Sportive Origin of the State', Chapter I in his *Toward a Philosophy of History* (W. W. Norton and Co., New York, 1941).

well-defined characteristics. The individual being initiated is established in a special 'marginal environment' so that the puberty rites are accurately styled by A. van Gennep *rites de passage*. The past of the individual is considered to be cut off, and certain excesses – licence, theft, arson, violence – are often allowed. This sense of a break from the past may be dramatized, for example, when the home of the boy destined to undergo the rites is invaded by those who are to initiate him and who tear him forcibly from the company of the women, and sometimes physically from the very arms of his mother, who puts up a show of resistance, half conventional and half real. During the period of initiation the boy is made to do many things that are hard, often, it appears, simply because they are hard. In some cases, special taboos are enforced. Thus a boy may not touch his own body anywhere with his hands, but only with a stick – if, for example, he wishes to scratch himself. An atmosphere of continual excitement is cultivated to enlist the youth's interest. As Nathan Miller states it, 'Put on edge through ingenious torments, sleeplessness, and nerve-racking frights, the candidate becomes keenly sensitive to the power of his preceptors and indelible, life-long impressions are made.'[1]

The role of the preceptor is important, for the puberty rites are essentially didactic, 'the chief vehicle to link generations in the transmission of the culture complex'.[2] The climax is reached in the inculcation of lessons in tribal law, morality and tradition. Bushman puberty rites, for example, feature religious dances in which animal masquerades predominate. Over all these presides the belief that the youths must be made by their preceptors to assimilate their lessons the hard way. Among the Bechuans, the boys in a state of nudity engage in a dance during which the men of the village pummel them with long, whip-like rods while asking such questions as, 'Will you guard the chief well?' or 'Will you herd the cattle well?'

Needless to say, because they incorporate youth into the tribe rather than into the family, puberty rites involve sexual segregation. The rites for boys are for boys alone. There are comparable rites for girls, but we are concerned with the boys alone here, for, generally speaking, it is boys alone who are taught in Renaissance schools, or who are given a systematic formal education. There are some few rare references to school education for girls in the Renaissance,[3] but commonly the girls of the time learned what reading and writing they learned outside the schoolroom, in the privacy of the home.

[1] Nathan Miller, 'Initiation,' *Encyclopedia of the Social Sciences*, Edwin R. A. Seligman and Alvin Johnson (eds), Vol. VIII (Macmillan Co., New York, 1937), pp. 49–50.

[2] Ibid.

[3] See Norman Wood, *The Reformation and English Education* (George Routledge and Sons Ltd., London, 1931), pp. 77–8, 181–2; cf. ibid., pp. 3–7, 28, 159 ff. Cf. Carroll Camden, *The Elizabethan Woman* (Elsevier Press, New York and London, 1952), pp. 44–50; Ruth Kelso, *Doctrine for the Lady of the Renaissance* (University of Illinois Press, Urbana, Ill., 1956), pp. 58–77, especially pp. 66, 68, 73 (girls' reading to be in the vernacular); A. F. Leach, *The Schools of Medieval England*, 2nd edn (Methuen and Co., London, 1916), pp. 88–9.

Puberty rites are thus ceremonial inductions or initiations of the youth into extra-familial life which involve a sense of break with the past (a 'marginal environment') together with segregation from the family and from those of the other sex, and chastisement under the direction of elders for didactic purposes. Any system of schooling which separates boys from girls and is carried on outside the home will, of course, to a greater or lesser extent involve all these things, with the possible exception of chastisement. And it is common knowledge that in the school from early Greek and Roman times well through the Renaissance, chastisement was definitely involved. Thus any formal education through the Renaissance might well tend to activate the complex of behaviour on the part of preceptor and student characteristic of puberty rites, and, indeed, almost any conceivable educational procedure outside the home will to some extent do the same thing. The coincidence of various forms of hazing with schooling everywhere is ample evidence of this fact.

The point of this article is that, although there are these general connections between school education and puberty rites, in Renaissance times (and to a great extent through the Middle Ages, as these led into the Renaissance) the status of Latin encouraged in a special way the development of a puberty rite setting and puberty rite attitudes in the educational activity of the time, and, incidentally, that traces of these attitudes can be found in the few places where Latin lingers on the educational scene today. This is thus an attempt to explore certain of the complex social implications of Latin as a learned language.

These social implications were large. For when Latin passed out of vernacular usage, a sharp distinction was set up in society between those who knew it and those who did not. The conditions for a 'marginal environment' were present. Moreover, the marginal environment was one between the family (which as such used a language other than Latin) and an extra-familial world of learning (which used Latin). The fact that the marginal environment was primarily a linguistic one only heightened the initiatory aspects of the situation, for the learning of secret meanings and means of communication is a common feature of initiatory rites. It is through ability to communicate that man achieves a sense of belonging.

III

The cleavage between the vernacular world and the Latin world did not coincide with the division between literacy and illiteracy, but it did coincide with the division between family life and a certain type of extra-familial life and with a division between a world in which women had some say and an almost exclusively male world. Literacy could be, and frequently was, acquired at home, often under the tutorship of women in the family. But this literacy, which can be distinguished from 'learning', was commonly restricted to ability to read and write the vernacular. Schools often prescribed that a boy be able to read and write at least the alphabet as a requirement for admission,[1] for it was the business of the school proper to teach, not reading and writing, but the Latin language. This medieval and Renaissance situation still registers in our vocabulary, where elementary schools are called not reading and writing schools but grammar schools – the 'grammar' here referring historically to the teaching of beginners' Latin, which was Latin grammar. This situation meant that, in general, girls, who were educated at home and not in schools, could be quite literate without having any effective direct access at all to the learned world, which was a Latin-writing, Latin-speaking and even Latin-thinking world. There were only occasional exceptions such as Hroswitha, Lady Jane Grey, Margaret More and Queen Elizabeth – or perhaps Shakespeare's Portia – to ruffle the masculine sense of self-sufficiency. Because their sex was so committed to the vernacular, women could become – as Raymond W. Chambers and others have shown they did become – both a major audience for English literature and some of its chief patrons.

Closed to girls and to women, the schools, including the universities with their own 'schools' (*scholae* or classrooms), were male rendezvous strongly reminiscent of male clubhouses in primitive societies. At the top of the academic structure, in the universities, with the exception of doctors of medicine, who at Paris, for example, were allowed after the year 1452 to marry and continue as regents,[2] teachers through the Middle Ages and the Renaissance (and in many universities much later than the Renaissance) were obliged to remain unmarried so long as they continued active teaching, and this whether or not they were clerics in the ecclesiastical sense at all. Peter Ramus, his erstwhile secretary and biographer tells us, often spoke about marriage but decided to forgo it because if he had married he should have had to resign as principal of the Collège de Presles and as a university master.[3]

Somewhat mysterious in its origins and implications, this specially closed environment of the universities was maintained by a long apprenticeship or bachelorship (common to medieval guilds of all sorts) terminating in the *inceptio* or inaugural act of teaching. Today the *inceptio* is echoed really but faintly in the now wholesale ceremony known by the mystifying name of commencement, and words surviving on university diplomas, *periculo facto* or 'having undergone the (requisite) danger or trial', bear witness to the old feeling that education was an initiation. But in helping to maintain the closed male environment the psychological role of Latin should not be underestimated. It was the language of those on the 'inside', and thus learning Latin at even an infra-university level was the first step towards initiation into the closed world. Earlier groups of learned men – the Academy, the Stoa, the schools at Alexandria – seem never to have achieved the

---

[1] For example, the statutes of Canterbury School and St Paul's School so prescribed in the sixteenth century – Wood, *Reformation and English Education*, p. 3.

[2] Hastings Rashall, *The Universities of Europe in the Middle Ages*, new edition edited by F. M. Powicke and A. B. Emden, Vol. I (Clarendon Press, Oxford, 1936), p. 446.

[3] Nicolas de Nancel (Nancelius), *Petri Rami . . . vita* (Paris, 1599), pp. 58–9.

close-knit, jealously guarded internal organization of the university. It seems not irrelevant that they did not have a secret language to nourish their *esprit de corps*.

The humanists, who for various reasons often thought in terms of a home-centred system of education, were hard put to find a substitute for the closed male environment of the school. One recalls the embarrassment of Erasmus, More and Ascham when they speak of rearing a youngster in a home where he would hear the proper use of language at an early age. These educators of course mean the proper use of the Latin language – they are giving no thought to the vernacular at all – and they are visibly nonplussed by the fact that this means that the youngster will be in the company of women, since it had proved impossible, even for the humanists, to have homes without women in them. Roger Ascham speaks rather glibly of the way in which Tiberius and Caius Gracchus were brought up in the home of their mother Cornelia, where 'the dailie use of speaking were the best and readiest waie to learne the Latin tong'.[1] But Ascham here is not merely resorting to humanist piety by preferring a classical example to a current one. He is bowing before historical fact. There were no current examples, and could be none. We can be sure that no English mothers cooed to their children in the language native to the mother of the Gracchi, and thus we find Sir Thomas Elyot more realistically stating, 'After that a childe is come to seven years of age, I holde it expedient that he be taken from the company of women, savynge that he may have, one yere, or two at the most, an auncient and sad matrone attending on hym in his chamber.'[2]

Sir Thomas pleads here that this arrangement will remove the child from temptations against chastity. However, although this reason might conceivably at times apply with references to servant girls or other attendants, the separation of the child from his own mother which Elyot seems to envision here, and which families such as Sir John More's practised (his son Thomas grew up in Cardinal Morton's household), is here generating its own special warrant in humanist educational aims. In cultivating the young boy's ability to speak Latin, women, not being part of the Latin world, were commonly of no use to a child after the age of 7, for this is the age when Elyot and others prescribe that a boy begin to learn and to speak Latin – and, for that matter, Greek as well. The difficulty was that if there were too many women around, the child would speak English, not Latin. He would slip back into the vernacular family circle instead of being forced out already at this tender age into the world of the 'tribe', of men. We are faced here with a rather precocious appearance of the puberty rite situation around the age of 7, but the humanists favoured precociousness and promoted it when they could.

Sir Thomas More and others, more realistic, would try to remedy the situation

---

[1] Roger Ascham, *The Scholemaster*, Edward Arber (ed.) ('English Reprints'; London, 1870), p. 28. Subsequent references here are all to this edition.
[2] Sir Thomas Elyot, *The Boke Named the Governour*, Henry Herbert Stephen Croft (ed.), 2 Vols, Vol. I (London, 1883), p. 35 (Bk I, Chap. VI).

by educating the women of the household, making them not only literate but learned (that is, in Latin). But their efforts would meet with no large-scale success. For some mysterious reason Latin was tied up with schools, and by the time it became accessible to women generally in schools, it had practically disappeared as a medium of communication. Even in its present attenuated form Latin has never been assimilated in the curriculum for girls' schools as it has in certain curricula for boys. One suspects that something of what it stood for, and in a certain degree still stands for, cannot be assimilated. It is a matter of record that the women students who today matriculate at Oxford or Cambridge Universities, where some classical tradition remains fairly strong, are almost invariably less well prepared in Latin than the men matriculating from the English public schools. Curricula are the product of complex and fugitive forces, but the forces are real and cannot be gainsaid.

IV

Flogging was a common practice in the schools of antiquity, as we know, for example, from St Augustine's rueful remarks in the *Confessions* about his own boyhood experiences.[1] The fact that school pupils were all boys of course encouraged rule by the rod. In the Middle Ages not only does this environment and rule persist, but there is evidence that the specifically initiatory cast of the punishment grew more intense and evident. This is made abundantly clear by Leach, who collects stories about the flogging in school of boy aspirants to monasteries which accompanied the early stages of initiation into monastic life, and quotes from Ælfric's *Colloquy* the 'highly characteristic' question which Ælfric has his typical master put to his typical pupils: 'Are you willing to be flogged (*flagellari, beswungen* or *swinged*) while learning?'[2] To this the boys – in this case not monastic aspirants – answer at once that they prefer flogging to ignorance. The question, answer and setting suggest the initiation practice among the Bechuans mentioned above. The boy must acknowledge the equation of learning and flogging, and thereby face courageously into learning as into an initiation, something of itself taxing and fearsome.

Renaissance educators did not, on the whole, abate the ferocity of medieval or ancient school punishment. Pictures of Renaissance classroom activity, such as Pieter Brueghel the Elder's engraving 'The Ass at School', feature bundles of switches as regular classroom equipment. 'Advanced' ideas on education did not necessarily entail diminishing physical punishment. Whereas an earlier tradition had, in Erasmus' phrase, tended to regard pupils as merely small-sized men, the Renaissance educator was often quite sensitive to the immaturity of his charges

---

[1] St Augustine, *Confessiones*, Lib. I, cap. ix, in *Opera omnia*, Vol. I ('Patrologiae cursus completus,' Series prima [Latina], J.-P. Migne (ed.), Vol. XXXII (Paris, 1841), cols. 667–8.

[2] Leach, *The Schools of Medieval England*, pp. 81–2, 89.

and to the psychology of child education. But for him psychology included the use of the birch. In Thomas Murner's *Mnemonic Logic* (*Logica memorativa*, 1509, etc.), which in an extremely 'progressive' fashion purveys the otherwise terrifying logic of Peter of Spain in the form of a logical card game, one of the woodcuts of 'cards' features a master holding three bundles of switches.[1] These, we are told, are to suggest the three questions, 'What? What kind? and How many?' used in handling enunciations, for, as Murner explains, it is with the aid of the switches that the answers to these questions are extracted from the pupils. Switches serve as mnemonic devices in both the real and the allegorical orders.

It is well known that the Renaissance Jesuit plan of education provided for a *corrector* for the 'little boys' (in effect, those still studying Latin) to 'keep them in fear', although the plan registers an oblique protest against beating as compromising good teacher–pupil relations, for it provides that this *corrector* never be one of the Jesuit teachers but either a person specially hired to do the beating or another student.[2] We should not suppose that punishment in Renaissance schools was always mild. Nicolas de Nancel, Peter Ramus' biographer and erstwhile pupil and secretary, a physician who goes into biographical detail with a whimsical clinical objectivity, reports that Ramus, who was a highly successful educator with 'advanced' ideas, often punished his pupils in savage outbursts of temper, not only whipping but also kicking them until they were 'half dead' (*semineces*) although – and Nancel adds wistfully here, 'for this he must be praised' – during all this process he never swore.[3]

However, although Renaissance reliance on physical violence as a teaching device was not new, the connection of this punishment with Latin teaching acquired a greater urgency. This was due to the greater prestige of Latin established by the humanists, but also to an increasing divorce between Latin and extra-curricular life and communication. In the Middle Ages, for casual communication between scholars, young or old, Latin was unblushingly vernacularized. Hence the venture into Latin, while a break with the past, was a relatively less violent break. For the humanist, only 'correct' classical Latin should be spoken, even by small boys beginning the language. The break with the past thus reached a kind of maximum in the Renaissance, and the sense of the Latin school as a special marginal environment reached its greatest intensity. The break with the past – that is, with the vernacular of one's childhood – was further enhanced by the concurrent growth of vernacular literature and its greater and greater independence of Latin which marked the Renaissance period.

[1] Thomas Murner, *Logica memorativa, Chartiludium logice, sive Totius dialectice memoria; et Nonus* [*i.e. novus*] *Petri Hispani textus emendatus, cum iucundopictasmatis exercitio* . . . (Strasbourg, 1509), fols. Bv^v-Bvi^r.

[2] See the documents in George E. Ganss, S. J., *Saint Ignatius' Idea of a Jesuit University* (Marquette University Press, Milwaukee, Wisconsin, 1954), pp. 26, 309, 331.

[3] Nancel, *Petri Rami . . . vita*, p. 60.

V

In the Renaissance the association of violence with teaching takes another special and interesting turn, for the Renaissance educator appears aware of the teaching environment not only in terms of the violence sometimes resorted to on the side of the teacher but also in terms of the courage which he hopes to develop in his pupils. This emphasis seems connected with the tendency of the humanist educator to think of educating his pupil as a whole person. Humanist teachers frequently functioned less as members of teachers' unions or university faculties than as *familiares* or even employees of bourgeois or noble families. Hence they show an interest in the pupil's total upbringing not so often met with in the medieval university, where all pupils were by definition (if not always in actuality) mere apprentices learning the more or less highly specialized teaching trade.

The new interest manifests itself in the many courtesy books and in the various *rationes studiorum*, or works on educational procedure, which were turned out in the humanist tradition and which connect in many ways with the courtesy literature. In this setting, where educational objectives are formulated under the more or less direct influence of well-to-do or noble households, concerned with family tradition and prestige, there flourishes the Renaissance cult of 'glory' and there develops the curious interest in the epic poem, together with the typical Renaissance view that such a poem is the highest creation of the human mind and consequently the normally preferred focus of literary (as apart from oratorical) study. By the same token there develops, under the concurrent influence of Plato's *Republic*, a keen interest in courage (which makes the glorious epic hero) as an express objective in the education of boys.

It has not been sufficiently remarked how much Renaissance poetic and other language study finds itself wandering from the consideration of poetry or language to the consideration of courage, or of its opposite, softness or effeminacy. In part this common deviation is undoubtedly due to the fact that in the Renaissance generally poetry tended to be exclusively a matter for education at what we should consider the secondary school or even the elementary school level. With our present upper division courses and graduate courses in poetry and literature, we are likely to forget that the ordinary Renaissance student finished his rhetoric and poetry in his early teens and went on immediately to 'philosophy' and shortly after, if he continued his formal education, to medicine or law or theology.[1] On his own initiative or in some more or less special circumstances a student could study literature at an advanced level, and in the later Renaissance students, in Great Britain at least, tended to linger on in Latin for a longer time, but, by and large, literary studies in the Renaissance were for youngsters. In the mid-six-

[1] See Ganss, *Saint Ignatius' Idea*, p. 45. The curriculum and students' ages here outlined may be taken as fairly representative of Continental practice generally, since the Jesuit programme of studies was conceived on an international basis and drawn up by pooling international educational experience.

teenth century Peter Ramus had explained how his students had finished not only rhetoric (together with what poetry was included in this 'art') but philosophy as well by the age of fifteen.[1] Rationalizing about the existing situation, Ramus states that poetry is taught at a very early age because the logic in it is diluted and thus assimilable by the tender youthful mind, unable to absorb the more concentrated logic of philosophy.[2]

This statement that poetry respects young boys' weakness is, of course, another way of saying that it gets them over the weakness. The Jesuit savant Martin Antonio Delrio a few years later will explain how the lowly humane letters toughen the young boys who suffer from too great tenderness in age and mind, preparing them for the weightier disciplines of philosophy, medicine, law and theology. He goes on to add that not only poetry, but drama, history, oratory and literature generally should be studied only by young boys, not by adults, whose sole concern with these things should be to edit texts for boys – Delrio is here apologizing for his own preoccupations, for these remarks of his occur in the preface to his collection or 'line-up' (syntagma) of Latin tragedies, which turn out to be entirely Senecan.[3] The idea that Seneca is exclusively for children may strike us as amusing and might have seriously upset even the Stoic Seneca himself, but Delrio's views represent one standard Renaissance position, supported chiefly by two considerations. First, in the actuality of the curriculum, if literature was to be studied at all, it had to be studied in the early years of school, for literature was used in the schoolroom chiefly to perfect the boy's competence in Latin so that, as soon as possible, he could move on to philosophy and the sciences. This was not Erasmus' ideal, but then Erasmus' ideal of an education terminating not in philosophy and science but in language and literary study, with theology itself cast in a grammatical rather than a philosophical mould, was never effectively realized.

A second consideration moving Delrio would have appealed to Erasmus: Seneca was a stern Stoic moralist and could thus be counted on to make the young boy manly and courageous. At this point we are reminded of the tendency of Renaissance educators to assimilate to the linguistic portion of the curriculum not only literary works of Stoics such as Seneca or his nephew Lucan, but also more properly philosophical works, such as the Enchiridion of Epictetus, which appears in a great number of Renaissance editions, often together with the Tabula of Cebes. The somewhat aphoristic character of the philosophy of the Enchiridion made it a congenial adjunct of rhetoric, which often cultivated the

---

[1] Peter Ramus, Oratio de studiis philosophiae et eloquentiae coniungendis, in Peter Ramus and Omer Talon (Audomarus Talaeus), Collectaneae praefationes, epistolae, orationes (Marburg, 1599), pp. 248–50; Peter Ramus, Pro philosophica Parisiensis academiae disciplina oratio, in his Scholae in liberales artes (Basle, 1569), cols 1019–20.

[2] Peter Ramus, Oratio initio suae professionis habita (Paris, 1551), p. 31.

[3] Martin Antonio Delrio, Syntagma tragoediae Latinae (Antwerp, 1593), Preface, fols. *3ᵛ, **1ʳ. A translation of Delrio's Preface by Richard G. Wittmann is available in typescript at St Louis University on application to the present author.

epigram. But, more than this, its strong moral and ascetical bias fitted the Stoic philosophy to the puberty-rite mentality which we have been considering here as connected with language study. Epictetus' was a toughening philosophy in a way that Aristotle's was not.

The Renaissance humanist could be disturbed by the plausibility of the charge that literature, and poetry in particular, was actually soft or effeminate, so that, being purveyed to youngsters at the very age when they should be maturing in manliness (the puberty rite attitudes clearly evince themselves here), it actually only weakens him. This is the burden or background not only of Ramus' opinion that poetry has little 'logic' in it but also of Gosson's attack on poetry, revealed by his charge, taken up by Sidney, that poetry is 'the schoole of abuse'. Although Gosson's principal concern is not poetry taught in schools but drama seen in the playhouses, his resort to the school symbol not only in his title but constantly through his argumentation – 'I have been matriculated my selfe in the schoole [i.e., of the stage], where so many abuses flourish. . . . I should tell tales out of Schoole, and be Ferruled for my faulte. . . . Liberty gives you head [i.e., in the playwright's world, conceived of as a school], placing you with Poetrie in the lowest form'[1] – leaves no doubt that the case for or against drama and literature generally is to be adjudicated in a pedagogical frame of reference: Do these things serve to make boys men (or men more manly)? Sidney works in this same frame of reference when he asserts that he knows *men* – the word is deliberately pointed and is Sidney's own – 'that even with reading of *Amadis de gaule* (which God knoweth wanteth much of a perfect Poesie) have found their hearts moved to the exercise of courtesie, liberalitie, and especially courage'.[2]

In Gosson and Sidney the connections between poetry, courage (or the lack thereof), and the education of young boys are suggested rather than explicitly dealt with. But in specifically educational treatises connected with the courtesy tradition they come definitely to the fore and show some of the real grounds for the Renaissance educator's preoccupation with the hero and with glory – these grounds being in this case associated with the proper toughening of the youth in initiation into extra-familial society.

Thus in Book I, Chapter X to XVI, of *The Boke Named the Governor* (1531) where Sir Thomas Elyot treats the scholastic curriculum of his youthful pupil, it is striking that at every juncture where he mentions the age of the boy, he brings in courage or 'corage' for explicit comment.[3] At seven, we are told, the child begins grammar, but not in too great detail, for too detailed grammar 'mortifieth his corage' (Chap. X). Up to his thirteenth year, 'the childes courage, inflamed by the frequent redynge of noble poets, dayly more and more desireth to have experience in those things that they so vehemently do commende in them they

[1] Stephen Gosson, *The Schoole of Abuse*, Edward Arber (ed.) ('English Reprints'; London, 1869), p. 24.

[2] Sir Philip Sidney, *The Defence of Poesie*, in *The Complete Works*, Albert Feuillerat (ed.), Vol. III (The University Press, Cambridge, 1922–6), p. 20; cf. ibid., p. 28.

[3] All quotations from Elyot are from the edition cited in Note 2, p. 237.

write of' (Chap. X). After 14, and some study of oratory and cosmography, it is time, says Elyot, 'to induce a childe to the redinge of histories; but fyrst, to set him in a fervent courage, the mayster . . . expressinge what incomparable delectation, utilitie, and commodite shall happen to emperours, kinges, princis, and all other gentil men by reding of histories' (Chap. XI).

The connection of literature (Latin) with toughness of moral fibre is here explicit, and this toughness of moral fibre goes with physical toughness as well. Thus, says Elyot, 'for as moche the membres by movyng and mutuall touching do waxe more hard', physical exercise must be insisted upon for boys, 'specially from the age of xiiii yeres upwarde, in whiche tyme strength with courage increaseth' (Chap. XVI). However, by the time the boy comes to the age of 17, a different emphasis must be given, for at this age 'to the intent his courage be bridled with reason, hit were needful to rede unto him some warkes of philosophy, especially . . . morall' (Chap. XI).

The picture is here complete. By 17 the child has become something of a man, his courage has been proved and he must now practise what one practises after crossing the threshold of maturity, namely, control. For our present purposes what is of interest is the absolute coincidence in the ending of language studies and the ending of emphasis on developing and proving courage. Both mark the ending of a period of initiation. Courage or 'corage' (heartiness, strength of heart) designates for Elyot something definitely connected with the process of maturing, not merely with high spirits, although it would include this. And this strength of heart is communicated by the study of literature – that is to say, of Latin literature (with some smattering of Greek).

It is true that Elyot is interested specifically in educating a 'governor', or, as he puts it elsewhere, a 'gentleman', one who rules or at least is part of the ruling class of a *respublica*. Still, his programme of Latin and Greek studies for his governor-to-be is basically no different from that of Renaissance schools generally, where it would presumably inspire the same kind of 'courage' in the sons of merchants and tradesmen as in prospective governors. In showing how the typical ideal Renaissance educational programme built around Latin is suited to nobles – the fighting class, who, above all, must pass through the puberty rites ('Will you guard the chief well?' ask the Bechuans) – Elyot is revealing something of the way this programme was felt as operating. In books such as Elyot's the humanists set out to show that even the nobles should be educated men – which, from one point of view, means that the humanistic study of Latin was a good and desirable substitute for more barbaric practices of initiation. In this context, how could it be entirely dissociated from such practices?

A cluster of forces sustaining and sustained by the Renaissance cult of the epic hero and of the epic can be seen here. This view of literature as inculcating 'courage' both nourishes and feeds on the cult of the hero and his 'glory' which the epic fosters. This cult, which affected governors and governed alike, has far-reaching and mysterious roots in human history. At this point we can only indicate that the position of Latin in Renaissance culture, the way in which this Latin was taught, the things it was supposed to do to the pupil, and the interest in the epic which by the seventeenth century in Western Europe amounts almost to a frenzy are not unrelated phenomena.

It is true also that Elyot's focus on courage in his educational plan is related to a similar focus in Plato's *Republic*, the major source for much that was explicit in the Renaissance cult of courage. However, the point here is not whether or not Elyot has assignable sources but rather where such sources strike root in his thinking – for not everything that Plato said manages to root itself in Renaissance educational theory or practice. What interests us here in Elyot is the association of courage with language study, and in particular with Latin. The study of Greek for Plato's pupil involved no break with the past. For Elyot's pupil, the study of classical languages did. The Renaissance environment for Platonic ideas was different from the original Greek environment.

Moreover, because of the attitude towards the classical languages peculiar to the humanist tradition, for Renaissance boys the learning of Latin represented, like the passage through puberty rites, not only something difficult but precisely a transit from ignorance to tribal wisdom, that is, to the accumulated wisdom of mankind. This wisdom was thought of as stored behind doors linguistically controlled from the inside. 'In the Greeke and Latin tong,' writes Ascham, 'the two onlie learned tonges, which be kept not in common taulke but in private bookes, we finde alwayes wisdome and eloquence.'[1] In any generation the wisdom of the past, which is not only the matter communicated to neophytes in puberty rites but a major item in all formal education, may be thought of as 'situated' somewhere. The only point we are making here is that Renaissance man regularly located this somewhere in linguistic terms.

The connection of the teaching of Latin and of literature with puberty rites is further manifest to us, if it was not manifest to Renaissance educators themselves, when these educators explicitly discuss the problem of physical punishment. In the long dialogue on the pros and cons of corporal punishment with which Roger Ascham opens his famous educational treatise, *The Schoolmaster*, he provides glimpses of issues relevant to our present subject which he never really fully exposes. Some pupils have recently run away from Eton, we are told in the course of this dialogue, 'for fear of beating', and the discretion of schoolmasters is called into question because they may flog to punish 'weakenes of nature rather than the fault of the Scholer', thus actually driving boys from learning.[2] This seems a clear indication that, whether it should be or not, punishment is felt by some masters as advisable for reasons other than the encouragement of formal learning.

We note farther on in the dialogue that Master Mason and Master Haddon vastly enjoy reminiscing about schoolboy escapades (one recalls that in puberty

[1] Ascham, *The Scholemaster*, p. 117.
[2] Ibid., p. 18.

rites the ordinary rules of behaviour are often suspended and outlawry is regarded with approval). Master Mason proves 'very merry with both parties, pleasantly playing with shrewd touches [trials – i.e. of the schoolmaster's patience] of many cours'd [flogged] boys and with the small discretion of many lewd schoolmasters', and Master Haddon remarks that 'the best Scholemaster of our time [we know that he refers to Nicholas Udall] was the greatest beater'.[1] Masters Mason and Haddon here plainly speak not as scholars but simply as men who had 'gone through' the *rites de passage* and who look back on such experiences, with their aura of lawlessness, as trials which others should perhaps go through not so much for learning's sake as simply to prove their prowess as members of the 'gang' and to achieve a sense of belonging. This is a line of argumentation which Ascham, like earnest educators today, does not like, but the fact that it is used and reported testifies to an existing state of mind.

Ascham himself suggests that native ability, not attributable to their experience of Udall's birches, might account for the success of Udall's pupils and leaves no doubt that he himself is against flogging as a device for teaching Latin. He himself does not state that there were other things besides the mere learning of Latin in the back of Renaissance educators' minds when they beat their boys. Yet the fact that there were, that the flogging served the purpose – unstated, unformulated, but real – of initiating boys into a tough, man's world, as suggested by Masters Mason and Haddon, is curiously confirmed by the example which Ascham himself brings forward to prove that beating is not necessary. The example has become classic. For it is an example not of schoolboy or budding young gentleman, but that of a girl, none other than the young Lady Jane Grey, whom Ascham, to his delight, found one day reading Plato's *Phaedo* while the more boisterous members of her family were out hunting.

Lady Jane was at great pains to explain how nice a person was her teacher, 'Master Elmer', by comparison with her strait-laced parents, by whom she was constantly 'so sharplie taunted, so cruellie threatened, yea, presentlie some tymes with pinches, nippes, and bobbes'.[2] Ascham does not pause to note that, rather than straightforwardly contrasting schooling based on kindness with schooling based on physical punishment, his example really contrasts the romantic world of a maturing young girl with the rough-and-tumble world his society prescribed for young boys. Despite Ascham's attempt to make something else out of his example, what is remarkable about Lady Jane is not that she is not being flogged – Master Elmer certainly could not have flogged her – but that she is studying the classics *instead* of hunting. This suggests that Lady Jane's approach to literature was somehow radically different from that of the ideal Renaissance gentleman, who liked both the classics *and* hunting. Had not Ascham himself written a treatise on the use of the longbow?

The *rites de passage* prescribed for the Renaissance gentleman were to initiate

[1] Ibid.
[2] Ibid., p. 47.

him into an aggressively competitive man's world. For Lady Jane, too, the study of literature was a kind of *rite de passage*, an initiation into a new world ahead and a break with the past. But the breakthrough was at a different point. It opened out upon a pleasant, fanciful, romantic world. As a *rite de passage* the study of literature here meant to a girl something different than to a boy. One made the *passage* to Lady Jane's world precisely by staying away from the hunt, just as the medieval lady, intrigued with vernacular romances, had done. One thinks of the Green Knight's lady in *Sir Gawain and the Green Knight*, or perhaps even of Paolo and Francesca.

I do not wish to pass on the relative merits of the two worlds, that of literature-and-hunting and that of literature-and-Master-Elmer, or to speculate as to where in the dialectic between the two we are at present situated, but only to point out that they can engender a dialectic because they represent different and opposed positions. In view of this fact, however, it seems not entirely irrelevant that *The Schoolmaster*, never published during Ascham's lifetime, is presented to Sir William Cecil and to the world by a woman, who writes the preface, Ascham's widow, Margaret. Nor does it seem entirely irrelevant to this dialectic that corporal punishment and the stress on Latin in school have, pretty generally, been disappearing in modern times with the emergence of co-education.

VI

This study has been a sketch of certain forces at work in the Renaissance attitudes towards Latin, towards literature and towards education. It could be elaborated indefinitely, and no doubt refined in many ways, by exploiting more and more examples, of which there is certainly 'copie' in Renaissance documents. Here we have limited ourselves to samplings from better-known sources, chiefly British. Perhaps further development is worthwhile, perhaps not. In either event, we can sum up our present conclusions.

First, I have not sought to maintain that Renaissance educators explicitly thought of Latin study as a puberty rite. They had no definable, abstract idea of what a puberty rite is or was – and neither, for that matter, do the primitive peoples whose puberty rites we have taken as a term of comparison. Renaissance educators, like primitive peoples and like ourselves, have no rationalized explanation for everything they do. They do certain things because they feel these things should be done, finding reasons for them afterwards if at all – and, if they are observant and honest, often being surprised at the reasons which turn up on close inspection.

The basic conclusion is that when Latin, in which learning was encoded, became by the time of the Renaissance a 'dead' language – a language which, however widely used, was divorced from family life – initiation into the language of learning became more than ever a *rite de passage*. Thus, when other Renaissance courses were being labelled 'methods' and 'systems', Comenius finds it natural to describe his course in Latin and other languages as a 'door' – *Ianua Linguarum*. Thus, in a Western society destined to become progressively more humane in its educational procedures, the status of Latin helped maintain the relatively violent puberty rite setting, a sense of existence on a threshold, within a marginal environment (associated with forced seclusion from the company of women and to a certain extent from one's own family), in an atmosphere of continuous excitement and of that aggressive competition or *aemulatio* which, toned down or outlawed in modern de-Latinized co-educationalism, was a key principle of most Renaissance education.

This complex of attitudes, not new but concentrated with new urgency around language study, helps explain (although I do not wish to suggest that it entirely explains) the frenzied fascination with epic poetry (most of which was in Latin during the Renaissance), with the courageous epic hero (given to war much more than to love-making), with epic theory and with courage itself, which marks linguistic studies in the period when Renaissance Latin education was having its full effect on society.

Seeing Renaissance Latin teaching in the psychological framework of the puberty rite helps us to explain much in the later trajectory of Latin teaching. In the nineteenth century, when Latin was on its way out as the core subject of the curriculum, educators produced the theory that Latin 'strengthened' or 'toughened' the mind. This theory, which is still met with today, has been labelled new,[1] and it was new in the sense that earlier educators had not explicitly advanced it. But the complex in which Latin was normally taught had associated the language in a special way with some sort of toughening. Were not nineteenth-century educators, and are not the few twentieth-century educators who repeat their words today, merely giving voice to a vague feeling which has its roots in the psychological setting of the Renaissance Latin school – the feeling that the teaching of Latin, independently of the communication of the ability to read the language (the immediate aim of Renaissance Latin teaching), had somehow to do with toughening the youngster for the extra-familial world in which he would have to live?

Translated, this means the feeling that a boy's education was basically a puberty rite, a process preparing him for adult life by communicating to him the heritage of a past in a setting which toughened him and thus guaranteed his guarding the heritage for the future. Latin had indubitable connections with the past, and it was hard, indeed all the harder as motivation waned when real use for the language began to wane. This association of Latin with a toughening marginal environment of a puberty rite type was sufficient to keep Latin in its place as the basic discipline forming the prep school character, with its twin emphases on Latin and physical hardihood (modulated eventually into good sportsmanship).

The perspectives proposed in this paper are, of course, suggestive rather than complete, but they open the way, I believe, to a better understanding of some

[1] See Ganss, *Saint Ignatius' Idea*, pp. 210–11, 219 ff.

curious and important momentums developed by past ideas and practices. And, since it is impossible to study the past without reference to the present, they suggest matter for reflection – forward-looking, let us hope, rather than nostalgic – concerning the twentieth-century situation. Where are the *rites de passage* for youth today? Does a technological society have any? Should it have any? If so, what should they be?

6 Latin and the Élite Tradition in Education

F. CAMPBELL

The decision of the Incorporated Association of Preparatory Schools – that most conservative of educational bodies – to recommend that Latin should no longer be a compulsory subject in the Common Entrance examination for the Public Schools after 1970 draws attention once again to the anomalous position of the classics in the education of the upper classes.

Latin and Greek have been, as is well known, the core of the curriculum in most élite schools and colleges ever since formal education began in Europe.[1] England has a long tradition stretching from William of Wykeham and Colet, Locke and Cardinal Newman down to Sir Desmond Lee and Mr Anthony Chenevix-Trench in our own day that an essential foundation for a liberal, gentlemanly education is to be found in the writings of Caesar and Ovid, Horace and Virgil, Aeschylus and Sophocles. In such countries as Germany, France and Italy the very names of their middle- and upper-class selective secondary schools *gymnasium*, *lycée* and *athénée* reflect their origins in Greece and Rome.

A century ago when the cult of the classics probably reached its peak in England it was everywhere taken for granted in the boys' Public Schools, and to a somewhat lesser extent in the grammar schools, that at least one half and sometimes as much as two thirds of the curriculum should be devoted to the grammar and literature of the dead languages. In certain famous schools the proportion was as high as three quarters. Edward Thring, educated at Eton, Anglican curate,[2] Fellow of King's College, founder of the Headmasters' Conference and for over twenty years headmaster of Uppingham, wrote in 1864: 'Let the mind be educa-

---

[1] 'In the past classics reigned supreme throughout the whole sphere of higher education. There were no rivals; and accordingly all students were steeped in the classics throughout their school life, and its domination at the universities was only challenged by the narrow discipline of mathematics'. A. N. Whitehead, *The Aims of Education* (Ernest Benn, London, 1962 edn), p. 93.

[2] 'As late as 1872 seventy of the seventy-two headmasters of the leading boys schools in England were clergymen.' G. Baron, *Society, Schools and Progress in England* (Pergamon, Oxford, 1965), p. 5.

First printed in British Journal of Sociology, *Vol. XIX, No. 3 (September 1968)*, *pp. 308–25.*

ted in one noble subject. If this subject also embraces a wide field of knowledge so much the better. The universal consent of many ages has found such a subject in the study of Latin and Greek literature.'[1] The same year the Clarendon Report, which reflected progressive upper-class thinking about the Public Schools, advocated that in a large school there should be one 'principal branch of study, invested with a recognized, and if possible, traditional importance, to which the principal weight should be assigned, and the largest share of attention given'.[2] It was right and proper that Latin and Greek should hold a 'foremost place' in the curriculum because they provided the 'best materials' for the study of language and literature, and supplied the 'most graceful, and some of the noblest poetry, the finest eloquence, the deepest philosophy, the wisest historical writing'. Sir Henry Maine was so enthusiastic for the classics that he could claim that 'except the blind forces of Nature, nothing moves in the world which is not Greek in origin'.[3] At about this time Eton was reported to have 31 masters, of whom 26 taught classics, 6 mathematics, 1 history and none modern languages or science.[4] Generally, in the teaching hierarchy those masters who taught Latin and Greek stood at the top.[5]

During the Edwardian era, as Bolgar points out, the student of Latin still had reason to feel that he, if any man, possessed the 'magic key' which would unlock the kingdoms of the world.[6] In 1904 when the new grammar schools were

---

[1] Edward Thring, *Education and the School* (Macmillan, London, 1867), p. 46. Thring makes his attitude towards 'mental discipline' theory clear in the following quotation: 'The mind requires healthy exercise, the end proposed is strength of mind, and it is a matter of comparative indifference provided the result is true, whether the years of practice and preparation are full of immediate gain or not' (p. 39).

[2] J. Stuart Maclure (ed.), *Educational Documents: England and Wales, 1816–1963* (Chapman and Hall, London, 1963) quoted on pp. 84–7.

[3] Sir Henry James Sumner Maine, Rede Lecture, 1875.

[4] Edward C. Mack, *Public Schools and British Opinion since 1860* (Columbia University Press, New York, 1941), p. 36.

[5] This superiority in numbers was accompanied by the view that classical masters were also superior in social and professional status. Mathematicians were by this time tolerated in the Public Schools, but modern linguists, historians and even more so scientists were widely regarded as inferior members of the teaching profession. A headmaster of Eton, the Rev. C. O. Goodford, at about this time when once asked point-blank how he rated the relative value of classics, mathematics and modern languages for his pupils rather surprisingly put his thoughts into mathematical form and answered with the proportion 15:3:1. T. W. Bamford, *The Rise of the Public Schools* (Nelson, London, 1967), pp. 118–19.

Even in a school which had become famous for its science teaching it was said: 'The classical master has always had charge of a form of boys, and he has made his influence felt in every part of their school life. He teaches classics, but he teaches much more than classics; from him the boys get their inspiration and ideals.' Anonymous, *Sanderson of Oundle* (Chatto and Windus, London, 1923), p. 237.

[6] 'Fifty years ago the classical education still had an exceptional measure of public esteem. That training in taste and accuracy of thought, that lucid if somewhat factitious understanding of human institutions and human nature, which a close acquaintance with the Greek and Roman authors could give, were considered to fit the young supremely for the conduct of life. Those who had undergone the rigours of the traditional Humanist

beginning to take shape their chief architect and sponsor Robert Morant (who as an Old Wykehamist had little time for technical schools, and believed whole-heartedly in the academic, bookish approach to secondary education) recommended that if two foreign languages were to be taken by a pupil, then one of them must be Latin unless special permission was granted for an exception. In the 1920s and 1930s, about 40 per cent of all candidates taking the School Certificate examination offered Latin as one of their main subjects. The Spens Report of 1938 made much the same recommendation as had Morant.

As recently as 1959 a poll conducted by the *Sunday Times*[1] showed that 87 out of 146 Public School headmasters favoured retaining Latin as a compulsory subject for all students entering Oxford or Cambridge (including those who intended to read science, mathematics or technology), whereas only 59 head-masters were against such a requirement. The most famous Public Schools, though no longer so hostile to science or modern studies as they once were, are only very slowly and gradually retreating from the classical ground on which they once so firmly stood. In 1965, for example, Eton had 37 masters teaching classics, 19 science, 13 mathematics and 19 other languages including English.[2] The percentage of boys and girls taking Latin in schools may have fallen since the war but the absolute numbers have – contrary to common impression – actually increased as may be seen in the following table:

Year	No. of G.C.E. passes in 'O' level examinations[3]
1952	18,500
1963	34,000

Why the classics?

The arguments in favour of retaining the classics, and more particularly Latin, as a central theme of the school curriculum have varied from time to time, depending partly on the personal and social predilections of the teacher and partly on the circumstances of the era. From century to century and from school to school a great variety of views have been expressed as to why this group of subjects should above all others be given priority in the time-table. History, religion, culture, politics, psychology, vocational training and social status have

---

discipline in school and university were accepted by the majority of their contemporaries as an authoritative élite. The classical student of Edwardian times had reason to feel that he, if any man, possessed the magic key which could unlock the kingdoms of the world.'
R. R. Bolgar, *The Classical Inheritance and its Beneficiaries* (Cambridge University Press, Cambridge, 1954), p. 1.

[1] *The Sunday Times* (17 May 1959).
[2] *The Public Schools Yearbook, 1965* (Black, London, 1965).
[3] Ministry of Education, *Statistics of Education, 1963, Part Three* (H.M.S.O., London, 1964), pp. 9–10.

all been invoked at some stage or another. As Bolgar says: 'Men's approach to the classics altered in conjunction with their general outlook.'[1]

The Christian churches – which, it must be remembered, controlled most aspects of education in this country until about a century ago, and still strongly influence schools in many parts of the world – believed, for example, that most wisdom was to be found, not so much in the discoveries or attitudes of contemporary civilization, but in the ancient books and manuscripts. The schoolmen of the eleventh, twelfth and thirteenth centuries turned eagerly to the old texts as the only possible light to penetrate the Dark Ages. The Bible, after all, was written partly in Greek, and the Fathers of the Church communicated with each other, both orally and in writing, in Latin. Roman Catholics in particular regarded Latin as the international language of the Church binding together the priests and bishops, and through them the faithful of the whole world.[2] Moreover, for most good Christians the classics stood for something more than language and literature; they represented tradition and authority. For priests and ministers it is also possible that they involved the necessary esoteric 'mystery' which helped to make them awe-inspiring in the eyes of their congregations. Vocationally, they were thus important for entry to at least one major profession.

A wider argument in favour of teaching the classics, not necessarily religious in its impulse (indeed some of its implications are decidedly pagan in tone) was that based on the theory of the heritage of Greece and Rome. According to this thesis which received enormous stimulus from the literary discoveries of the fifteenth and sixteenth centuries, was developed by many distinguished writers and thinkers, and is set out at length in the Clarendon Report, the foundations of modern Europe were laid by two highly civilized nations on the shores of the Mediterranean. The classical languages, it was claimed, kept alive almost all learning during the Dark Ages. The Renaissance would have been impossible without the knowledge contained in the classical texts; and modern politics, law and philosophy as well as much literature, language and geometry could only be understood in relation to their origins two thousand years ago. Certainly no gentleman could claim to be liberally educated unless he knew something of the ancient world. 'The Roman Empire is a bottleneck through which the vintage of the past has passed into modern life,' wrote Whitehead.[3] 'So far as European civilization is concerned the key to history is the comprehension of the mentality of Rome and the work of its Empire.'

'We cannot escape from the consul and empire of Rome – from the buildings and sculpture of Periclean Athens, from the writings of Plato and Aristotle,

[1] R. R. Bolgar, *The Classical Inheritance and its Beneficiaries* (Cambridge University Press, Cambridge, 1954), p. 380.

[2] It is worth noting that the only teachers' training college out of about thirty in the London University Institute of Education area which intends to offer Latin as a subject for the Bachelor of Education degree is a Roman Catholic one, St Mary's.

[3] A. N. Whitehead, *The Aims of Education* (Ernest Benn, London, 1962 edn), p. 101.

from the museum of Alexandra – in a word from Greece and Rome,' said Livingstone.[1]

At first the main emphasis in this teaching, apart from the purely linguistic aspects, appears to have been largely *aesthetic* in tone. The poetry of Catullus and Virgil, the oratorical style of Cicero and Demosthenes, the dramatic qualities of Sophocles and Euripides, the sculpture of Phidias and Praxiteles, the architectural splendours of the Parthenon and Forum – all these were supreme themes to be cherished by men of taste and sensibility. Petrarch and Boccaccio in Renaissance Italy, Milton in Puritan England, Locke at the beginning of the Industrial Revolution and Matthew Arnold during the Victorian era might differ in time, religion and nationality but were united in their belief that the intelligent sons of good families should have the opportunity to study the noblest examples of art and literature from ancient Athens and Rome. When Keats composed his *On First Looking into Chapman's Homer*, or Byron wrote of

> The isles of Greece, the isles of Greece
> Where burning Sappho loved and sung,

they were thinking of a civilization in which beauty was created and worshipped in a unique way.

Later, and more especially during the latter half of the nineteenth and first quarter of the twentieth century, many teachers appear to have shifted their emphasis from the cultural to the more explicitly political and philosophical aspects of the classics. Language and literature continued to be taught, but Greek declined in relation to Latin, and more attention was paid to Roman as compared to Hellenic history. Gradually, as Imperialism gained ground in certain European countries there was a definite movement away from art and aesthetics towards social and moral implications in the classical texts.[2] The Platonic idea of leadership

[1] R. W. Livingstone, *A Defence of Classical Education* (Macmillan, London, 1917), p. 6.

[2] It is perhaps significant that the fervent imperialist Cecil Rhodes, who had a vision of an Anglo-Saxon Empire which would rule the world, was a keen student of the classics, and was pleased to be reminded that in appearance he resembled the Roman Emperor Hadrian. Although not in any sense a scholar (he had difficulty in translating from Latin and Greek) it is reported of him that his favourite reading on the African *veld* and amid the rough-and-tumble of the Kimberley diamond fields was *The Meditations of Marcus Aurelius*. He frequently read Plutarch's *Lives* and Plato's *Dialogues*, and took Gibbon's *Decline and Fall of the Roman Empire* everywhere with him in Africa. Indeed, so keen was he on the latter that he spent £8,000 having the sources Gibbon used translated into English by a London bookseller. J. G. Lockhart and C. M. Woodhouse, *Rhodes* (Hodder and Stoughton, London, 1963), p. 210.

The educational sociologist Clarke commented on the new trend in classical teaching during this period: 'Without ceasing to be linguistic and literary, it [Latin] became more philosophical, with attention concentrated both on the substance of ancient thought and achievement and on the relevance of these to the contemporary situation. Moreover, its philosophical content was studied in close relation with modern European philosophy. In a word, we may say that the whole tradition was *reassimilated* to the needs and conditions of a complex industrial and imperial society. . . .' F. Clarke, *Education and Social Change* (Sheldon Press, London, 1940), p. 25.

A staunch defender of the classics, Ogilvie, suggests that during the latter half of the

was more clearly formulated, and less said about Greek democracy; there was a great deal of stress on the civilizing mission of certain nations; and words like 'power', 'hierarchy' and 'order' were more thoroughly scrutinized. Texts which would illustrate the themes of work, sacrifice and duty for the greater order of the state were sought out and commented upon, particularly in the Public schools.[1] The British upper classes were convinced, like the Mandarin Chinese and Toguwawa Japanese, that a thorough grounding in the classics was the best training for a country's administrators, statesmen and military leaders.[2]

In Prussia, for example, it seems clear that the reforms introduced by the neo-humanist Humboldt in 1808–11, and which lasted virtually unchanged for over a century, strengthened the role of the classics in the middle-class *gymnasia* and were closely linked with the rise of German nationalism. Similarly in France the encouragement of the classics in the new *lycées* by Napoleon was deliberately planned to stimulate patriotism.[3]

---

nineteenth century it was the lessons of Greek philosophy which were so relevant. 'England was in tune with Plato and the education which she evolved under the influence of Plato's vision was an education well calculated to serve her purposes. It inculcated loyalty, courage, responsibility and truthfulness: four virtues indispensable to the new governing class of a great empire.' R. M. Ogilvie, *Latin and Greek* (Routledge & Kegan Paul, London, 1964), p. 115.

Ogilvie's philosophical and political outlook are made plain in the following further quotations: 'It was not the good or the kind or the meek who were venerated but the courageous and the handsome and the patriotic: for it was only they who secured England's position in the world. . . .' (pp. 134–5). '. . . there is no place for heroism in a Welfare Society. The heroic ideal entails inequality, distinction, success and the desire to shine; virtues (or vices) which a socialist society is committed to repressing.' (p. 176).

[1] In an eloquent chapter entitled 'Family and Social Life' by Hugh Last the writer goes to great lengths to explain and analyse certain key words which apply to these conceptions of order, discipline and authority. *Virtus* he describes as not so much meaning 'virtue' as 'manliness' and more especially 'physical bravery'. *Gravitas* implies resistance to unthinking enthusiasms of the moment, and submission to established institutions. *Pietas* he suggests means not what he calls 'sanctimonious other-worldliness' but a general acceptance of the powers-that-be, both human and divine, or in the widest sense an expression of discipline in relation to authority. *Simplicitas* could be interpreted as keeping one's feet on the ground, and not being too imaginative or speculative. Cyril Bailey (ed.), *The Legacy of Rome* (Clarendon Press, Oxford, 1923).

[2] 'Like the public schools, Confucian education instilled gentlemanly attitudes which in turn helped to perpetuate a public servant élite. Both systems taught morals by teaching manners: both moulded behaviour through etiquette, through aesthetic appeals to "good form". Similarly, both systems pursued an amateur ideal, the notion that manners (signifying virtue) and classical culture (signifying a well-tuned mind) were better credentials for leadership than any amount of expert, practical training. In China, no less than in Britain, this faith in the amateur was reflected by Civil Service examinations which placed the greatest emphasis on a classical, non-technical syllabus.' Rupert Wilkinson, *The Prefects: British Leadership and the Public School Tradition* (Oxford University Press, Oxford, 1964), p. 126.

[3] Consultative Committee on Secondary Education, *Secondary Education* (H.M.S.O., London, 1938), pp. 408–10.

'During the later half of the eighteenth and most of the nineteenth century the classics that were taught in the schools and universities so far from being a danger to any accepted system of thought, were the harmless instruments of contemporary educational fashions, and were used to inculcate a taste for rhetoric in France, patriotism in Germany and a

In Britain this imperialistic concept was stated quite explicitly by Sir Richard Livingstone in his influential *A Defence of Classical Education*, published in 1917, which sought to prove that the strength of Germany was not merely due to her excellent scientific education but also to the traditional virtues of work, sacrifice and resolution in the face of adversity which were supposed to be part of the classical heritage. Significantly in this book very little is said about grammar and literature but a great deal about what he called the 'heroic and imperial spirit' of ancient Rome. 'We must go to Rome for our lessons,' he wrote. 'To govern peoples who differ in race, language, temper and civilization; to raise and distribute armies for their defence or subjection; to meet expenses civil and military; to allow generals and governors sufficient independence without losing control at the centre; to know and supply the needs of provinces two thousand miles from the seat of government. . . . Latin then stands in our education partly on linguistic grounds, partly on the heroic characters in its history, or the interest of its political and imperial problems, and on the capacities of its peoples for government.'[1]

Lord Asquith showed a similar conviction about the political – and doubt about the cultural – aspect when he wrote: 'On what may be called the political side of her activities – the art of government and conquest, the statecraft of consolidation and expansion, the reconciliation of local diversities with imperial unity, the approximation to a world-wide Peace – there is no need to dwell. I endeavoured some years ago to give reasons for the opinion that, in the thousand years which followed the birth of Christ, there was no era in which the external conditions of life were so favourable to the happiness of mankind as the reign of the Emperor Hadrian. The great fabric in time succumbed, as all human institutions do, to the law of decay. But it is unique in history, and its memories and examples will not and cannot die.

It is much more difficult to describe the character and appraise the value of the intellectual and spiritual debt we owe to Rome.[2]

Asquith's comment is of particular interest in this connection because he was not only a fine classical scholar and educated in the conventional upper-class manner but he would also seem to possess many of the attributes of the philosopher-king – he was a man of wide background and culture, an outstanding lawyer and eloquent orator, morally of the highest integrity, leader of a great political party in peace and war, and Prime Minister for twelve years. Yet now from the vantage point of the mid-twentieth century he can be seen as a typically limited representative of his class and country; a man brave and sternly dedicated

---

public school morality in Dr Arnold's England.' R. R. Bolgar, *The Classical Inheritance and its Beneficiaries* (Cambridge University Press, Cambridge, 1954), p. 367.

[1] R. W. Livingstone, *A Defence of Classical Education* (Macmillan, London, 1917), p. 153.

[2] H. H. Asquith, Introduction to *The Legacy of Rome*, Cyril Bailey (ed.) (Clarendon Press, Oxford, 1923).

to his duty as he saw it, but fundamentally restricted in his understanding of history, with a poor knowledge of how ordinary people lived and suffered, unable to grasp what was happening to the British Empire abroad or to such under-privileged groups as women and the working class at home (he was hostile to both the Labour movement and the suffragettes), and confused about economic affairs.[1]

Transfer of training

The third fundamental premise on which the teaching of Latin was based during the late nineteenth century was the faculty theory of psychology which claimed that certain faculties of the mind such as memory, accuracy, quickness, observation, attention and so forth could be generally trained. Thus arithmetic developed reasoning powers; nature study improved powers of observation; learning poetry helped the memory, and so forth. The mind could be exercised almost like a muscle ('mental gymnastics'), and what was important in teaching a subject was not so much interest or relevance but formal training and mental discipline.

The study of language was widely regarded as the best all-round stimulus to thought – there was great emphasis on words rather than things – and Latin and Greek because of their syntax as much as their literary richness provided *par excellence* the highest form of education. They were orderly and systematic, they compelled pupils to prepare and arrange their work accurately, they were an antidote to slipshod constructions, they formed good habits of thought, they were a corrective dose to careless speech, etc., etc.[2]

Moreover, the mental skills acquired in this way by learning grammar, parsing sentences, translating into English and writing compositions could – it was alleged – be carried over or transferred to other academic subjects, and later even applied to problems of professional life and administration.[3] Mathematics was

---

[1] Bernard Shaw had some caustic things to say about statesmen such as Asquith after the execution of the rebel leaders in Dublin following the 1916 Rising. 'Nothing more blindly savage, stupid and terror-mad could have been devised by England's worst enemies,' he wrote. 'It was a very characteristic example of the conventional gentleman-militarist education of Marlborough and Sandhurst, and the conventional gentleman-diplomatist education of Eton and Oxford, Harrow and Cambridge.' G. Bernard Shaw, quoted *Dublin 1916*, Roger McHugh (ed.) (Arlington Press, London, 1966), p. 361.

Ireland seems to have suffered peculiarly from English admirers of Roman imperialism because Lord Clarendon of Clarendon Commission fame proved to be a more than un-usually inept Lord-Lieutenant of Ireland during the great famine of 1847–8.

[2] 'If ever in after life your job is to think, render thanks to Providence which ordained that, for five years of your youth, you did a Latin prose once a week and daily construed some Latin author.' A. N. Whitehead, *The Aims of Education* (Ernest Benn, London, 1962 edn), p. 100.

[3] 'In classics we endeavour by a thorough study of language to develop the mind in the regions of logic, philosophy, history and of aesthetic apprehension of literary beauty. The learning of the languages – Latin and Greek – is a subsidiary means for the furtherance of this ulterior object.' A. N. Whitehead, *The Aims of Education* (Ernest Benn, London, 1962 edn), p. 96.

welcomed in the schools as a rather similar discipline which was not only specific but also general in its application. From this doctrine flowed the theory that in adult life the liberally educated amateur was to be preferred to the vocationally trained specialist.

The very fact that the classics might be dull or difficult, or perhaps not especially relevant to the problems of modern life was not in itself a defect. Indeed it was important for a student's character – and the word 'character' appears almost as frequently in connection with Latin as it does with religion – to persevere at things which might be unpleasant but were otherwise thought to be worth while.

This mixture of psychology and Puritan ethics which seemed to imply that a child's learning processes should be regarded more as a stern duty than as a purposeful, potentially useful or even pleasurable activity flourished, of course, mainly in the late nineteenth century but still has a firm grip on certain sections of the teaching profession (mainly those in grammar schools or private sector) as may be seen in two recent reports on the teaching of classics.

'As a subject of study by a wide range of pupils', says a survey by the predominantly grammar-school orientated Incorporated Association of Assistant Masters, 'the disciplinary [sic!] value (of Latin) – and we stand by the phrase undaunted by bogey-words – is its greatest educational asset.'[1] The preparatory school teachers echo this viewpoint and use rather similar language when they state: 'We are, at heart, staunch believers in the value of Latin, and we would be reluctant to advocate either a late start or a lowering of standards in our forms unless we are convinced that the increased time devoted to other subjects gives a boy the same disciplinary mental training and sense of achievement – both underrated values in modern education – which our traditional classical training has succeeded in giving him in the past.'[2]

Foundations eroded

Some of these arguments were, of course, soundly based – there is a vast and wonderful literature in Greek and Latin which cannot be ignored; it would be wilfully stupid to neglect the tremendous heritage of ancient times; no person with any pretensions to learning or culture could disregard what happened around the Mediterranean Sea between 400 B.C. and A.D. 200 – but many of the other foundations on which the edifice of classical learning and scholarship was erected have long since been eroded. Vocationally it is no longer necessary for a student who wishes to enter a wide range of occupations to have qualifications in the classics. The scientific and technological occupations have grown enormously,

[1] Incorporated Association of Assistant Masters, *The Teaching of the Classics* (London, 1962), p. 5.
[2] Incorporated Association of Preparatory Schools, *Prospect: the Purpose and Practice of Teaching in Preparatory Schools* (London, 1965).

and even the oldest and most élite universities no longer insist on Latin as a preliminary qualification for all courses. Only the clergy, specialist historians and linguists need Latin as an essential professional requirement. Medicine and law can do quite well without it. Even the churches are beginning to concern themselves more with psychology and sociology, and less to some extent with Biblical exegesis. It is perhaps a sign of the times that the Roman Catholic Church, in which Latin is most strongly entrenched, is now using the vernacular in celebrating Mass in many countries.

The faculty theory of psychology has been under heavy criticism ever since William James and E. L. Thorndike showed experimentally at the beginning of this century that the carry-over of learning from one subject to another is very limited. Modern psychological theory – which has made comparatively little impression on the grammar and Public Schools – suggests that specific elements (e.g. Latin words may help the learning of French vocabulary) or broad general principles (e.g. the planning and organization of an essay) may be transferred, but that intelligence and motivation are by far the most important factors in education. Indeed, it is now generally accepted by educational psychologists that a pupil learns best when there is some pleasure in work, and that a subject becomes 'stamped in' when it is accompanied by a sense of relevance and achievement. The contrary feelings of pain, difficulty or irrelevance are a positive disincentive to learning. Thus a pupil who has studied Latin solely because of fear of punishment or merely to pass an examination will probably never open a Latin textbook after he has left school.[1]

As Thorndike said: 'The notion that doing what is irksome and distasteful in schools gives one power and willingness to work for truth and justice in the world is an example of the naïve verbal thinking that still often pervades education. In the first place, the habit formed is sometimes that of doing the disagreeable with blind confidence – a superstitious puritanism which expects that out of aimless subjection of oneself to the disagreeable, good will come by magic. It will not. . . . To suffer simply so as to stand suffering would be as foolish as to learn falsehoods so as to be able to unlearn them.'[2]

As for the cultural heritage argument there are two criticisms to be made. Firstly, if classics teachers were frank they would have to admit that for every hour normally spent on the study of Greek and Roman architecture, music, law, sculpture or philosophy they must spend a hundred on what Bolgar calls the 'dull preliminaries' of grammar, composition, vocabulary and so forth. Pure gerund-grinding occupies far more time in the syllabus than any discussion on

---

[1] Whitehead, a keen advocate of the classics, has the honesty to admit: 'The situation is dominated by the fact that in the future 90 per cent of pupils who leave school at the age of eighteen will never again read a classical book in the original. In the case of pupils leaving at an earlier age the estimate of 90 per cent may be changed to one of 99 per cent.' A. N. Whitehead, *The Aims of Education* (Ernest Benn, London, 1962 edn), p. 95.

[2] Morris E. Eson, *Psychological Foundations of Education* (Holt, Rinehart and Winston, New York, 1964), quoted on p. 126.

the beauties of the Parthenon or Aristotle's views on democracy.[1] Some history is taught incidentally (mostly Caesar's Gallic Wars), a few myths and legends may percolate through from the wanderings of Odysseus or Aeneas, occasional oratorical flourishes may be remembered from Cicero or poetic images from Virgil or Catullus, but (apart from sixth-form and university specialists) the language problem dominates everything else. The students of Balliol had a limerick which sums up the problem:

> There once were some lectures on Homer –
> But I think the name's a misnomer;
> Verbs, nouns and articles
> Verbs, nouns and particles
> But uncommonly little of Homer.

To bring the average and still more the slower pupil in the fourth and fifth forms up to the necessary examination standard it seems necessary according to the teaching methods used in so many schools to neglect a great deal of the general cultural and historical background.

In any event it can well be argued that to prepare a boy or girl for the complexities of the modern industrialized, urbanized and democratic state it is as important to teach about, say, Renaissance Italy, Elizabethan England, the Industrial Revolution, the emergence of nation states during the nineteenth century, the rise of the United States, the progress of science and technology or the lessons of the Russian Revolution as it is to describe what happened on the shores of the Mediterranean two thousand years ago.

Latin and social status

Why then, if its cultural and psychological bases have been so seriously undermined, does the classical tradition persist so strongly in certain sectors of the education system? Why do so many middle- and upper-class schools in Britain and other parts of Western Europe cling so resolutely to Latin?

The first answer is, of course, sheer educational inertia. Traditionally, élite schools and colleges tend to be inherently conservative in their functions, and may in practice jog along virtually unchanged for decades or even generations with curricula, teaching methods and value-systems which developed in an earlier epoch. There is always a time-lag in the growth of new curricula, and this applies especially to Latin and Greek not only because they are dead languages

---

[1] Lionel Hale writes in *A Fleece of Lambs* of a girls' school: 'It had never occurred to Sophia, nor to any of the other girls in the Latin class, to connect the words on the printed page with anything that had ever really happened. Men marched, camps were struck, winter quarters were gone into; but to Sophia the Latin language did not concern men, camps, winter quarters and cavalry. It existed to provide Subjunctives and Past Participles, and (oh golly!) Gerunds.' Rupert Wilkinson, *The Prefects: British Leadership and the Public School Tradition* (Oxford University Press, Oxford, 1964), quoted on p. 66.

but also because of their vocational irrelevance.[1] The mere fact that Latin has for centuries been taught in academically selective or high status institutions is in itself an important reason for its retention. The tradition that, for example, Winchester and Eton, Balliol and King's College are distinguished for their classical scholarship carries great weight with the educated public: and so do the vested interests – the entrenched statesman, judges, administrators, school governors, headmasters and other members of the liberal Establishment who were themselves classically educated, and attribute their success in life partly to this fact.

Secondly, there can be little doubt – if we analyse the language used, the individuals who use it, and look closely also at subconscious motives – that social and political considerations still weigh heavily with the defenders of the classics. The cruder forms of imperialism may be in disrepute but for certain teachers the classical tradition still stands, perhaps more than any other tradition in education, for order, discipline and authority. Ideas about leadership may have altered since Arnold's day but for many Public School masters Latin still stands, in ways which are not always explicitly stated or perhaps even consciously understood, for old-established conceptions of hierarchy and class structure.

The distinction between liberal and vocational subjects may not be as clear-cut as it once was, but some sections of the upper classes (and their would-be imitators) still cling to outmoded conceptions of a gentlemanly, non-utilitarian, largely ornamental education. Like Plato more than two thousand years ago they despise the 'mechanical'.

Indeed, in spite of all the democratic advances of recent decades they still regard the classics as an élite or essentially patrician study, possessing a magic quality not possessed by other more plebian subjects. To read an author such as Livingstone is to get the impression that the study of Latin and Greek will help countries survive the crises through which they are passing, counteract drift and confusion, restore unity to disrupted societies and build up moral and ethical principles which are alleged to be lacking in contemporary civilization.

Particularly will the classics reinforce the influence of the past, and act as a powerful barrier against all forms of modernity. The very fact that they are dead languages is a virtue in so far as they are incapable of further growth and development. By their emphasis on traditional forms and usages they act as an obstacle to everything that might be summed up under the heading of 'progress' – democracy, socialism, urbanization, industrialization, the advance of science, the growing power of the masses and the spread of popular entertainment.

[1] The dangers of this time-lag are admitted by the classical teachers themselves. In a recently published pamphlet they say: 'But it must be admitted that the innate conservatism of teachers of Classics does not augur well for the chances of a thorough reappraisal. . . . The greatest obstacles to the Classics in the post-Robbins era will be its own teachers. . . . In many public schools the classical staff are their own greatest enemy, for the idea of *disciplina gratia disciplinae* dies hard.' Joint Association of Classical Teachers, *Robbins and the Classics* (London, 1964).

T. S. Eliot, who as poet, anglo-catholic and royalist, might be taken as the archetype of the high Tory literary scholar, when defending the classics in an address to Harvard University, expressed his distaste for the modern curriculum when he wrote: 'The first task of the communities should be the preservation of education within the cloister uncontaminated by the deluge of barbarism outside.'[1]

Sir Richard Livingstone, a typical upper-class Oxford don, stated in his *A Defence of Classical Education* a similar rejection of modern trends when he denounced the 'peculiar vices of our age, materialism, commercialism, the narrowness, ugliness, rush and economic pressure of life . . . advertisements . . . cinemas, electric trains'.[2] Nearly twenty years later he returns to the same theme of dislike for our 'mechanized, commercialized, industrialized existence'.[3]

Latin and the school structure

The link between classics and the structure of the educational system can be shown more explicitly in another way if we examine the types of school and college which still teach the ancient languages in various countries.

In England, for instance, there is a direct relationship between a school's social prestige in the community and the extent to which it is classically biased. Thus the independent fee-paying and upper-class Public Schools all teach Latin to all their pupils at least up to the age of 15–16, regardless of their abilities, aptitudes or future careers. The upper-middle-class and academically very selective direct-grant schools teach a good deal of Latin, the aided grammar schools somewhat less, the maintained grammar schools still less again, and so down to the comprehensive schools which teach only a little. The working-class secondary modern schools usually teach none at all. The actual ratio of Latin and Greek teachers in six different types of London boys' school in 1966 may be seen in the table below:

School[4]	Type	No. of pupils	Classical masters No.	Ratio
A	Independent Public	653	6	109:1
B	Direct-grant	1,361	8	170:1
C	Aided grammar	672	4	168:1
D	Maintained grammar	450	2	225:1
E	Comprehensive	1,200	1	1,200:1
F	Secondary Modern	568	—	—

[1] T. S. Eliot, *Essays Ancient and Modern* (Faber, London, 1949).

[2] R. W. Livingstone, *A Defence of Classical Education* (Macmillan, London, 1917), p. 75.

[3] R. W. Livingstone, *Greek Ideas and Modern Life* (Oxford University Press, Oxford, 1935), p. 115. In this book he uses the same word 'barbarism' as Eliot to describe many of the manifestations of modern life which he does not like, and goes on to say: 'But those who knew Greece naturally turned from Cobbett and the Manchester school to Pericles and Plato, from Leeds and Wigan to Athens, from self-satisfied mercantilism to a civilization without machines or vast towns or great resources or a soul' (p. 31).

[4] Figures on which this table is based were obtained by the writer from the headmasters

Similarly the expensive fee-paying preparatory schools all teach Latin to their pupils, irrespective of the latter's intelligence, usually right through from 8 or 9–12 or 13 years, whereas in contrast the council primary schools teach none at all. In the same way in the field of higher education the older and socially more superior the college the greater the emphasis on classics. Thus Oxford University in 1965 had about 9,800 students with 116 dons classified under the heading *Literae Humaniores*, but only 88 lecturing in social studies.[1] The provincial redbrick University of Manchester had about the same number of students (9,700) with only 27 lecturers or professors of Latin, Greek and Philosophy, but 121 teaching economics, politics and so forth.[2]

In France much the same sort of social and cultural relationship exists; the staunchest defenders of the classics being found in the old-established and high-status *lycées*. In spite of the rise of the élite polytechnics, the irresistible pull of science, and the vocational opportunities which are available for technologists, a classically biased education still has an enormous appeal to middle- and upper-class parents in that country.[3] 'The fact that a classical education is held in high esteem,' writes Gal, 'means that fathers of bourgeois families, professional men, civil servants, heads of business concerns who themselves have had a classical training, insist on one for their children. The lower middle classes, clerks, artisans, small farmers prefer their children to take up modern studies. Thus we find in 1947, in the first years of the secondary schools, there were 6,470 children of civil servants following a classical course, and 5,420 doing modern studies, the corresponding figures in the case of children belonging to the professional classes being 2,858 as against 1,238, and in the case of workers 1,549 as against 5,590.'[4]

In Italy it was significant that when a debate took place in Parliament during 1962–3, about a proposal to keep Latin in the middle-class *lyceos* but not in the socially inferior *scule medie* the division tended to occur along political lines, with the Christian Democrats favouring Latin and the Socialists and Communists attacking it.

In the Republic of Ireland where secondary school curricula tend to be domi-

---

of six schools in the London area. In school A (independent public) there were three masters exclusively teaching Latin and Greek, and six combining Latin with other subjects. It is estimated that this would be equivalent to six full-time classical masters. In school E (comprehensive) there was one other master who taught Latin four periods a week.

[1] *Oxford University Calendar, 1966* (Oxford University Press, Oxford, 1966).

[2] *University of Manchester Calendar, 1965–6* (Manchester University Press, Manchester, 1965).

[3] 'The difference in prestige among the various fields of study (in secondary schools) cause the brightest students to enrol chiefly in the classical section, the next level in the modern section and those of lower ability in the technical and vocational programmes. Thus, the educational system reflects and at the same time reinforces certain stratifications within French society; and in this way whole lines of human endeavour and large groups of people become stigmatized.' George A. Male, *Education in France* (U.S. Dept. of Health, Education and Welfare, Washington, 1963), p. 85.

[4] Roger Gal in 'France', *The Yearbook of Education, 1950* (Evans, London, 1950).

nated by the two-fold influence of tradition and the Roman Catholic Church it was noted in a recent report that whereas 100 per cent of all male candidates in the Leaving Certificate or matriculation examination normally take Irish and English as subjects, and nine-tenths take Latin, only about a fifth take French and a negligible number take another modern foreign language. Indeed, the figures showed that it was customary for more boys to sit an examination in Greek than in German, Italian and Spanish combined.[1] So much for entry to the Common Market!

The most striking examples of the way in which historical and political rather than cultural or psychological factors influence the teaching of classics are, of course, the United States and the Soviet Union. The former country, with its strongly utilitarian bias in education and lack of hereditary aristocracy or professional class in society, gradually gave up the serious teaching of Latin in most of the high schools which were developed in the nineteenth century or later. The U.S.S.R. had no place for the classics, except for a tiny handful of linguists, in the schools and colleges which were expanded after the 1917 Revolution.

What of the future?

The identification of Latin and Greek with élite schools and colleges was, as we have seen, a source of strength to these subjects in the past. Whatever their intrinsic merits as languages or literature there could be no doubt that their connection with famous institutions and superior social occupations gave them a unique prestige in the community.

But in the future as democracy gains ground and the old hierarchies break up all this is likely to be changed. The more egalitarian society becomes the less sympathy there is for traditional concepts of status. The greater the demand for a utilitarian curriculum the less tolerance for outdated forms of conspicuous cultural consumption. The Platonic theory about the need to train special leaders is in decline, and the new meritocrats who are gradually replacing the old aristocracy and plutocracy are more likely to choose the natural or social sciences than the classics. In the industrialized and urbanized economies of the second half of the twentieth century the vocationally trained specialist will be increasingly preferred to the gentlemanly amateur, with profound long-term consequences for both the curriculum and structure of secondary and higher education.

Already some classical teachers in Britain are beginning to be seriously worried that the large-scale introduction of comprehensive schools will undermine the position of the grammar schools.[2] Fears are especially expressed about the pros-

[1] Republic of Ireland Ministry of Education and the Organization for Economic Co-operation and Development, *Investment in Education* (Government Stationery Office, Dublin, 1965), pp. 276–7.

[2] 'The first wave of educational democracy, the 1944 Education Act, left teachers of the Classics more or less untouched. Not through masterly inactivity will they survive the second and third waves – the expansion of the universities and the Common School.'

pects for Latin in the intermediate section of the three-tier school system. In the long run there are even worse anxieties that if the ultimate bastion of the Public Schools is weakened then the prospects for traditional classics could be very grave indeed. There is also alarm that the growth of the new universities (only a few have shown much interest in the classics) and the increased importance of colleges of technology, polytechnics and colleges of education will further isolate Latin and Greek from the main stream of higher education. Two officially sponsored reports reflect this concern when they speak of the 'altered climate of public opinion', 'the precarious position of Latin', and of the old image of the classics as having 'lost its shine'.[1]

The solution advocated by the Joint Association of Classical Teachers – and it is difficult to know whether they speak for the majority or only for a few of the more far-sighted specialists in Britain – is to introduce what they call a 'new Latin for a new situation'. Briefly, this would mean fairly radical changes in the content and method of teaching the subject. It would involve the abandonment of old ideas about mental discipline, and require that classical courses become more directly relevant to contemporary cultural needs. Under the proposed scheme it is suggested that much of the conventional grammatical and vocabulary drill be jettisoned and that teachers no longer ask most of their pupils to make serious attempts at composition. The new emphasis would be on translation; reading would be more important than writing. For the duller pupils who might find even this too difficult the classical literature should be available already translated into the vernacular. Such a curriculum, which might best be described as general classical studies, would include much more history and aesthetics than is at present taught under the heading of Latin and Greek. It would involve more team-teaching, and the co-operation of specialists from various departments. Moreover, it would be directed towards all normal children and not merely a cultivated minority.[2] The advocates of this new curriculum are confident that it would have wide popular appeal because of the growing public interest in archaeology, increasing travel to Greece and Italy, and the numerous magazine articles, television programmes and paperback books about Mediterranean civilization.

In this way the reformers hope to democratize – and also bring more into line with current psychological theory about how children best learn in school – an élite tradition of classical education which has not changed much in essentials for centuries.

Joint Association of Classical Teachers, *Classics and the Reorganization of Secondary Schools* (London, n.d.).

[1] Joint Association of Classical Teachers, *Robbins and the Classics* (London, 1964), and *Classics and the Reorganization of Secondary Schools* (London, n.d.).

[2] This theme of a wider and simpler course of classical studies suitable for the younger school leaver is developed in a recent Schools Council report. *An approach through Classics* (H.M.S.O., London, 1966).

7 Metallurgy and the Department of Science and Art, 1870–1900

P. W. MUSGRAVE

The Department of Science and Art was established in 1853 under the Board of Trade. The impetus for its creation came from the Great Exhibition of 1851. The Department was transferred to the new Board of Education when this latter body was established in 1856. A minute of the Department dated 2 June 1859 said that it would 'assist the industrial classes . . . in supplying themselves with instruction in the rudiments of . . .' a list of scientific and technological subjects. The maximum income level for grant was, for many years, £200 which was in those years a high enough limit to allow the lower middle class to take advantage of the Department's efforts, and it was this latter class which benefited most from the new system of examination, mainly because the working class on the whole had not yet a high enough standard of education to attend classes at this level.

Development of a system of examinations

By 1859 a system of technological examinations was established. It covered six subjects and was aimed at what we today would call the technician level. In the following May 104 candidates sat papers. By 1862 several more subjects had been added, one of which was metallurgy, though initially few sat this subject. It is important to realize the conditions under which these examinations were run (Foden, 1966, pp. 74–7). The state at this time took little responsibility for the provision of technical or, indeed, any education. The ideology of *laissez-faire*, symbolized by the publication of Samuel Smiles' *Self-Help* in 1859, was strongly held by most people and the expectation was that ambitious men would force themselves to attend evening classes that were provided by such bodies as the Department. On the other hand employers preferred practical men to those with a scientific education and opposed government support to technical or applied scientific education on the grounds that this was a hidden subsidy to the industries

First printed as pp. iii–vi *of 'Curriculum Development in Further Education: Two Case Studies',* Technical Education Abstracts, *Vol. IX, No. 3 (January–March 1969),* pp. iii–ix.

concerned (Musgrave, 1966). In addition there was a shortage of teachers capable of providing technological educational at this level. Therefore it is not surprising that grants were given to teachers on the basis of Payment by Results; initially the scale of payment was £4 per candidate who passed. For some years the Department ran courses to train teachers for these examinations. On the whole it was elementary teachers who responded to the chance of extra earnings by running evening classes, often on school premises, for these technological courses.

The syllabus in metallurgy

Where the quality of teaching is low the syllabus assumes great importance as a means of guiding the teachers concerned. The syllabus for the metallurgy course was laid down by the School of Mines in Jermyn Street, which was at this time under the control of the Department of Science and Art. This institution was given the title of Royal School of Mines in 1863 and eventually became a part of Imperial College. Though this School was constantly attempting to give a practical direction to its courses, its characteristic was a broad and theoretical approach to its various courses including that in metallurgy. This stress on principles was in line with the contemporary definition of technical education (Musgrave, 1964). One of the difficulties at the time was that the principles of most technologies were barely established and, therefore, textbooks and syllabuses could often be little more than descriptions of processes. However, in 1864 J. Percy, Professor of metallurgy at the Royal School of Mines, published the first modern textbook on this subject, *The Metallurgy of Iron and Steel*, which related the relevant industrial techniques to chemical analysis.

Despite the stress on theory, this was a technological subject and if the examination was to have practical relevance, the syllabus should have been kept abreast of contemporary technical innovations. If the Annual Directories of the Department are examined, the way in which the syllabus changed as techniques altered can be seen. The Bessemer process, invented in 1856, was not mentioned by name until 1869, though admittedly prior to this the syllabus was somewhat vague. In 1880 Professor Percy handed over as examiner to Dr Roberts (later Roberts-Austen), who succeeded him as Professor at the Royal School of Mines. Then began a series of changes. In 1880 the Seimens–Martin process, invented in 1866, is mentioned. In both cases the gap between invention and inclusion is about thirteen years. But in 1881 the Gilchrist–Thomas process appears in the syllabus three years after its invention. That year also saw the dropping of the old crucible process of making steel, despite the fact that it was still in use in some places. In 1882 the syllabus was recast and whereas beforehand 'iron', which included steel, had been one of a series of metals to be studied, a new subject appeared, 'iron and steel'. Greater emphasis was placed on the chemistry of the processes about which more was now known.

Although the syllabus at Elementary level had apparently not catered for modern techniques before 1880, from 1869 candidates for Honours could be given questions 'at the discretion of the Examiner, who will have regard to the present state of metallurgical science as carried out in this and other countries.' Throughout this period the examination was set by the Professor at Jermyn Street and later after the school had moved in the early 1880s, at South Kensington. The papers, therefore, bore the mark of the Royal School of Mines, namely a broad theoretical approach. From 1883 a practical examination was set, though as can be seen from Table I, there were always considerably fewer candidates for the practical than for the theoretical examination. The Theory syllabus in 1890 consisted of the following parts:

(1) Introductory subjects (i.e. ores and ore preparation) and fuel.
(2) Iron and steel.
(3) Precious metals.
(4) Metals other than the foregoing.

The Practical syllabus consisted at the Elementary stage of:

(a) Principles on which calcination, roasting and reduction are based.
(b) Testing of fire-resisting materials.
(c) Properties of common alloys (pewter, brass, bronze).

From the late 1880s, examiners' comments were published in the Reports of the Science and Art Department. These remarks show the trend of teaching and of students' interests throughout the country. Thus in 1888, 'Answers to questions still show the prevalence of the mistaken belief that chemical methods only suited to the laboratory can be applied on a large scale to the extraction of metals from their ores.' In 1895 some classes seemed too keen on 'details of processes and methods rather than principles'. In 1899 '. . . special attention seems to be devoted to Iron and Steel to the undue exclusion of other metals comprised in the syllabus'. In this same year the section on iron and steel was revised and given more stress, but in 1900 the examiner still complained of over-emphasis on iron and steel at the expense of other metals.

Clearly there was a constant tension between the demands of examiners and those of the Royal School of Mines as expressed by its professors of metallurgy who were responsible for running the examination and saw as a necessity, possibly rightly under the conditions of the time, that candidates should gain a sound basic scientific training in metallurgy. Yet the examination did seem to be answering a useful purpose in that candidates put their stress on practice rather than principles and on iron and steel rather than the broader range of metals. Arnold, the blunt and practically minded Professor of metallurgy at Sheffield University, summed up the examination in the *Iron and Coal Trades Review* of 14 February, 1896: 'The metallurgy of South Kensington was the metallurgy of the cram books, and not of the steel works.'

The candidates for the examination

How quickly and in what areas did this examination develop in Britain during the late nineteenth century? Table I shows the growth in the numbers of candidates sitting the metallurgy papers; for comparison the total candidates sitting all examinations set by the Department is shown together with two other subjects relevant to those in the metallurgical industries. There was a steady growth

TABLE I

Numbers of Students Sitting Certain of the
Department of Science and Art Examinations, 1870–1900

	Total examined	Pure mathematics	Inorganic chemistry Theory	Practical	Metallurgy Theory	Practical
1870	16,515	3,995	2,694	—	160	—
1875	27,985	6,370	5,262	—	173	—
1880	34,678	11,179	5,529	1,937	277	—
1885	48,497	13,392	9,620	4,602	351	126
1890	83,070	25,261	17,769	8,238	514	253
1895	108,193	29,692	23,787	15,128	534	391
1900	151,279	23,059	15,071	10,226	463	370

Source: *Yearly Report of Department of Science and Art.*

throughout the period up to 1897 when the reorganization of secondary education resulted in a withdrawal of the many school pupils who by this time were sitting the examination set by the Department. These examinations had come to serve a different function from that for which they were originally intended. If one looks at the Calendar of the Department, the nature of the examinees is fairly clear. It was not the 'industrial classes' who were entering these examinations after study at night school, but the adolescent sons of the lower middle classes, often while attending what today we would call secondary schools. In 1883 the Department requested that candidates who were clearly not ready for examination should not be entered and, whether because of this or because of the increasing entry from schools, the pass rate which had been around 65 per cent rose into the upper seventies.

Over this period there was a sevenfold increase in both total entries and in candidates for the two purely scientific subjects, while metallurgy, clearly unsuited to the needs of schools, increased only by about half that rate. However, this in itself is, perhaps, no mean achievement under the social conditions of the time. Furthermore, the period 1874–96 marked the Great Depression, and there is not the cyclical connection that might be expected between the numbers of candidates entering each year and the 'ups and downs' of employment due to trading conditions.

Some indication of the way in which the numbers under instruction grew at differing rates in different metallurgical districts can be seen in Table II for three areas that specialized in the manufacture of iron and steel. This table also gives a clearer picture than the global figures in Table I of what was happening at the level of the individual class. Thus the totals of ten candidates represent single small classes.

It would seem that in Sheffield, where there was much specialization in high-grade steels, the basic scientific education of lower management was taken seriously earlier than elsewhere. By the end of this period the metallurgy examination was attracting some support. Except in 1895, the support in Sheffield was largely for the practical examination and this symbolizes the crucial role played by the presence or otherwise of suitable laboratories for such courses. Thus, in Cumberland, the one area in Britain with an ample supply of haematite ores suitable for making acid steel, only in 1892 were any candidates taught metallurgy and then the theoretical course was taken, since there were no suitable laboratories (this same factor stopped the teaching of practical Chemistry). In Middlesbrough, a boom town of the late nineteenth century whose industry was based on the large deposits of basic ores in the Cleveland Hills, technical education was developed a little more rapidly (after allowing for differences in population) than in Cumberland, but in 1901, an H.M.I. said that Middlesbrough was 'far behind any other town of its size in the district in its provision for technical "instruction".' There was a specially equipped metallurgical laboratory, but in 1891 only ten candidates were taught for the practical metallurgy paper and due to this lack of demand the laboratory was used for the teaching of school physics. Significant of this lack of interest in technical education was the fact that the local authority never made full use of its powers to levy rates under the 1889 Technical Instruction Act.

The situation in the areas specializing in mixed metallurgical processes can be seen by examining the case of Swansea. In 1896 the figures for candidates were as follows: chemistry: theory 161, practical 54; metallurgy: theory 15, practical 15. In Birmingham and the surrounding areas, another mixed metallurgical district, a similarly favourable situation was found.

In sum, there was a growth in the use of the system of examinations run by the Department of Science and Art throughout this period, though after the early 1880s, this was mainly due to a demand from a direction other than originally intended, namely from schools. It was, therefore, subjects like mathematics and chemistry that grew most rapidly, while the more technical subjects like metallurgy were less in demand, due to the marked contemporary antipathy to all technical instruction given outside the factory, even when called practical. The support for these examinations seems to have been stronger in areas of mixed- or high-quality metallurgy such as Birmingham and Sheffield, rather than in the other more run-of-the-mill iron and steel areas.

TABLE II

Number of Students at Certain Towns in Science Classes, 1870–1900

	Middlesbrough					Sheffield					Cumberland*				
	Pure Maths.	Inorg. chem.		Metallurgy		Pure Maths.	Inorg. chem.		Metallurgy		Pure Maths.	Inorg. chem.		Metallurgy	
		Th.	Prac.	Th.	Prac.		Th.	Prac.	Th.	Prac.		Th.	Prac.	Th.	Prac.
1870	—	8	—	—	—	35	98	—	—	—	28	—	—	—	—
1875	—	10	—	—	—	31	50	—	—	—	9	—	—	—	—
1880	3	40	—	—	—	158	20	—	—	—	20	16	—	—	—
1885	65	42	38	30	20	366	380	374	30	10	12	42	—	—	—
1890	62	50	50	10	10	333	560	530	10	10	30	—	—	—	—
1895	240	40	40	—	—	394	364	360	85	—	115	156	—	—	—

Source: *Reports of Department of Science and Art.*

* Includes Maryport, Whitehaven, Workington.

Discussion of the case study

The aim of outlining this case study is to learn something about curriculum development, and the historical evidence given so far must now be interpreted in this light. Any curriculum or examination syllabus is governed by the goals of those who organize it (Musgrave, 1970). Therefore the first question to be asked about any syllabus is by whose authority it is set. There may be a monopolistic authority as was the case for this examination in metallurgy, or the authority may be shared among several persons who may act in their own right or on behalf of specific bodies, as is the case for most of the examinations of the City and Guilds today (D. E. Wheatley, 1959). Clearly, where several parties are involved, conflict of interests may occur. In the metallurgy examination, the clients (namely the candidates) had relatively little power, although they eventually forced those in charge to give more weight to one part of the curriculum, (i.e. iron and steel) than the academics in authority wished. The relevant industry, one of the main power groups in today's technological examinations, had no wish, at that time, to influence the syllabus. However, the still-common clash between an academic demand for theory and an industrial demand for the practical was to some extent mediated through the candidates.

The creation of any syllabus can be seen as the setting and detailed implementation of relevant goals. Therefore, attention must be given to the ideologies held by those who take part in this process. In the metallurgy examination the Department was in a monopolistic position and those in authority believed in an academic approach that was in direct conflict with the beliefs and wishes of the candidates and those who employed them. It may well be that under certain conditions a benevolent despotism of the nature that the Department then exercised is one of the most efficient methods of opening up an under-developed subject, where texts are inadequate, and where teachers are poorly trained and scarce. Yet a sole authority may not be the best way to keep a syllabus up to date so that it meets the needs of industry. New goals are, from time to time, given to educational bodies such as the Department, and at the detailed level these include the teaching of newly discovered technological processes. In the case of the metallurgy examination alterations in curriculum seem to have been slow to come, before the 1880s. This raises the problem of whether such changes would come more easily with a single authority or with a co-operative authority. It may be that the type of administration machinery varies by type of industry, by social circumstances and according to the state of development of the technology. However, one of the advantages of the co-operative type of authority that is common today is that the body responsible for the syllabus can, by co-option, draw on a greater knowledge of the problems faced by the candidates, the teachers and the relevant industry (Thompson and McEwen, 1958). Clearly during the late nineteenth century the Department was trying to set one syllabus in metallurgy to suit a clientele of very varied ages and interests, who were taught under very different conditions.

Perhaps greater knowledge of the conditions might have led to a different and less rigid policy.

We have very few case studies of the life histories of examinations or of how decisions are made about the content of curricula. Clearly such studies raise problems that are central to any discussion about how we should set about developing curricula in the future. Relevant questions would be: what is the most apt mechanism (*a*) to organize (*b*) to change and (*c*) to keep up to date either a curriculum or an examination? Does the stage of development of a subject influence the answers given to the last question? And, finally, what is the nature of the power and the beliefs of those who hold it, which governs the process of setting curricula?

BIBLIOGRAPHY

F. E. FODEN, 'Technical Education in England', *Paedagogica Historica*, Vol. VI, No. 1 (1966), pp. 68–97.

P. W. MUSGRAVE, 'The Definition of Technical Education', *Vocational Aspect*, Vol. XVI, No. 34 (Summer, 1964), pp. 105–11. (Included in this Reader, Part One, No. 5.)

P. W. MUSGRAVE, 'Constant Factors in the Demand for Technical Education, 1860–1960', *British Journal of Educational Studies*, Vol. XVI, No. 2 (May 1966), pp. 173–87. (Included in this Reader, Part Three, No. 4.)

P. W. MUSGRAVE, 'A Sociology of the Curriculum', *Paedagogica Europaea*, forthcoming, 1970.

J. D. THOMPSON and W. J. MCEWEN, 'Organizational Goals and Environment', *American Sociological Review*, Vol. 23, No. 1 (February 1958), pp. 23–31.

D. E. WHEATLEY, 'City and Guilds Examinations', *Vocational Aspect*, Vol. XI, No. 22 (Spring, 1959), pp. 31–59.

8 Public School Town in the Nineteenth Century

T. W. BAMFORD

Any school influences a community both directly and indirectly. Masters, groundsmen, caretakers and domestics all earn money and support households, while food and drink, repairs and buildings bring trade to the locality. The effect is much greater for boarding than for day schools and was particularly interesting in the last century when the prosperity of schools varied so much. Normally we look at schools purely from the point of view of the pupils and are apt to forget that they are sources of wealth and can be considered an asset on the same footing as an industrial concern. Their prosperity or decline is a matter of vital interest to both traders and pupils. A school full to capacity is a successful one, while any headmaster unfortunate enough to witness a decline in numbers is written off as a failure. On the other hand, a golden age to which Old Boys and traders look back with reverence is reserved for those headmasters who have rescued the school from obscurity and produced a new reputation and increased numbers of pupils. In the nineteenth century a large boarding school in a small town dominated local affairs. Not only could it choke or enlighten the local community both culturally and industrially, but it could alter the whole aspect of town life in every phase, encouraging some projects and condemning others. Rugby School may be taken as a good example of all these trends.

Between 1806 and 1874 there were six headmasters – John Wooll, Thomas Arnold, A. C. Tait, E. M. Goulburn, Frederick Temple and Henry Hayman. Of these, three are usually reckoned to be failures since the school declined in size rapidly before they left. These are Wooll, Goulburn and Hayman. One, Tait, was successful since he maintained the flourishing state left by his predecessor (Arnold), while two are generally reckoned to be great headmasters since they rescued the school from failure – Arnold and Temple.

Before 1820 Wooll had himself been successful with the largest intake in England, but somehow within eight years, numbers had fallen to 123 from the prosperity total of over 380. On the level of subsistence this meant a loss of revenue to the town in several ways. Less food was eaten, less beer drunk, less

First printed in British Journal of Educational Studies, *Vol. VI, No. 1 (November 1957), pp. 25-36.*

fuel consumed, less washing done, fewer servants employed. In those days the average amount spent on food, lodgings and welfare, including pocket money, was about £60 a year, so that from this source alone the town lost over £15,000 p.a. through the failure of Wooll. The effect was aggravated by the fact that the masters' income varied with the number of boys, so that declining prosperity meant less money for the staff to spend. Fortunately this factor was less severe for the days of Wooll than those of Arnold and the headmasters who followed. In Wooll's day the staff were curates as well as schoolmen and this supplemented their teaching and made them less dependent on the classroom. The dual role had advantages. It made the link between neighbourhood and staff more personal and the school a spiritual focus point. In those days the boys boarded in the town, in large houses dotted about the main streets and the Market Place. Sometimes they were looked after by their own masters, but more commonly the houses were run by local people – the wives of solicitors and professional men, with the homes of surgeons particularly favoured by parents. The boys had their meals in shops in the main streets and were part of the intimate life of the town. The profit from boarding – as much as £10 per boy – was spread over the 'ordinary' residents. When Wooll went in 1828 all this was changed, for a key point in Arnold's policy was to raise the status of his staff by increasing their incomes. Apart from an actual increase from fees, by which the masters shared six guineas for every foundationer and nine and a half guineas for each of the other boys, Arnold changed the oc-casional case of a master keeping a boarding house into a general rule. As 'houses' became vacant he bestowed them on his staff in turn and the profits from the boys' maintenance went to swell the teacher's salary. By 1862 this income, as profit, was officially estimated as £14 per boy per annum.[1] If a master had twenty boys in his house, this meant a profit of £280 to add to his salary and a corresponding loss to a townsman as compared with the system of Wooll. So the salary of the assistant masters leapt to figures varying from £600 to £1,617, with the upper levels occupied by house masters. The staff saved a good deal of this salary, as indeed they had to, for permanent entrenchment at Rugby was not encouraged. Even so they each spent about £600 every year, most of which went through the hands of local traders or servants. With nine such masters in 1830 the total sum involved was over £5,000, and with growing prosperity and staff increases this amount was almost doubled in the sixties.

Another matter of economics concerned the buildings. While the school was declining outwardly in numbers under Wooll, a major reconstruction scheme was under way to prepare for future expansion. In the course of fourteen years, a headmaster's house, a new school and other buildings besides a chapel were built at a cost of £46,000. Most of the money benefited the town, and on paper this offset some of the loss due to the shrinkage of trade. The work was finished in 1823, so that there were still five years left before the coming of Arnold. The

[1] Report of H.M. Commissioners appointed to enquire into the Revenues and Manage-ment of certain Colleges and Schools (1864). (Public Schools Commission.)

building programme therefore could not have eked out the leanest years of all. In any case the townsfolk who benefited by building projects were not those who prayed for the maximum number of boys. As for the reputation of headmasters, it is a strange thought that if only the permanent and tangible things like buildings are considered, then Rugby has much more to thank Wooll for than Arnold, and similarly Goulburn, another outward failure at a later date, was far more successful than his illustrious successor, Temple.

Apart from the boys, the masters and the buildings themselves, there is yet another feature of town life that was affected directly by the school. The last years of Wooll which saw such a decline in numbers also saw the coming of the first upper-class parent. That was in 1821. These parents came to live in Rugby while their children studied at the school, and once schooling days were over, they moved on again. In the first year of Arnold, ten new boys were admitted in this way, and seven in his second. So it went on, varying from eight or ten to fifteen.[1] In the twenty years from 1844 to 1863, 110 families took up residence long enough to be traced through local directories. All these were gentry, and so were another twenty families whose length of stay was either too brief or too intermittent to be recorded. All came for the express purpose of being in the town while their sons were being educated. Of these families, thirty-four had only one child at the school. Two or three boys per family was common while nine families had four boys at the school, seven five, and one parent sent as many as seven boys there. The total stay varied, therefore, according to the number of their children who had to work their way through, but the pattern remained the same – arrival and departure corresponding strictly with the son's career at Rugby. Of all the 110 only nine stayed on any appreciable time after their sons had left. Only ten took any real part in local affairs, and for six of these it was only a temporary part. Nevertheless, three were very prominent citizens indeed,[2] and, together with the Rector and the Headmaster, became leaders of the town as patrons and as magistrates.

The main mass of local gentry in the period 1840–80 was therefore migrant. Locally they were called sojourners and stayed for five years or so on the average before they went away. Many of them had no settled homes of their own elsewhere, so that their departure meant not only leaving friends behind but plunging again into the problems of new surroundings. It meant that Rugby as a town held no attractions for them; even repelled them.

It has been suggested that the sojourners came to obtain a cheap good education; and in families where several boys had to be educated this was undoubtedly the case, but there are several objections to it as a general theory. For one thing several of these people were wealthy and kept up very large establishments, even to butler and footmen.[3] There are many widows in the list, and at first sight this

---

[1] Some of these, of course, would be brothers of other boys at the school.
[2] Fryer, Atty, Campbell.
[3] See, for example, J. Featherstone of Newbold Road in the 1851 Census details.

would seem to indicate a need to economize, yet many bought houses and furniture in the town and sold them at the end of their stay. This could hardly be done without considerable capital and the risk of grave financial loss, since house prices in Rugby were exorbitantly high in times of shortage and correspondingly low after long lean periods. Moreover, in the whole of the twenty years under review there was only one attempt to share a house.[1] This fact is all the more surprising when it is realized how large some of these houses were, even after accommodating a typical case of widow, son and servants. This phenomenon of sojourning was obviously a complex matter, and undoubtedly there were other motives which influenced parents. For one thing, there was the very natural desire of widows to be near their sons, especially when they were young. This was still the day of stern discipline in the classroom, when Public Schoolmasters – and Rugby was no exception – thought that corporal punishment was just and essential. Far more fearful, however, than the master's cane, which at any rate was usually wielded for good reason, was the bullying in non-class hours. The current idea that freedom was the right of boys as individuals, and that they were therefore entitled to unsupervised time, might have delighted the hardy males, but it produced a nightmare in the hearts of affectionate mothers. However, if a parent lived in Rugby, all this could be avoided. All the advantages of education at a school of the highest prestige could be obtained, and the penalties of boyish feuds eliminated, by the simple expedient of making the son a day scholar. Moreover, Rugby was a popular school and in good years large numbers were unable to get in. Sojourners, however, could guarantee (as residents of Rugby) entry of their children into the school, whereas application from outside stood risk of refusal.

Occasionally, gentry tried to make business arrangements, as the following advertisement shows:

> Exchange. A clergyman, desirous of drawing near to Rugby for benefit of the school, would not object to exchange benefices at a loss. His own worth £225 p.a. and an excellent house. Apply——[2]

Upper-class migrants became a prominent feature of the town, and among the first was Mrs Fletcher. In May 1829 she took a cottage in Bilton, became intimate with Mrs Arnold and exerted great influence over the family, even taking over Thorney How in the Lakes specially to be near the Arnold residence of Fox How. Many of these sojourners were used to a wandering life and might well be described as empire builders. In the family of E. Peters successive children were born in the East Indies, Middlesex, Naples, Gloucester, Sussex and Rugby. Another's children came from Woolwich, Ireland, North America and Rugby;[3] another from the East Indies and Mauritius.[4] Occasional members had children born in various parts of Europe. The Ramsay children were born in France, and the de Satge children in Cradley, Lausanne (2), Bridgnorth, Lausanne again for the

---

[1] Hatchell – Underwood.
[2] *Rugby Advertiser* (29 July 1854).
[3] R. Poulden.
[4] C. W. Radcliffe.

third time, and Pau. Many of those who had kept to these islands were widely travelled too. The Worsley children were born in King's Lynn, Harpenden, King's Lynn (2), Oakland, Woodhill, Camberwell and Rugby. Another case in Ireland, London, Brighton (2), Rugby.[1] When families were mixed, one obtained a mixture of both empire and home. Thus in the Hatchell household were children born in Ireland, Cheltenham, Jersey, the Cape of Good Hope and Madras.

All this lent a flavour not only to the school but to the town itself. It meant that there was a living resident expert on many parts of the globe and a real wealth of first-hand material. No doubt it had a subtle general effect in widening horizons, but records show the deliberate efforts to spread this experience can be counted on the fingers of one hand in the lectures of Fryer and Campbell.

Even if they were reluctant to spread their culture in the town, the sojourners with their big families were a great financial asset. Large new houses, each with servants' quarters, were built on the southern side, forming a select neighbourhood about the school itself, with quiet tree-lined streets on the windward side of the piggeries and cesspools of the lower-class areas. In 1851 there were seventy-six such families resident in the town. These would account for £2,250 in rent and almost £12,000 in trade.[2] This excludes the regular money brought in from rates, while in addition they employed a whole army of servants – 179 of them in the year 1851, ranging from a tutor and governesses to scullery maids. No wonder the traders looked on the gentry as a desirable asset and extolled sojourning as a virtue, even though there was the inevitable antagonistic minority who accused the newcomers of snobbery.[3]

Between the coming of Arnold in 1828 and the departure of Tait in 1850 the school was prosperous, the number of sojourners large and the traders contented. Goulburn, however, was unsuccessful. Within three years numbers began to fall, and with the decline the number of sojourners fell off rapidly too. The town was hard hit on two counts – lack of boys and lack of resident parents. Money was short, and the years 1853–7 were times of declining prosperity. In the middle of this period we read:

> Four years ago there was much difficulty in procuring a house suitable for a family in Rugby. We wish it was the case now, but the ticketed windows on the once favoured Hillmorton Road tell a different tale.[4]

or again:

> Here in Rugby we have not much to boast about in the annals of the departing year. The few houses erected and the number unlet are not signs of prosperity.[5]

[1] Baroness Maria Clanmorris.
[2] See *Rugby Advertiser* (10 February 1855), where the effect of 100 such families is discussed.
[3] Ibid. (23 April 1864 and 22 June 1867).
[4] Ibid. (27 January 1855).
[5] Ibid. (29 December 1855).

The years from 1855 to 1857 were the depths. Whereas in a good year like 1850 (the last year of Tait) the number of gentry houses advertised in the local press for letting was only three, by 1855 this figure had risen to twenty-six. In the last year of Goulburn the comparable figure was twenty-three, and this dropped immediately to four in the very first year of Temple. No wonder that the locals, in the midst of their depression, fixed their complaints directly on the headmaster. They looked on the era of Tait and wished he were back. When Tait was appointed Bishop of London a leading article in the local paper congratulated him warmly and hoped at the same time that the rumours of Goulburn's resignation were true. Even though the hopes failed to materialize on that occasion, it was taken as an indication of events. Finally, when he did in fact resign, we get: For the sake of the school, however, we are rather pleased at the prospect of a change which we truly believe was required.[1] At the same time it was important that another Goulburn should not succeed to Arnold's chair. All good men interested in Rugby School will join us in the prayer that the Trustees may be Divinely inspired in their choice.[2] Although the Headmaster was universally blamed within the town, other explanations for the school decline were also offered. For instance, in 1830 it had been decided that any newcomer must live in the town for two years before he could benefit by the foundation and thereby obtain relief from fees, and this was given as a reason for the empty houses along the Hillmorton Road. The explanation, however, does not bear investigation. If the rule had made little difference for twenty years, then why should it become suddenly effective in 1852–3? Moreover, the same situation still existed when Goulburn went and Temple came, and yet the prosperity of the town was almost immediately restored.

Unfortunately the troubles were not over with the new headmaster. Local businessmen were soon to learn that times had changed, and that their trade and wealth did not increase automatically with the prosperity of the school. This new phase is part of a pattern starting with the railway, in the siting of which the school played a vital part.

Originally the London and Birmingham line was scheduled to pass to the south of the school, and the railway station would then have been at the foot of the Catholic hill, close to the bottom of the school playing fields. This would have meant that the houses of the workmen, and indeed a whole new town, would have arisen in the valley with Rugby School sandwiched between the old and new towns. Whether this was the reason that prompted the school into action we do not know, but the Directors considered on 3 December 1830 a complaint about the line passing near the school.[3] A survey committee went to Rugby to investigate very early in the new year. Again, what transpired is unknown, but the business-

[1] Ibid. (27 June 1857).

[2] Ibid.

[3] British Transport Commission Archives, Minutes Book of the London and Birmingham Railway, LBM 1/26, p. 72 (see also references under 17 December 1830 and 7 January 1831).

men must have been convinced, for Robert Stephenson reported on the matter to his Directors on 7 January and the line was redrawn in its present position to the north of the town. Rugby was small then, merely 2,500, so that its modern character was moulded in that winter. It was perhaps the most significant decision in its history, for with the railway to the south there would have been no industrial expansion in the flat lands to the north, and Rugby would probably have remained a country market town on a main line railway. Moreover, if the old route had been the final one, it is very doubtful indeed if the town would ever have become a major railway junction.[1] For good or evil, the school made a successful challenge to the new way of life and was probably the first to interfere positively in the railway spread.

The railway brought London within two hours to the south, and Birmingham less than an hour in the opposite direction. The gentry and the school no longer had to rely on local trade, for the speed and reliability of the new service made a new mail-order business possible. By the seventies the school and local gentry were already bypassing the local traders and dealing directly with the 'Civil Service' and other similar stores in London.[2] The practice was already well established by 1874, so that the decline in school numbers under Hayman from 1871 to 1873 was taken more calmly. The traders were beginning to realize that their future prosperity lay with the permanent residents. If wages were low, at least the turnover was more stable. Efforts were made to attract industry, and in 1878 the opening of the railway sheds with 500 employees and a wage packet of £650 a week was welcomed with delight.

> Time was when the trade of Rugby depended almost entirely on the school and the residents attracted here by it. But in these days of Civil Service and other kindred associations to compete with local tradesmen, the school trade has shrunk into insignificance compared with the ready money custom of railway servants and others earning weekly wages.[3]

If the school affected the railway directly, the railway affected the school in its turn. Before it began to operate in 1838, boys arrived from all parts of Britain by stage coach, with several days' allowance for the frequent delays of the road, and two long terms a year to cut down the inconvenience. The railway brought in the fixed timetable with a punctual start, and three terms a year instead of two. Rugby was well favoured, for it became a railway junction and the only place for many years through which a journey north and south was possible.

The combination of a great Public School and a unique rail centre made the town ideal for other purposes too. Thus when Thomas Arnold managed to eliminate the Lower School (boys of 7–12) it effectively meant that education

---

[1] Mr Clinker of Rugby holds the view that there were very good railway reasons for moving the line from the south to the north. Personal information from Mr Clinker.

[2] *Rugby Advertiser* (25 April 1874).

[3] Ibid. (21 November 1874). See also ibid. (2 March 1878).

started at 13 or so instead of 7 or 8. To enter a boy meant a preparatory school course with training in the classics, and Rugby became a centre for the establishment of preparatory schools. They catered for the sons of gentry, and so were situated in select parts of the town, mainly under the shadow of the School itself, and never in middle- or lower-class areas. Like the sojourners, the proprietors took over large houses with high rates and rents. When the school was large, like Bloxam's, then it involved two large houses for boarding purposes. Although Bloxam's was not the first it was the only successful school in the early period. By 1850 a rival had appeared, and ten years later there were six schools altogether. When Bloxam retired the number stayed at five till 1880. However, with the growing industrialization Rugby became an unsuitable spot for young boys whose parents preferred a healthy country setting. By 1900 only two remained, and none survive nowadays within the town limits. At their height – in the sixties – they catered for two hundred boys, with fees ranging from 60 to 100 guineas according to age. Altogether, allowing for money saved and spent elsewhere, the town's trade benefited by about £10,000.

Like the boys' prep. schools, upper-class schools for girls grew up after 1850, catering for boarders and the daughters of sojourners and others. Again this formed part of the education industry directly attributable to the Big School, and accounted for trade to the amount of some £2,000.

It is possible now to arrive at some estimate of the value of Rugby School to the town. A convenient point of reference would be the census year of 1851, the last year of prosperity just before the depression of Goulburn. Taking into account the boys, masters and buildings, schooling meant £50,000 in trade, and £70,000 if the sojourners' contribution were added. The amount grew rapidly in the late fifties and sixties with the increase in size of upper-class schools, but after 1870 there was a decline, as the locality was bypassed for the main stores in the big cities.

On the human side the families of the staff and sojourners account for 285 people, and the servants directly dependent on them and the school for another 363. In other words the school was directly responsible for the presence in Rugby of 648 people other than the boys themselves. If the boys are added, then out of the total population 6,866 in 1851, over 1,100 were directly due to the school.

Many more were indirectly concerned. Forty merchants and small businesses grouped around the centre of the town handled the trade and found in it the basis of their prosperity. Even more intimately concerned with the upper classes were the washerwomen. They lived in immediate contact with the people they served. Altogether there were ninety-six of them in this particular year of 1851, and fifty-two in the streets overlooking and near the Close on the south and west.[1] In the old part of the town most households felt the positive influence of the school, from the Spread Eagle in the Market Place, which catered for visiting parents, to Mr William Lines, who manufactured ink at No. 4, New Street. If, on a con-

[1] Dunchurch Street, Union Street, Oak Terrace.

servative estimate, we reckon that half the trade of the shopkeepers came from school and sojourners, and if we include their dependants, and similarly the washerwomen and others, together with their dependants, we arrive at an additional figure of three hundred souls. In other words, directly and indirectly, Rugby School was the life blood of 1,400 inhabitants.

Apart from the economic and numerical side, there was too a cultural relationship between school and town. From the beginning of the century the staff preached in the churches as active curates, and took an active interest in all parish affairs, while Arnold went out with all the zeal of a missionary to bring the Word to the navvies working on the railway.

The staff were equally prominent in the educational field. At the adult level they helped with the Mechanics' Institutes and Art Societies. In the very first Institute, which had a short career in the thirties, Arnold was prominent. He lectured on history with elaborate visual aids and was not above telling his audience of the shortcomings:

> The very matters which concern us most nearly (our duties as men and as citizens) are exactly those on which the rules of this and similar institutions forbid us to enter. I do not dispute the expediency of these rules or their necessity in the present state of party feeling, both religious and political; but so long as they are observed it is idle to call Mechanics' Institutes places of education.[1]

In spite of his eminence, the Institute had closed over two years before he obtained the Professorship at Oxford.

> At Rugby I learnt that, notwithstanding the support which the institute there had derived from Dr Arnold and other gentlemen in the neighbourhood, it had ceased to exist.[2]

By 1846 the second Institute had come into being with the Rector as President and the new Headmaster, A. C. Tait, intimately involved. Throughout the forties, fifties and sixties the venture struggled on. It was always in financial difficulties, and the classes poorly attended. On paper, the instructors were ideal. From Rugby School, at one time or another, came Dr Tait, Jex-Blake, J. M. Wilson, F. E. Kitchener, A. W. Potts, all brilliant men and three indeed on the threshold of great careers.[3] In spite of it all the classes dwindled. In some years they had to be abandoned because no one registered, and yet identical classes held elsewhere in the town at less convenient centres, at considerably greater cost to the students, and with less able teachers, thrived. The mystery of the missing students was debated continually through the years, but no practical solution was ever found. Many

[1] Lecture to Rugby Mechanics' Institute (1838).

[2] T. Coates, *Report of the State of the Literary, Scientific and Mechanical Institutions in England, etc.* (1841), p. 9.

[3] Tait became Archbishop of Canterbury, Jex-Blake Headmaster of Rugby School and Wilson Canon of Worcester.

possible causes were put forward, and among them the fact that the Institute was too mixed a body, drawing from both rich and poor, ignorant and wise. The working classes, for whom the Institute was founded, were not on the same social plane as the more prominent members and the lecturers. The lecturers were in fact gentry, and all the gulf provided by two major social barriers separated them from their audience. For almost thirty years the Public Schoolmasters did what they could. They gave their services free; they dug deeply into their pockets to settle the accounts. However, by 1870 it had been made quite obvious that gentry-taught classes were not popular, and accordingly the sight of Rugby School names disappears in this connection.

If the linkage of Rugby School with the Mechanics' Institute ceased in one way, it persisted in another. Occasional public lectures given by the staff attracted large audiences who, to judge by newspaper accounts, were enthusiastic. The series of lecture-demonstrations on chemistry by J. M. Wilson in 1861 were outstanding, while the Rev. T. N. Hutchinson gave two notable series on electricity in 1867 and 1870. As for single lectures, the efforts of J. M. Wilson on 'Meteors', 'Geology of Rugby', 'The Sun', 'The Aurora', 'The Comets', as reproduced at length in the local paper, make fascinating reading even today. They stand as monuments by any standards, even those of Tyndall and Huxley. Why then were these lectures successful and the regular classes not? The lecturers were the same, and many of the audience at the special lectures were lower class. Perhaps the comparative rarity of the occasion had something to do with it, and possibly the size of the audience was a help in hiding the uneasy intimate relationship of the gentry–lower class conflict of a smaller group.

In the late sixties and seventies, when the country was becoming examination conscious, local organizations, called Rugby Education Board, Evening Classes for Young Women and Rugby Council for the Promotion of the Education of Women, set out to satisfy the demand for courses with a definite goal. The wives of the gentry were the driving force behind these ventures, and they prepared their students for the Cambridge Local examinations and the awards of the Society of Arts. Still later, when successful classes of high standard were being run by the Railway, the Co-operative Society and the Institute, the School influence was still seen in the Barby Road Art Classes under Mr Lindsay.

One of the more obvious characteristics of the gentry throughout the century was their interest in 'good works'. This was seen in their eager efforts for the Church, at home and overseas, their organization of appeals during and after every war, their deep interest in charity generally, and specifically in the aid of those suffering from local disasters in Britain. Their interest in adult education, in the Mechanics' Institute, was part of this theme; so was their influence in the development of lower-class education. When Arnold died there were only two lower-class schools in the town. One was an old foundation dating back to 1707, the other comparatively new, only twelve years old, started and financed by Thomas Caldecott, the Lord of the Manor. These two schools catered for just over half the children,[1] the rest having little or no instruction apart from the many Sunday Schools catering for all denominations. With the railway, Rugby grew rapidly. Lower-class workers came from all over the country, so that the School and its growing cluster of sojourners had plenty of material for charitable concern. Some of them focused their attention on lower-class education, and worked to this end through the Church. As a result, Rugby Education Society was founded to give guidance and common management. One of their first acts was to persuade Mr Caldecott to hand over the school that he himself had endowed. Thus the only non-sectarian establishment became strictly Church of England. Not only was the school renamed the Parochial, but all connection with the old régime was drastically cut by the resignation of the teachers, who had given long and valuable service.[2]

This society did not have a long life, for it ceased to exist in May 1854; yet in this short period it had made remarkable progress with the building of two new schools, besides aiding others. Its great aim had been to support and preserve the Church. With the competition from 'Romanists' and other sectarians, they were afraid that the poor would be inveigled from the bosom of their maternal Church.[3] Organized education was intended therefore to be a bulwark for the Church. But the efforts of Anglicans only stimulated the other denominations, so that both Wesleyans and Roman Catholics opened day schools in this period. As a result the numbers of lower-class children at school per 100 of lower-class population rose from 9·4 in 1841 to 11·2 ten years later, and to 17·2 in 1861. This meant that by 1861, in spite of a rapidly increasing population, there was a place in day school for every child. It was a remarkable achievement and it meant that the 1870 Act was inoperative as far as Rugby was concerned, and Rugby in fact never had a School Board. This can be traced to the fact that the town had always been education conscious, spurred on by the gentry, whose very presence was largely or entirely educational.

There was not a phase of the town's life in the nineteenth century that the School did not penetrate and influence. It dominated the town in the early and middle periods economically, culturally and educationally. The story, however, is by no means complete, for the positive contribution is only one side of the picture. There were times when the town had to fight the School for its rights, particularly so over the education of the middle classes. That, however, is another story.

[1] Actually 9·4 lower-class children per 100 lower-class population.
[2] William Ironside Tait and Euphemia Tait.
[3] See Annual Meeting of 6 March 1850: *Rugby Advertiser* (16 March 1850).

Index

Note: for Acts of Parliament, see under that heading.